Praise for *The Exchange Artist* by Jane Kamensky

"With her dramatic history of a building's—and a man's—meteoric rise and stunning fall, Kamensky unearths a gem in the tale of America's first great financial scandal. Wonderfully rendered with all the soot and tallow of the day, her portrait captures Boston in the throes of change, a dazzling place where farm boys became captains of industry." —*Boston*

"The images she evokes—of how our early cities were built, of the creation of the moneyed classes, of hustlers in knee breeches and suckers in artisans' aprons—are vivid." —*Fortune*

"An absorbing tale of one man who transformed outlandish promises into a fleeting illusion of success and then, finally, ignominious failure." —*New York Post*

"This is a fascinating historical narrative of Dexter, his associates, and events surrounding the nation's first bank failure." —*Booklist*

"Engaging social history by a talented scholar with a distinct gift for narrative." —*Kirkus Reviews*

"*The Exchange Artist* is a dazzling, disturbing account of rising and falling in early America, a tale of towering ambition and catastrophic collapse. How can millions of dollars of investment vanish into thin air? In beautiful, lyrical prose, Jane Kamensky artfully exposes the fragility of the paper economy in a nation one British visitor called 'the land of speculation.' This book is as much a history of a banking crisis as an excavation of the foundations of the American economy. It will astonish."

—Jill Lepore, author of *The Name of War: King Philip's War and the Origins of American Identity* and *New York Burning: Liberty, Slavery, and Co   Eighteenth-Century Manhattan*

"The book is a ripping good read and an instructive one. It's also testimony to the pleasures and privileges of serious scholarly research. Kamensky loved doing this book and her writing shows it. So much greater, then, the reward to her readers."
—David Landes, author of *The Wealth and Poverty of Nations* and *Dynasties*

"This shrewd and eloquent biography of a building, a man, and the speculative culture they reflect is bound to delight as well as disturb. Americans are indeed hustlers, and none so unabashed as the scions of Puritan New England. Bravo, Kamensky!"
—Walter A. McDougall, author of *The Heavens and the Earth: A Political History of the Space Age* and *Freedom Just Around the Corner: A New American History, 1585–1828*

PENGUIN BOOKS

## THE EXCHANGE ARTIST

Jane Kamensky is the chair of the history department at Brandeis University. Her other books include *Blindspot*, a novel written jointly with Jill Lepore, and *Governing the Tongue*. She lives in Cambridge, Massachusetts.

# THE
# EXCHANGE
# ARTIST

A Tale of

High-Flying Speculation

and America's First Banking Collapse

## JANE KAMENSKY

PENGUIN BOOKS

PENGUIN BOOKS

Published by the Penguin Group

Penguin Group (USA) Inc., 375 Hudson Street, New York, New York 10014, U.S.A.
Penguin Group (Canada), 90 Eglinton Avenue East, Suite 700, Toronto,
Ontario, Canada M4P 2Y3 (a division of Pearson Penguin Canada Inc.)
Penguin Books Ltd, 80 Strand, London WC2R 0RL, England
Penguin Ireland, 25 St Stephen's Green, Dublin 2, Ireland (a division of Penguin Books Ltd)
Penguin Group (Australia), 250 Camberwell Road, Camberwell,
Victoria 3124, Australia (a division of Pearson Australia Group Pty Ltd)
Penguin Books India Pvt Ltd, 11 Community Centre,
Panchsheel Park, New Delhi – 110 017, India
Penguin Group (NZ), 67 Apollo Drive, Rosedale, North Shore 0632,
New Zealand (a division of Pearson New Zealand Ltd)
Penguin Books (South Africa) (Pty) Ltd, 24 Sturdee Avenue,
Rosebank, Johannesburg 2196, South Africa

Penguin Books Ltd, Registered Offices:
80 Strand, London WC2R 0RL, England

First published in the United States of America by Viking Penguin,
a member of Penguin Group (USA) Inc. 2008
Published in Penguin Books 2009

3   5   7   9   10   8   6   4   2

Illustration credits appear on pages 441–442.

THE LIBRARY OF CONGRESS HAS CATALOGED THE HARDCOVER EDITION AS FOLLOWS:
Kamensky, Jane.
The exchange artist / Jane Kamensky.
p.   cm.
Includes bibliographical references and index.
ISBN 978-0-670-01841-3 (hc.)
ISBN 978-0-14-311490-1 (pbk.)
1. Boston (Mass.)—Social conditions.   2. United States—Social conditions—To 1865.
3. Dexter, Andrew, 1779–1837.   4. Businessmen—United States.   I. Title.
HN54.K36   2008
307.76'4097446109034—dc22      2007014318

Printed in the United States of America
Designed by Carla Bolte • Set in Granjon

FOR

CALVIN AND MALCOLM

Rags make paper,
Paper makes money,
Money makes banks,
Banks make loans,
Loans make poverty,
Poverty makes rags.

—Anonymous

# CONTENTS

# LIST OF ILLUSTRATIONS

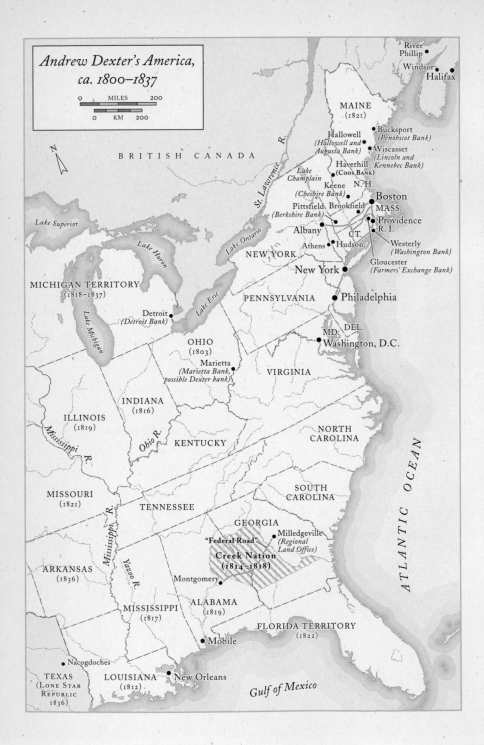

Andrew Dexter's America,
ca. 1800–1837

0    MILES    200

0    KM    200

BRITISH CANADA

River
Phillip
Windsor
Halifax

MAINE
(1821)

Hallowell
(Hallowell and
Augusta Bank)

Buicksport
(Penobscot Bank)

Wiscasset
(Lincoln and
Kennebec Bank)

Haverhill
(Coos Bank)

Lake
Champlain

Keene    N. H.
(Cheshire Bank)

Boston

Pittsfield  Brookfield
(Berkshire Bank)

MASS.

St. Lawrence R.

Albany

Providence
R. I.

Lake Ontario

Athens   Hudson

Westerly
(Washington Bank)

NEW YORK

Gloucester
(Farmers' Exchange Bank)

New York

Lake Superior

Lake Huron

PENNSYLVANIA    Philadelphia

Lake Michigan

Lake Erie

MICHIGAN TERRITORY
(1818–1837)

Detroit
(Detroit Bank)

MD.   DEL.
Washington, D.C.

OHIO
(1803)

Marietta
(Marietta Bank,
possible Dexter bank)

VIRGINIA

INDIANA
(1816)

Ohio R.

ILLINOIS
(1819)

KENTUCKY

Mississippi R.

NORTH
CAROLINA

MISSOURI
(1821)

TENNESSEE

SOUTH
CAROLINA

GEORGIA

Milledgeville
(Regional
Land Office)

"Federal Road"

Creek Nation
(1814–1818)

ATLANTIC OCEAN

ARKANSAS
(1836)

Mississippi R.

Yazoo R.

Montgomery

MISSISSIPPI
(1817)

ALABAMA
(1819)

FLORIDA TERRITORY
(1822)

Mobile

Nacogdoches

TEXAS
(Lone Star
Republic
1836)

LOUISIANA
(1812)

New Orleans

Gulf of Mexico

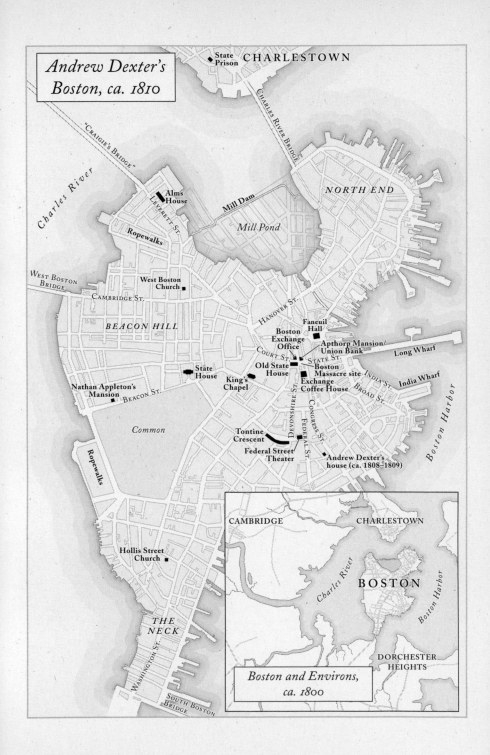

Andrew Dexter's
Boston, ca. 1810

State Prison
CHARLESTOWN
CHARLES RIVER BRIDGE

"CRAIGIE'S BRIDGE"

Charles River

Alms House
LEVERETT ST.

Mill Dam
Mill Pond

NORTH END

Ropewalks

WEST BOSTON BRIDGE

West Boston Church

CAMBRIDGE ST.

HANOVER ST.

BEACON HILL

Faneuil Hall

Boston Exchange Office

Apthorp Mansion/ Union Bank

Long Wharf

COURT ST.
STATE ST.

State House

Old State House

Boston Massacre site

INDIA ST.
India Wharf

Nathan Appleton's Mansion
BEACON ST.

King's Chapel

Exchange Coffee House

BROAD ST.

DEVONSHIRE ST.

Boston Harbor

Common

Tontine Crescent

Federal Street Theater

CONGRESS ST.
FEDERAL ST.

Andrew Dexter's house (ca. 1808–1809)

Ropewalks

Hollis Street Church

THE NECK

WASHINGTON ST.

SOUTH BOSTON BRIDGE

CAMBRIDGE

CHARLESTOWN

Charles River

BOSTON

Boston Harbor

DORCHESTER HEIGHTS

Boston and Environs, ca. 1800

# THE
# EXCHANGE
# ARTIST

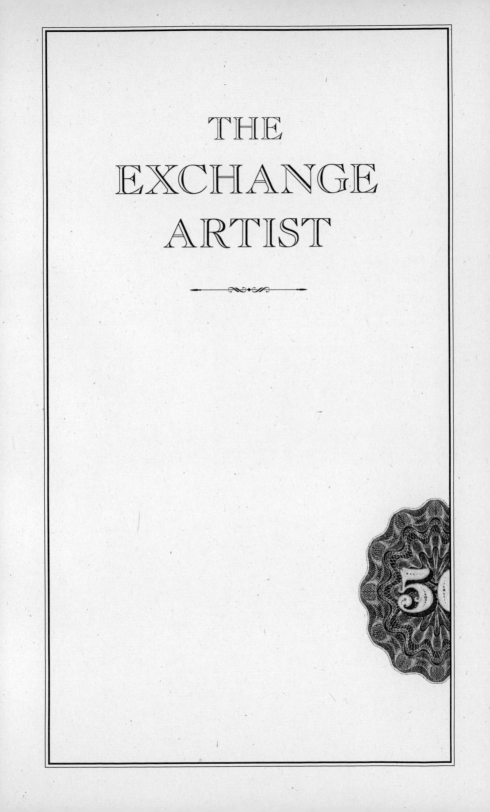

# RUINS

*The collapse,* long expected, came suddenly.

When night fell on Tuesday, November 3, 1818, Boston's Exchange Coffee House was one of the tallest, strangest, most talked about buildings in the English-speaking world. For a decade, people had called it too high, too ugly, too costly, too empty: just too much. None of that mattered now. By sunrise Wednesday, it was gone.

The blaze started in the billiard room on the building's seventh floor, three stories above neighboring rooftops. Just after seven o'clock, alarm bells summoned help from every corner of the city. With practiced speed, hundreds of stalwart Bostonians assembled. Several fire companies owned engines of the latest design, hand-cranked machines that could shoot water a remarkable five stories skyward. Hope flickered.

But a five-story spray left two floors undefended, a simple equation with a fateful result. Flames engulfed the building within half an hour. Around nine, the Exchange's gleaming tin-sheathed dome plummeted to the cellar with a deafening crash. The roofless shell burned furiously, belching fire like a volcano. Sky watchers in distant Connecticut, New Hampshire, and Maine noted an unaccustomed glow on the horizon.

After fire consumed the building's wooden vitals, its brick carcass imploded, wall by massive wall. The entire city—some of it built on land only recently reclaimed from the harbor floor—shook with the impact. By midnight, when the crowd began to disperse, only the Exchange's eastern elevation stood, an unsupported facade more than one hundred feet square. The next day, that trembling curtain of warped brick and blackened marble came down, too. Then the scavengers who eked a living from the city's detritus picked the site clean. A week later, all that remained was a yawning rubble-choked pit that would smoke for months and linger in ruins for nearly three years.[1]

Millions of bricks, tons of marble and granite, miles of lumber, reams of velvet and satin and paper: ashes. In a matter of hours the city looked different, as if a hole had opened in the skyline. Groping for words to describe the transformation, the man who had managed the Exchange's Reading Room dusted off his Shakespeare. "That magnificent structure is no more," he lamented.

> Those "cloud capt towers" which were yesterday the pride of our town, and which seemed as permanent as the foundations on which they stood, have disappeared like the enchantment of a dream, and left nothing but a heap of smouldering ruins, the melancholy monument of their former grandeur.

Much as Prospero, *The Tempest*'s sorcerer-protagonist, dissolved reality with a whisper, the Exchange had simply melted into thin air.[2]

Word of the conflagration spread almost as rapidly as the fire, and much farther. Within hours, the murmurs on Congress Street had condensed into handwriting, script into type, type into images and keepsakes. The day after the fire, five witnesses composed long letters for publication. Local papers began to report the spectacle on Thursday. By Saturday, people in New York City—more than two days' hard ride from Boston—could read two competing versions. Writing to his brother that day, a seaman stationed in Charlestown harbor placed "The destruction of that Elegant Building the Exchange Coffee House" in quotation marks, as if to indicate the title of an already well-known tale.[3] And so it became—a tale with legs, and wings. By mid-November, bulletins variously headlined GREAT FIRE, DESTRCTIVE FIRE, DESTRUCTIVE CONFLAGRATION! and, in German-speaking

Tremendous Fire!! *Broadside, ca. November 4, 1818.*

parts of Pennsylvania, FÜRCHTERLICHES FEUER! had appeared in every eastern state. The story reached London in December; by February, it hit Mississippi.[4]

Settled near the hearth in a library, a tavern, or a coffee house, the reader of these endlessly recycled news items experienced the delightful chill of the armchair spectacle: a guided tour of somebody else's tragedy.[5] Or near-tragedy, at any rate. For when the sights, sounds, and smells of the disaster faded, it became clear that the Exchange fire had not been especially ruinous. Given the building's enormity, given the neighborhood's density, given the chronic threat fire posed to cities built of wood, heated with flame, and defended by bucket brigades, the *limits* of the catastrophe appeared more startling than its toll. The

3

tale's horror turned on what ifs and might have beens. What if November winds had howled? Fire might have enveloped the city. Yet the night was eerily calm, and only the buildings attached to the Coffee House had been lost. What if the Coffee House had been packed with guests? Hundreds might have died, trapped in smoke-filled corridors and "buried in the mass of the falling walls." But everyone left the building calmly, and the fire had not claimed a single life.[6]

Why, then, the rivers of ink? Why did people who had never glimpsed the Exchange—who had never set foot in Boston, much less witnessed the fire—bother to take stock of its passing? The final collapse of Boston's Exchange Coffee House was a short-lived, low-rent spectacle. But the *story* of its collapse was a tale for the times, less a local comedy of errors than a national tragedy of value. The burning of the Exchange held a portent, an object lesson: the end of an Icarus tale written first in paper, then in bricks, and now in ash.

৵৴

Fire and gravity proved a pitiless combination, but an efficient one. Soaring had been the harder part. On Boston's Congress Street, as everywhere else in the young United States, *ascent* was the spectacle that mattered. *"Be Up and Doing!":* a call to arms during the war for American independence, the slogan became a call to commerce in the years thereafter. A generation after the Revolution, many Americans imagined rising as both a personal birthright and a collective destiny. "Happy America!" exclaimed Nathan Appleton in 1802, "where the poorest of your sons, *knows* that by industry & economy, he can acquire property & respectability, and has ambition enough to make the attempt—which seldom fails of success." A middling New Hampshire farm boy turned Boston shopkeeper, the twenty-three-year-old Appleton wrote this paean to the new American dream from England, where he was busily remaking himself as an international merchant. His own career proved his theorem: industry plus economy equaled prosperity.[7]

Appleton was wrong in supposing that purposeful striving almost always netted success. But he was hardly alone in believing it. In fact, the writer Charles Ingersoll noted in 1810, Americans' shared faith in the fruits of industry was as close as this mixed, restless, "adolescent people" came to having a national character. "Each individual feels himself rising in his fortunes; and the nation, rising with the concentration of all this elasticity, rejoices in its growing greatness." Wary of "every sensation of restraint," and "infected with the lust for novelty," Americans reached, strived, *climbed*.[8]

The gospel of ascent seeped into every sphere of life in the early republic, from farm house to schoolhouse to courthouse to counting-house to meetinghouse. And wherever it touched, aspiration took shape. In the slaveholding south and the rural north and the ever-expanding western backcountry, aspiration pushed relentlessly at the horizontal: a hunger for more acres, farther shores. But in the coastal port towns—especially in older, tightly bounded cities like Boston— the axis of aspiration was vertical. More than any other structure in the United States, Boston's Exchange Coffee House embodied the vertical imagination of the early American Republic.[9]

The building sprang from the dreams of one young man whose life shared the building's steep upward pitch. Like Nathan Appleton, whom he would come to know well, Andrew Dexter Jr. was an upstart, one of millions of boys and girls who grew up in the wake of the Revolution longing for more than their fathers had. Born in rural Massachusetts in 1779, he spent his youth in Providence, where he soaked up the gospel of aspiration at home and in church, in the press and in the streets. In his salutatory address to the Rhode Island College class of 1798, Dexter envisioned an almost martial striving. He assured his seventeen classmates that if they clung to their republican virtues, the "hatchet of industry, wielded by the strong arm of freedom, shall resound from the shores of the Atlantic to the banks of the Mississippi."[10]

After graduation, Dexter shouldered his hatchet of industry and headed for the forest of ships' masts and church spires that was

Boston. A small peninsula crowded with nearly twenty-five thousand inhabitants, the town suspended between the Atlantic and the Charles River was the fourth most populous in the United States, less than half the size of New York but more than three times bigger than Providence. Amid the bustle, Dexter studied law and fine manners under the guidance of his uncle Samuel, a prominent Federalist attorney and officeholder.[11]

By the first years of the new century, Andrew Dexter was rising in earnest, amassing credentials and connections, a bit of cash and some securities, a few small lots of land. In 1806, his aspirations fastened upon a particular object. He would build a temple of finance that towered over the tangled center of town. Under one roof he would concentrate "all the conveniences for every transaction which the multiplied negociations of commerce can require." There would be a central space where merchants could trade goods and paper, and well-appointed booths where they might deal more discreetly. A variety of offices—brokerages, insurance concerns, print shops—would surround the 'Change Floor, offering services now dispersed across the city. Business travelers would find suitable rooms to let, and news mongers would discover a library of the latest papers and shipping reports. No Dexter Tower, this he would christen the Exchange Coffee House, a label that honored his ideal of unfettered commerce, and called to mind like-titled establishments in England and America.[12]

Dexter and his architect, Asher Benjamin (another aspiring country sort), designed the Exchange Coffee House to elevate all of Boston, which seemed "fated to sink in every honourable comparison" to other great Atlantic ports. Just as its sheer height would declare an end to a hundred years of economic flatness, so the grandeur of the Exchange would ennoble the money trades that many derided as stockjobbing, speculating, or worse. Practical as well as "*patriotic* motives" recommended his "scheme," Dexter said. The building would profit investors handsomely. Commonwealth and personal fortunes would rise in tandem.[13]

For two years beginning in the spring of 1807, Bostonians could witness Dexter's ascent take physical form. Diggers and joiners and masons and carvers massed about the building site, assembling mountains of materials hauled from every corner of New England. The work—carried out by hand, by pulley, by horse, and by cart—was herculean, a Federalist Fitzcarraldo. Day by day and brick by brick the Exchange rose, passing three stories (the height of fashionable homes and shops), past four (the profile of the newest, most ambitious countinghouses), past five stories, then six (only one building in town stood that tall), finally topping off at an outlandish seven stories (unheard of, even in New York). And there was more to come: a triangular pediment pointing skyward atop the eastern elevation, and finally that tin-sheathed dome, a cap that outshone every other surface in town.

Nobody had seen anything quite like it. One British traveler pronounced the Exchange "very lofty and extensive"; another, from Connecticut, deemed it a "monstrous building." (This he intended as praise.) A more critical observer saw a mirror of Dexter's own hubris: "a building which almost intercepts the rays of the sun from the immensity of its elevation."[14] Other famous piles—Charles Bulfinch's new State House up on Beacon Hill, Benjamin Latrobe's Capitol in the new federal city, Thomas Jefferson's Monticello—were more expansive, with wings that embraced the horizon in a gesture of simultaneous dominion and repose. The Exchange did not embrace. It yearned, it loomed, it "reared to a giddy height." A tower to mirror a vertical America: this was the architecture of aspiration.[15]

Though it boasted more floors (and inspired more stories) than any other building in the United States, the Exchange was no engineering marvel. With masonry walls nearly five feet thick at their base, its structure hearkened back to the medieval castle more than it anticipated the "high Romance" of the steel-framed skyscraper. But if the builders on Congress Street heaped up stone and brick in traditional ways, the pay they received for their labors was novel. Dexter built the

Exchange Coffee House for paper, and he built it *from* paper. At once a fortress and a bubble, the brick tower rose upon a pyramid of bank notes.[16]

From Boston to Cathay, paper money fueled the rise of the young United States. It wasn't the nation's only medium of exchange, or the most solid one. The federal government minted coins from precious metals, "hard" money or "specie" in the parlance of the day. Hard money had many advantages. Its value, understood to inhere in the substance from which it was made, held stable. Hard money also translated well, crossing local and national borders without losing sense. But coins were difficult to transport in large numbers, not least because their supposedly transcendent value made them natural targets for thieves. Supply was a more profound limitation. Centuries of searching for a North American El Dorado had failed to turn up significant deposits of gold or silver ore within the boundaries of the American nation. For all these reasons, hard money made a poor medium of aspiration. This, Adam Smith theorized, was always the case. "The gold and silver money which circulates in any country may very properly be compared to a highway," he wrote, "which, while it circulates and carries to market all the grass and corn of the country, produces itself not a single pile of either." Hard money was heavy stuff. For better and for worse, it clung to earth.[17]

Few such ties tethered paper. Issued by private corporations rather than by the states or the federal government, early American bank notes were convenient and abundant. Beyond abundant—virtually unlimited. During Dexter's lifetime the number of state-chartered banks grew many times over, and the notes they issued multiplied exponentially. This tendency to climb, as Smith suggested, was characteristic of the medium. Where specie paved a commercial highway, paper forged "a sort of waggon-way through the air." Loosely moored to "the solid ground of gold and silver," the economy "suspended upon the Daedalian wings of paper money" took flight easily. Where coin held you down, paper lifted you up. But it could not keep you aloft.[18]

With much less capital than ambition, Andrew Dexter was well suited for a set of Daedalian wings. Bank shares numbered among his first investments. As his vision of the building on Congress Street came into focus, he quietly acquired a controlling interest in several banks, each of them cash-starved and remote, both from Boston and from each other. From their notes—which he issued in the millions— he built the Coffee House. Throughout 1807 and 1808, Dexter passed his doubtful paper in distant markets, perfecting a recipe for making something out of nothing. Gold into paper, paper into bricks: this was the alchemy of bank notes. Hard-money men resisted the spell. In December 1808, Nathan Appleton (shopkeeper no more) cautioned his fellow merchants against this "grand inchanter, whose touch converts every thing to paper—whose wand calls up a castle more stupendously magnificent, than any described in Eastern romance." Still the tower and the pyramid grew, inching further from their foundations. The real magic lay in not looking down.[19]

⁓

Dexter's collapse, the Exchange's first fall, went down hard.

By the spring of 1809, many merchants had noticed how close to the sun Dexter's wings were carrying him. One of his banks, as Rhode Island legislators discovered that March, had emitted more than $600,000 in notes during the previous year—promises backed by exactly $86.48 in specie. By any measure, this was far above solid ground.[20] The state closed that bank, making it the first bank to fail in United States history. Two more banks, one in western Massachusetts and another in the Michigan Territory, quickly followed suit. Others teetered on the edge of ruin. Everywhere, Dexter's alchemy reversed itself. Bank notes in the pockets of hundreds of laborers on the Exchange and thousands of people with whom they had traded goods and services were transmuted from money back into paper. Printed promises that one day bought food and clothing and shelter revealed themselves the next as mere wisps, drawings on pulped rags. One writer called the wreckage an "immense floating mass of . . . paper TRASH."[21]

9

In May, Dexter gathered up what little was left to him and fled the country, beginning decades of earthbound flight that took him from rural Nova Scotia to the Alabama woods. Others lacked even his clipped wings. As spring turned to summer, Boston's municipal jail grew crowded with "respectable mechanics" rendered insolvent by the "miserable stuff . . . tendered to them as money." Like Appleton and Dexter, these men were strivers, "men who have, till of late, seen better days," the papers said. Yet prison, not success, was the harvest of their "industry and genius." Prison, and the Exchange building, the "GREAT HOUSE [they] erected on this *paper foundation*."²²

That summer, as honest laborers sweated in jail, and Dexter cowered in Canada, news of the debacle overspread the country, traveling backward along the paths of Dexter's bank notes. People from Rhode Island to Detroit declared themselves "astonished"—by the height of the pyramid, by the shakiness of the ground beneath it, by the speed of the fall and the breadth of the fallout.

Shocked, yet again.

For they had known other collapses, too many to count. The fates of Holland's tulip market in the seventeenth century and London's South Seas Company in the early eighteenth remained legendary. More recent and local instances abounded as well. Doubtful schemes in western lands stained the reputations of many heroes of the founding generation, from George Washington to Robert Morris to Andrew Dexter's uncle Samuel. In 1807, President Jefferson himself had punctured the nation's commercial prosperity with his misguided embargo. Each time, each crash *astonished*.

Like those burst bubbles, this one carried a whiff of venality. It was, as it had to be, somebody's fault. A peddler of promises turned confidence man, Dexter made a splendid, smirking villain. "The astonished multitude gape at the edifice," one Boston pressman reported, "while the *projector behind the curtain,* smiles with a *horrid grin,* to think how *dexterously* he has managed the business."²³

But the image of the grinning bogeyman concealed scarier truths. Early capitalism was more existential comedy than Gothic horror.

Value was an illusion with no magician conjuring it. Dexter's downfall astonished not because it was monstrously singular, but rather
because it laid bare the rules of the game. A web of increasingly remote,
sophisticated, and abstract market connections made all Americans gamblers, as it blurred the line between daring and fraud. One
writer mocked Dexter's investors as "adventurers in a legerdemain
project"—willful suspenders of disbelief, as indeed they had proven
to be. Just like everyone else. Their collective sleights of hand fabri-
cated an economy that lurched between inexplicable booms and
unpredictable busts. Post-Revolutionary America was Andrew Dexter's America, a place crisscrossed by new roads to success, which in
turn were riddled with new pitfalls.[24]

In the end, Andrew Dexter's paper promises were backed by the
same airy stuff as Nathan Appleton's vision of a "happy America" of
boundless opportunity: an almost mystical faith in the rising future.
That faith was a powerful engine. But it was often misplaced. Industry and economy might yield "property and respectability," as
Appleton assured himself. Then again, they might not. Upstanding
people like Appleton aspired and dared and soared, while other moral,
hard-working people yearned and risked and failed. By the time Dexter and Appleton began their dramatic rises, roughly one in five
American householders could expect to face insolvency at least
once. In a world of abundant leverage, little regulation, and less insurance, almost nothing checked their falls. Like a latter-day Jonathan
Edwards, Andrew Dexter reminded believers in the gospel of aspiration that only the thinnest thread of confidence suspended them over
a bottomless pit.[25]

୰

After Dexter crashed and fled, after the banks shuttered, after the
insolvent mechanics suffered and starved and saved themselves, or
failed to, the Exchange building endured, an American monument to
soaring and stumbling. Appleton called it a "modern Babel."[26]

Divine wrath had leveled ancient Babel's cloud-piercing height.

And when Boston's tower, that shrine to destruction, was itself destroyed, some of those burned by the first collapse delighted in the cosmic comeuppance. "This stupendous edifice was erected during the most pernicious periods of speculation," lectured one Republican correspondent. "It arose on the ruins of many industrious citizens." But the wheel had turned. Now "the rubbish now lying in the cellar of the building" had precisely the same value as the "bank bills which gave rise to this modern Babel." The lesson was clear: "all speculative projects founded on injustice, eventually prove ruinous to the projectors." An aging Revolutionary who witnessed the fire rendered this Old Testament verdict more starkly. The Exchange, he remarked, had been "conceived in sin, brought forth in iniquity, but it is now purified by fire." Ashes to ashes, ruin to ruins.[27]

This was a stern moral, and yet a soothing one. In this version, divine gravity reversed the unearned rise and redeemed the undeserved fall. God was still watching, the "City on a Hill" still holding aloft its beacon of righteousness to a fallen world.

That, at least, was the story.

One story.

In my version, the rise and falls of Andrew Dexter and his Exchange Coffee House offer different lessons. Andrew Dexter and Nathan Appleton, the con man and the businessman, emerge as remarkably similar creatures, their different fates as much the result of chance as of character. Neither a mustache-twisting villain nor a vengeful god controls the action. Only Prospero—Shakespeare's cold, capricious enchanter—lurks behind the curtain, conjuring cloud-capped towers out of words and dismantling them without reason or warning.

In Andrew Dexter's day, Americans knew their Shakespeare, and they often used Prospero's lines to think about the wreckage that accompanied the here today, gone tomorrow world of paper money. (Prospero's name punned on prosperity.) But they needn't look to Elizabethan England for a poet of ruin. Every crossroads had a tavern, and every tavern had a homegrown Prospero, a man who had ridden fortune's merry wheel top to bottom, and liked to sing of modern life's capriciousness.[28]

In Pittsfield, Massachusetts, the Berkshire town where Andrew Dexter commandeered his first bank, one bard of chance put it this way:

> FORTUNE will various gifts impart,
> Sometimes she'll smile & sometimes frown,
> 'Tis best to keep a cheerful heart,
> Some will go up, and some go down.

He called the tune "The Bankrupt's Soliloquy After Going Through the Mill." It features no sin, no iniquity, no heaven-sent fire: just fickle Fortune, blinder than Justice. Some went up and some went down. And others, as Dexter was soon to demonstrate, spun round and round, bottom to top and through the mill again.[29]

# ONE

# PROMISES

*The Age of Paper,* an American publisher called the late eighteenth century. The label fit his era in more ways than he intended. More printers labored at more presses, cranking out a fast-growing supply of newspapers, novels, engravings, laws, and maps that still failed to meet the exploding demand. Stationers stocked blanks for letters, diaries, and account books, instruments of self-fashioning that increasing numbers of the nation's self-made men and women required. Indian treaties and slave sales, two-dimensional instruments of the three-dimensional violence upon which Jefferson's empire for liberty rested, transformed paper into land and labor. Underwriting all of these, paper was the stuff of money.[1]

Shells, silver, pelts, plants, gunpowder, gold: colonial North Americans made these things, and many others, into mediums of exchange. But by the turn of the nineteenth century, almost everyone had grown accustomed to trading their crops, their goods, their land, and their sweat for paper. From the farmer's scribbled IOU to the merchant's note of hand to the corporation's engraved stock certificate to the government's bond, a multiplicity of credit instruments circulated in the young United States, paper building a nation. By far the most common among them were banknotes.[2]

Printed on white paper thin enough to make them portable—stackable—bank notes came in every color of ink, so long as it was black. They came off the presses in sheets, a vertical column of four bills to the page, ready to be cut apart, when the ink dried, into small, rectangular slips about the size and shape of today's dollar bills. Their designs varied, but all notes followed the same basic plot line. In print appeared the denomination, the bank's name and place of business, and, most centrally, its pledge to pay the specified amount, in coin, to anyone who presented the note at its counters. A clerk's careful hand filled in blanks for the serial number, the date of issue, and the original holder's name. (She or any subsequent "bearer" could redeem the note.) Two signatures—one from the bank's president and one from its cashier—guaranteed every one. Written with hand-cut quills in iron gall ink, these were autographs, not engraved facsimiles. Evidence of hand and heart, these signatures proclaimed that bank bills embodied the real obligations of real people. The early American banknote was a frozen gesture: a handshake caught mid-grip, a speech act committed to paper and stretched over time and space. "The President, Directors, and Company promise . . . ," the formula ran. *We do.*[3]

The trick came in reckoning the value of such a promise. Banknotes were money, passing from hand to hand in exchanges of every sort. But they weren't legal tender. Nobody—not shopkeepers, not laborers, not the post office or the tax collector—had to accept them. Nor did any public body endorse them. The hyperinflation of the Revolutionary War had cured the federal government of its short-lived addiction to paper money. To spare the country a repeat performance, the Constitution declared that no state would "coin Money; emit Bills

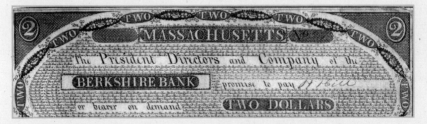

"*. . . Promise to Pay,*" detail, Berkshire Bank $2 bill, 1809.

of Credit; [or] make any Thing but gold and silver Coin a Tender in Payment of Debts." Into the void stepped banks. State legislatures chartered them as corporations, but bank directors, not the state, guaranteed their issues. So if you chose to credit a given note, you needn't take it at its word. How well you thought its value matched the amount on its face depended on a dense web of local knowledge: the bank's reputation for probity and promptness, the good names of its directors and its debtors, the fullness of its vaults, and myriad other factors, a complex calculation whose variables increased with the number of note-issuing banks.[4]

In 1784, a Philadelphia financier called the "new science" of banking "a pathless wilderness, ground, but little known to this Side of the Atlantick. . . . a mystery." He exaggerated. Colonial Americans had dabbled in this new science for nearly a century. Victims of the chronic imbalance of payments that pulled specie toward the empire's center, Britain's North American colonies had experimented with a variety of innovative banking schemes, creating paper currencies backed by land, by crops, by future tax receipts, by faith and desire. The first paper money issued by a government in the Western world came not from the sophisticated financial centers of England and the Netherlands, but from the cash-poor colony of Massachusetts Bay. Not quite a pristine wilderness, then. Still, banking was hardly well-trodden ground in the early American republic. Pennsylvanians incorporated the Bank of North America, the first in the United States in 1782; as of 1790, there were but four in the country.[5]

But the "pathless wilderness" soon grew crowded. By 1800, the legislatures of the various states had chartered twenty-eight banks, authorizing each of them to raise a specified amount of capital, to pay dividends to its stockholders and interest to its depositors, and to charge a fixed percentage for making loans. A decade later there were four times that many, and by 1820, the number of American banks had reached 328. Each new settler in the erstwhile wilderness of banking printed its own notes to lend, typically in four or more denominations.

Three hundred banks meant at least twelve hundred kinds of bills, all staking their claims to be money.[6]

And so every working day, as you traveled or traded, your pocket-book filled with promises, some from distant parts and most signed by people whose names you failed to recognize. It was impossible to determine their value by weight, as you could with coins. Nor could you do so by sight, simply adding the numbers printed on their faces. No, dealing with banknotes took literacy. Early American money had to be carefully read. Once or twice a week, newspapers published rates of exchange for the notes of local and regional banks next to tables listing the latest value of the English pound, the Indian rupee, and the Spanish *reale*. Adding to the confusion were bills the individual states had issued three decades before. The Revolutionary-era currencies lingered on as ghosts in Americans' psyches, if not often in their pocketbooks. Into the 1800s, almanacs enumerated shifting rules for "reducing" these bygone state notes. (To change New York's into Georgia's, add 1/16 and divide by 2. To render South Carolina bills into those of Pennsylvania, multiply by 45, then divide by 28.) The sums were hard to reckon, and the old state monies didn't trade much any more. But relative to the cacophony of newly issued bank paper, they made stable units to think with.[7]

If legitimate notes demanded fancy ciphering, a rising tide of fakes required still closer scrutiny. How much "easier to make and utter counterfeited bills," noted one antibank editorialist, "when thirty different kinds of bills are in circulation, having sixty different signatures, than when the notes of one, two, or three Banks circulate."[8] Some moneymakers (as counterfeiters were called) invented spurious banks in whose name they issued broken promises. Others mimicked or modified the notes of actual banks. Ones morphed into fours and tens; the occasional audacious three became a thirty. In self-defense wary note handlers embraced a new genre, the counterfeit detector, which first appeared in Boston in 1806. For a mere twelve and a half cents, printers Samuel Gilbert and Thomas Dean promised, their *Only Sure Guide to Bank Bills* would teach money readers to distinguish the real from the near-real. Doing so required a jeweler's eye. In a fraudulent Farmer's Exchange Bank note, they instructed, the *"plough . . .* joins the tails of the oxen, which in a genuine it does not." A Maine bank's "true tens" depicted a dockside "work-shop *with windows,"* where "the false have a shop *without windows*."⁹

Counting windows less than one thirty-second of an inch square on a building smaller than the tip of your pinky. Recalibrating the prices in your store according to the bills a customer offered in payment. Buying Rhode Island money cheap in New York, redeeming it at par in Providence, and reversing the gambit to fund your return trip south. These were among the scholasticisms of early American paper. With the circulating medium a Babel of promises, the most basic of exchanges required careful conjugations and declensions, a grammar that changed shop by shop, bank by bank, day by day. Every man his own arbitrageur.

Phillip Ammidon, a Boston merchant who stocked his store on Long Wharf with flour from Pennsylvania, cotton from Georgia, leather from Spain, and wine from France, struggled to balance a drawer full of currencies as polyglot as his wares. "Sir," he told a trading partner in late 1804,

> I have sold your exchange today at 1 pct. discount which was the best I could do, for Foreign [that is, non-Boston] Money; a part of which I have gotten exchanged for Eastern money, but as everyone deposits in the Banks; it is almost impossible to obtain any particular money we want—Exchange has been purchased to day at 2 pct. discount, foreign money & is very difficult selling it at all for Cash . . .

This confusing monetary climate had doubtless contributed to his failure a year earlier, when the commissioners of bankruptcy assigned a young lawyer named Andrew Dexter Jr. to collect from the merchant's debtors, sell off his assets, and divide the proceeds among his creditors. Settling these claims marked Dexter's first foray into the giddy world of postwar urban real estate, his first attempt to exchange earth for paper.¹⁰

∽

Andrew Dexter Jr. was the scion of a paper dynasty that stretched back two generations before his birth in 1779. The Dexters had been in New England much longer than that. Irish Protestants, the family fled religious upheaval in Ulster's County Meath in 1641 and left England for Massachusetts soon after, landing in Boston at the tail end of the Puritans' "Great Migration." For the next hundred years, the Dexter clan pressed paper into service in traditional ways, signing deeds granting them title to lands near Boston, and conversion narratives attesting to their stringent faith.[11]

For Andrew Dexter's great-grandfather, paper meant scripture. Born in 1700, the Reverend Samuel Dexter graduated from Harvard in 1720, a dedicated preacher if only an average scholar. A portrait of him depicts a stern-faced Calvinist with his hand in the Bible, a coarse square neck cloth resembling the pages of an open book his only other ornament. Dexter ministered to the First Church of Dedham for more than thirty years, a settled career that belied a restless temperament that he—in good Puritan style—turned to vigorous spiritual scrutiny, and that his worldlier descendants—also in good Puritan style— would apply to the market. "[M]ellancholy is so much my natural disposition that it makes my life very uneasy," he confessed to his diary. He took offense quickly and often found himself "very painfully, affected with oppositions and troubles," including financial woes. The living his parishioners paid him barely made ends meet, and Dexter supplemented his income by digging graves, with help from an enslaved man whom neither penury nor piety moved him to free. Aside from his religious texts, he left little paper behind when he died in 1755: an estate worth less than what his weaver father had bequeathed to him decades earlier.[12]

Paper meant something different to Reverend Samuel's eldest surviving son and namesake, born in 1726. His preacher-father instructed him tirelessly, preparing him for a place at Harvard. But the younger Samuel manifested what his own son would later call "a strong disinclination for the profession his father had chosen." A strong independent streak led him to question received wisdom, including the verities of Calvinism. He embraced instead the morals of trade, beginning with an apprenticeship to a Boston dry goods merchant. Before he turned twenty-four he had parlayed his middling birth, hard work, and an advantageous marriage to the daughter of a Huguenot merchant into a shop of his own. At his store near the Mill Bridge, the minister's son sold the fruits of the vast and growing empire to which the North American colonies belonged: Jamaican sugar, Bohea tea, Scottish linens, East Indian spices. He promised cheap prices and easy credit to "Country Customers and others who buy to sell again."[13]

Most of Dexter's country customers paid him with paper money. New England's colonial governments had printed bills of various sorts since 1690, and paper had become the dominant medium of exchange for everyday transactions well before Samuel set up his shop.

The trend eased the constraints of colonial trade, but paper money also opened deep fault lines among colonists, and between the colonies and Parliament. Farmers who needed to wring cash from their lands and shopkeepers who sought a ready means of exchange tended to support the new monies, arguing that a currency's use determined its worth. "What intrinsick value is there in Silver, or Gold, more than in Iron, Brass, or Tinn?" asked one advocate of banking in Massachusetts. "Is not every thing in this world, just as men esteem and value it?" Larger merchants, fearful that paper would dilute their purses and their power, called for tighter controls over bills that "have no intrinsick Value, and . . . are no better than waste Paper." Eager to keep the colonies fiscally dependent, Parliament concurred; the Currency Act of 1751 prohibited New England legislatures from issuing more fiat paper. But the pause was short-lived. Three years later the outbreak of the French and Indian War brought new demands for cash, and colonial printing presses went back to work making money.[14]

Hungry for currency to lubricate his growing trade, Samuel Dexter endorsed the colony's experiments in banking. But like many merchants in his day, he was quick to insist that he didn't chase paper for its own sake. He "had no relish for the glitter of wealth," Dexter's son later noted, "and no avarice to lead him to hoard it." By the age of thirty-six he had amassed "property sufficient to satisfy his moderate desires." In 1762, with business booming, he closed up shop and returned to his native Dedham, where he remade himself as a country squire. He built a Georgian mansion, one of the finest in town. (In 1776, George Washington really *did* sleep there.) But he paid more attention to filling his library than his purse. "His mind had never been limited to his compting-room and ledger," his son insisted. To the preacher who would deliver his eulogy, Samuel Dexter left instructions to remind the mourners not "to 'lay up treasures on earth,' while they are indolent with respect to their well-being hereafter."[15]

His sons expressed less ambivalence about earthly treasures. Andrew Dexter, the first of them to survive infancy, was born in Boston in 1751, just as his father became an independent proprietor. For him there was no battle between scholarly tomes and account books. ("Not brilliant," his own obituary would label him.) With none of the angst that had marked Samuel Dexter's choice of calling a generation earlier, Andrew followed his father into trade. When he came of age, he opened his own shop on Hanover Street. There he sold "GOODS of various sorts," wares whose finery he was reluctant to tout lest "some folks would call it puffing, and others would give it even a worse name." He named the shop Andrew Dexter's Cheap Store, and sought customers who felt "*disappointed* and *deceived,* when allured by pompous Advertisements." With something of the diction of his minister-grandfather, he told those who patronized the Cheap Shop that they would "not have the least Reason to repent of it afterwards."[16]

Andrew Dexter made that particular promise in December 1773. On the sixteenth of that month, Boston's Sons of Liberty, dressed as Mohawks, dumped hundreds of crates of East India Company tea into the harbor to protest British taxation policies. To revenge what would later become known as the Boston Tea Party, Parliament billeted thousands more red-coated troops throughout the town, shut down the local government, and sealed the port. By summer commerce had slowed to a standstill: no goods, no work, no cash. One Boston merchant complained that "you might as well ask a man for the teeth out of his head as to request the payment of money that he owes you."[17]

The deepening hostilities between Crown and colony touched everyone in Massachusetts. The Dexters aligned with the patriot cause, and for a time Samuel Dexter numbered among its leaders. His son, still a young man, embraced the Boston boycott movement, a difficult choice for a fledgling merchant. In November 1774, Andrew reminded would-be customers he had "conscientiously refrained from importing any Goods since the Act for blocking up the Port of Boston took place," and affirmed that he nonetheless had items for sale, "Very Cheap Indeed!" But on Hanover Street as elsewhere in town, buyers remained scarce.[18]

Six months later, the long cold war turned hot on Lexington's village green. In the aftermath of the battle, as many as twenty thousand colonial militiamen massed at the edges of Boston, laying siege to the more than ten thousand British regulars garrisoned in the city. Civilians fled in droves. By the time the British evacuated, in March 1776, the city's population had fallen by more than 80 percent, to fewer than three thousand.[19]

Andrew Dexter escaped to the countryside, one among thousands streaming across the Neck every day of the siege. First he berthed with his parents, who had removed to Woodstock, Connecticut, a small town in the center of the state. ("We seem as if we were out of the world here," Samuel Dexter said of their remote situation.) It was there, in the spring of 1778, that the twenty-seven-year-old Andrew married Mary Newton, daughter of a well-to-do merchant from Rhode Island. The next year the young couple followed the Connecticut River north to Brookfield, Massachusetts, an ardently patriot village where Andrew's brother-in-law thundered the American cause from the pulpit. In Brookfield the following March, a bare ten months after her wedding, Mary Newton Dexter delivered their first son.

With less than his characteristic modesty, Andrew named the boy after himself.[20]

By then the rebellion in Massachusetts had ripened into a bloody and protracted war of colonial liberation whose front lines extended from Quebec to Savannah. Waging it required vast reserves of commitment, daring, and luck. And cash: like all wars, America's Revolution devoured money—money to outfit and transport soldiers; money, sometimes, to pay them. Like most postcolonial polities, the new United States had virtually none. The abrupt end of trade with Britain left state coffers bare. The national treasury had only just been called into being, all but empty. With little specie on hand and no gold or silver mines in eastern North America, printing presses held the only feasible remedy.

Massachusetts issued its first war bonds in May 1775, less than two weeks after the battles of Concord and Lexington. Samuel Dexter's was one of three authorizing signatures that transformed them from paper into money. In June the Continental Congress approved the printing of a national paper currency, issuing $2 million worth that month alone. Ten times that much was circulating by the following July, when the nation formally declared its independence. "Floods of Paper Money," an anxious John Adams called the massive issues that dwarfed earlier colonial experiments. But the "floods" could barely float a growing army. Congress called for new disbursements every month, then every two weeks. By the end of 1779, when they halted further emissions, the delegates in Philadelphia had printed more than $226 million in the small square bills called 'Continentals.' Over $100 million more came from the states, each of which printed its own bills. And still the war dragged on.[21]

The value of the Continental hinged on people's confidence in the American project, and on Congress's fiscal restraint. Both were in short supply in the first years of the war. The British held a decisive military advantage and gained crucial early victories. Congress simply could not afford monetary prudence. By turns unable and unwilling to wring taxes from a struggling people at war over taxation, legislators failed to prop up the dollar by taking money out of circulation. Infusions of specie from France, Spain, and Holland helped, but ultimately proved too small to stem the rising tide of paper. For the army to keep eating, the presses must keep running.

As an ever-increasing number of paper dollars chased a dwindling number of goods, prices soared. "My son . . . used to sell tow cloth at a pistareen a yard, now sells for two," wrote Samuel Dexter in the fall of 1775, when the war had barely begun. By 1779, the year his grandson Andrew Jr. was born, the Continental traded against specie at a rate of forty-two to one, and falling. Samuel Dexter damned the makeshift paper currency, calling it "no better than the *wampum* of the savages." All the "solid coin" he had saved, fruit of a lifetime of *"rising early and sitting up late and eating the bread of carefulness,"* now was "sadly metamorphosed into this vile trash." It grew more vile still. By 1781, it took $147 in continental paper to match the purchasing power of a single silver dollar. A sackful of paper couldn't fill a sack with groceries.[22]

That summer, Samuel's son Andrew returned to Boston, one among waves of dispossessed émigrés. He was thirty years old. His wife, Mary, was twenty-three and pregnant, with their toddler, Andrew Jr., in tow. Raised in a fine home in prosperous prewar Newport, she would have been shocked by the ravaged town. The fighting, nearing its end, was now confined to the southern states. But five years after the siege, the ruins remained. Churches, houses, fences, trees, piers, mills: anything made of wood had fallen victim to the occupying army's relentless quest for fuel. Schools, wharves, shops, even graveyards awaited repair. The Hollis Street Church, a simple wooden meetinghouse well south of the town center, had escaped unscathed. The Dexters baptized their newborn there in July, naming him Samuel after his grandfather and his great-grandfather. For good measure they asked the preacher to cast the devil out of three-year-old Andrew at the same time.[23]

Though its privations had eased since the starving winter of 1779,

Boston still bore war's deep scars. Discharged infantrymen roamed the streets, pressed (sometimes unsuccessfully) into service with the "corps of invalids." Smallpox stalked the wharves. Sick and wounded soldiers languished in warships in the harbor, while the town struggled to muster enough men to fulfill the quota it owed the Continental army. The selectmen collected corn and guns, live beef and old shoes, to send to the troops in Virginia. Paper money remained abundant and worthless, provisions scarce and expensive. Starving families filled the almshouse to near bursting, so many that the Overseers of the Poor could not provide them with sufficient bread and other "Necessaries of Life."[24]

As in all wartime economies, scarcity for most meant opportunity for some, laws against profiteering notwithstanding. Smugglers and privateers flourished, as did merchants who had stockpiled goods before the blockades to sell them dear afterward. Unpersuaded by hungry city customers who accused them of extortion, farmers commanded record prices for grain, meat, and milk. People with ready cash bought homes that Loyalists had abandoned when they fled— some of the finest property in the city—at fire-sale prices. Those who could afford to hoarded money itself, confident the government would someday make good on the promises it printed. Spontaneous paper fortunes blossomed and died. One Massachusetts revolutionary described "a world turned topsy turvy." He was "still drudging . . . for a morsel of Bread, while others, and among them fellows who would have cleaned my shoes five years ago, have amassed fortunes, and are riding in chariots."[25]

Despite or because of the giddy economic climate, the elder Andrew Dexter didn't make a go of it this time. If he managed to reopen his Cheap Shop, he didn't advertise. Perhaps he lacked the steely nerves or the full purse or the malleable ethics needed to succeed in postbellum Boston. Or maybe Mary Newton Dexter wanted to live closer to her family. (Newport, too, was suffering terribly in the aftermath of British occupation.) For whatever combination of reasons, the couple soon pulled up stakes, their fourth move since their marriage. By the summer of 1783, Samuel Dexter was sending parcels for his two young grandsons to Providence, Rhode Island.[26]

A river town of some six thousand inhabitants and fewer than a thousand dwellings, Providence was roughly a third the size of the city the Dexters left behind. Yet the small capital of the tiny state of Rhode Island was, for better or for worse, the paper money mecca of the United States. Since the colony's founding as a refuge for dissenters in the early seventeenth century, Rhode Islanders had defied conventions of all sorts—religious, political, and fiscal. The colonial legislature emitted no fewer than eight waves of paper bills between 1715 and 1750. Its easy money policies made Rhode Island's economy especially dynamic, and earned the opprobrium of more conservative New Englanders. As early as the 1730s, merchants from neighboring colonies had begun refusing Rhode Island bills.[27]

In Rhode Island as across the United States, the Revolution greatly increased the thirst for paper. Before the fighting was done, the state had printed nearly $1 million of its own bills. Given its small population—around fifty thousand by the war's end—this was an enormous sum, more than enough to spark hyperinflation. In 1779, one Providence merchant spied a beaver hat priced, exorbitantly, at $400. When he returned to the shop after lunch to offer the merchant a stack of bills, the cost had risen to $450. He bought it, sure that it would command $500 by the next morning. Yet the flood of paper was not nearly sufficient to finance the state's public debts, which spiraled in the 1780s. Specie flowed out of Rhode Island as its taxes reached crippling new heights. Desperate for cash, farmers sold off lands at a fraction of their value. In Providence and Newport, merchants resorted to barter.[28]

The state legislature responded to a worsening depression with a familiar remedy: by authorizing large new emissions that they declared legal tender in all contracts. The cure quickly proved worse than the disease. Printing began in May 1786, and by August, the new paper was trading at a third the value of specie. Increasingly stiff penalties against people who refused to accept the bills at face value failed to check their fall. When the state retired the notes three years later, they were worth just 6 percent what they promised.[29] Paper money opponents again used "Rogue's Island" to illustrate the medium's dangers. One French traveler claimed he could read on the faces of Providence merchants "the imprint of the contempt which the other states feel for Rhode Island[,] and of the inhabitants' awareness that they deserve this contempt." The poets known as the Connecticut wits lampooned the state for making the "press [its] mint, and dunghill rags [its] ore." For the "wiser race," they insisted, there was only one recourse: "Like Lot from Sodom, from Rhode Island run."[30]

Some of Providence's more established merchants *did* flee the state without looking back. But Andrew Dexter Sr. ran *toward* this paper paradise, a porous place, less hide bound than the venerable city on the Charles River. As Providence recovered its prosperity, he climbed through the city's fluid ranks. Dexter opened a new Cheap Store on the first floor of his home on Main Street. He bought and sold town lots, making land into another commodity to exchange for paper.[31] Decades ahead of the textile boom that would make New England an industrial center, he tried his hand at cloth production. In 1787, he and two partners opened a small manufactory in the warren of dilapidated buildings known as the "Rotten Row." Prince Hopkins, an enslaved black man who had lost a leg and an arm fighting the British, worked their crude spinning jenny, making thread other servants wove into rope or coarse cloth.[32]

But Dexter soon decided that his future lay not in rags, but in the paper made from them. He gave up the spinning concern and stocked his shop with lottery tickets as well as cloth wares. He went to Philadelphia to broker shares in the Bank of the United States for would-be purchasers in Rhode Island, and he joined forces with the Providence gentlemen agitating for a local bank. After a seven-year struggle, they gained their charter in the fall of 1791. That October, the stockholders of the new Providence Bank—the nation's fifth—gathered at the courthouse to pay in their shares and elect nine men to head the enterprise. Andrew Dexter Sr. was eighth among them. He served as a director of the bank for the next five years. In 1797, the freeholders of Providence ratified Dexter's status as a leading money man by electing him town auditor.[33]

Great-grandson of a minister, grandson of a merchant, son of a banker, Andrew Dexter Jr. spent his boyhood in a spacious home in the commercial heart of Providence, a house that paper built. He, too, must have demonstrated early promise handling paper, for he read, wrote, and ciphered well enough to become the second Dexter in two generations to seek higher education. Before the summer of 1796, he enrolled at Rhode Island College, the humble local institution that a Providence merchant's bequest would soon rechristen Brown University. The classical curriculum he studied there resembled the course his great-grandfather had followed in Cambridge in the 1720s. But the little Baptist college was no Harvard. Nor was university training any longer the preserve of would-be clergymen. Other paper trades beckoned Dexter and his classmates. Among their cohort future lawyers and merchants outnumbered future ministers by more than two to one. None of the eighteen young men who comprised the class of 1798 knew his destiny, of course. But like many inheritors of the Revolution, they placed great confidence in their ability to shape the future, the nation's as well as their own.[34]

In the fall of 1798, with terror overspreading France and the Adams administration embattled in Philadelphia, the future seemed especially unsettled. "You, gentlemen, have the singular fortune to complete the course of your collegiate education at a period the most alarming and interesting that the world ever saw," the college's thirty-year-old president told them. With everything up for grabs, the graduates must remember to strive for success in the next life as well as in this one. "Not only remember that you are immortal, but that you are accountable creatures," he urged. Andrew Dexter Jr. took at least part of this lesson to heart. An accountable creature indeed, he had worked hard at his studies. When the tutors handed down class ranks, he came in second, thereby earning the chance to address his peers at commencement on September 5.[35]

Picture him, clad in the black bombazine robe and four-cornered cap that mark the occasion, striding past the hawkers and dram shops along Main Street to enter the Baptist Meeting House at the head of his class at ten that morning. After the opening hymn and benediction, Dexter takes the podium to offer a salutation in Latin and a ten-minute speech in English. He has wavy auburn hair, piled high and loose in the day's youthful fashion. His eyes are light, his gaze penetrating. He blushes easily, and the close quarters and hot words must bring color to his face as he uses his bully pulpit to caution against "the intrigues of ambition," a deluding passion that leaves those in its thrall "jealous" and "discontented." Despite the warning, careful listeners can tell that Dexter is flush with ambition, and with pride. He directs his homily not just to his seventeen confreres, but to "the youth of America." "By us alone," he insists, must the "invaluable legacies" of the nation's founders "be transmitted to posterity. Yes, upon us depend the freedom and happiness of millions left unborn."[36]

*Upon us alone*: young Dexter imagined his classmates as accountable creatures, yes, but also as moral free agents, making themselves as they made their way in the world. In this respect he shared the core ideology of the nation's aspiring men, the restless youth whom everyone called "the rising generation." Providence city fathers hoped the town's rising generation would make its ascent *there*. They had created the bank, in part, to hold on to such comers. Absent such "a Spring to promote Our Young Men in Buissiness hear," one of the bank's founders warned, "they must & will Continue to go to Such places as will Aid them with the Means of Buissness." His logic had prevailed, and now the Providence Bank provided "a Good & Substantial Foundation for the Commertial, Manufactoral, & Macanical Riseing Generation": a paper foundation, a reservoir of ready capital.[37]

But Andrew Dexter Jr. wanted a bigger pond. As he proclaimed at commencement, his vision of the nation was expansive, stretching "from the shores of the Atlantic to the banks of the Mississippi." His sense of his own industrious future extended at least to the banks of the Charles. So at the age of nineteen he bid Providence farewell and headed north to seek his fortune in the city that had beaten his father a decade and a half before.

✑

The pathway from Charlestown's Main Street to his uncle's front door was tiled in black and white marble and flanked by two hundred poplar trees arrayed in almost military precision. Shortly after his graduation, young Andrew Dexter walked up that shade-dappled allée to the estate Samuel Dexter had built in the shadow of Bunker Hill, upon the ashes of the town leveled in the late Revolution. Formal gardens edged in boxwood fronted the five-thousand-square-foot mansion, which (its owner boasted) had "pretensions equal, if not superior to any within the Commonwealth."

Andrew had grown up in a solidly built house on a tight urban lot. His uncle's domain was something altogether different. Its orchards and greenhouses, its "pure country air" and urbane conveniences marked it as the "Elegant Seat" of a distinguished gentleman. From the cupola you could see for twenty miles, the endless vista anchored by a commanding "prospect of the Harbour of Boston."[38]

With its eighty-odd wharves reaching into the Atlantic like so many grasping fingers, the harbor was the nerve center of New England's trade, and trade was thriving once again. "Boston is barely reviving from the horrors of civil war," one French traveler noted in 1788, "but its commerce is flourishing." The boom would continue for nearly two decades. For as the European powers went back to the business of warfare, the United States got down to the business of business. The nation's declared neutrality proved as lucrative as it was precarious. The per capita value of Boston's exports nearly doubled between 1790 and 1800; customs receipts quadrupled. Laden with fish, beef, pork, grain, lumber, furs, soap, oil, candles, rum, cloth, and much else besides, ships out of Boston traversed the globe, returning with holds crammed full of sugar, tea, coffee, wine, silk, and porcelain. From Samuel Dexter's cupola, his curious nephew could see hundreds of masts stretching skyward, the steeples of trade. Peering down upon this maritime theater created what one traveler called the "singular and beautiful" illusion that ships' rigging spanned Boston's streets while "the colours of all nations" hovered "over the tops of the houses." On a clear day, an aspiring young man might imagine he glimpsed the coast of far-off Canton.[39]

Samuel Dexter's reach did not extend quite that far, but it was broad indeed. Young Andrew's father had achieved a decent station, earning his neighbors' esteem and the wherewithal to retire from trade to country life, much as his father had done before him. But Samuel, the elder Andrew's youngest sibling and only brother, had done better. He took the Dexter family's peculiar blend of daring and restlessness and vulnerability to the national stage. When Andrew crossed his uncle's threshold, he entered the realm of Big Paper.[40]

Books, for starters. Born in 1761, Samuel Dexter rose from a comfortable childhood to a stellar university career. In a poem he wrote for his Harvard brethren, Samuel disavowed the "wild ambition" that animated the day's more "martial souls." He protested too much. "Modesty is young Ambition's ladder," one of his many critics later scoffed. The jab, lifted from Shakespeare, neatly captured the Janus-faced character of young Samuel, who blushed as he looked skyward. In July 1781, when Harvard celebrated its first public commencement after seven years of war and strife, Samuel Dexter delivered the valedictory address. From triumph in the classroom he vaulted to renown as a lawyer. Intuitive, fearless, sometimes cutting, he made an unrelenting courtroom advocate. His "gifts. . . . are those of the tongue," said an observer who had watched Dexter out-talk his opponents. This was not a compliment. Some damned him as a tongue-for-hire, arguing every side of every issue. One who doubted the firmness of his party allegiances suggested that Samuel "change his Christian name, and to sign himself in the future Ambi-Dexter."[41]

Samuel Dexter's growing reputation soon took him past law books and into the congressional record. No town offices for him: he entered the state legislature before he turned thirty, and had finished a term

Samuel Dexter *(1761–1816),*
*by Charles Harold Macdonald, 1893,*
*after Gilbert Stuart.*

in Congress by the time he passed thirty-five. Just before his nephew joined him in Charlestown, Samuel Dexter—styled *Hon. Samuel Dexter* now, and not yet forty—got the Massachusetts legislature's nod for a seat in the United States Senate.

Then and afterward the Boston press lavished ink on Samuel Dexter's eccentric political career. Yet the paper that compelled him wasn't newsprint. It was money. "Dexter is very able, and will be an Ajax at the bar as long as he stays," the arch-Federalist Fisher Ames noted. But "if he did not love money very well, he would not pursue the law." By all accounts Samuel Dexter *did* love it, a fact that made him different from his father. The old merchant, his son insisted, "saw nothing lovely in money, but the means of enjoyment and kindness." The deprivations of wartime had turned him into an ascetic; he refused well-paying commissions, lived on little, "squandered nothing," and gave away much. The son responded differently. In the dizzy postwar world Samuel Dexter joined the fast-growing clan that many damned as "the *speculating tribe*."[42]

Before the eighteenth century, *speculator* meant roughly the same thing as *spectator*. He (the speculator was male) was a contemplative type, a watcher. But by the time of the American Revolution, its meaning had begun to change. Writing in 1776, Adam Smith felt the need to define "what is called the trade of speculation" for his readers. The "speculative merchant," he explained, "exercises no one regular, established, or well known branch of business. . . . He enters into every trade when he foresees that it is likely to be more than commonly profitable, and he quits it when he foresees that its profits are likely to return to the level of other trades." "Sudden fortunes" and sudden losses were the equally likely results. No longer an observer, the speculator had become a doer—and sometimes an undoer.[43]

Smith called the speculative merchant a "bold adventurer." Post-Revolutionary Americans had other names for him. Jobbers, jackals, and jockeys: these were but a few of the epithets leveled at the men who made fortunes out of paper. Their enemies, who were many, cast them as sharks, hawks, wolves: "artful" predators glutting themselves upon "honest" hardworking prey. They were diviners, reading entrails for a hint of what the future held, or alchemists, using thick smoke to mask the underlying hollowness of their promises. One Connecticut critic joked that the paper money speculators so loved should be emblazoned with the image of "Dr. Faustus paying the Devil for the black arts."[44]

These were dark assessments of the speculating bent, yet not wholly inaccurate ones. Paper men openly pursued private gain, which many of their countrymen deemed incompatible with the public good. And they chased fortune not by working up a sweat, but by playing hunches. Paper men bet on everything from banks to bridges. Paying pennies on the dollar, they bought up moribund Continentals and other public securities, holding them against the day the federal government would make good its debts. Such maneuvers defied the labor theory of value, which said that work made worth. Speculators had different ideas about the nature of value. Let others invest their toil; they would peddle confidence.

And confidence mattered. If they were gamblers, paper men were also *believers* in the unlikely new nation's future greatness, and their faith—their bets—created capital that helped to make it so. It is no accident that so many of the country's founders—George Washington and Thomas Jefferson, Benjamin Franklin and Alexander Hamilton, Robert Morris and William Duer—were brazen speculators of one kind and another. Under their leadership, Americans developed a reputation as a speculating people. "Were I to characterize the *United States*," said one British traveler who toured the country in the 1790s, "it should be by the appellation of the *land of speculation*."[45]

Like the great paper men of his day, Samuel Dexter bought into what schemes he could with what resources he had. In his early twenties when the war ended, he may have had the foresight to buy up the depreciated Continentals that had threatened his father's well-being. Certainly he sought other opportunities to make money out of money. Like his brother, he was a bank man, subscribing largely to Hamilton's Bank of the United States in the summer of 1791. As the price of shares soared from $25 to more than $300 in a matter of weeks, Samuel grew a paper fortune, only to lose it just as quickly as prices tumbled back down. The ride seems only to have emboldened him. For he soon joined forces with a cluster of Bostonians who sought to make money out of another sort of paper: land titles.[46]

Anglo-Americans had always been hungry for land, whose acquisition by treaty, contract, and outright theft formed the backbone of the colonial experience. In the late eighteenth century, after war removed imperial barriers to westward migration, that hunger turned to mania. As its population swelled—more than doubling between 1776 (when it stood at about 2.5 million) and 1800 (when it topped 5.3 million)—the United States began in earnest its relentless push toward the Pacific. This great surge westward meant different things to different Americans. The mass migration of whites dispossessed natives by the pen and the sword, and visited a second middle passage upon millions of the African Americans enslaved in the land of liberty. To ordinary white men the West spoke the American vernacular of fresh starts; to their wives it whispered of isolation and desperate toil.

For speculators like Samuel Dexter, the West was strictly a paper affair, a derivative of the dreams of others. These dreams grew feverish in the 1780s and 1790s, as state legislatures sold off the huge tracts known as their western reserves. Opponents of speculation argued that such legislative acts amounted to a sort of magic, turning "acres by [the] millions" into "transferable, personal, moveable property"— that is, into paper. Private land companies sprung like rabbits from so many hats, turning the deeds they bought from their governments into stocks, bonds, mortgages: paper one step further removed from the soil it represented. In and out, that was the land company's gambit, as one Connecticut letter carrier rhymed:

> No matter what's the land nor where:
> Such things are not the seller's care.
> And no one buys them to retain,
> But to grow rich and—*sell again*.

Often, these sales turned out to be what the Connecticut cleric Timothy Dwight called "fairyland transactions." Ordinary purchasers signed away real money, only to discover they had bought lots that were already owned, or under water. Some found themselves proud owners of "tracts which never existed."[47]

Nowhere was the transformation of earth into paper more frantic than in Georgia's western reserves, the vast region that would later congeal into the states of Alabama and Mississippi. Fertile soil and a long growing season made those lands especially suitable for cotton, a crop that the recent invention of the cotton gin was beginning to make profitable. Political circumstances made titles to those lands especially convoluted. The Cherokee, the Creek, the Choctaw, and the Chickasaw; Spain, France, England, the United States, and the state of

Georgia all claimed dominion over what came to be known as the "Yazoo" lands, after the Mississippi River tributary that cut across its northwestern corner. Daring investors loved the chaos, which held prices down and kept timid buyers out. Southern land companies multiplied, and with them pamphlets touting the untapped riches of the Yazoo lands. However cloudy the titles on which they were based, shares in these ventures sold briskly, touching off what Dwight called an "ocean of speculation. . . . throughout the Union."[48]

Samuel Dexter set sail upon that shimmering ocean in February 1796. On the thirteenth of that month, a group of investors calling themselves the New England Mississippi Land Company purchased 11 million acres of the Yazoo tract from agents of the Georgia-Mississippi Company, who journeyed 1,100 miles to Boston to deliver the deeds and collect promises amounting to $1.4 million. (The price represented a profit of 650 percent to the Georgia Company, a feat all the more remarkable since the state of Georgia nullified their titles the very day of the transaction.) Samuel Dexter was one of the New England Mississippi Land Company's founders, and he numbered among its largest shareholders. Measured in acres, his Yazoo domain encompassed a land mass half again as large as the state of Rhode Island. He measured it in dollars, a rapidly increasing number of them.[49]

During the second half of February the rage for Georgia lands overspread Boston "like a destructive kind of epidemic." Those who caught the fever—"all classes of people," according to one skeptic—left their shops and work yards and boardinghouses to search out Yazoo paper. Their "whirl of . . . giddy pursuit" ended when they set their hands to New England Mississippi Land Company notes, "transported with the idea that they had made their fortunes" with a signature. Share prices climbed. The speculator's alchemy transmuted Dexter's imaginary property into a fortune of more than one hundred thousand dollars, about fifty times what his grand Charlestown estate was worth.[50]

Then, in mid-March, Boston newspapers confirmed what merchants had been whispering for weeks. Knowingly or not—opinions varied—the New England Mississippi Land Company had purchased invalid titles from unscrupulous men. The securities based on those titles rested not on land but on air. It was an all-too familiar tale. ("LAND JOBBING has become so common of late," mused one Federalist editor, "that the bursting of the Georgia bubble, affords matter only for a 'tooth pick conversation.'") The familiar sequel followed. Rudely awakened from their "golden dreams of wealth and fortune," small investors dumped their shares, whose value approached zero.[51]

At which point, like any good speculator, Samuel Dexter bought more. Nobody supposed that he meant to move to Georgia and bushwhack his way through a million acres of wilderness. No, the game was to hold these Yazoo cards until his hand improved. Eager to stack the deck in its favor, the New England Mississippi Land Company transformed itself into a lobbying organization. When Andrew Dexter Jr. arrived in Charlestown in the fall of 1798, he found his uncle and the other leaders of the company enmeshed in what became a decades-long legal battle to clear their titles or extract compensation for their losses, a fight they would take to Congress, the Supreme Court, and the president himself.[52]

Andrew had come to Boston to study under his uncle, a one-man law school charged with preparing the young collegian for admission to the bar. (The Suffolk Bar examined Harvard graduates after a year or so of such tutelage, but Brown wasn't Harvard, and Andrew would have been expected to study three times that long.) Every morning save Sundays, the pair might take the fifteen-minute walk from the Charlestown heights across the Charles River Bridge and down Hanover Street to Samuel Dexter's office on Tremont. There Andrew could slog through Samuel's extensive library, soaking in the arcane vocabulary of pleading and the accumulated wisdom of the English common law. With their intricate claims about history, jurisdiction, and property rights, the New England Mississippi Land Company's pleadings offered an education in themselves, a hands-on internship in American contract and constitutional law.[53]

But forget the court papers and the treatises. Andrew's apprenticeship began with the academic study of law, but it did not end there.

As important to his future, and far more captivating, were the personal connections his uncle forged for him. At Samuel Dexter's office, in his parlor, and especially on 'Change—the open-air stock market stretching east along State Street, where, rain or shine, men about town gathered at midday to trade gossip and swap paper—Andrew Dexter made business and social contacts (often the two were the same) that carried him through his life.[54]

Samuel Dexter's Yazoo brotherhood counted a dozen or so men, three of whom extended their patronage to his protégé. Born in the early 1750s, William Hull, Samuel Brown, and Perez Morton came to think of the younger Dexter as something between a business partner and a kinsman. Each had a generation on Andrew, and a crucial decade on Samuel; all three fought in the Revolution whose freedoms and challenges the Dexters had inherited without blood sacrifice. (Then as now, a war record was a vital political credential, one Samuel Dexter conspicuously lacked.) Hull, a Connecticut farm boy and then a Yale man, had triumphed at Trenton and suffered at Valley Forge with George Washington before commanding his own detachment in New York. After his regiment disbanded, Colonel Hull opened a law office in Newton, Massachusetts. When he needed cash, he mortgaged his large brick estate to Samuel Dexter, whose Federalist sympathies didn't get in the way of his friendship with Jeffersonians like Hull.[55]

Samuel Brown moved from Newport to Boston just after the siege and quickly proved his mettle as one of the war's young "worthies." By 1779, he had amassed enough Continental currency to buy much of the property confiscated from the exiled Loyalist governor, Thomas Hutchinson. After the war, Brown set up shop as a merchant. In the 1780s, not content with the crowded West Indies trade, he sponsored one of the first voyages from Boston to China. At the same time he began to climb the rungs of local officialdom, rising from watchman, to selectman, to membership in the troika who audited the town's accounts. Shortly after Andrew Dexter Jr. arrived in town, Brown became Boston's navy agent, negotiating contracts with the merchants and manufacturers who provisioned New England seamen. Commercially ambitious, Brown was politically unpredictable. He supported the construction of a grand Boston theater, a project that old guard revolutionaries construed as a sign of Federalist degeneracy. Yet he also served as a director of the Union Bank, whose founders the Federalists denounced as "Jacobins." Like Samuel Dexter and William Hull, Brown also chased Yazoo land. On paper—hotly contested paper—he owned a hundred twenty-five thousand acres of Georgia.[56]

Perez Morton shared Brown's allegiances—to the Dexters, the theater, the Union Bank, and the Yazoo faith. But in each case Morton's stake was larger. He was the theater's main champion, the Union Bank's landlord, the crux of the Dexter family network, and one of the largest Yazoo landowners. Morton claimed exactly 389,375 Georgia acres, not a rod less. The obsessive reckoning—retotaled in a close hand, many times, over many years—suited a man who could be calculating and reckless by turns. A combination of roofless ambition, hard work, and simple good luck had taken him from a family of modest means to the zenith of Boston society. Morton's unruly passions threatened that position. But he kept careful accounts of how he had gotten there.[57]

Morton's father had owned the White Horse Tavern, a Newbury Street institution where political banter flowed as freely as ale. But Joseph Morton groomed his son for a different sort of bar, sending him to the Latin School at the age of ten, and then to Harvard, where Perez distinguished himself in student politics. He graduated in 1771 and won admission to the Suffolk Bar three years later, at the age of twenty-three. Morton began his legal career in the summer of 1774, as Boston struggled under the Intolerable Acts that had shut down the port and the courts. Full of youth's heedless daring, Perez turned the widening political chasm into a space of opportunity. Pleading the cases of others persecuted in the patriot cause, he grabbed the attention of the rebellion's leaders. Samuel and John Adams both favored him. A portrait engraved in 1807, when Morton was a corpulent and bewigged fifty-six-year-old, shows traces of the fiery gallant he was in

Perez Morton,
*by Charles Balthazar Julien*
*Févret de Saint-Mémin, ca. 1807.*

those days: the jutting chin he led with, the high forehead that con-
noted his powerful intellect, the deep-set heavily fringed eyes that
advanced his claims as a man of feeling.[58]

Like his friend Samuel Dexter, Morton garnered his first real fame
for public speaking. In April 1776, he delivered a stirring oration at
King's Chapel, during a ceremony for the reinterment of Joseph Warren, who had fallen at Bunker Hill. Turning Warren's death into
martyrdom and his remains into relics, Morton called for a complete
break with Britain, still a radical proposition that spring. Abigail
Adams sat among the throng, electrified by Morton's words. The
"Subject must have inspired him," she told her husband, adding that
"a young fellow could not have wished a finer opportunity to have displayed his talents." Adams hoped the speech would go into print and

indeed, before a month had passed, book buyers in Boston, New York, and Philadelphia could purchase copies of Morton's *Oration* for a sixpence. Schoolboys read it for years to come. Andrew Dexter Jr. had yet to meet Morton when he cribbed from the *Oration* in his salutatory address to the graduates of Rhode Island College.[59]

The *Oration* made Perez Morton's war, and the war made Perez Morton. Not so much the fighting, though he briefly saw action in Rhode Island. But mostly Morton talked his way through the war, dazzling audiences in the courtroom as well as in the coffeehouses, where patriot committees plotted strategy. Detractors called him simply "the Orator," hinting at the slipperiness of his arguments, which he often deployed against fleeing Tories, and sometimes marshaled on their behalf. A poet satirized his flexible gifts:

> Thy tongue, shrewd Perez, favouring ears insures,—
> The cash elicits, and the vote secures.

Clever with deeds as well as words, Morton grew rich trading abandoned Loyalist property. As the war drew to a close, he grabbed a particularly plummy parcel for himself, the old-fashioned way: he married it. In February 1781, he wed Sarah Apthorp, a celebrated belle who belonged to one of the town's wealthiest Loyalist families.[60]

Twenty-two-year-old Sarah Apthorp had spent her childhood up in the Palladian mansion her grandfather built in the 1750s. Three stories high and five bays across, the brick home on elegant King Street was as imposing as it was ostentatious. An ironwork balcony, two white pilasters spanning its entire height, and a battlement railing crowned by the Apthorp family crest proclaimed the importance of its owners. A "polish'd world," Sarah called the home of her youth, a place where "taste and talent" flourished and "brilliant bounties shone." The town of Boston assessed the estate at $22,000, more than ten times the value of Samuel Dexter's Charlestown pile. From their exile, the Tory Apthorps sold it to their patriot son-in-law for £150.[61]

Old State House, *by James Brown Marston, 1801.*
*The Apthorp mansion is the second building from the right.*

King Street was State Street now. Amid the bare-knuckle jostling of republican life, the Apthorp mansion hearkened back to an imperial age. The Mortons embraced its English-style refinement, using the home to showcase dazzling, cosmopolitan lives. More strenuous Bostonians despised these "mushroom gentry," as they called the empty-headed bon vivants who slept till ten, breakfasted at noon, and passed their days in a whirl of tea and talk. Satirists ridiculed the Mortons as *Messieur et Madam Importance.* "I mean to be remarked for splendour and luxury," proclaims a fictional Sarah Morton, "to ascend to the pinnacle of politeness and the tip top of the better-most genii." Where she chases fashion, her consort seeks fame. "I have ever thought that keeping aloof, and only appearing at times, when some important questions were agitated, would be most likely to secure my importance," he muses. We embrace the "principles of republicanism," explains the mock Perez, "but now we soften them down in the school of politeness, and make them wear a more pleasing garb."[62]

Sarah Morton reigned in the parlor, lounging on her damask sofa and trading bons mots with carefully composed groups of worthies. According to one regular guest, Sarah—"Philenia," as she styled herself in print—assembled a heady mixture of men and women, "Jews & Gentiles," "people of all *party* colors; but no low people . . . no hewers of wood nor drawers of water." For Perez Morton, 'Change—just steps from his ornately carved front door—was the masculine antidote to his wife's salon. There the lingua franca was money, and any man who spoke it fluently was welcome. In place of couplets he traded rumors about cargoes and contracts, land deals and law cases: stories with prices attached, but gossip just the same.[63]

Perez Morton's appetites didn't stop at paper, alas. In love as well as commerce, he was something of a speculator, subject to consuming if short-lived infatuations. (His "transient flame," Sarah Morton called the passion her husband so liberally bestowed.) Well before Andrew Dexter entered his life, Morton had transformed his glittering home into what one contemporary called a "conspicuously infamous" one. Early in 1787, Perez Morton seduced his wife's younger sister Fanny, who had lived for a time with the Mortons on State Street. That autumn, he became a father twice over. In September, Sarah Morton gave birth to Charlotte, the couple's fifth child in six years, and their last. Fanny delivered her child—Morton's daughter *and* his niece—shortly afterward. A friend whose adulteries Morton had once helped to conceal returned the favor, spiriting away the baby to be raised in a nearby town. As Fanny resumed her affair with Morton, local scribblers picked up the scent of scandal, which they broadcast in coy verses:

No longer by vain fear, or shame control'd
In guilty amours, grown securely bold,
Mocking rebuke, they brave it in our streets,
And ******, even at noon, his mistress meets.

So public in their crimes, so daring grown,
They almost take a pride to have them known.

Known they soon were. And when Sarah's brother James demanded
a duel with the man who had betrayed one of his sisters by seducing
the other, Fanny took poison. She left a rambling suicide note insisting that "my once lov'd Morton is the first & last man I Ever knew,"
and begging him to care for her "sweet Infant . . . if ever you lov'd its
mother."[64]

News of the tragedy swept through the streets and lingered on the
page. The press bristled with veiled allegations and equally veiled
defenses. Morton knew paper, knew he would outlast the letters and
columns and poems, which depreciated more quickly than banknotes.
But in the winter of 1789, a thinly disguised version of the tale showed
up in *The Power of Sympathy,* a two-volume, three-hundred-page
novel complete with a prefatory lecture on the dangers of seduction
and an engraving of the debauched and abandoned girl. (*"O Fatal!
Fatal Poison!"* the caption reads.) Morton tried vainly to suppress the
book, which, as one satire held, would "brand him a villain [for] centuries to come."[65]

Not centuries, perhaps, but shame clung to Morton for years. His
professional star dimmed. In 1790, he was elected a counselor to the
Supreme Judicial Court, a group of esteemed lawyers that included his
friends William Hull and Samuel Dexter. But within several years, he
gave up the practice of law. His politics, vaguely Republican despite his
high-toned personal style, likewise grew tentative. He held local office
intermittently but never advanced to the national arena. Emboldened
by the whiff of scandal he trailed, Morton's political opponents mocked
his morals, his manners, and especially his love for money:

O, Perez, *thy case* might a hero abash,
Thou fearest thy neighbors—thou *lovest French cash*—
Sanscullotes, with scorn,
Behold thy dissembling,
Thy blustering and trembling—Huzza![66]

And indeed, from the 1790s, the pursuit of cash—French or otherwise—became Morton's overriding goal. Ever more the paper man,
he speculated in lands from Maine to Georgia. He turned his wife's
gay salon into a countinghouse, selling the Apthorp mansion to
the Union Bank, which lined its magnificent ballroom with desks
and hung a shop sign beside the grand entrance. (Sarah Morton eulo-
gized the "defaced" mansion: "How art thou changed! and mammon's
store/ Proclaims the reign of soul is o'er!") When young Andrew Dexter met him, Morton was ensconced in a grand new home in
Dorchester—financed, perhaps, with imaginary Yazoo winnings—
where he devoted himself to his various and growing commercial
interests.[67]

The seducer, the *salonière,* and the speculator had a great deal in
common. They inhabited a world of masks and mirrors—of *artifice*,
as their critics often said. Whether they chased love or money, they
used the same ammunition: the false face, the feigned promise. Yazoo
securities *"stand on the same footing as counterfeit bank bills,"* argued
Abraham Bishop, a Connecticut Republican who had bought some
himself before he began to inveigh against them. Those who sold the
stuff, he said, were no better than highwaymen. "Formerly the enemies of man frequented the public roads—put pistols to the breasts of
unsuspecting travellers, and robbed them of the valuables they had
about them," Bishop fulminated.

> We live to see robbery in a more refined stile. Men who never added
> an iota to the wealth or morals of the world, and whose single
> moment was never devoted to making one being wiser or happier
> throughout the universe—riding in their chariots—plotting the
> ruin of born and unborn millions—aiming with feathers to cut
> throats, and on parchments to seal destruction.

Like poor Fanny Apthorp, the people who bought what Morton, Dexter, Brown, and Hull sold staked their futures on empty words. As if
to drive Bishop's point home, booksellers advertised Bishop's *Georgia*

*Speculation Unveiled* alongside the scandalous *Memoirs of Stephen Burroughs*, son of a preacher turned conman turned counterfeiter.[68]

Speculators were not in fact counterfeiters. Not usually, anyway. However obscure their provenance, Yazoo securities were as different from Burroughs's fakes as wishing was from lying. Yet Bishop was right when he said that the Yazoo fraternity struck "at the foundation of many generations." The claims of tradition meant little to them. Preferring fickle fortune to steady competence, they chased the main chance. In this sense the Yazoo men were exemplary Americans, as Hector St. Jean de Crèvecoeur had so famously described them. Heedless of "ancient prejudices and manners," dogged in their pursuit of *"self-interest,"* devoted to "new principles . . . new ideas . . . new opinions," they were self-consciously *new men.*[69]

And like Crèvecoeur's Americans, the Yazoo men were promiscuous, in the eighteenth-century sense (Morton in the twenty-first-century sense as well . . . ). Faith in the rewards that attended risk imparted a shared identity to an otherwise diverse and fluid group. They came from different ethnic and family backgrounds and pledged different parties. They attended different churches, but these good paper men shared a reverence for Mammon. Money's god prized novelty and flexibility, tenacity and daring. Morton expressed something like their catechism when he pled the New England Mississippi Land Company's case to Congress: "Whatever is not forbidden by law, is permitted," he argued, "and whatever is permitted, is lawful."[70]

Paper's novice, Andrew Dexter rehearsed that creed at his uncle's side, shuttling between Charlestown and 'Change throughout 1798 and 1799. In the spring of 1800, he followed his mentor to Washington, the new national capital on the Potomac. The town was not so much rough as raw, its appearance the product of a decade-long orgy of speculation that had created more building sites than buildings. "If I wished to punish a culprit," said one congressman, "I would send him to do penance in this place, oblige him to walk about this city, city do I call it? This swamp—this lonesome dreary swamp, secluded from every delightful or pleasing thing." It was with considerable reluctance that Samuel Dexter accepted John Adams's nomination as secretary of war, at which post he worked until January, when he took the helm at Treasury. That job made him the nation's chief paper man, with Andrew Jr. as his private secretary.[71]

In a city of work yards and hovels, the Dexters were fortunate in their six-bedroom home on F Street, near the temporary quarters of the War Department. For the most part, though, their two years in Washington amounted to a hardship tour for the family, as painful as it was instructive. As the contest for the presidency deepened into partisan warfare in the final months of 1800, Samuel Dexter discovered anew how vicious politics could be. While Congress struggled to break the deadlock among Adams, Jefferson, and Aaron Burr, Republican newspapers heaped vitriol on the current administration. Before Jefferson's inauguration, Samuel Dexter had been called a doddering grandmother, an arsonist, and a "dexterous" thief, an irresistible pun that would follow the family for years.[72]

Through it all Samuel Dexter offered his nephew a model of calm endurance, as well as an object lesson in the bitter fruits of public service. Andrew could be forgiven for supposing the world of paper money a gentler one than that of newspaper politics. Let the Republicans heap scorn on the Yazoo brotherhood. Call them crooks and liars, men "bankrupt of character as well as fortune," in *Philadelphia Aurora* editor William Duane's stinging phrase. Never mind their avarice, their cunning, their fluid understanding of value. Andrew Dexter had seen more honor among them than in the halls of Congress.[73]

By the fall of 1803, he had joined them in earnest, as an equal partner in his uncle's Boston law practice. He lived in the back room of their office on Court Street, among the bankers and merchants who peddled paper on 'Change. The Dexters rented the space; Andrew owned no real estate, nor much else besides. In addition to his profession—a credential of still uncertain value—his buffer against economic disaster was personal property that Boston's tax assessors valued at $250, the rough equivalent of six months' wages for a skilled laborer. Andrew Dexter greeted his twenty-fifth year with much more in his head than in his pockets. Turning his soaring ambitions into something at once liquid and concrete was the goal he would chase, with great daring and startling initial success, for the rest of his life.[74]

⁓

"Boston is so grown you would scarce know it for your native place," Susan Apthorp Bulfinch told her brother in 1804. Imposing new buildings contained the poor and displayed the powerful. Well-stocked shops enticed "the Young and the gay." A glorious new State House on Beacon Street had replaced the old town house on State; the Apthorp family's ancient home was now a bank. Bulfinch, who held a much higher opinion of the mansion's makeover than did her first cousin Sarah Morton, pronounced its new exterior "handsomely orna-mented." She had good reason to boast. Her son Charles was the architect of Boston's face-lift, which had made him famous even as it made him poor. (Build a city, lose a fortune.) Still, she cherished those few places her son and his friends with money hadn't changed. "The Common still remains free," she noted ruefully, "and we hope always will, as we really begin to be crowded."[75]

In fact, its topography ensured that Boston had *always* been crowded. The Puritans' would-be City on a Hill huddled upon a clover-shaped peninsula less than two miles long and at most a mile across. The water that surrounded the near-island contained its spread, while the three peaks that dominated the town's west side—Beacon Hill, Pemberton Hill, and Mount Whoredom, the colonists had called them—pushed settlers toward the eastern half of the isthmus. There they built a maze of streets so crooked and narrow that they teemed even when the town had housed no more people than an English village.[76]

Still, the decade since 1794 had done more to transform Boston than the three score and ten years of fire and war, boom and bust that Susan Bulfinch had endured there. ("In so long a life there is much of sin, much of folly, to be lamented," she reflected.) Almost overnight, the wooden village of her youth vanished as fat purses and changing tastes claimed what the British occupation had spared. Swords into plowshares: masons pulled down the walls that had fortified the city during the Revolution, cleaning the bricks to make streets and bridges, schools and houses. Like an adolescent, Boston shot up suddenly, its gangly new skyline growing from two stories to three, even four. As speculators carved up the edges of the city, the town grew wider as well as taller. Nearly "every spot of land is cover'd with brick build- ings," Bulfinch marveled. "The buildings are continu'd so far that you must ride many miles before you can arrive at the country."[77]

Stylish Bostonians like the Bulfinches fancied a ride into the free air of the countryside. But more of the traffic flowed in the opposite direction, moving down country arteries toward the port whose pop- ulation had more than doubled since 1780. More than twenty-five thousand people lived in the transformed city Bulfinch described, and their number was still growing fast. Like all early Americans, Bosto- nians had large families. But nearly half the increase came from an influx of newcomers, migrants from rural New England and immi- grants from overseas. They came in boats and stages and private carriages, sailing into the harbor or walking up the Neck or rumbling across one of three new bridges connecting the peninsula to the main- land. They were farmers who would be clerks, artisans in search of bigger markets for their crafts, laborers haunting the wharves and building sites. They were growing families and, especially, young men on the make: men like Andrew Dexter Jr. and Nathan Appleton.[78]

For the well-traveled, college-educated Dexter, the passage from Washington back to Boston had been a homecoming, an exile's return. For Nathan Appleton, Boston meant something quite different. It was the metropolis glimmering in the distance, seventy miles and a world away from the New Hampshire farm where he was born in October 1779, six months after Dexter. Much like Dexter's birthplace of Brook- field, New Ipswich was a frontier town with village aspirations. But where the Dexters were city folk who retired to the country to play at farming, the Appletons were the real thing. They had worked New England's rocky soil for generations, and by the time Nathan came along, they owned more acreage than any other family in town. "I came to Boston a poor boy," Appleton later recalled, an exaggeration but not quite a lie. His family prospered, but they were not cultivated, not *worldly,* as Nathan yearned to be.[79]

Like many rural boys in the fast-changing world after the Revolution, Appleton aspired to more than a farmer's hard-won competence, even at the risk of ending up with less. During the winters, when farm chores were lighter, he attended the village's one-room school. He excelled at math, soon besting his teacher, and continued on to the town's new academy, which prepared promising young men for college. In the summer of 1794, he passed the entrance examination for Dartmouth, but he or his father decided upon a practical education instead. That fall, the sandy-haired boy of fifteen rode off to Boston— whence his brother Samuel had preceded him—bent on "trying his luck" in trade. Many years later, Nathan would render the journey as a pilgrim's progress toward an almost celestial city. Just across the Massachusetts line, Nathan's ten-year-old brother turned their horse toward home. From there Nathan "footed it" for miles, carrying everything he owned ("beside what was on my back") tied up in a small bandana. The next day, he picked up the Boston mail stage, which crossed the Charlestown Bridge at dusk. When he wrote his memoirs in the 1850s, Appleton could still picture the lamps lining the bridge that night, beacons hinting at his bright future.[80]

The "truth is," Appleton later insisted, "that my mind has always been devoted to many other things than money-making." Many nineteenth-century merchants chanted this mantra as they grew rich. "I can't help seeing openings for profit, neither can I help availing of them," explained Appleton's cousin William, born in Brookfield a few years after Andrew Dexter. "I pray God to keep me from being avaricious, and proud of my own success." If not smugly "avaricious," such young men were eager unto restlessness. ("I must be busy," William Appleton confessed. "I don't know how to stop.") Hunger for a future that was busier, bigger, and, yes, *richer* than the present had pulled many of them toward Boston in the first place. Nathan Appleton quickly got to work making that future. By day he kept the books at his brother's shop on Cornhill; at night he studied accounting and dabbled in French. In 1804, a decade after the mail stage dropped him at a boardinghouse on Quaker Lane, the teenage clerk had become a merchant worth over ten thousand dollars. Boston had once been his farthest shore. Now his contacts stretched from Liverpool to Calcutta.[81]

Nathan Appleton and his brother kept a set of scales to weigh gold and silver coins, lest somebody try to shortchange them. But at the Marlborough Street counters of S & N Appleton as everywhere else in the city, most customers paid with banknotes, another import whose supply grew ever more abundant and variegated, much like the cloth the Appletons sold. By the end of 1803, there were seventeen banks in Massachusetts; the next year, the state chartered four more. One diarist called the surge a "Bank Mania," fretting that "every company of boys, which had a stock in marbles" would soon seek incorporation as a bank. Just as people and goods flowed into the bustling port, paper money pooled in Boston, an emblem of the city's dominant place in regional trade. A writer in the *Palladium* imagined the picaresque journey of a five-dollar bill from country to city. Stuffed into pockets, purses, "watch cases, snuff-boxes and iron chests"; forced "to associate with a dirty handkerchief and a comb, bunch of keys, strips of poetry from newspapers, and a lucky-bone"; passed from hand to hand in shops, at work sites, and during "the midnight orgies of rakes"; the bill saw most of the state before landing, at last, in Boston, where he was crammed into a drawer with other members of his fast-growing family.[82]

This motley paper clan built everything Susan Bulfinch described. The buildings, the bridges, the newly paved streets themselves: all rested upon a paper foundation. Paper turned land and crops and even people into capital. It released wealth, and thus *created* wealth—not always fairly or painlessly, not always permanently, but ineluctably just the same. More than furs, more than whale oil, more than stone or lumber or bricks, paper revived Boston's sagging fortunes.[83]

But as one Boston banker wrote in January 1804, "blessings *misused* are the worst of evils." Having long bemoaned the dearth of ready cash in their city, the small fraternity of rich men who ran its banks now found themselves in the novel position of protesting too much. Too much of the wrong kinds, anyway: paper streaming toward State Street from rough, remote places, far from the old-line ports run by old-line families with old-line principles. Country financiers believed their new banks added money to the system, an assumption Boston's moneyed elite deemed "fallacious in the extreme." The size of the pie—the country's *real* capital, its specie—was fixed; only the size of the slices varied. As investors chased each new, new thing, the outlying banks drained specie from Boston coffers. In exchange they offered promises of uncertain value, money too far.[84]

*Distance*, the established bankers said, was money's worst enemy. Mostly Federalists, Boston's money men feared the creeping democracy all around them, in banking no less than politics. To them, good order was the soul of republicanism. Distance undermined it, making people difficult to govern, truth difficult to determine, and worth difficult to establish. For these reasons, they explained, banknotes held only "local and circumscribed value." Distinguishing "prudent and judicious enterprizes" from "bold speculative adventures" was more art than science, and each additional mile deepened its mysteries. Credibility couldn't be weighed on a shopkeeper's scales. You needed to look up State Street and see a bank's tidy brick building to take the measure of its officers on 'Change. Outlying banks frustrated such judgments. Nor could Bostonians easily redeem country notes for their equivalent in gold or silver—not when thirty miles represented a day's hard travel, a day's income forfeited. So canny city merchants discounted country notes, and the cheaper paper threatened the dearer, the *better*.[85]

Fearing that Boston would lose its monopoly on capital, and that they would then lose their hold on Boston, the city's bankers met off and on over several years to bemoan the surging tide of country paper. Finally, in the fall of 1803, the directors of Boston's four banks banded together to put up a flood wall. They pledged to discount the notes of outlying banks steeply, and to dispatch runners to the country to redeem their bills for specie. Then these "men of sound judgment" took to the press, urging their peers, "the Fathers of the State," to deny requests to create more banks.[86]

As others were quick to point out, these claims of "sound judgment" barely disguised the bankers' self-interest. Having won their own charters just a few years before, these "rich men" would now deprive others of "the fat things of the land." To their enemies, the bankers were an exclusive "fraternity," a *privileged order,* a "band of usurers." "They meet at their banks and plot evil," one critic alleged. They paid clerks "to ride into all the obscure towns," planning to turn paper back into gold and "to instruct and enlighten the people in the ways of wisdom." But their wisdom was false, an artifact of their outmoded notion that precious metals possessed deep, immutable value. They did not, any more than cowrie shells, or paper, or any other substance chosen to represent money. All these were but proxies, tools, the "labor-saving machinery" of commerce. "*Real value*" was itself an illusion.[87]

And their pursuit of that illusion had backfired. Instead of making paper more like the "solid money" they imagined gold and silver to be, the Boston fraternity's war on the country banks made the circulating medium more erratic. Shopkeepers hesitated to accept the paper their customers tendered, lest bankers refuse country notes in payment for shopkeepers' debts. Country banks grew anxious about emitting bills that paid riders might return en masse. The chaos give rise to a new sort of paper men whom Appleton called "money brokers." Pricing different notes according to secret formulas based on rumors filtered over distance, brokers made a fine profit. But their machinations made paper's value shakier. By design and by accident, the banking elders thus managed to check the ascent of their less established brethren. With money "continually fluctuating," wrote one opponent of the city bankers' campaign, "*no industrious young man can rise . . . for what he gains in one day is lost the next.*"[88]

In February 1804, a group of self-styled upstarts turned the existing debate on its head. The threat posed by country paper, they said, was imaginary, a "pretended deluge" manufactured by "a small powerful party." But the counterfeit crisis had provoked a real one. In response, this "Committee of . . . Shop-keepers and traders"—men "not so affluent as many of their fellow-citizens"—petitioned the state legislature to endorse a "novel system of banking": an institution that would issue no bills of its own, would but serve instead as a statewide clearinghouse for other notes. This was "ground untrod," they said, and they seemed uncertain about what even to call their project. They tried various labels: it was a "Guarantee Fund," a "Deposit Bank," an "Association Fund." The one that stuck was the Exchange Office—the Changery, for short—a name that neatly summarized the group's abiding faith in perpetual motion.[89]

The Changery proposed to raise a capital of two hundred thousand dollars, most of it in the notes of Massachusetts banks. *Any* of them. The office would accept bank bills "indiscriminately" and lend them out "promiscuously, as they are received." Like a bank, it would charge interest on loans. The Changery would also levy a commission, a fee pegged to the face value of the notes exchanged, rather than the perceived quality of any given breed of paper. Here the exchange men differed from brokers, who arrayed bills in concentric circles radiating out from State Street, the farther the bank, the deeper the discount. To the Changery, a bank's distance from Boston was irrelevant, since the enterprise would "supersede the inconvenience of returning [bills] home." Money *had* no home. So long as a bill passed from hand to hand to hand, it did what it promised. At rest it regressed to paper. The exchange men pledged not to redeem the notes they took in. By promoting a truly "free circulation," the office would "render the nominal value of said Bills permanent," and "one paper cent . . . as good as another."[90]

And paper, the exchange men said, was as good as anything else. No: better. The "ponderous gravity of specie" only retarded the flow of commerce. The Exchange Office agreed to maintain a reserve of fifty thousand dollars in coin, but its founders saw this fund as vestigial, ceremonial: "neither more nor less, than simply a guarantee of public confidence." If jittery investors liked shiny things, the Changery would show them metal. Beyond such display, "gold and silver . . . would be useless in its vaults." The *what* of money was arbitrary, so long as the chosen representative of value was "convenient, easy of transfer, and not liable to depreciation." Paper had the first two qualities. Now, the Changery's steady guidance would make it stable, too. Then, as rain nourished crops, free-flowing paper would nourish "all classes of men":

> Society, enlivened with pleasing prospects, will be dil[i]gently engrossed in scenes of employment, irksome indolence become unfashionable, and beggarly despondency find no congenial abode in the human breast. Commerce . . . will walk hand in hand with industry, and the community subsist on the fat of the land. Public spirit, elbowed by opulence, will step nobly forward . . . to throw magnificence over towns.

Turnpikes, bridges, buildings, and many other "glorious fruits" would grow in this new commercial Eden, its fertile plains well watered by a smooth river of bank bills.[91]

One part Adams (Samuel), one part Smith (Adam), and two parts Wordsworth (William), the exchange men were capitalists as well as republicans, and romantics as well as capitalists. They believed in the moral economy and the invisible hand, in feeling and in reason. To their detractors, this hodgepodge of ideas bespoke the exchange men's lack of station. The Changery was a "preposterous, heterogeneous absurd kind of a—nobody knows what," a "mere rattle" for these "factious, over-grown boys" to shake at their "elder brethren." This "pennyless pack" of "young comebychances" refused to play their assigned part in the great chain of being: the role of "submissive shopmen."[92]

Like all caricatures, this one built upon underlying truths. Many of the Changery's founders *were* young. The score or so of men who shepherded the enterprise included a few elder statesmen; Samuel Clap, the operation's president throughout its existence, and Samuel

Sumner, the lead petitioner, were in their late fifties when the legislature agreed to consider their plea in the spring of 1804. For the most part, though, the exchange men belonged to the post-Revolutionary generation. Born in the late 1760s and 1770s, they grew up in an infant nation, with all the expectations and tribulations it bred.[93]

When the Changery's supporters called these men "young dolphins," they referred to more than their age. The exchange men weren't just youthful; they were leaping, *rising*. They came from decent families, had academy (rarely college) educations, and wrote with practiced business hands. Like Andrew Dexter and Nathan Appleton, both of whom would join the enterprise, many of them had forsaken village life for city ways. In Boston they clustered "in the ordinary walks of life" (as one of them said), selling everyday items to the very customers who tendered country banknotes in payment. David S. Eaton's store on Market Street stocked peas, flour, cheese, and molasses. Samuel Sumner dealt in earthenware. Brothers George and Thomas Odiorne, migrants from New Hampshire, sold hardware and called themselves simply "shopkeepers," as did many of their fellows. Nathaniel Parker and a few others used the loftier title of "merchant."[94]

If the exchange men weren't quite as humble as their petition held and their critics mocked, neither were they "India Nabobs." Men on the make but not yet made, the Changery's backers were, as they said, a "Middling Interest," a label that described their politics (Republican-leaning Federalism, or occasionally the other way around), and also captured their liminal station in life. Owning, on average, about six thousand dollars' worth of property, they had resources a common laborer could scarcely dream of, but remained less wealthy and less liquid than other Boston money men. (The average director of the Union Bank possessed nearly four times that much and held a greater percentage of it in paper; directors of the Massachusetts Bank owned *eight* times more than exchange men.) Like Dexter, like Appleton, the typical exchange man counted one significant asset—a plot of land, a partnership, a professional credential—as his hedge against sliding backward.[95]

Or, as the first step up ambition's ladder. For exchange men, the next thing was all. The banking brotherhood tried to keep them in their places, insisting they were "better what they are, than what they would be." But the Changery's supporters were projectors, not stewards. Leave the glorious past to the fat bankers with their "ordained rules, and established precedents," their "skinflint avarice" and "bloodshot ideas." The exchange men embraced the "new fangled" future. Dudley Bradstreet Story, one of the office's trustees, rechristened himself Dudley S. Bradstreet when he arrived in Boston, adopting a more established-sounding lineage in his quest to establish himself. Crowell Hatch, likewise a Changery officer for several years, cherished the relics that the crew of the famed *Columbia* brought him from the Sandwich Islands. Thanks to them, he could find his name on the map of the North Pacific: "Hatch's Island" honored his co-sponsorship of their voyage. Poets as well as shopkeepers, Samuel Sumner and Thomas Odiorne wrote the swooning sorts of verse that their fellow exchange man John West stocked in his bookstore on Cornhill. More than age, status, origins, and occupation, the exchange men shared a way of being in the world. Call it the exchange persuasion: a hunger for mobility, a taste for far horizons over nearer ones, a fantasy of perpetual becoming that grew with the Revolution and would long outlive it, an American dream.[96]

This persuasion persuaded. In June, the exchange men's petition reached the State House, provoking heated debate. But as soon as "the thing was understood," one pressman noted, "it was readily assented to." Perez Morton and William Hull both voted with the majority that made the Exchange Office Boston's fifth bank. With its charter to begin the first Monday in August, the Changery's founders scrambled "to construct this experimental idea into masonic work," as Thomas Odiorne later wrote. They elected officers, sold equity, and found space for their operations in a yellow brick building at the corner of

Wilson's Lane and State Street, the heart of 'Change. (Samuel Dexter had rented space in the same building for his law practice two years earlier.) They hired a phalanx of clerks and messengers: younger men from poorer parts of town, much like the person Nathan Appleton had been when he got to Boston. "First teller" William Flanagan boarded in a house on Russell Street, a grubby block near the rope-walks in the seventh ward. Beginning in late August, he welcomed customers to the Changery, logging deposits on Wednesdays and recording loans (discounts) on Tuesdays and Fridays, between the hours of nine and three.[97]

Flanagan must have been busy, for the Changery was an instant success. Investors snapped up its fifteen hundred shares for one hundred dollars each, payable (like everything else at the office) in country bank bills. Shopkeepers touted their willingness to take any notes acceptable to the Exchange Office for the muffs and tippets and silver plate that signaled their customers' burgeoning gentility. Merchants presented their factors with checks drawn on the Changery, explaining that the new breed of amalgamated paper represented "a mixture of allmost all kinds" of money. In perhaps the surest sign of its triumph, the Exchange Office became in January the subject of an affectionate satire, a forty-eight-page "allegoric memoir" celebrating the daring of the exchange men and lampooning the fusty bankers who conspired against them. According to *The Changery,* even some of those hoary-headed elders had become grudging admirers. For a time, it seemed, ordinary people were fulfilling the Changery's most extravagant prophecy: that their shared faith could make the "paper medium, equal to what its face represented."[98]

By the summer of 1805, the Changery had become a cultural as well as an economic touchstone. Though the establishment bankers excluded the exchange men from their joint meetings, and though the legislature voted down its requests to begin printing small banknotes, the Exchange Office's future appeared promising.[99] Its supporters were passionate and plentiful; both political parties courted their favor. The concern's balance sheet looked healthy enough, with deposits (liabilities) amounting to just over $250,000 and loans (assets) that slightly exceeded them. In addition, the Changery had taken in a little more specie than the $50,000 its charter mandated. Owing roughly five times as much as it held in hard money made the Exchange Office aggressively leveraged by the standards of its day, but not frighteningly so. Those who bought in early received regular dividends on their stock, four percent every six months. Come-lately investors hunted for shares to purchase.[100]

Andrew Dexter Jr. was one of the latter. He had not signed the exchange men's initial petition in February 1804, but several of his acquaintances had. Through them or through others, he began to amass stock in the venture. In June 1805, when seventeen of the leading exchange men applied (for the third time) to transform their business into a note-issuing bank, Dexter's small, precise signature endorsed their appeal. When the Exchange Office elected a new slate of officers that August, he became a superintending trustee. Every few weeks, he took his turn behind the counters on discount days, where Flanagan or one of the other clerks presented him with loans to approve and deposits on which to pay interest.[101]

◇

Within six months of Andrew Dexter's election to the board, he began to change the Changery. The office's founders had envisioned it as a vehicle to *keep* country bank notes in circulation. Dexter went them one better. He used the Changery to *put* bills into circulation. As he took control of the organization, the Exchange Office would come to value a bank's money not in spite of its distance from State Street, but because of it. In the winter of 1806, the exchange men began to seek deposits from the remotest banks—even, in two important cases, to help charter new ones. In the process, Nathan Appleton recalled, they made a new discovery: "that a bank could be made profitable, in proportion to its distance from Boston, and the difficulty of access to it."[102]

Like all inventions, this one was partly the child of necessity. Amazed at the Exchange Office's success, Boston banks fought to regain the exchange business they had earlier sloughed off. (The author of *The Changery* imagined how reluctantly the pure-breed bankers imitated "those mongrels, whom we have tried hard to belittle.") By calling their loans and raising the prices they paid for out-of-town bills, they pulled country banknotes out of circulation—"kidnapped" them, the Changery's supporters said—and ransomed them for specie. The tide of country paper crested, and then began to ebb. The Changery needed more money flowing over its sluices, and Dexter set out to find it—to *make* it, if need be.[103]

But the Changery's reformulation of distance was born of philosophy as well—Dexter's philosophy. Combining the exchange man's faith in motion, the gambler's belief in the long shot, and the Yazoo speculator's trust in the boundlessness of the nation's interior, Andrew Dexter treated banknotes like grown children. He wanted them to go out into the world, to hang on to their values, to be well thought of wherever they went—so long as they didn't come back to live in his basement. As he told the officers of one country bank in which he took a large interest, bills sent "to distant parts" might be "disposed of in such manner that they cannot return to injure the Bank." The Exchange Office played a crucial role in making good this promise. Taking all money at face value, the Changery could turn obscure bills into familiar ones. As Appleton saw it, Dexter converted the Exchange Office from a "nondescript association" into "an engine . . . for the purpose of circulating the notes of particular banks," banks he happened to own. In other words, Andrew Dexter turned the clearinghouse into a money laundry.[104]

First stop, Pittsfield, near the western edge of Massachusetts, where the turnpike leading north from New York crossed the one heading west from Boston. The convenience these roads afforded traders—you could reach Boston in less than three days, New York within five—coupled with the region's fertile soil and abundant waterways, made Pittsfield prosperous by country standards. The town boasted neat farms, busy forges, quarries, and mills, ambitious schools, and well-stocked shops. But a truly vibrant commerce demanded cash, and

Pittsfield's town fathers wanted a bank. Early in 1806, a bipartisan group of local notables (a physician, a lawyer, a pair of merchants, the innkeeper) asked the state for a charter. In February, the General Court approved their petition, making the Berkshire Bank the commonwealth's westernmost by a factor of two. The bank could raise a capital of $75,000, which tied Northampton's for the smallest in the state, yet offered a lot of liquidity to this village of two thousand people. Locals appear to have been surprised by their own success in the matter; two exclamation points followed the news in the *Pittsfield Sun*.[105]

Subscription books opened in May, and the bank's 750 shares quickly sold out. Joseph Goodwin, a farmer from neighboring Lenox, bought 100; a score of other Berkshire county gentlemen purchased blocks ranging from 1 share to 17. The remaining 513 shares—nearly 70 percent of the total—went to Andrew Dexter Jr., who became in July the only nonlocal director of the enterprise. Joining forces with the Pittsfield bankers forced him to cede his place on the Changery's board. (The charters of both organizations forbade interlocking directorates.) When they met in early August, the stockholders of the Exchange Office elected other money men in his place. Some of them—his uncle Samuel, his kinsman Artemas Ward—shared Andrew's view of money. Others found it less congenial. Nathan Appleton was one of the latter. Married since April to a daughter of Pittsfield merchant Thomas Gold, he knew perhaps too much about the Berkshire Bank and its out-of-town owner.[106]

At a hundred dollars per share, Dexter's stake in the Berkshire Bank cost more than fifty times his net worth. The funds can only have come from the Exchange Office. The Pittsfield bank's charter required buyers to use gold or silver for its shares, and Dexter may have put up part of the price in coin. (In the year after June 1805, the Changery's specie reserves fell by more than 90 percent.) The rest was paper, drawn from the Exchange Office's miscellaneous supply. Dexter used the notes of existing country banks to buy a controlling interest in this new one. Then he turned the wheel again, asking the Berkshire

Bank—*his* bank—to invest in the Changery. On the first page of the Pittsfield bank's cash book, the cashier recorded a debit of $75,000, for two bundles of notes previously sent to Dexter. As collateral for the loan, Dexter had put up his Berkshire Bank shares, securing promises with promises bought with promises. Signed and cut and stacked and wrapped, the Berkshire notes became the first bricks in his pyramid.[107]

By mid-September, when the Berkshire Bank opened for business on the ground floor of a small brick building, just below Michael Bird's hairdressing shop and directly opposite the Congregational meetinghouse, thousands of its notes had made their way 140 miles east, to State Street. The Exchange Office offered them (at face value, of course) to loan applicants, who in turn paid their suppliers, their workers, and their landlords in Berkshire bills, who then used them to buy groceries, medicine, firewood. If any of those notes reached Pittsfield again, the Berkshire cashier redeemed them with drafts payable at the Exchange Office, weeks hence, in country notes. At which point the cycle could begin again. Other Berkshire notes moved north and east on Changery business. By year's end, Dexter had offered smaller, quieter versions of his deal with the Berkshire Bank to at least five cash-poor banks in northern New England. He lost a small traveling trunk as he caromed across Maine and New Hampshire. When he posted a reward for its return, he did not mention whether the trunk was stuffed with paper.[108]

The northern banks whose fortunes Dexter tied to the Changery's lay farther from Boston than Pittsfield did; it took so long to reach the Penobscot Bank, 250 miles east in Bucksport, Maine, that its notes virtually never returned home. But the distance between State Street and Maine's middle coast paled when compared to the outermost island of Dexter's paper archipelago. In the summer of 1806, the Exchange Office sent emissaries past the Berkshires, past Albany, past the far edges of New York and Pennsylvania, past even the brand-new state of Ohio, deep into what eastern Americans called the "Western World."[109]

*Berkshire Bank $5 bill, dated September 17, 1806, the bank's first day of operations. Note the high serial number, 13112. Many of the notes already in circulation had gone to Andrew Dexter and the Exchange Office.*

Detroit was a dot at the edge of the map, the sort of place where medieval cartographers etched dragons. Even its name—from *de'troit,* or the strait—bespoke a fluid, foreign world peopled by European traders, native trappers, and people in between. France had claimed the post at the neck of Lake Erie until the British and their Indian allies won it in 1763. England held it for more than two decades after that, finally ceding the lucrative territory to the United States in 1796. In January 1805, the United States incorporated the region as the Michigan Territory, turning the crumbling encampment of Detroit into an American capital city—at least on paper. On the ground, the Wyandot, the Delaware, the Shawnee, the Ottawa, the Chippewa, the Potawatomi, the Miami, and the Wea still had the real power.[110]

That year, Bostonians monitored Detroit's fortunes in the press, not thinking they would ever go there—few would—but because Jefferson had tapped their own William Hull to be its governor. (Patronage of the rankest sort, Federalists sneered.) Hull didn't want the job. He took the commission because he needed the money; the Yazoo bubble had ruined him. When he left Boston in May 1805, he knew he had chosen a difficult post. But what greeted him, his wife, and three of their children at the end of a five-week, thousand-mile journey by carriage, boat, horse, and foot was worse, far worse, than the Hulls could have imagined. They arrived on July 1 to discover that fire had consumed the entire town—every house, every picket, every "convenience"—twelve days before.[111]

After a wretched summer huddled in tents and sheds, Hull took his family back east to Washington, both to plead the territory's interests and to join Perez Morton, Samuel Dexter, and the other New England Yazoo men pressing their claims before Congress. The House put off debate on the contentious matter twice before rejecting the latest compensation plan in March. (If "he could give a death-blow to the Yazoo business," said Virginia's John Randolph before the vote, "he should die in peace.") Gossips in Detroit wagered that their governor would never return, but Congress's decision sent the still-impoverished Hull back to Michigan in April 1806, an outcome he found almost unbearable. "Placed on the frontiers, separated from the States by a wilderness and by savages, every moment being liable to be assailed by a superior force, among a people who have received very little, very little but neglect from the government, the prospects appear gloomy indeed," he wrote. To live in Detroit was "to remove from the World, and barely exist."[112]

No wonder Hull relished the interest some of his eastern friends expressed in his place of exile. Before he decamped Boston, he passed along good news to Augustus B. Woodward, the eccentric young scholar-cum-speculator whom Jefferson had made Michigan's chief justice. "A very rich & respectable Company of Merchants, in Boston, have agreed to make an establishment in our Territory to carry on the fur Trade," Hull wrote. There were a dozen of them, men of great "wealth, intelligence, & Spirit." Expert paper men, too, for many of them served as trustees of the Boston Exchange Office. On the long journey west Hull clutched their petition to create a "Bank at Detroit, to consist of a Capital not less than Eighty nor more than Four hundred thousand dollars."[113]

A *"bank of discount and deposit in Detroit!"* John Gentle marveled.

To "discount what? cabbages and turnips—to deposit what? pump-
kins & potatoes"? He pronounced the Bostonians' motives as dubious
as their capital. Many suspected they were "*Yazoo* claimants," Gentle
hinted. A nonnaturalized Brit whose land titles Hull and Woodward
had negated, Gentle had an ax to grind. But disinterested Detroiters
likewise found the banking scheme puzzling, if not sinister. "No honest man here can conceive for what purpose *this Bank* is intended, to
such an amazing amount," wrote Stanley Griswold, another New
England Republican whom Jefferson had consigned to the Michigan
government. Even at the low end, the amount of the bank's proposed
capital truly was "amazing." Eighty thousand dollars was more than
double the value of what Michigan produced in a year, nearly six times
the combined worth of Detroit's burned buildings. This far into the
backcountry, there was simply no cash to speak of, nor much else a
banker could turn into money. Which is why no bank existed west of
the Alleghenies.[114]

The would-be Detroit bankers agreed with their critics: the district
was cash-starved. Upon this desert they promised to rain money. The
bank would promote trade, improve transportation, support agricul-
ture, and nurture a "laudable spirit of enterprize." Solicitous of the
public good, attracted by the obvious "private advantages," migrants
would rush to the "flourishing" territory. Hoping against hope that
the Boston adventurers were right, Hull championed their cause. "I
have ventured to give them such assurances, that they will immediately make all their arrangements," he told Woodward. Immediately,
they did so; a day after the Boston company signed their petition, Hull
reported that "all the shares are now Subscribed for excepting one
quarter part, which is left for the People of the Territory." If Detroiters didn't want their 25 percent stake—well, the Boston gentlemen
were happy to take that, too.[115]

Hull arrived in Detroit in early June, trailing a retinue of carpenters, bricklayers, and building materials. William Flanagan followed
in July, having quit his post as first teller of the Exchange Office to
serve as cashier of the "contemplated" Detroit Bank. Flanagan, who

escorted Hull's wife and children, probably followed the route the family had taken the previous year, going by stage from Boston to Albany, and then proceeding by boat: north on the Hudson to Lake Champlain and the Saint Lawrence, then southwest across Lake Ontario, with a portage around Niagara Falls before the final crossing of Lake Erie. It was fortunate that so much of their journey took them over water, for their burden was massive. A pair of "strong iron doors, and several tons of bar iron, to strengthen the vaults"; a sixteen-inch lock with a foot-long key; three sets of scales to weigh coins; a half dozen Windsor chairs and a writing desk; ink stands, ledgers, and rulers: Flanagan brought the outward trappings of credibility.[116]

"Nothing was done that summer—nothing was thought of, but the bank," John Gentle recalled. Soon after Flanagan arrived, the mechanics at work on Hull's residence (a "stately mansion," no, a "palace," Gentle scoffed) stopped abruptly to construct a bank next door. That the Boston group didn't own the land proved no obstacle. The bank went up quickly, a squat little box a story and a half high and less than thirty feet square, the first brick building in Michigan. However unassuming its design, the Detroit Bank's roof marked the highest point in a hamlet surrounded by hundreds of miles of unbroken forest. The

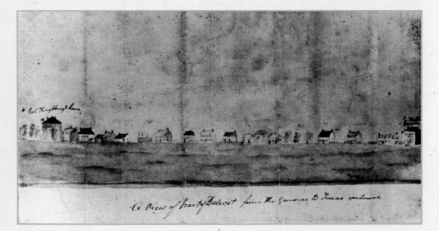

*"View of Detroit Drawn by Geo. W. Whistler in 1811."*
*The Detroit Bank is the third building from the right.*

bank made a statement, a loud one. By midsummer, word of its existence had surfaced in the New England press.[117]

In the last days of August, another magnificent convoy came from the east. This one included Judge Woodward, whose long-awaited return from Washington at last gave the territory's Supreme Court a quorum to hear the bankers' petition. "Several active young gentlemen" from Boston accompanied him. Exchange men Nathaniel Parker and Dudley S. Bradstreet (né Story), who together would own more than 70 percent of the new bank, numbered among them. But Gentle counted *"two or three . . . principal owners"* of the bank in Detroit. The next largest shareholder, with 10 percent of the total, was Andrew Dexter Jr., there on paper, if not in the flesh. Into the woods the Bostonians had carried talismans to convert Flanagan's hollow brick shell into a bank: sacks of gold—about $19,000 worth—and paper, reams and reams of paper, "an immense cargo of bank bills, not filled up."[118]

For what remained of the summer, Hull and Woodward, Bradstreet and Parker, and maybe, just maybe Dexter, set to work turning those blank forms into money. One Boston newssheet reported that some Detroit notes had "reached town" in late July. In fact, the bills had barely made it to Detroit, let alone back to Boston; there was, as yet, no bank to issue them. But on September 19 the territorial legislature (that is, Hull, Woodward, and a second judge, Frederick Bates) approved the Bostonians' petition. Because Michigan was federal territory, the bank's charter would not become official until the U.S. Congress confirmed it. But provisionally, at least, the bankers got everything they had asked for, and more. The new bank could raise a million dollars, over twice what its founders requested. The corporation would last 101 years, ten times the usual lifespan. It could spread through space as well as time; the bank's officers might set up loan offices "wheresoever they shall think fit," another unheard-of provision. About specie reserves or limits on note issues—centerpieces of every other such charter—this one remained mute.[119]

As Woodward explained, these unaccustomed freedoms testified to his belief that money was but a shared fiction, "an artificial mode of representing the necessaries and comforts of life." Its value resided in what it did, not what it was. When "exchangible at pleasure" for worldly goods, gold, silver, paper, and many other things became money. When their exchange function ceased, coin reverted to its "raw material," bank bills to "worthless paper." A government need do nothing—*should* do nothing—to "regulate the quantity of coin, or of bank bills in society. The good sense of society always regulate[s] both, without any aid, and much better without aid than with it." The Detroit Bank charter read as it did because Woodward and his Boston backers thought "all attempts . . . to assign limitations to capital, or quantum of medium, are fruitless and unnecessary . . . a mere relic of popular prejudice and mistake." Unencumbered by such limitations, the Detroit Bank was an *extendo ad absurdum* of the logic of the Boston Exchange Office. This was no accident. As soon as the bank was operational, the exchange men officially applied to Detroit's bankers for a loan. Applied, in effect, to themselves. Their wish was granted.[120]

The morning after the legislature approved its charter, the Detroit Bank offered its 10,000 shares for sale at Smyth's Hotel, a ramshackle affair down the street from the new bank building. The nominal price was a hundred dollars a piece, but Woodward's charter allowed buyers to put down just 2 percent of that, making the total equity roughly equal to the amount of specie the Bostonians had lugged to Detroit. The subscription books stayed open for four days, during which the Boston faction engrossed 9,507 shares. Over the next several weeks, the proprietors doled out the remaining equity privately, to a "chosen few" Detroiters whose support the enterprise would need. On October 11, the owners elected four of the local shareholders as directors. Woodward would serve as president. But with less than 5 percent of its equity held in the Western world, the bank was a Detroit institution in name only.[121]

Exactly as the founders intended. For although its solid brick building, its thick iron doors, its imposing desk and precise scales lent a luster of credibility to Michigan's waterfront, the Detroit Bank's real audience lay hundreds of miles east: in Dexter's anointed banks in Pittsfield, in Bucksport, in Keene, in Wiscasset, in Augusta. And especially at the Changery on State Street, the hub of Dexter's intricate web of exchange. There, the only names that mattered were the ones on the bank bills that Parker and Bradstreet carried out of the woods.

Immediately after their "election," the new officers of the new bank filled out the bills the Bostonians had printed so confidently in Newburyport, Massachusetts, months before, notes of the latest design. Every promise needed a serial number, a date, and two signatures. William Flanagan inked his name on the cashier's line in the lower left in a plain, even hand that evoked a clerk's loyalty. President Augustus B. Woodward gripped his quill as lightly as he wore his liberal learning; beside Flanagan's precise autograph, his signature swoops and dances. On a ten-dollar note signed three days after the bank was organized, Woodward's name is smudged, the date carelessly scrawled, a clue to the haste with which the pair worked their way through the stack of paper before them. As if the Boston investors could not wait for the ink to dry.[122]

At the end of October, just before winter sealed off the Western world, Parker and Bradstreet headed back to their snug New England firesides hauling promises: at least $80,000 in Detroit Bank notes, and

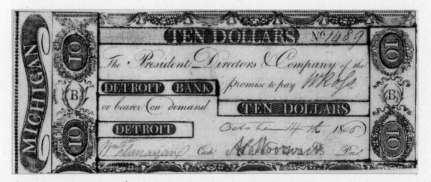

*Signed in haste, Detroit Bank $10 bill, October 1806.*

perhaps twice that much. (John Gentle derided this initial shipment as "a small venture of 163,000 dollars.") Parker stopped in New York to trade, but by late November he was back in Boston. Installed once again behind the counter of Changery, he and Bradstreet, along with their fellow directors Nathan Appleton, Samuel Dexter, and the others, worked the banker's magic, launching Detroit's paper into the slipstream of circulation whose currents made it into money.[123]

# TWO

# ICARUS

*December 1806,* barely winter by the almanac. Chilled bones know better. Snow came in mid-November, "with considerable violence." New England's skies remain "dark & lowry," the fields a hard brown, the produce markets sparsely stocked. Packed with gawkers drawn to the "political heat" of a spectacular trial, the old County Court House is the warmest spot in Boston. Thomas O. Selfridge, a rising lawyer, stands before the bar, finally called to account for a killing on a sweltering Monday last August, at high noon, in the middle of 'Change. The victim, Charles Austin, was an overheated teenager bent on avenging his father. Benjamin Austin, the longtime editor of the *Independent Chronicle* and Boston's least temperate Republican, had insulted the Federalist Selfridge in his pages, provoking the affair of honor. Selfridge meant to refuse the challenge. But in the end he panicked and fired his screw-barreled pistol. Armed with a stout hickory cane, young Austin crumpled and died at the corner of Congress and State. His funeral convulsed the town, much as the trial does now. It is a political circus. Republican prosecutors square off against Federalist defenders. Samuel Dexter leads the defense, and his golden tongue carries the day; the jury acquits his client in fifteen minutes. Bonfires follow hot words. From Boston to New York crowds hang Selfridge in effigy. Austin's *Chronicle* muddies Samuel Dexter's name. Again.[1]

Amid this cacophony, Detroit Bank bills slip into Boston quietly, on little paper feet. The Changery lends them to borrowers, who pay them to creditors, who trade them for rent and food and firewood. "[S]truck on *Perkins'* newest Stereotype" plates, a patented printing process designed to produce unforgeable results, the Detroit notes *look* like money. Perkins-style notes, the *Boston Gazette* acknowledges, "are now the handsomest Bills in circulation," and the ones labeled "Detroit Bank" appear no less solid than the thirty-one other flavors they come in. Indeed, "most of the bills in circulation are exactly like them," one critic explains; the Detroit Bank's "can be known only by examining the name of the Bank, President and Cashier." Whether lulled by their familiar appearance or convinced of their credibility, many shopkeepers take them at par, "the same as other bills," as one dry goods seller advertises. Which makes the Detroit notes *work* like money. By the time Selfridge's trial opens, the bills have become part of the circulating medium flowing through Boston and beyond: faces in the crowd. They look like money, they work like money, they *are* money—at least to those who believe that money is as money does.[2]

The Detroit notes don't stay quiet for long. Boston's leading bankers and "principal merchants"—the same loose coalition of powerful men that fought the Changery—see paper as a proxy for gold more than for goods. The promise that these bills might be redeemed for specie is plainly absurd; their journey east was a one-way trip. The gainsayers warn credulous clerks against crediting them. "How, in the name of common sense, are these bills to be sent home—who would travel 12 or 1400 miles to carry them?" asks a writer calling himself "A Friend to the Public." "Who would risk sending them?" another skeptic wonders. "Suppose, for instance, 50 or 100,000 dollars worth of them were collected, would it, *even then,* pay for the risk and trouble" of a bank run on Detroit? What would these moneymakers dream up next—perhaps "a rival Bank at Nootka Sound—with one branch at Cape Horn, and another at the bottom of Hudson's Bay"? The Detroit Bank is nigh unto fiction, they insist; its notes all but fakes. One caution against them runs alongside news that the notorious counterfeiter Stephen Burroughs has broken jail in Montreal. A two hundred dollar reward is offered for his capture—payable, presumably, in something other than Detroit Bank bills.[3]

Those who damn the Detroit Bank know its paper hasn't merely appeared; there are agents spreading the notes. The critics have a good idea who they're up against. "There are a few individuals in this town who wish to get these bills into circulation," the *Gazette* hints. Some writers—wishfully? misleadingly?—express relief that the Exchange Office has agreed to refuse Detroit notes. The opposite is true. In all but name the Detroit Bank, like the Berkshire Bank before it, is a wholly owned subsidiary of the Exchange Office, which in turn has become Andrew Dexter's pet. To the extent the Detroit bills are being shoved rather than slipping into circulation, he's the one doing the shoving.[4]

Many know, or at least suspect, that Dexter is the man behind the money. Few have any inkling of what he means to do with it. Not even the local tax assessors can see the contours of his unfolding plan. Last spring, when they made their annual pilgrimage through the town to discover who does what, owns what, and owes what, they noted nothing exceptional about the twenty-eight-year-old attorney who lives in the Court Street law office where he plies his trade. By their reckoning his fortune had doubled since they had started tracking him in 1803, a fact that only confirmed its modest size: $400 in real estate (his half of the rented space he shares with his famous uncle Samuel), and $500 in "personalty" (furniture, paper). They may know that he's a bank director, and a member of several charitable societies where he can support good works (kindness to animals, fire prevention) while rubbing shoulders with the elite. But in a city that plays home to a small but growing number of near-millionaires, Andrew Dexter's total worth doesn't reach $1,000. He is one more striver with an attitude.[5]

That's what the tax men see, anyway. But their appraisal is a snapshot, and Dexter's life a blur of motion. For he has begun to play at one of Boston's most popular pastimes: the real estate game.[6] Last May, if not before, Dexter singled out a densely peopled tract in the eighth ward, south of State Street and west of Congress. From a widow and a shopkeeper he purchased four small parcels of land lying between Devonshire Street and the courtyard known simply as Salter's, after the brewer who once owned it.[7] Nothing about these lots stands out. They are tiny—less than 2,300 square feet combined. Devonshire, the byway they front, is more alley than street, a twisting path lined with the shops and homes of working people: three grocers, an engraver, two blacksmiths, a mariner, two bookbinders, a shoemaker, tailors, a wheelwright, and a boardinghouse keeper. The structures upon Dexter's properties—which include a small brick building, several tenements, and the remains of a wood house—fit comfortably into a landscape where ordinary people eke out a modest living amid what one British traveler calls the "litter and confusion" of Boston's *Old Town*."[8]

Through a summer made hectic with travel on banking business— hard travel to Pittsfield, to Maine, to New Hampshire, perhaps to Detroit—Dexter has worked to complete the puzzle, collecting a half dozen similar jigsaw pieces (more tenements, another pump, a "necessary house") before November. By year's end, the collective price of these lots tops $110,000. Dexter owes much more than he owns, naturally. In each case he has put a little money down, mortgaging the balance, usually to the sellers. His purchases are as interconnected as they are leveraged; he secures each new lot with his equity in the previous ones. These loans—some $65,000 worth—will begin to come due in January, shortly after the Detroit Bank notes arrive to ease his burden. In six months, he has worked a minor real estate miracle: starting with almost no money to his name, he has amassed over twenty thousand square feet of property, a trapezoid stretching south from State Street to Salter's Court, and east from Devonshire Street all the way to Congress.[9]

The neighborhood is not especially glamorous—not *"delectable,"* as Nathan Appleton calls the new Beacon Hill. Dexter's holdings lie within the town's crooked, organic, almost medieval core, very close,

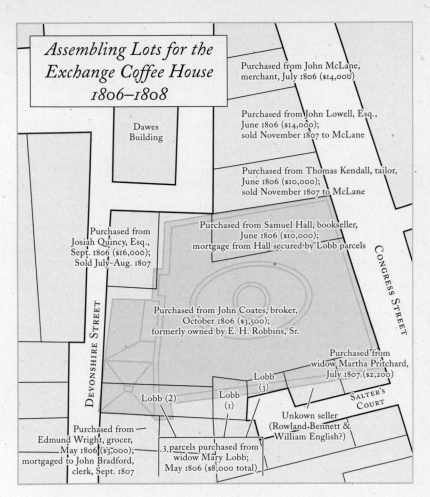

**Assembling Lots for the Exchange Coffee House 1806–1808**

Dawes Building

Purchased from John McLane, merchant, July 1806 ($14,000)

Purchased from John Lowell, Esq., June 1806 ($14,000); sold November 1807 to McLane

Purchased from Thomas Kendall, tailor, June 1806 ($10,000); sold November 1807 to McLane

Purchased from Samuel Hall, bookseller, June 1806 ($10,000); mortgage from Hall secured by Lobb parcels

Purchased from Josiah Quincy, Esq., Sept. 1806 ($16,000); Sold July-Aug. 1807

Purchased from John Coates, broker, October 1806 ($3,500); formerly owned by E. H. Robbins, Sr.

CONGRESS STREET

DEVONSHIRE STREET

Purchased from widow Martha Pritchard, July 1807 ($2,200)

Lobb (3)

Lobb (2)

Lobb (1)

SALTER'S COURT

Unkown seller (Rowland-Bennett & William English?)

Purchased from Edmund Wright, grocer, May 1806 ($3,000); mortgaged to John Bradford, clerk, Sept. 1807

3 parcels purchased from widow Mary Lobb; May 1806 ($8,000 total)

in fact, to the heart of the maze. The nerve center of the seventeenth-century Puritan village, State Street remains the spine of the rising commercial city. Stretching east from the front steps of the Old State House, passing banks and coffeehouses and shops and warehouses, it becomes Long Wharf, reaching nearly a thousand feet into the harbor that brings Boston its fortunes. For nearly two centuries before any playhouse graced the town, *this* was Boston's theater: the place where the struggling remnant of the godly erected their humble wooden church in the 1630s, where the bloody Boston Massacre exploded in

1770, and where outraged patriots in turn staged their protests. The church has long since crumbled to dust, and ten years ago Bulfinch's iconic new State House on Beacon Street replaced the Old. Trade endures. For nearly two centuries, the State Street corridor has comprised Boston's "general mart of business," as one eighteenth-century gazetteer put it. Hackney coaches and horse-drawn trucks still line its sidewalks, bringing travelers and goods and news. The Puritan fathers are gone. But for those whose religion is commerce, Dexter owns something very close to sacred ground.[10]

He means to consecrate the space after the fashion of the day: by leveling everything on it. "Bostonians with all their good qualities, seem to disregard whatever was venerated by their fathers," notes Shubael Bell, a housewright who has pulled down his share of buildings while nursing quiet qualms about the "spirit of improvement (so called)." Such halfhearted nostalgia cannot halt the frenzy of creative destruction. By the time Dexter gets to the party, the orgy of building has been going for more than a decade. The boom has remade the map of the town, and reshaped its people as well.[11]

The whole process of building has been magnified, elaborated, segmented—in a word, professionalized. The number of carpenters in Boston has nearly doubled since 1800, growing twice as fast as the population of adult men. By 1810, there will be nearly six hundred of them in town. What laborers in the building trades gain in numbers they lose in independence. A generation ago, joiners and masons worked for themselves, honing their trade through years of apprenticeship that taught them to fashion a simple dwelling from cellar to roof. Now builders labor under middlemen who break their jobs into ever-smaller component parts, piecework. Near the top of the pyramid are self-styled "architects"—men (often gentlemen) with book learning, international horizons, and professional aspirations—who dream the buildings that laborers realize, never touching earth or bricks or wood themselves. (In Boston three men—Peter Banner, Charles Bulfinch, and Asher Benjamin—call themselves architects, at least some of the time.) Above the architect stands another middleman, the capitalist. The money required to create today's brick-and-mortar fantasies comes not from architects, or carpenters, or even future owners, but from bankers, insurers, and speculators: men who would make bricks the handmaidens of paper profits. It is their ranks that Andrew Dexter seeks to join.[12]

Working in tandem if not always in harmony since the mid-1790s, the joiners and bricklayers, the architects and capitalists, have razed whole blocks and raised entire new ones. In 1803, a group of gentlemen calling themselves the Mount Vernon Proprietors began to create Boston's first gridded neighborhood almost literally out of thin air, paying throngs of workers to hack away the top fifty or sixty feet of the westernmost peak of the Trimount, as the three hills above the Roxbury flats were called. Wagonload by wagonload, the gravel fills the salt marshes lining the town's western edge to make the long, wide avenue known as Charles Street. This year Beacon Hill, "that commanding eminence," Bell calls it, began to bow its "venerable head" as well; next summer another corporation will start to fill in the Mill Pond, building a checkerboard of new streets by mixing the tops of the erstwhile hills with cellar earth, oyster shells, pot shards, and animal waste: the detritus of city life. South of Long Wharf, surveyors and diggers carve wide avenues into land stolen from the harbor. Broad Street—earning its name at more than seventy feet across— slashed its way onto the map this year, impressing observers used to Boston's tangle with its straight sides and right angles.[13]

All along these new blocks, buildings of every sort pop up "almost as suddenly as the genii of Aladdin's lamp," the writer Samuel L. Knapp observes. Aspiring capitalist princes cover the west side of town with the mansions Bell calls "Citizens' Palaces." New steeples pierce the skies over Hanover and Park and Cambridge and Charles streets; a Catholic church—in Puritan Boston!—is risen on Franklin Street. Two theaters vie for patrons in the town that had banned theatricals into the 1780s. Scores of other buildings celebrate the rivers of capital coursing through the mansions and theaters and even the churches. Bulfinch and others design banks and insurance offices, shops and warehouses, countinghouses too numerous to count. On Broad Street, a row of "about 60 large and elegant brick stores . . . of uniform height and appearance" rose, all of a piece, just this year. At the center of town the money counters and theatergoers and mall strollers rest secure in their elegance, while Bulfinch's new state prison in Charlestown and his almshouse on Leverett Street move the wretched and the poor to the edges of their field of vision.[14]

However diverse their patrons and purposes, the new buildings share a great deal. For the most part, they are skinned in brick, the new face of the city. As late as 1794, the merchant Thomas Pemberton had lamented that Boston's "houses are built chiefly of pine and oak," materials "not only perishable, but . . . dreadfully accessible to all the dangers of wind and fire." (The frequency of building-consuming blazes in the eighteenth century helped clear the ground for the building binge of the early nineteenth.) In 1803, a decade of debate and seven major fires later, the selectmen ordered that "all buildings exceeding ten feet in height shall be built wholly of brick or stone . . . and covered with Slate Tile or other non-combustible composition." Law and taste conspired to ensure that the rising city would be built to last.[15]

More durable than their colonial ancestors, the new buildings are also out of scale with the past. Some are expansive, with symmetrical wings that command their lots. Others ascend through space. The stately homes of the 1790s regularly included a third story, and now many elite Bostonians consider a fourth floor de rigueur. Some of the new stores along Broad Street have five stories, while the central pavilion of Bulfinch's India Wharf complex will stand a full six floors tall when completed next year. This bloated scale comes with bloated price tags. Elegant private homes regularly fetch $10,000, and the finest command twice that—still just a fraction of what civic buildings cost. In 1804, the Suffolk Insurance Building, one of the new palaces of finance on State Street, sold for nearly $40,000, about the cost of the West Boston Church. The State House, the Leverett Street almshouse, and the renovation of Faneuil Hall each consumed more than $50,000. It was a rare building whose price reached six figures; the massive state prison may be the only such project in Boston.[16]

*North and east elevations, India Wharf,*
*by Charles Bulfinch, ca. 1803–1807.*

The town's new redbrick face, its breadth and its height, its startling cost: all of it represents an investment not just in practicality, but in *taste*. The new buildings affirm Boston's membership in a refined transnational community. With his college education and keen eye for detail, Andrew Dexter understands their engagement with ancient forms, however distantly refracted. Greek and Roman ruins had inspired Italian Renaissance architects, whose works in turn informed the English classicists of the seventeenth and eighteenth centuries. Carried across the Atlantic in pattern books, treatises, and the sketches of gentlemen returning from the grand tour, drawings of the buildings of Inigo Jones, John Soane, the Adam brothers, and other leading London architects became hugely influential in the port cities of the United States. Shubael Bell is proud that so many of his town's "elegant" and "lofty" new buildings have been fashioned "after the modern English models." A writer in Philadelphia finds the

American deference to English precedent slavish. "Our domestic architecture is for the most part copied, and often badly copied too, from the common English books."[17]

However large, self-conscious, and expensive, these English models lend a visual stillness to the new Boston, a quietness that mocks the constant rumble of wheels over cobblestones. What Bell calls the "improved style of architecture" pays homage to classical precedent through restraint in ornament and gesture. The new buildings are "uniform and chaste," he says. Etched lines replace extravagant curves. Massy pillars yield to graceful columns whose proportions communicate form's relationship to function. The Adam brothers, among the leading English exponents of the new classicism, argued that the "gracefulness of form . . . courted by the ancients" would free buildings from the shadow of "the gothick style," with all its "massive" and "ponderous" details. Straining skyward, Gothic cathedrals soared. Embracing the horizontal, classical buildings repose. Symmetry, order, elegance, and above all *control:* these are the maxims of the new classicism.[18]

Andrew Dexter longs to join the gentlemen who make architecture their language. The building he dreams for his Congress Street lots will make a statement—several, really. The structure must assert a sense of *belonging,* his right of place within the new merchant city. Large, elegant, refined, made of brick, it will speak the vernacular of classicism. But it will *not* repose. Surrounded by the architecture of aspiration, Dexter imagines a tower that will outreach everything he sees. He cannot possibly finance the project on his own, so he begins, early in the New Year, to hawk its virtues in the press.

⟰

January 1807, November's snowfall a distant memory. "Weather still mild & the earth uncovered," Salem minister William Bentley writes in his diary. "Business active in all its branches and our ports not obstructed with ice." The harbor is clear, but Boston's streets are clogged with crowds protesting the release of Charles Austin's killer.

Selfridge's freedom has "enraged the people of Boston," Bentley says, and "the public mind is not easily quieted." Blazing straw replicas of the murderer and the judge light the long winter nights, and mobs threaten the homes of any who cut the figures down. The defense lawyer, Samuel Dexter, escapes this particular ignominy. He is scorched only in the press. The *Independent Chronicle* urges polite readers to shun him. Dexter has shown "meanness, that no man could be capable of, who possessed the feelings, the principles or the spirit of a *gentleman*," the paper declares. "Dexter must be a stranger to all."[19]

Samuel's ambitious nephew Andrew faces challenges of his own. This month he starts to chip away at his mountain of real-estate debt. The mortgages that lot sellers so generously extended him last spring had been short-term loans—two or three years at most—with large annual or semiannual payments due along the way. Beginning now: on January fifth—five days late—he pays off a $2,000 loan to a merchant named Thomas Pollock. Several days later, he must scrape together seven times that much, the first installment of what he owes Congress Street merchant John McLane for his parcel near State Street. The line of creditors unwinds behind Pollock and McLane. Three more payments will come due in June, another three in the fall: some $35,000 to pay off before year's end, which will mark only another turn in the cycle of buying and owing and hoping that is the speculator's lot.[20]

As Dexter's obligations loomed, solid and real, his assets seemed ever more vaporous. If he had imagined that Detroit Bank notes, loaned through the Exchange Office, would answer his needs, events threatened to prove him wrong; both institutions were under attack. By December, the whispering campaign against the Detroit Bank had reached Washington, D.C. President Jefferson himself received warnings from several quarters: newspaper editor William Duane passed along dark rumors from John Gentle. Treasury secretary Albert Gallatin conveyed Detroiter Stanley Griswold's assessment that the "establishment must be either a landed or a swindling speculation," and recommended that "some inquiry . . . be made respecting the motives of the governor." Jefferson shared his doubts with Secretary of State James Madison, who asked William Hull to send him a copy of the law creating the bank. Hull complied, also enclosing a treatise from Augustus Woodward extolling the provisional charter's virtues. The matter sits on Madison's desk now, awaiting its day before Congress. Meanwhile, along with the usual flurry of petitions for new banks, the Massachusetts General Court will hear a committee report laying open the activities of the Changery.[21]

Faced with accelerating demands for money coupled with a crimp in his supply lines, Andrew Dexter deems New Year's Day "a propitious juncture" to solicit, at last, "public attention" and "general encouragement" for his plan: "the building of an elegant Exchange and Hotel in this metropolis." During the first week of January, the project's backers publish, anonymously, two long essays outlining their "new schemes." (That Dexter penned these essays seems certain. He is still the lone investor in the venture and will later be credited—and blamed—as the building's sole author, the "struggling Genius" whose "firm *unaided* hand" raised its lofty walls.) Both columns bear the headling PUBLIC WORKS, and promise readers that the project will foster private wealth and commonwealth. (Like many of his class, their author believes these are one and the same.) The articles, which constitute a sort of prospectus for the massive undertaking, set out to answer three questions: Why now? Why here? and Why *this*?[22]

The author begins not with the building itself, but with the city that surrounds it. He means, first and foremost, to elevate "the reputation and consequently the advantages" of Boston, to lift its standing in the eyes of the nation, the world. This is a tall order. For all the growth the town has witnessed in recent years, it remains a defensive place, more confident of its glorious Revolutionary past than its prosperous republican future. There is no denying that this tenth-generation descendant of John Winthrop's City on a Hill fails some of the most important tests of a modern metropolis.

During the last generation if not long before, North American cities from New York to New Orleans have adopted the relentless logic

of the grid, a systematic landscape designed for coherence and legibility. They have begun to separate trades and homes, sorting people into
districts according to status and occupation. All the while Boston has
clung to what one traveler calls its "coquettish negligence." The town
is picturesque, but it is not rational—*not straight,* as so many observers
put it. Its variegated topography and proudly independent culture
combine to lend the city an irregular, haphazard quality: the very
antithesis of a plan. Here "every one builds to please his fancy, so that
at every corner you turn you discover a new whim," one visitor notes.
Its helter-skelter appearance gives Boston "more the aspect of an European town, than any other city in America."[23]

Boston is charming, but you can't eat charm. "*Boston* is not a thriving, that is, not an increasing town," one British observer comments.
The village on the Charles *is* growing, just more slowly than its competitors. The demographic boom of the last quarter century has
managed only to restore the population to the level it had reached in
the 1720s. Still first among Anglo-American cities in 1750, it fell to
second, after Philadelphia, by 1760, and then to third, behind a surging New York, a decade later. Even the upstart Baltimore had passed
it by 1800, the year Jefferson's election to the presidency further mar-
ginalized the town. Ever "the headquarters of federalism," Boston
faces east; England is the touchstone of its economy, and its imagination. Jefferson's America faces west, toward the nation's dynamic and
ever-expanding backcountry. Even if Boston wished to reorient
itself—it does not—the city lacks the rich hinterlands that nourish
New York and Philadelphia, and give those who live there an easy
conduit to "that new and vast emporium" beyond the Alleghenies.
What Boston exports, writes one traveler, are "inhabitants, a commodity which, I am informed, they send in numbers greater than from any
other quarter." Losing money to New York, power to Washington,
culture to Philadelphia, and people to the Ohio country: Boston is an
aging matron recalling her youthful glory.[24]

Dexter refuses to join the chorus of "degradation" that faults Bostonians for "cautious enterprise" and "niggardly patriotism." To the

contrary, he insists, the town's best days have only begun. After languishing "lethergied in inactivity, for many tedious years," he writes, the city has lately "awakened from her torpor":

> There never has arisen a time when commerce more generally flourished, when public Works were more freely undertaken, and when the spirit of improvement seemed more generally to inspire all classes of the community, than that which is chosen for the accomplishment of the present design.

His project will capitalize, quite literally, on this *"never-to-be-recalled* conjuncture" of good luck and "pristine enterprize."[25]

Yet this "spirit of improvement" has somehow neglected the city's most glaring need: the creation of "a regular Exchange" for the conduct of trade. Public Works offers only the barest outline of what he means by this. The building must be "placed in the most central and conspicuous situation which can be found," someplace "[c]ontiguous to business" (south of State Street and west of Congress, for example). It must feature "all the conveniences for every transaction which the multiplied nego[t]iations of commerce can require," including an exchange room with ample public space and discreet private stalls, a reading area stocked with up-to-date business "intelligence," decent rooms to accommodate travelers (he proposes seventy-six of them), a bar and dining room where they can take meals. Simple enough. Yet visitors and locals alike complain that Boston remains "utterly deficient in those public conveniences, which are usually attached to every city of trade in the world."[26]

This is a pitchman's self-serving hyperbole, to be sure. But it is not a lie. European cities had domesticated their financial markets centuries ago. Completed in 1382, Bologna's Loggia dei Mercanti was among the first exchange buildings in the West. From there the form quickly moved north, with capitalism itself. By 1700, temples of trade could be found in Amsterdam, Antwerp, Augsburg, Barcelona, Berlin, Bruges, Cologne, Florence, Lille, London, Milan, Palma, Perpignan, Rome, Rotterdam, and Venice. Most of them followed a similar plan: an open trading plaza surrounded by arcades lined with shops and services. In the late seventeenth century, European exchange builders began to replace central courtyards with covered halls. Some of these indoor exchanges boasted peaked arches and elaborately carved spires—soaring Gothic details that marked them as cathedrals of commerce. A trading floor, ringed with pillars, might ascend two or more stories before terminating in a rotunda or vaulted ceiling, making a space quite like the nave of a church, with merchants' stalls standing in for pews, money for missals. To the English writer Joseph Addison, London's Royal Exchange marked the epicenter of empire. It was an *"Emporium* for the whole Earth," he noted in the *Spectator* in 1711, and its denizens formed "a great Council, in which all considerable Nations have their Representatives." The man-about-'Change, Addison continued, was truly "a Citizen of the World."[27]

Few of Dexter's readers—only leading merchants such as Nathan Appleton—had seen the exchanges in London, Bristol, and Liverpool firsthand. But as Public Works points out, Bostonians can find prods to "public rivalship" much closer to home. America's *"Southern Cities"*—south of Massachusetts—boasted commercial buildings that Boston would do well to envy. Regardless of whether he ever made it to London, Dexter had seen these for himself, beginning in his boyhood home of Providence. He grew up in the shadow of that city's center of trade, a plain three-story wooden affair dating from the 1790s called the Exchange Coffee House, an establishment whose modest scale and appearance matched Providence's own. Nonetheless, the Providence Exchange offered merchants a place to take coffee and play cards and read the papers, a central hall where they could trade the kinds of gossip that passed for business news (at least on days when the weather made their usual meeting spot, on the Great Bridge, unpleasant), and a handful of attic lodging rooms to accommodate out-of-town traders. If eighteenth-century Providence offered much less than Dexter dreamed of, it had more than Boston, at least in this one respect.[28]

Dexter's journey with his uncle to the new federal city on

the Potomac exposed him to grander and more flamboyant public buildings—exchanges, coffeehouses, hotels, and sometimes combinations of all three. Heading south by coach from Boston to Washington in 1800, he would have sojourned in New York (always "the City" to Boston's "town" or "village"), where he had the chance to tour two of the most celebrated buildings in the new nation. Perhaps Andrew and his uncle passed the night in the City Hotel, which occupied an entire block of New York's famed Broadway. (Boston's new "Broad Street" is diminished by the comparison.) Five stories tall, the brick building had 48,000 square feet of interior space crammed with 130 guest rooms, along with offices, parlors, stores, and even a circulating library.[29] The luxury the City Hotel offered to travelers, New York's Tontine Coffee House extended to merchants. Situated at the corner of Wall and Water streets, the crossroads of mercantile New York, the elegant four-story brick-and-stone structure rose in 1794, built upon the remains of the old Merchants Coffee House and the purses of more than two hundred hopeful subscribers. A view of the building painted in 1797 shows its terrace thronged with well-dressed men about their business as the

Tontine Coffee House, New York City, *by Francis Guy, ca. 1797.*

American flag flutters overhead and ships' masts crowd the sky behind them. Even on a sunny day when they chose to trade outside, these New York moneymen raised themselves from the muck; their balcony hovers above the laborers and carters busy on the street below.[30]

In Philadelphia, the next stop on the Dexters' trip south, men likewise did their trading indoors. Since the heady days of the Revolution, merchants there had repaired to the City Tavern, known locally as the Exchange. Its owners supplied this plain but ample three-story brick building with newspapers and coffee. In the exchange hall adjoining the coffee room, merchants manned stalls after the European fashion. Just across the street stood the spectacular new Bank of Pennsylvania, which the European-trained architect Benjamin Latrobe was finishing as the Dexters passed through town. If Philadelphia's Exchange, so called, was not much grander than the one Andrew Dexter had left behind in Providence, Latrobe's bank—a classical temple centered around a rotunda much like the Bank of England's—was one of the most celebrated buildings in the new nation.[31]

Washington, the terminus of a journey that took the Dexters nearly two weeks, had no exchange to speak of in 1800, or much of a mercantile community to demand one. Yet despite the new town's famously primitive conditions, it claimed one of the grandest public buildings in the United States. Completed in 1793, long before the federal government decamped from Philadelphia, the Union Public Hotel was the third-largest structure in the capital, surpassed only by the yet-unfinished president's house and the Capitol itself. Renowned for its cost as well as its scale, the building spanned nine bays and stood nearly seventy feet tall, its four stories looming over the hovels and swamps that comprised most of Washington. In addition to numerous bedchambers (these perhaps too pricey for the Dexters, who took rooms in the more modest City Hotel), the Union Public Hotel offered a variety of civic spaces to an emergent polis, including assembly rooms, a theater, and a post office.[32]

Across the European continent, and all along the eastern seaboard, ambitious buildings catered to the merchant's pursuit of happiness and the stranger's search for comfort. The models to which Dexter alluded in his prospectus for the Boston Exchange varied in many ways. Some were new and others well worn, some dramatic and others drab. Yet all of them, from the most humble to the most opulent, acknowledged the preeminence of commerce by giving it a roof, a room, a central place within the cityscape. To a significant degree, they were also Federalist projects, their backers sharing not only Hamilton's economic vision, but a partisan aesthetic of grandeur, order, and exclusivity. And not one of them rose in Boston.[33]

The city Dexter calls home has commercial buildings of course: banks, coffeehouses, insurance and brokerage offices, warehouses aplenty. These are private concerns, scattered around the city. Merchants seek out these "various strange places" to pursue specific transactions at appointed times. But for the most part, traders do business out of doors. When a Boston merchant says he is going to the Exchange—"on 'Change," in the day's vernacular—he means the stretch of State Street between the front of the Old State House and the corner of Congress. As his commercial brethren across the country and around the world demand nobler surroundings for their craft, Bostonians stubbornly insist on "remaining in the open street in all kinds of weather, and through all seasons."[34]

The "open street": Dexter hates the promiscuous hurly-burly of 'Change, "the wet and mud, and dirt" of it all. He hates trading paper alongside horses that foul his path and hawkers whose cries drown out his sober dealings. Like another anonymous writer in the *Gazette*, he wants to enforce "a distinction between the ordinary negotiations of merchants, and that of apple and potatoe carts." Unlike that author, Dexter wants to abandon 'Change, not to reform it. For 'Change is a place without boundaries, without barriers, without order. It is a likelier setting for a murder—rash Austin's murder, poor Selfridge's undoing—than for dignified enterprise.[35]

Dexter's critique evokes the English writer Daniel Defoe's famous description of London's 'Change Alley, the open-air trading nexus that spills alongside the Royal Exchange. At the hour of 'Change, Defoe wrote in 1719, "the Alley throngs with Jews, jobbers, and brokers; their names are needless, their characters dirty as their employment." The alley's denizens slithered from the street into smoky coffeehouses and taverns. They nabbed potential customers in doorways and conducted their deals with winks and whispers. To Defoe, this paradox of open stealth was the essence of speculation, governed by neither the restricted access of a gentleman's club nor the public scrutiny of a well-regulated market. Amid the jostling of sharpers and double-dealers it was impossible to distinguish the honest few.[36]

Unlike Defoe, Dexter finds the trading of paper an honorable calling, worthy of more controlled surroundings. Jefferson's men embrace the world out of doors, from the rural pastoral to the rude democracy of city streets. Dexter yearns for walls and doors, for civic order. This is his politics of real estate.[37]

Like a good politician, Public Works inspires and shames his readers by turn, daring them to let Boston continue to "sink in every honourable comparison" with its sister cities for want of a proper Exchange. But business is business, and he knows that appeals to "*patriotic* motives" will not suffice. An investor also needs the promise of a "sure and definite profit" to "compensate him for the risks he may encounter." An optimistic man in optimistic times, Dexter does not dwell on the risks. Instead, he vows that "the probable profits arising from the proposed scheme will be sufficient to induce the rich and the patriotic to unite" behind it. The proposed building's location ensures heavy traffic, and its amenities will compel "the general attendance of Merchants," all for a price. Where the use of the streets is free—too free—merchants will pay to attend this new Exchange. Rents from the offices and brokers' boxes, fees from annual subscriptions to the reading room, and "above all, the income from the Hotel" should assure investors a return of 10 or 11 percent per year after "the contingent expense of repairs, &c" had been deducted: nearly double the legal interest rate for banks.

Beyond this, the details of the investment remain hazy, as befits a building that exists only in its author's fertile mind. Public Works does not tell his readers what it will look like or exactly what it will contain. He is somewhat more specific about how much capital the venture requires. The "building and land will cost about one hundred thousand dollars," he estimates. (Considering that Dexter has already spent rather more than that on the land alone, this reckoning is conservative indeed.) As to how he will raise the funds, Public Works says nothing. Last month, Dexter floated a plan to create an "Annuity Fund," a life insurance pool whose premiums would be wholly devoted to building the new Exchange. Such an investment, he argued, would "enhance the income" to subscribers and "at the same time, . . . accommodate and embellish the Town." As this proposal wends its way toward the General Court, Public Works alludes only to the "Corporation."[38]

Neither the vagueness of Public Works's plan nor the aggressiveness of his pitch distracts readers, who know the Exchange Dexter proposes is both novel and expensive. Its city-within-a-city plan, its massive scale, its monumental *ambition* abrade the sensibilities of a town steeped in tradition and suspicious of luxury. Opposition mounts, offering Public Works further evidence of the peculiar civic "fatality" that makes Bostonians "so negligent of their reputation, and at the same time so tenacious of it." He declares himself "disgusted with the vain and overbearing self formed argumentators" who protest his plan. They are denizens of "our Insurance Offices," gamblers who hate risk, the same sorts fighting the Changery and the Detroit Bank. They see "no need of an Exchange or Hotel in Boston," preferring instead to associate with the "clans of politicians, knots of scandalizers, and clubs of empty-headed, local, hood-winked reasoners, with which some of our public streets are filled." For them, 'Change is exchange enough. They decry almost every aspect of Dexter's proposed colossus. The "merchants would not frequent it," they say. The "cost will be extravagant, the situation ineligible, and the speculation dangerous."[39]

About the last they are surely right. The very buildings that inspired Dexter's quest—costly "public works" built with innovative, and risky, private financing—amply demonstrated just how dangerous such a speculation could be. New York's Tontine Coffee House, like Bulfinch's Tontine Crescent on Franklin Street, was named for the seventeenth-century Neapolitan banker Lorenzo Tonti, who had devised a form of lottery where shares devolved to the surviving investors, the youngest growing rich as their elders died off. The scheme had succeeded on Wall Street in 1794. (New York had scale in its favor.) But in Boston such leverage bankrupted Bulfinch the following year, for the first if not the last time.[40] Samuel Blodget, the New England–born merchant-turned-architect behind Washington's Union Public Hotel, likewise ruined himself trying to fund that project through a lottery. Public interest abounded; nearly half the town's population turned out to celebrate the laying of the hotel's cornerstone. But costs spiraled and lottery ticket sales couldn't keep up. Funding collapsed even as the structure rose.[41]

Such tales abound, one for every big building, maybe more. Blodget knows, Bulfinch knows: fortune is capricious, unfeeling. Projects engrossing huge capital over long periods run overtime and over budget. Buyers evaporate while creditors multiply. Trade slows. Tastes change. Prices that rise giddily fall hard. Even in cautious Boston. Harrison Gray Otis, one of the town's most successful real estate magnates and a sometime-Yazoo man, tells a friend that "money is the object here with all ranks and degrees, and though a great deal is accumulated . . . still more is distributed." The situation everywhere is "much the same," he suspects:

> The minds of men teem with projects, & because everything has hitherto succeeded owing to the unprecedented circumstances of our Country, the conclusion is that nothing can miscarry. Hence bridges, turnpikes, canals, houselots and every species of property are under some aspect or another objects of speculation, and I hope we may never see the ruin as broad as the enterprise.[42]

Andrew Dexter's mind is teeming, and he would do well to listen to such warnings. But he does not, cannot. His vision, his land, his temperament, his debts: all these compel him not just to dream Boston's Exchange, but to build it. Now.

April 1807, the days still cold and the skies leaden after the New England fashion. Political clamor provides the only reliable heat. January's bonfires have burned out, but the Selfridge affair continues to simmer along Boston's crooked alleys and narrow streets, which again play host to the tax assessors. As they survey the fourth ward, they discover that Andrew Dexter's fortunes have changed, dramatically. He now owns the Court Street building in which he makes his home and law office, renting out space to a merchant, a student, and several attorneys, including Perez Morton, Samuel Dexter's sometime Yazoo partner. He has paid John Cody, a laborer who lives down the block, to "improve" the parts of the structure Dexter uses as a dwelling place, perhaps adding refinements that reflect his own ascendant status.[43]

Dexter is no longer a creature of the fourth ward alone; he owns property all over the city. Northeast of his office, near the grog shops and brothels lining Fish and Ann streets, he owns a wharf that last year was called simply "Lewis's." Dexter has renamed it Exchange Wharf. A half mile south of the wharf, on Devonshire Street, he has demolished the structures on some of the lots he purchased the previous year, erecting five "new stores" and part of a sixth in their stead. Elsewhere within the block marked off as the site of the future Exchange Coffee House, buildings stand and tenants remain; a tailor, a merchant, a gilder, a printer, a common laborer, and, ironically, the proprietor of a coffeehouse count Dexter as their landlord. Thus the assessors find an entire neighborhood of people—black and white, Irish- and French- and American-born—whose lives and livelihoods Andrew Dexter has tethered to his ambitions. He is their neighbor, their employer, the collector of their rents. He will evict some of them to level their houses and shops, and will house others in splendor once his planned palace is complete. Totaling up the bits and pieces, the tax men value Dexter's personalty at $6,000, and his real estate holdings at $68,700 more, an eighty-three-fold increase in twelve months.[44]

To the assessors his debts remain invisible. But Dexter knows those obligations only too well. As both the markets and the mercury rise, he is scrambling for cash. In February, the state legislature refused to charter his Massachusetts Annuity Fund, which was to raise capital for the Exchange. He asks subscribers to consider proceeding without an act of incorporation, but they are loath to risk it. March brought definitive word that Congress had nullified the Detroit Bank's charter. Andrew Dexter responds to the news precisely the way his uncle Samuel greeted the revocation of his Yazoo land titles two decades before: he increases his holdings, buying out Nathaniel Parker's and Dudley S. Bradstreet's shares of the defunct bank, probably for pennies. The investment would appear hopeless. Detroit bills are now officially spurious, irredeemable promises from a nonexistent company. Some shopkeepers continue to accept them at a discount, prompting warnings from Boston bankers. Paper money is twice removed from reality, they remind its captive users. Gold and silver represent wealth, and paper represents gold and silver. The soundest banknote is merely the "sign of a sign, the shadow of a shade." The Detroit Bank's bills are less solid still.[45]

Unable, at least temporarily, to turn this ectoplasm into bricks, Dexter tries to transform earth into money. On March 3, the day Congress dooms the Detroit Bank, he advertises "Lots of Land, situate between *Congress-street* and the areas of the contemplated Exchange, so that each Building will have two fronts," one on the street and one on an imagined pedestrian mall. Dexter promises "liberal credit" to buyers and says the parcels will go fast. The notice runs several times in several papers. He finds no takers.[46]

Dexter needs a reliable and ample source of cash to contract with the army of workers and suppliers whose skill, imagination, forbearance, and sweat the Exchange will consume in great quantity. Already, the future leaders of this gang of laborers have committed to the project. Samuel B. Jarvis, a housewright from the city's emerging South End, will oversee the artisans whose medium is wood, men whose hands and hearts will frame and finish the Exchange. Jonathan Whitney, a bricklayer who lives in the enclave of building tradesmen in the shadow of the new almshouse, will supervise the scores of brick and stone workers the building will employ. Jarvis and Whitney may have worked with Dexter on the just-completed Devonshire Street stores that will connect to the western elevation of the Exchange. On this much larger project, he will come to feel "greatly indebted" to their "skill and unremitted attention."[47]

With at least part of his construction team in place, Dexter certainly has a set of plans for the building, plans drawn by the architect who will help him to realize his vision. In every way, Charles Bulfinch is the obvious choice for so large a commission. The most eminent among the handful of architects in the city, Bulfinch has designed nearly every significant Boston building since the mid-1790s, from the iconic State House to the lavish Park Street mansion in which Samuel Dexter now resides. (In fact, so much of the town's post-Revolutionary face-lift redounds to his credit that the entire period is sometimes labeled "Bulfinch's Boston.")

By 1807, Bulfinch has known artistic success and financial defeat— "loss and mortification," as he puts it. His bankruptcy a decade before bled away his family fortune, leaving him "reduced to [his] personal exertions for support." Why not exert himself on Dexter's project? Bulfinch could get the job done; he possesses the experience—not to mention the reputation, the *credit*—to pull off a high-wire act like building the Exchange. Despite his money troubles, he is accomplished, even famous. He is also a gentleman. Ties of status, party, and family link Bulfinch to the Dexters. Like them, Bulfinch is a Federalist in his politics as well as his aesthetics. The connections between the families run deeper, closer as well. Bulfinch is a first cousin of Sarah Wentworth Apthorp Morton. He and Andrew Dexter must occasionally play whist in the Mortons' Dorchester salon, while Dexter talks business with Perez Morton and trades blushing glances with Morton's daughter Charlotte.[48]

Yet Dexter does not choose Bulfinch—or Bulfinch, however strapped for money, does not agree to take on so complex a client, even one who will soon become a cousin by marriage. The man who takes the job is Asher Benjamin, a not-quite-architect and not-quite-gentleman whose life story resembles Dexter's own. Where Bulfinch descended from wealthy Boston Loyalists, Benjamin—like Andrew Dexter—is an upstart. A carpenter's son from central Massachusetts, Benjamin came to seek his fortune in Boston around the turn of the century—again, just as Dexter did. Where Bulfinch honed his sensibilities by gazing upon Europe's ancient ruins during a youthful grand tour, Benjamin earned a housewright's practical education in the Connecticut River valley, fitting joints and carving ornaments on other men's projects. (He seems to have worked under Bulfinch, in fact, crafting the spiral staircase in the Hartford State House in the mid-1790s.) And where Bulfinch articulated his vision in brick, Benjamin (again like Dexter) as often made paper his métier, conveying his wisdom in a series of printed guides that translated the lofty principles of neoclassical architecture into the everyday practices of ordinary American builders.[49]

Asher Benjamin, *anonymous, ca. 1830.*

In January 1807, while Dexter unfolded his plan for the Exchange in the press, Benjamin announced the publication of his second book, the *American Builder's Companion*. The *Companion,* its author declared, was eminently practical, a compendium of "neat, elegant and useful designs." The book was also resolutely *American* in its compass. "Devoid of that heavy, expensive, and colossal mass of work, so common in European publications, designed for wealthy and luxuriant cities," Benjamin's treatise proudly featured "buildings adapted to the taste and genius of the United States." The *Companion,* Benjamin promised, would convey not only practical wisdom, but local knowledge: "useful information for the American workman." English inspirations (Benjamin borrowed heavily from London's Adam brothers in particular) are adjusted, which is to say *diminished,* to meet American realities. Marble becomes wood. "[F]ancy orders" are "reduced to a regular system." Readers learn how "to lighten the heavy parts, and thereby lessen the expense of both labour and materials."[50]

If Benjamin's watchwords are *lighten* and *lessen*, Andrew Dexter's aesthetic runs along a different track. *More is more* is his motto. Far from wanting to bow to New England parsimony, Dexter seeks to raise Boston to the level of those "wealthy and luxuriant European cities." He embraces rather than disdains "heavy, expensive, and colossal mass." And so he would seem an unlikely convert to Benjamin's sensibility, and Benjamin an unlikely architect of Dexter's vision.

Benjamin's books are widely used, to be sure; his 1797 *Country Builder's Assistant* has gone through four editions in ten years, and the *American Builder's Companion* will see six printings. These and other accomplishments have earned him the respect of Boston's artisanal community, which elected him an officer of the Associated Housewright's Society. But in the winter of 1807, a prospective client can count Benjamin's Boston commissions on one hand. The only public buildings among them, the newly completed West Boston Church and the Charles Street Meetinghouse, are elegant but derivative, monuments to Bulfinch's influence as much as to Benjamin's unique sensibility. Indeed, in the *Boston Directory* Benjamin lists himself as a housewright, not an architect. The assessors, making their rounds through the seventh ward, call him a carpenter.[51]

For Benjamin, the attraction of Dexter's project is easy to imagine. Neither especially accomplished nor financially secure, the housewright on the make could hardly refuse such a major commission. Like many artisans, Benjamin and his family move house regularly, pulling up stakes when leases expire in the spring. These annual removals have marked out a path of modest betterment. Just last year, in fact, the family relocated from the old West End—where their neighbors included a motley assortment of tinsmiths, seamen, and well diggers—to a house of Benjamin's own design in the newer, straighter, more respectable environs of Beacon Hill.[52] But this progress up the city's social and occupational ladder is both halting and tenuous. Dexter's project offers money and a chance for acclaim. Benjamin needs both. Drawing the plans for the West Boston meetinghouse had netted him eighty dollars, and this ambitious project was sure to be worth more, if not in cash then in the currency of reputation.[53]

What recommends the modest young housewright to Dexter is less obvious. Perhaps it is not so much that Benjamin is knowledgeable—Bulfinch, after all, is much more so—as that he is malleable, willing to bend his own good judgment to a client's taste when he cannot move the client to his. Perhaps, indeed, *Dexter* fancies himself the true designer of the pile, and Benjamin more of a general contractor.

There is precedent, on both sides, for such arrangements. These days, gentlefolk like to style themselves as architects. Sarah Morton, for example, relished designing her own country estate. "I am practicing, without having studied, Architecture," she gaily told the poet Joseph Dennie in March 1797, "and have, from my own whimsical Plan, built a House in Dorchester."[54] This spring, James Smith Colburn, an ambitious young merchant, is designing "two beautiful houses" on Beacon Street, one for himself and the other for his sister. "They were planned by myself," from the "bowfronts, circular dining rooms, and drawing rooms . . . with folding doors" to the "new and elegant furniture" that filled it, he later boasted. The vision of "fashionable style" had been his own, "and the work executed by A. Benjamin, Architect." Benjamin may bite his tongue while realizing this patron's design, especially when installing the elongated three-story pilasters so plainly at odds with his own aesthetic of "proportion and harmony." (So overdone are the homes when Benjamin finishes them that Colburn's sister declines to purchase hers, prompting Colburn to sell the house to the up-and-coming merchant Nathan Appleton.) But Benjamin "executes" the job nonetheless, dutifully translating Colburn's vanity into marble and mortar. Perhaps he offers the same chance to Dexter. Certainly Benjamin takes no special pride in the Coffee House. It is (and will remain) the most ambitious project of his career, yet he will never so much as allude to it in the five building manuals he is to publish after its completion.[55]

From the ground up, the building Dexter commissions presents challenges. The lot is large and irregular, a trapezoid measuring nearly 100 feet on its shortest side and over 120 on its longest, covering nearly 13,000 square feet of ground in all. On this awkward footprint Benjamin plans a multipurpose structure centered around a covered interior court, the eponymous 'Change Floor. Below grade will be two stories housing the building's dependencies (pumps, kitchens, washrooms, wood storage) as well as some paying tenants. On the principal story, one floor above the street, a variety of commercial spaces—a Reading Room, a bar, and a post office as well as the Coffee Room that figures in the building's name—will surround 'Change. As the building ascends, public space gives way to private, masculine business to feminine leisure. Benjamin maps out a large dining room on the story above the 'Change Floor, and a double-height assembly room that will take up much of the next two floors. Hotel chambers, private dining rooms, and offices fill out the upper stories, a program that blends the countinghouse with the Palladian villa. How far the Exchange will rise beyond that may not yet be fixed, even on paper. Forget classical repose; Dexter wants to stretch the building as high as his finances permit. Benjamin plans five stories above grade, but Dexter will go taller if he can afford it. Benjamin needs to incorporate a measure of elasticity into his design.[56]

Even if Dexter chooses Benjamin for the latter's flexibility, there are compromises that even the most accommodating builder—the exalted architect and the humble contractor alike—must refuse. Toying with timing is one of them. Benjamin knows, the masons know, the carpenters know, every day laborer knows: if Dexter can hardly afford to begin, he cannot afford to delay. Building on such a scale is not only a highly leveraged enterprise, but, like all construction in these northern climes, a seasonal business. The winters are doldrums, too harsh to permit work on the exterior of a structure. The warmer months are frantic, too short to waste. And now it is spring, the moment in between, the fulcrum on which the construction cycle balances, heavy work held in delicate equipoise with the caprices of New England weather.[57]

If Benjamin's experience building the West Boston Church the previous year is any guide, and if Dexter has any sense at all, the crew that constructs the Exchange has used the "leisure moments" of January, February, and March to gather supplies: to "collect and bring on the Spot the various materials as Sand, Bricks, Lime &c."[58] Each of these they shall need in great quantity. The building will consume upward of two million bricks, with some fifteen hundred hogsheads of lime mixed into mortar to cement them. (For scale: two million represents nearly 10 percent of the bricks manufactured in the entire state during an entire year, a number that would take a four-man crew working six-day weeks more than two and a half years to produce, adding up to a weight that would fill the hold of a ninety-ton ship thirteen times over.)[59] When weather and cash flows permit, the head mason or his men take the ferry or the new bridge to Charlestown, whose rich beds of clay make it a regional brick-manufacturing center. There they can purchase bricks for anywhere from $6.50 to $30.00 per thousand from merchants like John Wait, who sells many different grades and colors at his store near the North Mills. From the Charlestown brick yards they transport the heavy cargo across the river to Dexter's Exchange Wharf, and then haul it by wagon across town to the Exchange's land. After stacking the bricks, the men can use the cellars of the new Devonshire Street stores as a staging area for "making up the mortar, and other preparatory steps" that will allow them "to be in full readiness" when the ground softens enough to yield.[60]

That moment—the "first pleasant day[s] in which it was safe to venture abroad without winter clothing"—is here, and fleeting. Like capital poorly invested, the cost of a month lost now would compound through the spring and summer, leaving the building unroofed when winter sets in. Every postponement pushes the imagined income from the imagined Exchange that much further into the future, out past the looming due dates of Dexter's very real mortgages. Indeed, he and Benjamin must sense that they are already behind. Last winter, the builders of the West Boston Church gathered bids from contractors in January and began work in earnest by early March. Already well off that mark, Dexter puts out the call to those with idle picks and strong backs. CELLAR TO BE DUG, runs the announcement in the papers on April 13. "Any persons willing to contract to dig the Cellar under the Exchange Hotel, about to be erected in Boston, will please apply at the office of ANDREW DEXTER, jun., Court-Street."[61]

The men who answer the call—the faceless number who break ground on the Exchange Coffee House—take on some of the hardest and most dangerous work involved in the enormous project. They will also be among the lowest paid, lowest status men on the site: black and immigrant laborers and carters with little in the way of craft skills or bargaining power. For their toil they earn barely sixty cents a day, less than half the wage commanded by a master carpenter or a skilled mason.[62]

Clearing the land is their first task. For two weeks or more the crew works not at building up, but at dismantling, brick by brick, the houses and tenements and outbuildings scattered across the site, structures Dexter bought at considerable expense only to tear down. With luck the work proceeds "orderly & peaceably," as the demolition preceding

Benjamin's last major project did. The tangled street lines of the old city prevent them from squaring off the lot. But they can reduce it, as nearly as possible, from three dimensions to two, transforming a living neighborhood into a set of property lines spelled out in deeds and ruled on a map. As they do so, the crew works to conserve both time and the used materials, which will see new life in other projects, much as the bricks reclaimed from the old West Church now form the walls of the new African Baptist meetinghouse on Belknap Street. The salvage is not worth much—the remnants of the old West Church fetched just $365 at auction last February—but Dexter must extract every cent he can to defray the cost of the building. Even the dirt removed to form the Exchange's foundation—more than three thousand wagonloads of it—commands a price in a town hungry for landfill.[63]

Excavating the Exchange's "spacious cellars" is especially hazardous work. The surface area is vast by the standards of the day, and the workers must delve at least fifteen feet into the earth to create a foundation sufficient to support the building's height and mass. In a pit this deep a collapse would be calamitous. (Several years later, Martin Nolan, "a labouring man" digging the cellars of Bulfinch's Suffolk County Court House, will learn this the hard way, when "the earth caved in upon him, and so injured him in the limbs as to confine him to his house 14 weeks." He was lucky.)[64]

But assume fortune and weather favor them, and the crew is large enough for the task. Soon the workers are ready to shore up the basement walls. For this phase of construction Benjamin relies on Jonathan Whitney, the head mason, to assemble a team of stone workers to add their craft knowledge to the diggers' and carters' muscle. A life member of the town's leading artisan fraternity, Whitney likely puts out the call among his brethren in the Massachusetts Charitable Mechanics Association. He needs several three-man teams, each consisting of a master stone mason to build up the wall, a journeyman assistant to mix his mortar, and a boy to tote the "hod," or heavy wooden trough that carries their materials. Working deep within the damp ground of late spring, Whitney's crews cement large pieces of rough granite along the faces of raw earth, laying a wall some four feet thick to support the tremendous weight of the planned building. The task requires over a thousand "perch" of cellar stone, a quantity the workers weigh in pounds, in hours, and in pain. Dexter reckons the job in money; the rock for the cellar walls costs him more than $3,000, plus an additional $1,500 for the work of his men.[65]

Dexter's accounting makes him conscious, as well, of the chain of labor and power that brings these blocks of stone to the open pit fronting Congress Street: a braid of private effort and "public works" not unlike the future he dreams for the Exchange. The footing upon which the building rests began life well north of Boston, in granite formations running beneath the Merrimack River valley. After locating a promising bed of stone, workers cut trenches deep into the earth. (Battered by the harsh New England climate, the weathered rock nearer the surface neither bears weight nor holds a fine polish.) Cleaving veins of rock along their natural grain, they use drills and wedges and sledgehammers to pry loose huge blocks. Simple levers help the miners ease the massive stones—each cubic foot weighing 140 pounds or more—onto wooden sledges, which they drag up to ground level with the aid of hoists and cranes. But such labors, however herculean, cannot move the stone from Chelmsford to Boston. For that they need water. Not until the Middlesex Canal opened in December 1803— itself the product of eight years' hard digging—did it become feasible for Boston buildings to rise from granite foundations.[66]

Four years later, there is a system in place. Barges float the pale stone some twenty-seven miles from landings near the quarries to the canal's southern terminus in Charlestown. From there the blocks are hauled by horse- and manpower into the work yard of Bulfinch's state prison, itself wrought from Chelmsford granite just two years before. At sunrise each day, jailers lead the convicts through the iron doors of their cramped cells, each "just large eno' to contain a Bed, a small table and a chair," Bulfinch's mother notes, into the yard to break rock. Wearing the uniform that marks them as prisoners—a suit of "party

coloured clothes, with each half of their jacket and trowsers of a different colour"—they toil with picks and chisels until dusk, "hewing
blocks of granite into graduated shapes and sizes for building." From
this backbreaking work the keepers grant them but short reprieve:
fifteen minutes for breakfast and for supper, half an hour for their
midday dinner. Still, a Scottish traveler who observes them at the rock
pile finds the prisoners "as busy and as attentive to their work, as if it
had been their chosen and voluntary employment." Which it isn't. Yet
these men, no less than the proud artisans under Whitney's direction,
are bound by crime and punishment to the refined palace Dexter is
building across the harbor. Dexter's supply of ready granite hinges not
just on the whims of the market and the activism of laboring men, but
on the machinery of the state.[67]

The fates of the workers who dress the raw stone that becomes the
Exchange's granite base are yet one more reminder that the business
of building in an early American city is a maze of *ifs*. Human effort
controls some of these. If the wheels of justice grind out a steady supply of incarcerated criminals, and if the prisoners work their blocks in
steady fashion, and if free workingmen in Boston answer Dexter's call
for labor promptly, and if their injuries are few, and if he manages to
pay them well enough, and regularly enough, to keep them on the job,
then construction may proceed. Other contingencies belong to the natural world. If severe storms like the violent hail that lashes Boston on
April 30 remain infrequent, if the "long fogs" of spring part to allow
the canal boatmen to float their cargo from Chelmsford, if all of
these acts of god and men cooperate, then and only then can the cellar
walls of the Exchange rise to meet Congress Street before the end
of May.[68]

Typically this moment prompts ritual, an open-air coming-out
party to announce a civic birth. One morning the previous April, the
pastor, the lead stonecutter, and "several Ladies and Young Persons"
from the congregation gathered to lay the cornerstone of Asher Benjamin's fast-building West Church. Holding a ceremonial trowel, the
Reverend Charles Lowell led the crowd in a short prayer. Perhaps,

when Whitney sets the Exchange's cornerstone, Andrew Dexter offers his crew some inspirational words about the altar of commerce, much as Lowell knelt before "the throne of Grace" on Cambridge Street last spring. Or perhaps not. Given their late start, the time to stage such a moment is a luxury the builders of the Exchange do not possess, any more than they can count on a large, welcoming audience for their new arrival.[69]

Ceremony or no, time remains of the essence. Work multiplies from the ground up. Spring's outlays of money and manpower, granite and mortar, have brought the Exchange only to street level, leaving at least five stories to complete before the roof goes on. And the roof must beat the winter.

The next phase of construction belongs to the carpenters, who protect the cellars by "lay[ing] the Floor of the House." The team working on the West Church, with its footprint of 5,600 square feet, began that task one Monday morning in April 1806 "and completed the same before night." The Exchange covers twice that expanse and so requires both more men and more time. One group of Massachusetts housewrights estimated that a carpenter could lay 200 square feet of board planking in a day. Working at that rate, it takes a dozen men four full days to floor the Exchange's basement.[70]

More men, more time, and, at every stage of its construction, the Exchange also consumes more *lumber* than almost any other building project of the day. The enormous brick-skinned building conceals an intricate skeleton of wood. Where the cellar's granite walls link the Exchange to the quarries of Chelmsford and the work yard of the state prison, the girders and joists and planks that frame the building connect the commercial temple erecting south of State Street to the New England interior. The timbers that Dexter's crews fasten together during the spring of 1807 descended from the forests of New Hampshire and Maine a year and a half earlier. Loggers felled their spruces, pines, and hemlocks in winter, when deep snow made for (relatively) easy transport by sled, and deep cold kept sap from flowing and spoiling the wood. Sawed into rough boards at any of the hundreds of mills that dotted the riverbanks of those northern districts, the wood was then lashed to form large rafts—as big as 200 feet long and 40 feet across—and guided down river by three- to six-man crews. Like loggers, millers and raftsmen measured their lives in seasons, condensing much of their work into the brief interval between the breakup of the ice pack in early spring and the slowing of those rushing waters in late summer. The proprietors of the urban lumberyards where these rafts came to rest also found themselves dependents of time—and space. Green wood required as much as a year's seasoning before it was ready for sale. In Boston, the still-uncrowded streets along the town's "Neck" played host to most such businesses. It is likely to those yards and wharves that Samuel Jarvis repairs to purchase wood for the Exchange.[71]

When Jarvis's men finish flooring the basement it is Whitney's turn again, time for the masons to build up from the cellar walls. Now, instead of granite, their medium is brick, laid several deep and then faced, on this first floor, with the same white marble that will grace the exterior of the Exchange in lavish abundance. Securing a supply of marble—a luxury material that costs him a dollar for each linear foot, or more than three thousand dollars to surface the basement's exterior walls—adds yet another spoke to Dexter's busy construction hub. The veins of marble that will eventually decorate the Exchange course through the cliffs along the Hudson River. Well north of New York City, towns like Athens grow prosperous wrenching the stone from the earth. Near the quarries sloops piloted by men like Captain Samuel Edmonds stand ready to ferry the snowy blocks away for processing. Some of the finish work on the Exchange's marble takes place in New London, Connecticut, whence the carver Chester Kimball ships polished stone to Boston, probably to be off-loaded at Dexter's Exchange Wharf.[72]

Floor, walls, windows, walls, floor, repeat. Week by week and story by story, building the Exchange becomes routine during the summer of 1807—an intricate dance pairing quarries and forests, ships and wharves, bricks and boards, carpenters and masons, all keeping time to the music of the weather—but a routine nonetheless. Potential delays abound. The lead mason and head carpenter fret about undisciplined laborers and tardy suppliers. For if the carpenters lack wood when the masons reach the window line, or if the masons want for brick when the carpenters finish framing a floor, work grinds to a halt. Haste likewise threatens their progress. One bright June day last year, master mason Warren Jacobs tumbled from the top of the West Boston Church as he hurried to finish the cupola. He died hours later, "notwithstanding he had the best medical aid." Asher Benjamin, the architect on that project, doubtless remembers the horrible scene: the mason's broken body, his shaken comrades, his grieving wife and children. Not to mention the time and money lost to his burial. Taller and more complex, the Congress Street worksite is inherently more dangerous than the church had been. Jarvis and Whitney urge their men to work quickly but carefully, with *deliberate* speed. They comply; whatever small calamities befall them do not make the papers.[73][74]

The summer proves exceptionally wet, even by New England standards. "All speak of the extraordinary rains of this season," William Bentley notes. Even so, the shell of the Exchange inches higher, a plant fed by immense toil. Four stories, then five, and still reaching upward. The scaffolding spans more than one hundred feet, a third again as tall as the cupola of the West Church. Craftsmen and their apprentice boys clamber up ladders into the latticework bearing unwieldy loads of wood, brick, and mortar. A windlass helps them to haul the heaviest pieces. The builders race the calendar, aware that autumn's falling light will rob them of time soon enough. And time, as Franklin said, is money.[75]

Five stories from the street, and the money holds. Six, and yet one more. Now seven stories above grade, Dexter's palace outdoes the only six-story structure in Boston—the central pavilion of Bulfinch's India Wharf. (There, the top floors serve only as warehouse space. Nobody would dream of inhabiting such an aerie.) The Exchange towers over its surround. Looking south, it dwarfs the ramshackle Quaker meetinghouse across Salter's Court and eclipses the row of three-story

Frontispiece, J. Leadbeater,
*The Gentleman and Tradesman's Compleat Assistant, 1770.*

buildings that the merchant Benjamin Joy has lately put up along Congress Street. To the north, the Exchange casts a pall over Bulfinch's Suffolk Insurance Building (home of the chattering naysayers Dexter despises) and the Old State House, that aging monument to Boston's Revolutionary glory. As the days grow shorter, the Exchange's shadow lengthens.[76]

The number of people working at the site grows with the building. At midsummer, there are easily a hundred and not yet enough. Dexter puts out word in the papers: STONE CUTTERS WANTED TO HIRE . . . TO WORK ON THE BUILDING FOR THE EXCHANGE COFFEE HOUSE. The men who answer the call litter the site with sheds and improvised workshops, where they cut stone and polish the ornaments for their heroic enterprise.[77] The block is crowded with men and boys who work with wood, rock, metal, and glass, and with all the others who attend them. Carters bring them supplies and remove debris. Blacksmiths shoe the carters' horses. Wheelwrights keep the wagons in order. Grocers keep the workers in food, and boardinghouse keepers put roofs over their heads. Bonesetters repair their mangled bodies in the event of injury. Ship captains and canal boatmen float marble, brick, and boards to the site. And on and on, from Congress Street to the shops and workrooms, to the wharves, to the prison yard, to the quarries and the forests: the intricate fabric of exchange expands strand by strand. The diverse laboring people ensnared in this far-flung web hold at least two things in common. All are working, in more and less direct ways, to complete an implausible building. And Andrew Dexter owes money to each and every one of them, each and every week.

The Exchange grows with time, the crew grows with the building, and the cost grows with the crew. Bills outpace the most aggressive forecasts. His own experience, Bulfinch said years before, had taught him "the fallacy of estimates in general, and especially in buildings of a public nature." If Benjamin has learned this lesson, he has not convinced his client. However unforeseen, the overruns of cost and time are more predictable than Andrew Dexter's income. As workers scramble to shore up the walls, Dexter scrambles to scare up revenues.

He enlists others in the cause, taking on two partners who already belong to his insider network of family and finance. In early June— twelve thousand dollars in mortgage payments due this month alone!—Dexter, his Exchange Office confrere Crowell Hatch, and Samuel Brown, long embroiled in the Yazoo affair with Samuel Dexter and Perez Morton, petition the state legislature to incorporate them "by the name of the Proprietors of the Exchange Coffee-house." On the twentieth the governor signs a bill that allows Dexter, Hatch, and Brown to sell four hundred shares in the venture, now defined as *"a building on an extensive plan, Containing an Exchange, a Coffee-house, and different apartments for other uses, which will be conducive to public accommodation."* The charter declines to limit the personal liability of the investors. Should they default on their promises, each will lose his money and property. And the legislature restricts the trio in other ways as well, decreeing that "the value of the land and building to be erected thereon, shall not exceed two hundred thousand dollars." Still, this is wide latitude, an enormous sum, twice what Public Works projected the building would cost only six months before. It is not enough. In the end it will represent less than half of what Dexter lays out.[78]

And so, in addition to opening an office, electing directors, and selling equity in his new corporation, Dexter embarks on other quests for funds to pay his workers and his lenders. Outlandish quests: while his petition wends its way through the State House on Beacon Street, Andrew's father and his brother Samuel forge west, beyond the pale, back to Detroit. In a letter introducing them to Augustus B. Woodward, Dexter explains their mission. "They are authorized to cooperate with you," he tells his old friend, to restart the Detroit Bank "on proper principles as may be deemed most beneficial and proper." Reorganizing the defunct Detroit Bank *would*—briefly—prove beneficial, if not exactly proper. For now, it remains a mere whisper of hope.[79]

A whisper against an outcry. The collapse of the Detroit Bank and the evident strain on several others (among them the Berkshire, the Coos, and the Penobscot, all in Dexter's fold) has emboldened the opponents of country paper. Some blame the Exchange Office, turning its proud promiscuity into a vice. "Who aids and countenances the emission of . . . Bank Notes, which are no better for the public than blank paper"? one anonymous writer asks. "*Answer.*—A certain Office in *Boston,* which by reason of the '*miserable falling off'* of its deposits, is reduced to the practice of every *expedient* to increase them. At this office these bills are palmed upon the ignorant and unwary, who think a public institution 'can do no wrong.'" As the outlying banks increase their issues, Boston moneymen increase their skepticism. One critic uses a construction analogy the workers on Congress Street would appreciate: "[T]hese banks are digging a pit for themselves," he writes, "and the time is fast approaching when country bank bills will depreciate as fast as the old continental money." In August, the directors of the Massachusetts Bank vote to refuse checks drawn on the Exchange Office. When the Changery elects trustees that month, Nathan Appleton parts company with them, while Andrew Dexter takes up a new position as their solicitor.[80]

Dexter also pursues more concrete possibilities, pawning precious earth to raise paper. By early September, he has sold most of the Devonshire Street buildings and mortgaged the remainder, raising $24,600 to offset his obligations. In October, he borrows against the wharf. In November, he diminishes the Exchange itself, selling a lot lying north of the building that was to provide the viewing site for its grand architectural theater.[81] What he can't sell or leverage he rents out, promising tenants of the Devonshire Street buildings that their "Stores, Shops, Offices or Counting Rooms" will communicate "with the principal Room of the *Exchange Coffee-House,* now erecting." (The engraver Thomas Wightman is one of the handful who respond; he will later fashion the image of the building emblazoned on its stock certificates.) Compared to the demands Dexter faces, these leases generate paltry sums, hundreds of dollars where tens of thousands are needed. Still, any money is some money to place in the daily extended hands of the long-suffering workers on the overextended building. Money for which they must now be especially grateful.[82]

For as the laborers know all too well, it is not just Dexter who is struggling in the second half of 1807. All Boston is suddenly as cash poor as it is building mad. Dexter, Benjamin, their workers, and their tower exist not just in the microeconomy of the chaotic building site, but also in the larger political economy of the United States. And the new nation's long cold war with England—a battle over the legality of the lucrative American re-export trade to Europe's warring nations—has lately grown dangerously hotter. On June 22, two days after Massachusetts chartered Dexter's Exchange Coffee House corporation, the waters off the coast of Virginia witness the first skirmish of the still-distant War of 1812. A delegation from the *Leopard,* a fifty-gun British warship, boards the American frigate *Chesapeake* to demand the return of deserters from the Royal Navy. The American captain refuses, and the *Leopard* opens fire. When the smoke clears, three men lie dead on the *Chesapeake*'s decks. Eighteen more are wounded, some mortally.

The *Chesapeake* affair, as the clash is dubbed, instantly becomes a cause célèbre. Jefferson proclaims the assault "an enormity . . . without provocation or justifiable cause," and demands redress. Through the summer, his administration gropes toward a plan to avenge the nation's honor peacefully. They map a policy that substitutes commercial warfare for armed conflict. If American ships cannot safely remain neutral, they will not trade at all. On December 22, Congress passes Jefferson's Embargo Act, which declares "an inhibition of the departure of our vessels from the ports of the United States." All exports, all imports, all *ports* closed to foreign trade.[83]

Bostonians join the national hue and cry against what the town fathers call "a wanton outrage upon the lives of our Fellow Citizens . . . and an infringement of our National Rights and Sovereignty." But the town's merchants also know the *rage militaire* engulfing the country threatens their very livelihoods. Without cash crops, without significant manufactures, without rich hinterlands, Boston has only the sea. Cut off from it, the town's trade-based economy grinds to a halt. Ships idle at the wharves, their bare masts creating "the appearance of a forest . . . scath'd by the lightning of Heaven." "Almost every Person we meet, and almost every circle we visit are bitterly complaining of the hardness of the times and [the] scarcity of money," notes an advertisement in the *Chronicle*. A saying circulates: "Embargos will *cloath a Merchant* in rags."[84]

The embargo makes for "a sad ending of the year," as Bentley notes. Gloom envelops Dexter's construction site. Gentlemen whose deep pockets hold "large capital" put their schemes on hold and "wait for better times," Bulfinch notes. Dexter cannot. The month has been "hitherto mild," but the signs of winter are unmistakable. The sun sets by four. Nearly a foot of snow falls the day after Christmas. Work on the building must continue—must, indeed, accelerate.[85]

Sometime before the worst of the weather sets in, the laborers, paid in promises, close off the Exchange to the sky. Working on icy scaffolds high above the ground, they lay a flat roof across all but the center of the building. In order to contain the spread of fire, the town requires that all structures taller than ten feet be topped with "Slate Tile or other non-combustible material." The Exchange stands ten times that high. Sheets of copper or iron would satisfy the law, as would planking sealed with stucco or concrete. Builders' manuals feature recipes for fire-resistant "gruels" made of sand, lime, earth, and ash, priced at various costs for various purposes. Dexter does not pay for even the cheapest of these mixtures. The workers cover the Exchange's roof with "sheathing paper," which they coat with gravel and tar. The viscous black liquid seals the roof against rain, even as its flammability courts disaster. (Several years hence, the deadliness of the Richmond Theater fire will be blamed, in part, on such roofing material.)[86]

Rather than run through what little cash he has on fireproofing measures that nobody will see, Dexter spends extravagantly on the ornament at the center of the roof: a dome with a circumference of over a hundred feet. This is the Exchange's architectural signature, a nod to venerable English models from Saint Paul's Cathedral to the Bank of England, a thumb-in-the-eye from Benjamin to Bulfinch, whose State House is the only other domed structure in Boston.

Elliptically shaped to mirror the rectangular 'Change floor ninety-five feet below it, the Exchange's dome is a marvel of both engineering and craft. The carpenters and masons work together to build up its shallow contours. Around its perimeter they place sixteen windows to allow daylight into the building. Glass fitters carefully fill these convex openings with large panes, 384 in all. They glaze the round skylight in the center of the dome, the building's oculus, literally its eye onto "the starry world around." When the framing is done, the dome is plated in tin, "after the method practised in Montreal," as one early critic notes. Hard times be damned, Dexter brings experienced tinsmiths down from Canada to do the work. They skin the dome in gleaming metal sheets, a bolder, more optimistic finish than the flat yellow paint atop the State House.[87]

If ever the building is finished, merchants will be able to mount the stairs from the seventh floor to the roof, climb a ladder to the top of the dome, and open a portal admitting them to a railed walkway around the oculus. If ever the embargo is lifted, they will watch from

*Exchange Coffee House dome.*

this highest point along the harbor as their ships return home laden with the fruits of empire. If ever, but not now. There is no staircase, or any ships: nothing to gladden the merchant's "joyful eye," nothing to repay the Exchange's towering height.[88]

When the builders of Asher Benjamin's West Church completed the outer shell of that structure, some sixty-five carpenters and masons gathered at the Green Dragon Tavern for a "rational, friendly, and becoming" celebration, precisely eighty-four days after they had set the cornerstone. Dexter's vastly larger crew has toiled far longer and built far higher. In a project rife with deadly errors, they have done nothing wrong (or nothing wrong enough, at least, to leave a written trace behind). They have earned a little sober merriment in honor of their achievement.[89]

But circumstance has wronged *them*. The embargo—a policy dreamed up in Washington, beyond their control if not beyond their ken—has laid siege to their enterprise. And if Jefferson's sins aren't enough, their boss continues to violate the builder's first commandment. "A wise man buildeth his House upon a Rock," the gospel says, "so that when the rains descend and ye floods come and ye winds blow and beat thereon it falleth not." Every carpenter knows Saint Matthew's injunction. But every day Andrew Dexter flouts it. As the men on his crew will soon come to realize, his house rests upon paper.[90]

# THREE

# RECKONING

*A bit of luck* followed Charlotte Morton and Andrew Dexter to Gilbert Stuart's painting rooms on the last Wednesday of April 1808. Dressed in their portrait finery, they would have gone by carriage over the muddy roads (it had rained for two days) from the Morton estate in Dorchester, their wheels clattering over the slats of the still-new South Boston Bridge as they approached the city. Looking north from the causeway that lovers called the "Bridge of Sighs," they could see the Exchange Coffee House. Still unfinished and already taller than any other building in town, Dexter's tower mirrored the pair's own rising stature.[1]

So, too, did the day's errand. Andrew and Charlotte were fortunate to procure any appointment with the acclaimed portraitist, let alone this second chance, after Charlotte had "disappointed" Stuart by missing her session on Monday. Auspicious as well to see the great man before noon. The light was best in the morning, and so was Stuart, whose reputed genius went brush-in-hand with his rumored fondness for liquor. (He "loves a cheerful bottle, and does no work in the afternoon," one Boston matron warned her nephew before his sitting.) No proper home was complete without a brace of Stuarts, and the future Mr. and Mrs. Andrew Dexter Jr. wanted theirs ready when they married, less than two months hence. This was an impossibly tight deadline for the artist, who was known to be "very dilatory in finishing his pictures." But at least the project would have a sober start.[2]

And so they turned their backs on the heart of town and headed south toward Washington Street, where Stuart and his family rented rooms in the rambling wooden house of a distiller's widow. This was hardly a fashionable milieu for a painter of Stuart's stature, much less his clients. Taking advantage of cheap land, a variety of artisans—mariners and tailors, a fire engine builder and a fishhook maker, a cooper and a cobbler—established their manufactories along Boston's narrow Neck. If Charlotte Morton recoiled from the stench of the tallow works or the din of the blacksmiths' shops, it cannot have escaped Andrew Dexter's notice that many of the artist's neighbors worked in the building trades, some of them, perhaps, on the Exchange itself.[3]

Dexter and his bride followed a line of immortality seekers to Stuart's door. His reputation—earned in London and Dublin, burnished in New York and Philadelphia—preceded him to Boston, where he'd settled three years before. As Stuart had told a friend, "In England my efforts were compared with those of Vandyck, Titian and other great painters—but here! They compare them to the works of the Almighty!" Since the painter's arrival, local grandees had shelled out one hundred dollars or more to have their "inimitable likenesses" rendered by the master.[4] Stuart, whose large appetites and small business sense frequently took him to (and over) the edge of financial disaster, nourished their adulation. Fame was currency. He loved the epic canvas, grand commissions like the full-length *Washington at Dorchester Heights* he had unveiled at the Federalist celebration of the Fourth of July in 1806. But pleasing the wealthy by softening their flaws was the backbone of his trade. "I have a family," Stuart told a student. "I paint for bread."[5]

The furnishings in Stuart's painting room weren't much to speak of: six chairs, an old carpet, a supply table, and a looking glass where subjects could primp and preen. A thunderstorm on Monday night had left the place "leaking like the devil," Stuart noted in his appointment book. Crumbling plaster added to the usual jumble of paints and palettes, brushes and drafting instruments. (Stuart used these "pieces of apparatus" to trace copies of his famed images of George Washington, creating a steady stream of original imitations that proliferated—and then deflated—like paper money.) Along the walls plaster masks of sitters' faces jostled against partly finished portraits, some of them on canvas and more on scored wood panels. Since December, when Jefferson's embargo began to choke off supplies of imported cloth, Stuart had often used the latter support, which gave those portraits an especially sharp line.[6]

The clutter in the studio matched Stuart's own aspect, which owed more to Falstaff than to the late lamented Washington. The painter greeted customers in his shirtsleeves, the "disordered" linens stained with traces of the snuff he kept in a silver box the size of a small hat. His moods were as erratic as his dress. As Charlotte's sister Sarah later put it, "He seems to think that his genius gives him a right to follow

Mrs. Perez Morton, *by Gilbert Stuart, ca. 1802*

the entire bent of his temper & spirits, be that what it may." In his best humors, she continued, the painter could be charming, telling jokes and tall tales with a rapid-fire diction and "droll & peculiar" inflections.[7]

Despite the cancellations, the rain, the embargo, there is every reason to suppose that Charlotte and Andrew found the painter in good spirits. Stuart had known Charlotte's family for years, and her mother had inspired one the finest paintings of his career. Describing the image in the *Port Folio,* Sarah Morton called Stuart's brush a "[m]agician's wand": poetic license, not to mention vanity. Yet those who saw this luminous portrait of "the American Sappho" could witness the mutual enchantment of an artist and his muse. The temperamental painter would bring a special energy to his hours with Charlotte Morton and her fiancé that Wednesday morning.[8]

The Dexters' first session with the painter yielded little more than a foundation for their portraits: Charlotte's silhouette roughed out upon a wide mahogany board, Andrew's on a stretched canvas roughly the same size, the glowing flesh tones that marked Stuart's best work not yet visible. On Saturday, the couple returned for the second of what typically amounted to three sittings, each of which could last an entire day. This time they would have recognized a familiar face drying on the easel. Nathan Appleton had sat for Stuart the day after the Dexters' first appointment.[9]

Appleton's ghostly half-painted likeness must have disconcerted Andrew Dexter. The previous summer, Appleton had ended his brief affiliation with the Exchange office when Dexter resumed his, a telling move. This erstwhile ally of the Changery had become an implacable foe, not just of the office, but of everything Dexter believed about money and value.

Like Dexter and the other exchange men, Appleton had initially thought that Boston bankers acted "very unadvisedly" when they refused the bills of their country competitors. Recent experience had changed his mind. Increasingly, he sensed, the outlying banks were living beyond their means, flooding "the channels of circulation" with too many notes backed by too little specie. When those bills made their way home, country bankers evaded and delayed, redeeming their promises with new promises to pay later, in other paper, at the Exchange Office. Trips to visit his wife's family in the western part of the state allowed Appleton to see such tactics firsthand at the Berkshire Bank—the "poor Pittsfield Bank," as he would later call it.[10]

In the spring of 1807, just as Dexter broke ground on the Coffee House, Appleton began to publish his concerns in the press. He called attention to the wide and growing gap between the banks' paper capital and their specie reserves, and urged "the honorable and wealthy directors of the Boston banks" to rein in their country brethren. "To pretend that all the banks in this Commonwealth can pay their capital, is absurd," he warned. "Nominal capitals" rose ever higher above the solid ground of specie. "The difference is made up by mutual confidence," Appleton reminded his readers. "[D]estroy that confidence and the whole fabric falls at once."[11]

Paper money was a collective delusion, and Appleton despised what he called the "tricks of trade." A merchant's ethics, he believed, forbade even "the slightest prevarication or deviation from the truth." Stuart's painting room was a logical stop for this self-proclaimed apostle of candor. All portraits—including the quick pastel sketches William Doyle hawked for a quarter at his "New Exchange Office for Profiles" on Tremont Street—promised faithfulness to their originals. But Stuart's heads, among the best in the world, aspired to deeper truth. Freezing a lifetime of flickering moods and changing fortunes in a single, transcendent image, a Stuart portrait revealed an enduring *essence*. He painted "mind" and "*character*," not merely faces, his admirers said. "STUART, thy portraits speak," Sarah Morton wrote.[12]

Yet if Stuart was a seeker of truth, he was also a master illusionist. Magic mirrors, his portraits fawned and flattered, showing wealthy patrons the inner selves they wished to see. One Bostonian accused the artist of "Promethean impiety, in giving to some of his likenesses thought, feeling, taste, and soul, when the allwise Creator had denied these gifts to the originals." Precisely what Stuart was paid for. Conjuring a semblance of spirit out of pigment on cloth, Stuart "counterfeit[ed] the soul." To sit for Stuart was to embrace Appleton's intrinsic value logic and Dexter's paper money mores simultaneously.[13]

After Charlotte and Andrew finished their second sitting, Stuart's assistant, John Ritto Penniman, came to the painting rooms to "grind colors," mixing brilliant solids like Prussian blue and Dutch pink and Venetian red with oil to ready them for his employer's brush. A talented sign painter on his way to becoming an esteemed artist, Penniman had a highly trained eye. He knew the sleights of hand that allowed Stuart to turn flat paint into pulsing flesh and seeing eyes. If he paused to study the emerging portraits of Appleton, Morton, and Dexter, Penniman would have seen truths disguised as well as revealed.[14]

Appleton's likeness shows no trace of the New Hampshire boy who had "footed it" into Boston fourteen years earlier, his worldly possessions bundled in a handkerchief. He has worked hard since then, building the scale and complexity of his trading operation while remaining cautious, upright. Appleton has been lucky as well, receiving large shipments of foreign goods just before the embargo took effect, and commanding high prices for them in import-starved Boston: one of the few merchants to profit during the downturn. He will later describe the period as one of "varied success . . . with an average of prosperity." In fact, his ascent has never faltered. Year by year, the twenty-nine-year-old in the portrait has risen beyond the boarding-house that served as his first home in Boston. Not two weeks before sitting to Stuart, Appleton purchased a four-story bowfront mansion that Asher Benjamin was building on Beacon Street for the outlandish sum of $13,500. Stuart renders Appleton as a citizen of the world, equally at home in Europe as on Beacon Hill. The master's brush transforms the "common mouth, middling nose" and "round chin" described on Appleton's 1802 passport into the features of a gentleman

of distinction. Carefully coiffed, with light playing on his blond curls
and gilt buttons, Appleton appears confident and serene.[15]

This is a painter's trick. Honest he may be, but Appleton is not
serene. He is anxious about the torrents of country banknotes flowing
into his adopted city. He is angry at the way this tide of paper erodes
the bedrock of his growing fortune. He is also, increasingly, possessed
with a singled-minded resolve to purge Boston of the paper menace.

Stuart's Charlotte Morton, like his depiction of Nathan Appleton,
conveys deep truths and buries deeper ones. The painting glories in
her youth (she is twenty-one) and her startling beauty. She presents
what her mother called "a perfect face": "complexion of the most delicate bloom, large dark eyes of enchanting blue, long ringlets of flaxen
gold, in which no tint of the auburn nor approach to the red were
seen." If Charlotte withholds the smile that her mother likewise
deemed "perfect," she discloses something of her "sweetness, softness,
[and] elegance."[16] Solemnity lies beneath that sweetness. Charlotte is
a serious and accomplished young woman, "a musician, a painter, a
poet," her mother boasts. She has little patience for the glittering beau
monde inhabited by others of her age and status and sex. "The better
I become acquainted with the world," Charlotte wrote, "the more dis-
gusting do I find its cold ceremonies, & deceitful politeness." In the
"gay world," she complained, "gross deception" flourished and "real
friends" were few.[17]

The recipient of Charlotte's letter, a prominent hostess well schooled
in the ways of the polite world, could be forgiven for wondering
whether her young friend's yearning for authenticity was itself a pose,
a nod to the cult of "sensibility" that dominated the era's novels and
magazines. But Charlotte had good reason to shun the "gay world,"
whose argot of "gross deception" was her birthright. Charlotte had
drawn her first breaths in Boston in the fall of 1787, just as her aunt
Frances ("Fanny")—her mother's sister, her father's lover—delivered
Perez Morton's illegitimate daughter in nearby Weston. "*Child of my
sorrowing soul!*" Charlotte's mother called her. And Charlotte *had* been
a child of sorrow, her young life shaped by the shadowy knowledge

Nathan Appleton,
*by Gilbert Stuart,*
*1808 (detail).*

of her half sister, like some minor character in a romance novel. Charlotte Morton chased the authentic in a world of masks and mirrors,
much as Nathan Appleton did. Yet as her mate she had chosen Andrew
Dexter. Their June wedding would take place in Trinity Church, where
the Mortons had baptized Charlotte some twenty-one years before.[18]

The match is not an obvious one—not visually, at least. Dexter's
darkness is ill suited to his fiancée's near-translucence, and their tem-
peraments seem likewise opposed. As he surveyed the canvasses,
Penniman could be forgiven for coupling Charlotte with Appleton
instead. Their long fine noses, their delicately mottled cheeks, and
their angelic lightness make them plausible siblings. Formally, none
of the three was well mated. All faced left, leaving no "pendant pair"
among them, no set of mutually adoring gazes to be forever preserved
over some carved mantle. Indeed, the painted evidence offers cause to
wonder what has brought Charlotte Morton and Andrew Dexter to
the threshold of marriage.

Charlotte Morton
Dexter, *by Gilbert
Stuart, 1808
(ca. 1828, detail).*

Andrew Dexter Jr.,
*by Gilbert Stuart,
1808 (detail).*

Perhaps Charlotte Morton, like her future husband, was a devotee of exchange, hoping to trade her fallen family for his aspiring one. For some time now, her father's money and connections had helped to finance the real estate dreams of her intended. If Dexter wanted money for mortar and mortgages, Perez Morton needed a different sort of capital. None of his children—four daughters and a son, all in their twenties—had married. Perhaps there was an element of quid pro quo involved in Charlotte's engagement, where Morton's investments with Andrew Dexter amounted to a bride price. Charlotte Morton likely married for love *and* money, objectives not opposed in her world. If Andrew Dexter was the husband of her father's choosing, he was also, as her mother wrote in an essay on marriage, "the husband of her love." Which, then as now, was no guarantee of bliss. Marriage required vigilance, Sarah Morton insisted. Even the most loving wife might find herself

> harrowed by disappointment, . . . defrauded of that protection, and refused that fidelity, which she sought, in which she trusted, and would gratefully and eternally have cherished . . . at once pursued and repulsed—pure in conduct, perhaps beautiful in person—yet left to coldness, neglect and desertion.

From a woman who knew disappointment, a warning Charlotte Morton would do well to heed.[19]

Among the three portraits, Dexter and Appleton make in some ways the likeliest pair. Excepting minor variations in background— the hint of a pilaster behind Appleton, Dexter against a plain, dark brown—the images are more twins than cousins. Both men are shown in half-length bust, turned three-quarters toward the viewer. Their coifs, their coats, and their linens are virtually identical. (Dexter cannot afford the gold buttons that adorn Appleton.) They could come from an assembly line: young men of commerce, the basics blocked out by an assistant like Penniman and the details left to the master. The high-flying speculator and the prudent merchant are superimposed upon the same template, as if peering through a wooden cutout

at a carnival. *As if they are the same man*. The notion would horrify
Appleton more than it would Dexter. And there's something to it.
Country boys of '79, they have landed in the same city—even in some
of the same clubs. Both chase fortune, and they do it in quite similar
ways. Appleton traffics in cloth, Dexter in paper. Yet each makes his
living by playing the spread between the bid and the ask. To call one
a gambler and the other a trader is to make a subtle distinction. Yet
the portraits show the differences between them as well. Where
Appleton appears attentive, even curious, Dexter is bold, almost defiant. The trace of a sneer begins to curl his lip.

For all three sitters, commissioning a Stuart portrait was an act of
speculation. In their different ways, each placed a bet on a future that
would make such an object a logical accessory. Stuart is unwilling to
gamble on his clients, though. He does not work on credit. A once and
future bankrupt, the painter has been burned before. He has not for-
gotten the client who paid him in "uncurrent bank notes,"
exchangeable only at a discount. Now all subjects pay as they go: half
at the first sitting, more with every layer of paint, gloss, gilt, *soul*. Morton, Dexter, and Appleton had the means and the motive to ask Stuart
to begin these statements of self. Only two of them will possess the
wherewithal to redeem the portraits from the studio.[20]

John Ritto Penniman cannot see this in April 1808. He has a painter's eye, but he is not clairvoyant. Gazing out from Stuart's easel on
the last day of April, Andrew Dexter and his betrothed brim with
potential, much like the tower erecting on Congress Street, an unfinished monument that grows more imposing every day.

⁓

Winter had been cold and spring tempestuous, lousy weather for construction. But the builders managed to get the roof on the Exchange
before snow blanketed the city in January. Now, as snow yielded to
rain, the building's interior swarmed with workmen. The week Gilbert Stuart began his portraits of Dexter, Morton, and Appleton, a
British traveler in Boston heard news of "a very lofty and extensive

hotel" arising "under the direction of one of the principal merchants in the town," and headed to Congress Street to survey the scene. The "plasterers and carpenters were at work" inside, he reported, their pace indicating that the project would be finished by summer. Even in its rough state, the building unfolded on "a grand scale." If "properly conducted," he supposed, the Exchange would "far exceed any thing of the kind in the United States, and perhaps be equal in accommodation, as it is already in size, to any house of that description in London." It was sure to "form a very noble ornament to that part of the town."[21]

That part of town—the mercantile heart of Boston—had never needed a noble ornament more urgently. Not in a generation, anyway. Since the 1790s, commerce itself had provided all the ornament a traveler could wish for: the sights and sounds and smells and tastes of goods from around the globe. The soaring Exchange was a monument to this soaring economy. Dexter designed the building to stand taller, to see farther, to face more resolutely *east* toward the riches of London, to help merchants navigate the waves of currency that accompanied the waves of oceanic trade.

Yet for all but a lucky few—the Appleton brothers, for instance—the boom that inspired the building had already gone bust. In 1808, exports out of Massachusetts reached barely a quarter of the previous year's totals. Hundreds of once-proud ships—those "mighty riders of the ocean"—lingered still and shorn, their sails and spars stored until the glorious resurrection of trade. Merchants fretted over empty stores, knowing that each day brought them closer to falling "through the debtor's hatch."[22]

Idle ships meant idle hands, and idle hands left hungry mouths in the city's poorer wards. "I am in Boston in a starving condition," an anonymous young cooper told Jefferson. "I have by working at jurney work got me a small house but what shall I git to eat[?] I cant eat my house. . . . I wish you could feal as bad as I feal with 6 Children round you crying for vittles & be half starved yourself."[23] In January, driven by desperation and a keen sense of justice, scores of jobless seamen defied the selectmen's injunction and near-zero temperatures when they took to the streets. Playing military music and carrying a flag at half-mast, the group paraded to the governor's house where, the papers reported, they "demanded *employment* or *bread*." His voice barely audible over the assembly, the Republican governor James Sullivan condemned "their manner of seeking relief," extended his sympathies, and insisted that "he could do nothing for them." The crowd dispersed without violence, but more such protests would follow. The embargo, which would drag on until the spring of 1809, was but two weeks old.[24]

Andrew Dexter felt the weight of the embargo with peculiar force. Like Gilbert Stuart, Dexter practiced a breed of alchemy, transforming base materials into valuable ones. And just as the halt in overseas trade hindered Stuart's supply of canvas, the embargo—indirectly but surely—threatened Dexter's chosen medium, paper money. No trade meant no work; no work, no customers; no customers, no currencies; no currencies, no exchange. Every day of the embargo reduced the Exchange Office's chances to make something of nothing, while every day of construction on the Coffee House brought new demands for cash. One traveler's surmise notwithstanding, the immense building was nowhere close to completion. It was a hollow shell, its polished facades wrapped around a money pit.

In this sense, the building resembled Stuart's unfinished portrait. The young gentleman in the frame gave every appearance of rising. But in fact, by April 1808, Dexter was falling so fast he could be forgiven for not knowing if he was tumbling from the brightly tinned dome of the Exchange Coffee House or whether Congress Street was rising to meet him.

⁂

When does a scheme (a blueprint, a plan) become a scheme (a trick, a plot)? Both meanings attached to the word in the age of paper, though the former, more wholesome definition still dominated in Dexter's day. If the boundary between plan and plot is blurry now, it was less

clear then, in a culture that greeted self-interest with distrust and speculation with contempt. But however faint, the line between scheme
and scam existed in 1808. By the time he and his fiancée sat for Stuart
at the end of April, Andrew Dexter had crossed that line. And he
knew it.[25]

Looking back on Dexter's short, sad career at the end of his own
long and prosperous life, Nathan Appleton decided that his adversary
had laid a plot: "a tremendous speculation" to obtain "control of the
circulating medium of New England." That is the victor's story. Dexter would see it differently, not as a nefarious master plan, but as a
series of small gambles whose failure to pay off led to bigger risks, and
ultimately to desperate ones. Dexter approached the faint line separating scheme from scam slowly, year by year, and then brick by brick.
In 1804, he was a struggling young lawyer. The following year he
joined forces with the Exchange Office, thus declaring himself one of
the bolder Boston moneymen. By the end of 1806, he had helped to
create two highly leveraged financial institutions, the Detroit Bank
and the Berkshire Bank, knitting them together by routing their funds
through the Changery on State Street. Early in 1807, he had begun to
build the Exchange Coffee House—which he proudly promoted as a
"new scheme"—upon this paper foundation. In all this he acted aggressively, even heedlessly. But foolish daring does not a scam make.[26]

After Congress's disapproval of the Detroit Bank charter threatened the Exchange Coffee House, Dexter drew closer to the law's
fuzzy margins. In June 1807, he sent his father and brother to the
Western world to reestablish the bank as a private concern, entrusting
them with a small amount of specie to underwrite a large quantity of
new bank bills. The paper promises they brought back to Boston in
July looked much like the previous version. But there was no "company" mentioned on the new notes; only the president, directors, and
stockholders of the Detroit Bank "jointly and severally" guaranteed
their payment. In practice, this meant Andrew Dexter, who now
owned 9,999 of the bank's 10,000 shares. As the Exchange building
and its demands grew increasingly outsized, so too did Dexter's toler-

*Second Detroit Bank, $5 bill, July 1807.*

ance for risk, and so too did the boldness and doomed optimism of his plans, his *schemes*. But through the end of 1807—until the embargo married Dexter's bad judgment to spectacularly bad timing—these tireless machinations are better characterized as scrambling than as swindling.[27]

If it is difficult to say exactly when Dexter cast aside his principles, it is easier to discover where the transformation occurred. It surprised nobody at the time that the border between high finance and brazen fraud ran through Rhode Island, whose reputation for playing fast and loose with money was a century old by the spring of 1808. Andrew Dexter stepped off the edge of legitimate commerce in Gloucester, a hamlet of two thousand farming families barely twenty miles from his boyhood home in Providence.

Gloucester was Rhode Island's Detroit, a "small two-penny Village . . . containing about a dozen houses," one Philadelphia writer called it in 1809, after Dexter had made the place infamous. Tucked in the state's hilly northwestern corner, serviced by a stony, rutted road, it was farther from Providence and Newport than it looked on the map. In recent years, the spirit of "improvement" transforming rural New England had swept into Gloucester, leaving in its wake small monuments to civic life: a library (really, a locked bookcase in the back of the schoolhouse), a Masonic Hall, a post office, and no fewer than nineteen establishments licensed to peddle liquor. Still, there was no denying the town's remoteness. Without ready access to markets, Gloucester farmers tended their fields and flocks chiefly for the benefit of their own families, producing little more than they consumed. In the depression following the Revolution, they had reverted to barter, paying their rents with grain in the manner of medieval peasants.[28]

Like most rural Americans, Gloucester's citizens prized easy credit and soft money when they used cash at all. (Voters' loose money mores were largely responsible for the town's overwhelming opposition to the U.S. Constitution.) Bankers also saw the potential for gold in its hills. In February 1804, a group of the town's leading men—the same coalition of improvers who had built the so-called library and worked to better the dreadful roads—secured a charter for the Farmers' Exchange Bank, the ninth bank in the nation's smallest state. In the entire country, perhaps only Detroit's bank was less well connected to the infrastructure of commercial transportation. Even it had more dignified quarters. The Farmers' Exchange Bank rented space on the first floor of the Masonic Hall, a wooden house fronting the dirt path that passed for Gloucester's main street. A dry well beneath a trapdoor in the floor served as its safe. When a writer in the Boston *Repertory* suggested that the "cellars of the Rhode Island country taverns" should not be treated as "reservoirs where wealth is hoarded," he surely referred to the Farmers' Exchange.[29]

The lack of a proper vault may have embarrassed the directors of the Farmers' Exchange. (Recall that the Boston founders of the Detroit Bank dragged iron doors and several tons of bar iron overland from Boston for that special purpose.) Yet in practical terms, the vault secured very little. As the state legislature later determined, "the whole money paid into the Bank, at any period whatever" amounted to under $20,000, less than one-fifth what its charter authorized. That was the *cumulative* total. On the day Dexter got there, the merest fraction of that—$380.50—remained beneath the trapdoor.[30]

In the bank's early years at least, this persistent lack of funds reflected no lack of effort on the directors' parts. What the legislature termed their "new and strange expedients" to procure capital might be funny if they weren't so sad. In the spring of 1805, for example, they attempted to augment their small store of specie by buying sacks of Rhode Island corn and rye on the cheap to peddle at the markets in Hartford, a farmer's exchange indeed. The scheme failed, as did others that followed. The state examiners put it this way: "From the first commencement of the institution it has been conducted, as the perplexed and confused state of the books sufficiently evinces, negligently and unskillfully; . . . the Directors had at no time a proper knowledge of the affairs of the Bank."[31]

Perpetually short of cash, the Gloucester bankers often proved reluctant to redeem their notes. When William Foster, a merchant from Smithfield, turned up at the bank in April 1807 with $700 in its notes, the cashier refused to pay him specie, neither would he return the bills. Instead, the banker stashed the notes "in a box or drawer behind the counter, and, after equivocating for some time," offered a personal IOU in exchange. Rumors that the bank's bills were barely credible and its books poorly policed scared off legitimate customers. But counterfeiters swooped in where investors feared to tread. No sooner had one man convicted of "making and passing" Farmers' Exchange fakes escaped from the county jail than a "new gang of villains . . . who are *better workmen* than their *predecessors*" began producing phony notes that withstood "a close examination with the true ones." Distinguishing the "true" bills from the forgeries hardly repaid the effort; authentic Farmers' Exchange Bank notes were nowhere near as good as gold.[32]

Enter Andrew Dexter. His connection to the Farmers' Exchange Bank, a partnership that proved both his and its undoing, was in many ways unlike his commitments in Pittsfield and Detroit, or his role in the Exchange Office. He joined each of those ventures at or very near its founding. On State Street, in Pittsfield, and in Detroit, he was an organizer, a *believer* in the enterprise. Gloucester was different. The bumbling management of the Farmers' Exchange Bank, its depleted coffers, its allure for counterfeiters: all were public knowledge before the end of 1807, when Dexter proposed a partnership between it and the Boston Exchange Office. He did so not in spite of the bank's tawdry reputation, but because of it. If the perfume of success lured him west from State Street to the Berkshires to the Michigan Territory, the scent of failure drew him to Gloucester. Its funds scarce, its notes abundant, its credit doubtful, the Farmers' Exchange Bank was rotten fruit. Dexter plucked it not to save the bank but to save himself.

In December 1807, with the chill of Jefferson's embargo deepening on his Congress Street building site, Andrew Dexter wrote to the president and directors of what he termed "the Farmers' Bank." "Gentlemen," he addressed them, proposing that the Exchange Office should purchase half the bank's stock, in return for which the Farmers' Exchange would lend "fifty to one hundred thousand dollars in their bills" to the State Street concern at 3 percent annual interest. Dexter promised that the Gloucester bills would "either be kept from circulation entirely, or be paid out in such manner as will be most likely to prevent their return to the Bank." (He would send them to Detroit, to Pittsfield, to Wiscasset: details not worth specifying.) The Changery was "willing to receive the bills and make all the arrangements immediately," with the transfer of stock to follow shortly thereafter.[33]

When the directors of the Farmers' Exchange Bank refused his proposition, Dexter looked elsewhere—everywhere—for cash. Several wells seemed promising; each quickly ran dry. Squeezed by the embargo, he squeezed his debtors in turn, going to court to extract small settlements from tenants who failed to pay their rents. But verdicts awarding him $43 from a barber, $31 from a yeoman, and the $75 a tailor owed him amounted to little against the six-figure obligations he had run up since 1806.[34] Dexter earned some breathing room from the Massachusetts legislature in the first days of March 1808, when they amended the charter of the Exchange Coffee House to allow the proprietors to raise up to $50,000 toward the cost of completing the building by mortgaging their real estate. But a lack of investors

rendered the new line of credit useless. At the same time, Boston merchants began to lose faith in Berkshire notes, whose value started to
fall. Stern warnings against the new Detroit Bank bills prompted
shopkeepers who accepted those notes to demand a premium for
doing so. And the building craftsmen whose wages came due at the
end of each week were canny enough to demand inflated numbers of
these discounted notes so that they, in turn, could buy food and shoes
and firewood, could pay their rents to landlords like Dexter. As Dexter's paper depreciated, he needed more notes to do the work of fewer,
a vicious cycle.[35]

His debts mushroomed, and Gloucester beckoned. On Sunday,
March 20, Dexter set out upon the uncomfortable journey from Boston to northwest Rhode Island to press his case with the directors of
the Farmers' Exchange Bank. A cloudy day that yielded to heavy
thunderstorms by nightfall made for poor traveling weather. The
mean hostelries that awaited him at journey's end—the guest rooms
over Cyrus Cooke's tavern on Main Street, or the lodging chambers
of the Central Hotel (a grandiose name for the second floor of a har-
ness maker's shop)—cannot have delighted the man who was going
to such extraordinary lengths to build the most elegant hotel in North
America.[36]

The following morning, the bank's directors, a baker's dozen,
tramped through the mud into the Masonic Hall for their weekly discount meeting. Along with their other business, they engaged in
"conversation among themselves respecting selling their stock to
Andrew Dexter, jun." The Boston investor waited nearby to hear their
verdict, to no avail. "The result of the conversation at that meeting,"
the bank's cashier later recounted, "was that they concluded not to sell"
their shares.[37]

This news of a second rebuff failed to deter the bank's eager suitor.
Dexter's dealings in Detroit and Pittsfield had made him an expert at
wooing rural money men. Their shortsighted decision, their rotten
roads, their disagreeable weather be damned. At the next Monday's
meeting, Dexter was back. Seated at the table this time, he convinced

most of the directors to part with their stock. ("At last" they "agreed to sell," one of them said of the moment Dexter exhausted their resistance.) The resigning officers transferred their shares to their remaining associates, Simon Smith, one of the wealthier farmers in town, and John Harris, a lower court judge in Providence County who also served as the bank's president. In exchange, each of the departing directors received his freedom from the failing enterprise, as well as thirteen hundred dollars in Farmers' Exchange Bank notes. It can have surprised nobody that Harris and Smith, the last guardians of the institution's admittedly fragile virtue, were later revealed to have acted "as the agents of . . . [Andrew] Dexter," for whose sole "use and benefit" the shares had been acquired.

Harris and Smith were not sufficient, though. The new owner needed a new board. Dexter put forward one candidate, Elisha Fairbanks, but the nomination failed. (Fairbanks, with his name worthy of Dickens and his veiled ties to the Dexter family, would finally become a director in October.) Instead, Harris granted ten shares a piece to three men to allow their immediate election as officers of the reorganized Farmers' Exchange. The first was James Aldrich, a member of the old board whose debts to the bank kept him from making a clean getaway. The second was William Colwell, who had served as cashier of the institution for all of a fortnight. The other new director was the new owner's brother Samuel, an exchange broker from Providence.[38]

At the first meeting of the new directors, Dexter presented a document granting Harris, Colwell, and Samuel Dexter "full powers to make such negotiations and arrangements with Andrew Dexter, jun. from time to time as they may judge advisable." His handpicked board quickly assented. For its first official act, the committee loaned Dexter seventeen thousand dollars in Farmers' Exchange Bank notes, "for which they took his receipt."[39]

He knows there is nothing behind the receipt and nothing behind the notes, nothing of worth in the Rhode Island town, no hope of redemption for either the money or the bank. In Gloucester, Dexter is no booster. He is a parasite, feeding on a corpse. Three weeks before he sat for Gilbert Stuart, two months before he wed Charlotte Morton, the hemorrhage began. April 6, 1808: the day Andrew Dexter swapped his gentlemanly discretion for a con man's disguise, his scheme for a scam.

⌒

From April 1808 till its grand opening a year later, the story of the Boston Exchange Coffee House was less a builder's than a clerk's tale. Not, in the end, such a different story, for clerks and carpenters had much in common. Like woodworking and brick making, writing and ciphering figured as male job skills, the building blocks of many a middling man's republican independence. Both callings required considerable training. The housewright endured years of apprenticeship as he climbed the occupational ladder from wood-toting "boy" to journeyman to craft master. The clerk likewise relied on a variety of teachers, from his mother to the writing masters of the local primary school and academy. He had no clear path to college, nor any real use for it. Rather than liberal learning, the central goal of his education was the perfection of a "Clerk-like Manner of Writing, fit for the Dexterous Dispatch of Business." The clerk was a penman, a good "merchant's hand" one of his main craft skills. In this sense clerks, no less than building craftsmen, were manual laborers.[40]

In addition to writing fluidly, the clerk needed to reckon fluently. Looking back on his long and successful life, Nathan Appleton recalled with special fondness the moment he "learned the first principles of book-keeping by double entry." Accounting was a skill clerks ignored at their peril, Appleton believed. "I have always attributed a great portion of the failures which take place," he counseled, "to a want of attention, or a want of knowledge, in the proper principles of book-keeping."[41]

Like the journeyman carpenter outfitted with adze and level and compass, the clerk armed with steel-nibbed pens and tightly ruled ledgers *aspired,* seeking fortune in a culture that increasingly rewarded hard work over high birth. By the early nineteenth century, the clerk probably stood a better chance of achieving success than did the craft worker. While many of those who worked with bricks or boards or stone saw their autonomy challenged by capitalist middlemen and the new disciplines they imposed, the culture of the market brought opportunities to the penman. With diligence and luck the "SMART, active BOY, who can write a fair Hand, and is acquainted with Figures" might become a shopkeeper, and the shopkeeper a merchant. Appleton had done it, transforming himself from farm boy to penman to man of capital, moving from boardinghouse to Beacon Street in the process. His neighbor there, James Colburn, had made the same journey. A shopkeeper's helper in 1792, he climbed so far and so fast that by 1808, as he boasted, he was "worth over half a million dollars." This was the stuff of clerks' dreams, the dreams of New England boys who knew the merchant was the new century's master builder and paper its dominant medium.[42]

With its small population almost uniformly dedicated to the hardscrabble life of subsistence farming, Gloucester, Rhode Island, offered few jobs to the young man who preferred the pen to the hoe. But William Colwell had managed to find one. Like most young men with large aspirations and modest backgrounds, Colwell left few traces of his early life on the historical record. Born in 1780 to Quaker farmers in the neighboring village of Foster, he spent his youth there and in nearby Smithfield, arriving in Gloucester some time after 1800. There he worked, at least part of the year, teaching the rudiments of literacy to the children of the town's more ambitious families. Though he schooled their sons and daughters, Colwell did not reach the upper echelons of Gloucester's admittedly truncated society. His family did not number among the officers of the town's militia, the brethren of its Masonic Lodge, or the shareholders of its modest library—as the founders of the Farmers' Exchange Bank all did.[43]

Nonetheless, on March 15, 1808, the bank's board—for two weeks yet the old, pre-Dexter board—elected William Colwell to replace

*William Colwell's signature; detail from
Farmers' Exchange Bank $2 bill, May 1808.*

their retiring cashier. The job would make large claims upon Colwell's practiced hand and loyal temperament. In such a small operation, the cashier managed virtually all of the bank's daily operations. When the directors conferred, Colwell would record the proceedings and tally the votes. When the mail carriers fought their way to Gloucester, Colwell would repair to the post office to collect the bank's correspondence, logging checks received and discounts extended in an orderly set of ledgers. When customers came to the Masonic Hall to redeem notes for specie, Colwell extended his hand in greeting. Which was only fitting, since his hand held the pen that endorsed the promise that each of the bank's bills uttered. Inked onto the lower lefthand corner of every Farmers' Exchange note, Colwell's signature embodied the authenticity of the bill, transferring the institution's "fidelity and faithfulness" from handshake to paper.[44]

These were weighty responsibilities. To ensure that Colwell executed them faithfully, two of his kinsmen posted a bond of ten thousand dollars, indemnifying the bank against the unlikely event that Colwell should ever commit fraud. As one nineteenth-century critic pointed out, however, such bonds did "not cover loss by indiscretion, neglect, or errors of judgment, however gross these may be."[45]

Despite his vital role, at the end of the day the cashier remained a laborer, his status closer to the porters who transported a bank's capital than to the trustees and shareholders who raised and owned it.

Andrew Dexter took the unusual step of making his cashier a director of the enterprise. But despite the fancy title, at heart William Colwell was a clerk, exercising a clerk's earnest diligence in exchange for a clerk's modest pay: a wage of roughly $3.80 each week, $0.64 for every working day. The cashier of Boston's venerable Massachusetts Bank had earned five times that—back in 1784! In a city like Boston or Providence, a common laborer made as much as Colwell did, a skilled craftsman considerably more. But Gloucester was not Providence, much less Boston. And in a town with very little in the way of a cash economy, the cashier's meager wage amounted to more money than Colwell was likely to see any other way. What's more, by dutifully executing his office, the cashier helped to ensure the bank's credit, and thus to make that money good beyond the narrow confines of northwest Rhode Island.[46]

Colwell was not especially proficient at math. (In the coming months, Dexter's representatives would point out the cashier's frequent "mistake[s] in counting" banknotes.) But what he lacked in ciphering skill, he made up for in fealty. William Colwell possessed a clerk's habit of deference along with his steady hand, and his boss knew how to nurture a cashier's devotion.[47]

Two years before, Dexter and his partners had gone to the considerable expense and bother of bringing William Flanagan from the Exchange Office on State Street to the Michigan Territory, where they personally underwrote a fifteen-thousand-dollar bond to install him as cashier of the Detroit Bank. Flanagan had served them steadfastly ever since, weathering the bank's tempestuous fortunes without flinching. His signature on the bills of the new private bank read as clear and firm as it did on the old.[48]

Good help was nowhere near so hard to find in Rhode Island as it had been in Michigan. Even so, the new owner of the Farmers' Exchange Bank acted quickly to secure Colwell's loyalty—indeed, to encourage the cashier to identify the bank with Dexter. At a meeting soon after Dexter bought the concern, Colwell later remembered, "some of the Directors mentioned that it would be proper to increase" the cashier's paltry wage. The board failed to act on the proposal. But Dexter cornered Colwell afterward, pledging "that he should have twice as much as the Directors had agreed to give, and if the Directors did not pay it . . . he would." For once Dexter backed up his smooth words, promptly delivering Colwell "two hundred dollars in addition to his salary." This was a pittance when compared to Dexter's obligations, all the more so since the bonus consisted of Farmers' Exchange Bank notes. But to a man of Colwell's humble station two hundred dollars was a fortune, a sum that easily purchased trust and forbearance. And so, when his benefactor asked him to, Colwell "delivered the stereotype dies, used by said Bank, in impressing their bills, to Andrew Dexter."[49]

Those dies, eight nuggets of case-hardened steel, constituted the only real assets the Farmers' Exchange Bank possessed. The key component of the engraver Jacob Perkins's patented process for making fraud-proof bank bills, such dies protected a bank's good name from those who would falsely utter it. Under the Perkins system, a bank locked away the blocks bearing its name and location "for its own security" until it needed bills. Then the directors delivered the precious blocks to Newburyport, where the printer fitted them into a matrix comprised of some fifty-seven other elements, all bolted to "a strong iron frame, which is screwed to a metal plate of an inch thickness." Then, working alongside his brother and several assistants at the engraving plant built for the purpose, Perkins "impress[ed] all the bills required . . . as fast as they can be properly executed." Mindful of the security of his operation, Perkins accounted not only for each bank's dies, but also for every sheet of the specially watermarked paper on which he printed their mirror image. In return, Perkins asked "reasonable compensation": forty dollars to cast the dies, four dollars for every hundred sheets of bills he pulled from his press, and a rental fee for the use of his patent on the stereotype process.[50]

To determine this last component of his price, Perkins used a sliding scale based on a bank's paid-in capital, a formula that benefited the Farmers' Exchange. Even so, the humble Gloucester bank paid

dear to become an early adapter of the day's most advanced anticounterfeiting technology—and for good reason. Notes struck off on
stereotype plates conferred a certain legitimacy on an otherwise
obscure bank. A merchant in a distant city might not know much
about the good folks of Gloucester, but to his wary eye a Perkins bill
looked standard, current, *real*. A host of remote country banks across
New England and beyond—including the Berkshire Bank, the Detroit
Bank, and the Farmers' Exchange—made this bet, agreeing to pay
Perkins's price in 1805 and 1806, several years before Massachusetts
mandated the use of such notes.[51]

By the time Dexter got to Gloucester, however, skeptics were beginning to worry that the Perkins method contained the seeds of its own
undoing. The inventor touted his notes as a "completely mechanical
production" immune to human manipulation. But as one of the
engraver's competitors warned, the *"perfect sameness"* that constituted
the stereotype bill's sole virtue actually facilitated the counterfeiter's
task. "Where is the mighty difficulty of passably imitating *regular*
marks. . . ?" As every new technology begets its own larceny, standard
notes bred standard fakes. The Perkins system had given the public a
sense of "false security," leaving them deaf to the rustlings of money
makers in the woods, much less foxes in the henhouse, like Andrew
Dexter.[52]

In late May, secure at the helm of the Farmers' Exchange, Dexter
explained to his cashier "some ideas which myself and friends have
respecting the manner of managing" the bank's meager funds. Direc-
tive number one: hoard specie. "The general rule should undoubtedly
be to pay punctually," Dexter conceded. But there were "important
exceptions." Currency brokers and others who sought "profit out of
the injury and loss of the bank" should be "paid only by drafts on the
Exchange-Office, at forty days sight"—paper promising more paper,
elsewhere, later. Banks should fare worse, especially those close
enough to send runners to Gloucester on a regular basis. Dexter continued: "The Providence banks should, in my opinion, be plagued as
much as possible." He suggested that Colwell employ what had

become a familiar trick in the country banker's arsenal. He should honor the note's printed promise, but make it hurt, detaining the bearers "as long as it will naturally take to count out all the kinds of specie change, intermixed in the most deliberate manner." He might redeem a stack of five-dollar notes in *"four pence half penny pieces,"* turning each copper "between his thumb and finger several times, to discover" the coin's denomination, then using "pen and ink and [a] large piece of paper" to "set down several figures and make a long sum in Arithmetic." He could then set the change on the scales, demonstrating (again at length) that the bank's paper was worth its weight in gold. A cashier who acted his part well might run out the clock, closing for the day before the notes were paid. *Come back tomorrow,* he could (gently) tell the customer, recommending Gloucester's fine accommodations for the overnight stay. Days might drag into weeks. One creditor of the Nantucket Bank recalled that he had "attended the bank assiduously every day" for more than two weeks before the teller at last forked over the full sum the bank owed him: $472. Here was the logic of intrinsic value turned against itself, specie weaponized. The merchant who left Gloucester days late and burdened by sacks of silver and copper might think twice before taking a Farmers' Exchange note out of circulation again.[53]

In case this principle should confound the new cashier, Dexter dispatched an emissary to Gloucester to "assist" Colwell and his fellow directors. Dexter introduced Charles Edwards, whom he called "my clerk," as "a young gentleman of respectability, in whom you can place the utmost confidence." This description to the contrary, Edwards did not possess a gentleman's education. ("I called at your house . . . but you was not there," he wrote to Samuel Dexter, a slip in grammar that no gentleman would allow himself.) Rather, like all good clerks, Edwards earned his employer's recommendation through his fine penmanship; the *Boston Directory* listed him as a "scrivener and copyist." The young man's allegiance to Dexter also stemmed from the fact that his boss was his landlord. Edwards rented a small office in the unfinished Exchange building, the kind of mutual dependence that nourished an employer's "utmost confidence" in his subordinate, and vice versa. Over the ensuing weeks, Edwards traveled to Gloucester often enough to befriend William Colwell, whom he offered "a bed at my house" on Chamber Street whenever the cashier next found himself in the big city.[54]

With the benefit of Edwards's hands-on tutoring as well as Dexter's written instructions Colwell soon learned his new boss's second maxim: spew paper. Escalating with the claims of the Exchange building, Dexter's ravenous appetite for Farmers' Exchange Bank notes increased as summer wore on. Every day on Congress Street a battalion of skilled laborers—glaziers and plasterers and painters and paper stainers and carvers and gilders—worked to complete the last bits of construction. Every week, crews presented Dexter with their bills. Every month, the men who had loaned him money to buy the land sent their clerks to collect on the mortgages coming due. In July, Dexter asked Colwell to forward him "all the bills now hand" at the bank. After running through that supply in less than a month, Dexter "procured the paper" to have additional bills "struck off in Newburyport." These blanks he forwarded to Colwell for signature, sending some in care of Edwards and carrying others to Gloucester himself. At the end of August, Dexter returned to Boston with more than $40,000 in newly signed Farmers' Exchange notes, some 1,635 sheets of uncut bills bundled into three hefty parcels. A week later, a messenger brought Colwell another $200,000 in unsigned bills, along with Dexter's injunction to sign the largest denominations first. This was too big a shipment to wrap in paper. After signing the 8,000 sheets, Colwell was to "redeliver them to him packed in a box," along with any others he had on hand.[55]

Colwell must have come to dread his errands to the post office. For no sooner would the cashier set down his pen and unkink his hand than Dexter's next entreaty would arrive, always seeking "as large as possible" a shipment of bills. In return, his boss typically presented a generic paper marker, leaving the particulars for Colwell to ink in: yet more writing for the beleaguered scribe. "Received of the Committee of the Farmers' Exchange Bank," Dexter's IOUs read, "_____ in their bills, which I am to employ as their agent, for their benefit, accounting with them for such a portion of the profits, and at such times as may hereafter be mutually agreed upon." When even these vague assurances became too confining, Dexter replaced the stack of individual receipts with a blanket pledge:

> I, Andrew Dexter, jun. do promise the President, Directors and Company of the Farmers' Exchange Bank, to pay them, or order, _____ dollars, in two years from the date with interest, at two per cent. per annum; it being however understood that said Dexter shall not be called upon to make payment until he thinks it proper, he being the principal stockholder, and best knowing when it will be proper to pay the same.

By the time Colwell filled out this absurdly ambiguous receipt at the end of November, the number in the blank would exceed a half million dollars.[56]

When he could, Dexter annexed to these enormous notes of hand whatever blend of hard and soft monies he managed to scare up: here some "specie change" to frustrate runners, there a couple thousand dollars in the notes of other banks in which he held an interest, occasionally a few hundred dollars in current Boston money. For a time, at least, such small infusions might satisfy customers in Gloucester and thus help to keep whispering about the bank to a minimum. Yet the funds Colwell received from his boss never added up to more than pennies on the dollar against Dexter's mounting debts to the Farmers' Exchange.[57]

With his patron laboring to keep him both frantic and ignorant, Colwell could not see that the chain of paper stretching from his desk to Dexter's formed but one strand of a vast and intricate web of money crisscrossing the nation from its coastal ports to its westernmost edge. This much Colwell would have known: the vault, such as it was, lay empty. Only confidence backed the notes he was signing, unmerited confidence that ebbed with proximity to Gloucester. To pass as current money, Farmers' Exchange notes must escape the information orbit of Providence and Boston, must be set adrift far enough away, as Dexter had put it in his initial proposal to the directors, "to prevent their return to the Bank." Which meant that Dexter couldn't pay the Coffee House builders with Gloucester bills. Not directly, at least. He sent those bills west. Farmers' Exchange notes went to Pittsfield, where Andrew's youngest brother Simon Newton ferried Gloucester paper on a regular basis.[58] Dexter also shipped the bills to Michigan; merchants were seen "bringing Rhodeisland bills here to redeem the Detroit [notes]," and then "sending the Detroit money to boston" in return. He routed them to Ohio; "large quantities of the bills" turned up in Cincinnati, and some surfaced in Marietta. And they went other places as well, blazing a trail of paper that vanished from the historical record as soon as a banknote became a wage, a hat, or a bushel of wheat. In exchange, Dexter's runners returned to Boston with bills from the Berkshire Bank, the Detroit Bank, the Marietta Bank, and many others. Rendered current by the Exchange Office, *these* notes paid the workers on the Coffee House, paper brought back to life as brick.[59]

But no matter how far afield Dexter scattered them, Farmers' Exchange Bank notes found their way back east, where the demand for paper money was greatest. During the last months of 1808, as Dexter stepped up his demands and Colwell augmented his hours at the pen, Farmers' Exchange Bank notes crossed the counters of Boston merchants with ever-increasing frequency, coming to rest in stores such as the Broad Street countinghouse of Nathan Appleton.

Repeatedly, Dexter enjoined William Colwell to keep his signing sessions "profoundly secret." Eager to please his employer, Colwell filled out the bills "as privately as possible." The cashier didn't talk, but the money spoke volumes. Every time a customer paid for her calicoes with a banknote from Gloucester or Pittsfield or Detroit, Appleton heard the paper murmuring. Every time Appleton presented such bills at the Exchange Office only to receive equally dubious paper in return, he heard it shouting. And by the end of October, he decided that he had heard quite enough from the likes of Andrew Dexter.[60]

∞

November 1808 found Boston agitated. The weather, rarely pleasant this time of year, turned warm and wet and somber by turns. (The "great darkness," one diarist noted, resembled the fabled "dark day of 1780," when night inexplicably fell in the middle of a May afternoon.) Politics, rarely calm during an election season, were likewise more than usually fractious. Debate over the now-protracted embargo made for an especially bitter struggle at the ballot box, as Republicans decried Federalist treachery and Federalists mocked "Jeffersonian Gloom." Partisan bickering spilled into the streets. In a long-delayed aftershock of the honor killing of two years before, Thomas Selfridge came to blows with his victim's father, the contretemps ending only when the younger man "laid [Benjamin Austin] in the gutter."[61] Pessimism about the future—the country's, the town's—was infectious. "Our National Concerns are in a deplorable condition," a young painter noted in his journal. "America never saw so gloomy a day since the revolution."[62]

Despite the pressures bearing down upon him, Andrew Dexter had reason for cautious optimism. By hook and increasingly by crook, he had nearly finished the Exchange building. The exterior was complete, leaving a hundred thousand extra bricks that could be cleaned and resold to anyone foolish enough to embark on a large-scale building project in these days. The tower's lavish interior was almost done as well. Solomon Willard, a country carpenter who once labored with a broad ax splitting piles, used fine polishes to finish his dramatic contribution to the project: a spiral staircase that began in the basement and serpentined, floor after floor, until it reached the roof. Willard's seven-story helix was a marvel of engineering and art, the most amazing "piece of joiner's work in the country" by one estimate. He had struggled with it for months. But now he was smoothing the rough edges and readying his bill. Dexter still needed a crew of journeymen carpenters to work on various corners of the place for several weeks. But twenty months after workingmen first broke ground on the cellar, the end was at last in sight.[63]

Tenants were beginning to materialize. In August, real estate broker Rufus Davenport took an office below the Exchange's Congress Street entrance, along the same basement hallway as Charles Edwards's copying shop. Several weeks later, Lafayette Perkins, a sign and housepainter (no Gilbert Stuart), moved into a studio on the first, or "principal," floor. This month the town post office leases quarters just beside the grand staircase leading onto the main floor, its presence signaling to all of Boston the Exchange's importance to gentlemen in the know.[64] The building's new denizens brought a modest revenue stream, although it's hard to see how Dexter imagined that the post office's annual rent of $150, for example, would offset his costs, even when multiplied over scores of rooms, more of them ready for hire each day.[65]

Still, he was beginning to see income, however small, from a project that had known only massive outlays. For better or worse, Dexter still owned, at least provisionally, the whole magnificent pile and the ground beneath it. In fact, his mood buoyed by whatever combination of good news—his recent marriage, the rush of paper westward from Gloucester, the dazzling sight of the seven story building itself—he *added* two small parcels to his holdings. The first, a narrow corridor of land stretching east from the Exchange, would afford a dramatic vista culminating in the building's main entrance. The second, a "new brick dwelling house" on Round Lane, offered something more precious yet: a respectable place for Andrew and his bride of five months to set up housekeeping among neighbors who included emerging professionals (merchants, a lawyer, a schoolmistress) as well as humbler folk (a truckman, a bricklayer, a seaman). Here, one imagines, rose the staircase along which to hang their Stuart portraits (provided the Dexters could scrape together the funds to finish them). Here lay comfort if not grandeur. For polite entertainment, the rebuilt Federal Street Theater stood two blocks away at the head of Franklin Street, just east of the crescent of luxury residences that had bankrupted Charles Bulfinch: an elegant surround if a bitter reminder of the dangers of real estate speculation.[66]

Not that the Dexters were keeping up with the Appletons; Round Lane was no Beacon Street. Days after Dexter signed the deed for the south Boston home, Nathan Appleton and his wife moved into their mansion in what he called this "truly delectable" part of town, a home that cost nearly triple what Dexter's had. Contractors were still putting the finishing touches on the place, installing painted blinds behind the street-floor windows and sealing the skylights four stories above. While Asher Benjamin and his crew worried about the final details of the design, Appleton fretted over the decor that would proclaim his refinement to his "very stylish" neighbors. He asked his brother in London to send him "a pair of Grecian Lamps—rather elegant than showy, some handsome chimney ornaments novel and elegant—a pair of stylish Bell ropes for the drawing rooms," and "a great many pretty things" preferably in the "prevailing colors orange and light green." These "tasty" imported objets would decorate the room over which Stuart's portrait of the successful young merchant presided.[67]

High style cost money, and that fall, money—especially paper money—tormented Nathan Appleton as never before. Country banks had vexed him for the better part of a decade. Like other Boston merchants, Appleton watched the notes from distant banks flood into town, pooling in such numbers that their value plummeted, and their discounted price drove good Boston money out of circulation. (This he later described as a triumph of barbarism over "civilized Banks," whose bills were "pushed out of existence by the Goths and Vandals to the North, of the East, and the West.") Like other Boston merchants, he tried various remedies to stem the tide, even going so far as briefly to join forces with the Exchange Office.[68]

But Gloucester paper—*Dexter* paper—was different. Many country banks were poorly run, but the Farmers' Exchange Bank was degenerate. According to what Appleton called his "mercantile code," men of commerce must yoke their quest for "individual benefit" to an equally ardent passion for "absolute and undeviating justice. . . . The morals of trade are of the strictest and purest character," he insisted. "There is no class of men with whom the Christian rule of doing to others what we expect or require in return, is more strictly demanded, than amongst merchants." Every note issued by the Farmers' Exchange Bank violated those golden rules of honesty, charity, and transparency. Under Dexter's direction, the Exchange Office, too, had become "monstrous." Dilution, depreciation, and delay: these were unpleasant enough. But Gloucester bank represented "evil . . . of a magnitude too serious to be unregarded," and Appleton devised "a plan for putting an end to it." No hotheaded duelist in the model of Thomas Selfridge, he would not challenge Dexter in the street. Instead, Appleton would fight paper with paper: in the banks, at the bar, and in the press.[69]

Appleton enlisted the leaders of sixty-three other firms in the battle, marshaling a roster of combatants that reads like a who's who of business Boston. Save for a lone shopkeeper, his troops in the coming skirmish against country paper were merchants, men who trafficked in imported goods ranging from wine to cloth to "West Indies goods": rum and coffee and sugar and chocolate. Two-thirds of them sold their wares from shops along the wide gridded avenues adjacent to Appleton's own Broad Street countinghouse. These were the entrepreneurs of the new city and the new century. Since their compass extended beyond Boston—beyond the United States as well—they needed money that would remain current over distance. Toward that goal Appleton asked them to contribute one hundred dollars a piece to a war chest that would be used to dispatch runners around the region to redeem country bank paper.

Each member of the committee then set his hand to an open letter addressed to the cashiers of any banks found guilty of playing what Appleton called "the non-payment game." (The appended signatures, graced by ostentatious flourishes no mere clerk would employ, run a full two pages; Appleton affixed his own in a modest sixteenth place.) Since "many Country Banks" had "unwarrantably abused" the "confidence placed in their bills," the subscribers declared themselves "compelled to send the bills home." If a besieged cashier so much as hesitated before redeeming the notes in specie, the merchants would "proceed to the collection by due course of law."[70]

Appleton and his backers wasted no time making good the threat. In addition to seeking redemption at banks across the New England interior, the syndicate worked to undermine the credit of country paper in Boston. They refused such bills when customers offered them in payment, and they urged local bankers to do the same. Since their ranks included five directors of the leading Boston banks, it came as no surprise that by the end of the month both the Massachusetts Bank and the Union Bank had voted "not to receive Bills from Berkshire Bank, from the Farmers' Exchange Bank," and from several others rumored to be in Dexter's clutches. The group also ran on the Exchange Office in late November, filing suit when its treasurer equivocated about the terms of repayment.[71]

These were crucial early victories in Appleton's war on paper. But the stakes were too high to let the outcome rest in the hands of judges and merchants and bank directors. Since the ultimate fate of Dexter's paper empire rested upon public confidence, its adversaries would have to appeal not only to "commercial men" like themselves, but also to "the great body of the community": the shoppers and artisans and traders "who seldom reflect[ed] on the nature or tendency of the bills they circulate." A merchant's honor was "as delicate and fragile as that of a woman," Appleton believed. "It will not bear the slightest stain. The man in trade who has been found to equivocate or falter in his course, becomes a marked man. He is avoided." Dexter had faltered and must now be shamed and shunned. Just days after they began to work behind the scenes with the country cashiers and the Boston bank directors and the Suffolk County courts, the merchants Appleton organized laid out their arguments in the press.[72]

Appleton chose the pseudonym "Smith" (as in Adam?) for many of his efforts to win converts to the cause. Posing as a spectator with "no interest in the subject," Smith was pleased to discover "that the Merchants of this town, are about taking measures to put an end to the present shameful system of evasive speculation practised by many country Banks." In support of their (which is to say, of *his*) efforts, he offered "a few observations on the subject of banking generally" and "the abuses now practiced" in particular. "A perfect system of banking," Smith explained, "resembles the most perfect of all systems, that of animal life." Free "circulation" brought "health and activity to the remotest extremities, whilst the heart is kept active and vigorous, by the regular return of its own fluids." But New England's monetary hydraulics had gone badly awry. A once-healthy creature, the banking system suffered from "an unnatural and poisoned circulation, placed in his extremities" and "immense tumors forming in his very vitals." Only "convulsive throes" could "drive back the overwhelming pollution." Whether out of tact or out of fear of libel, Smith made no mention of Dexter. But canny readers could break the code. For poison in the extremities, read Farmers' Exchange Bank; for "immense tumors," substitute the Exchange building. Appleton's men themselves would provide the "convulsive throes."[73]

Anonymously but unmistakably, Dexter also pled his own case in the papers, playfully turning the rhetoric of Appleton's men against them. He derided "the ultimatum of the Boston Merchants," self-styled heroes who became the villains of Dexter's version. Their "underhand[ed], insidious practices"—traveling "miles a score," overcoming "perils 'by flood and field'" to run on lawful banks—had "rendered it absolutely necessary that Banks should procrastinate in their payments." And on whose authority? Had the leader of this group "been appointed, a *Dictator* to the public by law?" Or perhaps, "like Sir Launcelot, he is a self-appointed redresser of public wrongs?" Instead of jousting with phantoms, he should "sit down, adjust his own accompts, take down a volume of Shakespeare and listen to the advice of Lear's fool": *"Say less than thou Trowest"* and *"Pay more than thou owest."*[74]

By Dexter's logic, country bankers were the hapless victims of Appleton's self-serving crusade. Public-spirited men, they had watered the parched countryside with their circulating medium only to be greeted with contempt. First the "iron fangs of the merciless *embargo*" had paralyzed them. And now Appleton's crew massed like common thugs, adding injury to Jefferson's insults. "Red-hot gibbets are preparing!" Dexter warned. A "phalanx" of enemies gathered; a "mighty host" numbering "more than a hundred, young and old" had "subscribed the mighty sum of *one hundred dollars*" each to the "horrible and bloody" cause. *They* were the speculators, driven by "corrupt" self-interest. *Their* money was fictitious, the invention of "*ephemeral Merchants*" who floated the "absurd and *infamous*" idea of "creating a capital by *running* on a Bank." *They* were the savages, "dispatching *circulars*, heralds, pioneers, and tommyhawkers" across the region. And "all for what?" The high and eminent turned mean and barbarous just to bring a few poor country bankers "up on their marrow-bones." Coming as it did amid widespread economic hardship, the campaign's timing was opportunistic if not vicious. "Is this the time to hurl the gauntlet?" Dexter asked. "Have we not enough already to contend with?" He urged readers not to let "a *few* malicious individuals," men of "weak nerves" if not "sinister motives . . . set the whole community in an uproar." Like "Smith's" essay four days earlier, Dexter's was unsigned. But again the clever reader might guess the author's identity. The opposite of *sinister,* which still carried its original latinate meaning of "left," was *dexter*—"right."[75]

With each exchange of words the argument between Dexter and his pursuers grew hotter, and more personal. Appleton damned Dexter's "witty" ripostes as the work of an "arch magician": a "grand Inchanter, whose touch converts every thing to paper—whose wand calls up a castle more stupendously magnificent, than any described in Eastern romance—who devours . . . a brace of Banks for breakfast, and calls for more." This "Merchant" (as Dexter sometimes signed himself) was in fact a magus, Appleton proclaimed. (Perhaps "P," Appleton's pseudonym this time, was short for Prospero.) Meeting Shakespeare with Shakespeare, P. warned all "who handle such airy stuff" as the enchanter's bills to "take care lest it vanish like the 'baseless fabric of a vision.'"[76]

Appleton mocked Dexter's background. This arch magician was a counterfeit, a man "of little or no property" who would pass as a man of capital. In this respect, of course, the two were doubles. Appleton had traced the very same path. The roots of his own fortune lay no deeper. Nor was its foundation—the arbitrage of the import-export business—much more solid. But rather than taking the honest road from double entry bookkeeping to mercantile riches, Dexter had looked for a shortcut to self-making, some kind of diabolical spell. Writing again as "Smith," Appleton traced the progress of the scheme in his next installment. The nameless speculator had started with the Exchange Office, which he had quickly "seized on . . . as a fit engine" for his designs. From there he conquered outlying banks, one after another. Just "suppose," Appleton hinted, that "one individual owns such a majority of [a bank's] stock, that he controuls every vote," that he can "designate his own directors and officers." Would he not "find men who . . . may be induced to yield up the Bank," to convert it into "a machine devoted to his speculations"? Now imagine that the same individual has acquired "a monopoly of Country Banks": not just one remote outpost but a whole ghostly network of them. What prevented him from foisting "on the public MILLIONS of dollars in Bank Notes," all "dependent for payment on the success of the wild speculations and visionary projects in which [he] may be embarked"? What reader could "avoid shuddering at the idea of bursting such a bubble"?[77]

Coming from the man holding the pin, such deep concern about bubbles bursting sounds rather disingenuous. And indeed, in a series of light verses entitled "New Hobbies" that ran in the *Palladium* adjacent to Smith's essay, somebody—the wit and bravado smack of Dexter himself—made precisely that point:

Some Merchants in [Boston] to shew some new pranks,
Have mounted their Hobby "The breaking up banks"
But in this vain attempt they will surely be hinder'd,
For their Hobby-horse proves to be quite broken winded.
Alas, poor Hobby!

Public confidence first from these Banks they estrange,
To wit, *Berkshire, Vermont* and the *Farmer's Exchange:*
Many hands are employ'd from them specie to draw,
But their vaults are replenished by one "dexter" paw.
                    Change your Hobby.

Hobbyhorses and pranks: the clash between the magus and the merchants was a trifle, the poet suggested, mere child's play. And in this
game pitting brains (or dexterousness) against brawn (the clumsy
hands of the "many"), the author picked Dexter as the sure winner.[78]

The doggerel appeared on December 20, 1808, almost exactly a year
after Andrew Dexter first approached the Farmers' Exchange Bank,
barely a month after Nathan Appleton and his allies penned their ultimatum. The poet's posturing aside, the merchants' syndicate had
already punctured the "public confidence" on which Dexter's scheme
rested. In Boston the currency of Dexter's paper fell precipitously.
Some business owners refused Gloucester and Pittsfield bills outright,
while others discounted the notes by as much as 20 percent. (Even
those who claimed to accept such money "at par," Appleton alleged,
secretly inflated their prices in self-defense.) In Detroit, the bank suddenly "stopt the Payment of their Bills" on December 10, when the
Michigan legislature outlawed the paper of unchartered banks.[79]

Nowhere had the past month been more tumultuous than in sleepy
Gloucester. The literary pretensions of Appleton's newspaper war
with Dexter—its brushes with Shakespeare and Adam Smith—must
have eluded William Colwell. But the cashier didn't need the Boston
papers to tell him the Exchange Bank was under siege. The battalion
of runners descending on the bank told him Appleton's campaign was
on. Dexter hoped the waiting games that had carried the bank
through the fall would suffice, and again counseled the cashier to
slowly count change. But as the number of would-be redeemers grew
and the reserves of specie dwindled, that gambit failed, and the mood
in Gloucester turned from mild concern to full-blown panic. "The
present state of our affairs respecting the Bank is . . . truly alarming,"

John Harris reported on December 5. "We are threatened with pros-
ecutions and almost every thing else bad." Deferring to the Bostonian's
"superior knowledge and understanding in these things for my rule
and guide," Harris urged Dexter to stock the bank's empty vault with
"about eight or ten thousand dollars in specie, and about as much in
Berkshire bills." An infusion of that magnitude was, Harris insisted,
"our only remedy." *Just tell us what to do,* Harris pleaded: Dexter should
"communicate your advice and directions to us as soon and as often as
possible." *And tell us face-to-face:* Dexter's "personal attendance soon,
[and] on many occasions, is absolutely necessary." In language that
echoed at once the Old Testament and the sentimental novel, Harris
warned, "*If these things cannot be done we must unavoidably fall and not
rise again.*"[80]

Terrified of falling, Icarus flew still higher. Dexter made promises,
sending the Farmers' Exchange a little cash—a couple hundred dollars in Boston bills; a bit more from Marietta, Ohio, or Westerly,
Rhode Island (where he had recently commandeered another bank);
a couple thousand in Berkshire notes—with his assurances that more,
much more, would follow. He made excuses: sickness ("I should go
myself, but am prevented by illness") or frenzy (the "innumerable
engagements of business" that "occupied my mind incessantly") or bad
timing (it was "after Bank hours," it was Sunday) prevented him from
coming up with more money. In any case, he insisted, the real blame
lay with the "villainous combination of men" arrayed against him.[81]

But more than false promises or flimsy excuses, Dexter made
demands: incessant, insatiable demands for enough Farmers' Exchange
notes to shore up his crumbling pyramid. Forget the one hundred
thousand dollar cap Rhode Island's 1804 charter had imposed on the
bank's total capital; they had passed that mark long ago. Now Dexter
told the cashier "to employ yourself constantly in signing bills, except
during the time you are naturally in the bank." If Colwell were careful, he might "write in the day time as well as night, provided you shut
yourself up between the bank hours in your private chamber, letting
no one know or *suspect* your business." Colwell, ever dutiful, took the

injunction to heart. Another Gloucester man who rented rooms in "the house where the Bank was kept" heard the cashier "in the Bank at night time," sometimes arriving "as early as two o'clock in the morning, and very often at four o'clock."[82]

No matter how many sleepless nights he spent hunched over his pen, Colwell could not keep up with Dexter's hunger for paper. On December 10, Dexter sent him another two hundred thousand dollars' worth of unsigned notes, sixteen reams of Perkins's paper. In a letter accompanying the shipment, Dexter told Colwell that he must have the cash "immediately or it will be too late," and begged him "to fill up the blank bills . . . without one moment's delay." If the cashier could estimate at "what *hour* you will have ready for me fifty thousand, and at what *hour* afterwards [another] fifty thousand, and so on," Dexter would "have a safe messenger ready" to fetch each installment.[83]

Such desperation worried John Harris enough that he and Elisha Fairbanks headed to Boston mid-month to question Dexter face-to-face. Colwell stayed behind in Gloucester, pen in hand, signing more notes and receiving more pleas. "Thy letter with bills, &c. I have at this moment received," he wrote to Dexter in his plain Quaker idiom. "I shall sign as fast as I can," he promised. "I believe I can finish fifty thousand a week." (Some of these sheets he filled out "with so much precipitation" that the notes went off without dates or numbers.) Meanwhile, he told his boss, "Thou wilt have a full opportunity to discourse with Judge Harris and Fairbanks on the subject" during their sojourn in Boston. Dexter truly must have been an arch magician, because he managed to reassure Harris and Fairbanks of his good intentions. Their confidence if not the bank's credit restored, the pair returned to Gloucester without "the least doubt of [Dexter's] success."[84]

No wonder Colwell had begun to doubt the wisdom of his so-called betters. Stationed at the base of the pyramid, the cashier carried the weight of the entire ungainly structure on his back. "Our situation becomes every day more disagreeable," he told Dexter. "The discontent and irritation among the people is very great," the bank's distress a "common topic of conversation throughout the country." New runners turned up "daily," calling for "innumerable small sums" of specie. The contents of the makeshift vault had dipped below two hundred dollars, a situation Colwell found "inexpressibly troublesome." He begged Dexter, "Help us a little." *Please send money.* "I cannot but think that fifteen or twenty thousand dollars judiciously applied, and paid out in small sums at the Bank" would do much to remedy the situation, the cashier explained. But Colwell was being paid *not* to think, and his deference, deeply ingrained, died hard. Even now he pronounced himself "willing . . . to submit it all to those who have the direction of this business." He would "endeavour . . . to be as contented as possible, and bear my *heavy load without a murmur.*"[85]

Having confessed his fragile state, the cashier can only have seen Dexter's response as callow, pitiless. "[I] very much regret the unhappy situation in which you are placed," his boss averred. (*"You are placed"*: the passive voice a sop to conscience.) But enough sympathy; here is Dexter's real anguish: "I am sorry you have signed no more bills." Colwell should double his manic pace "to sign at least twice as many more during the next week. I wish you would work day and night so as to sign if possible twenty thousand dollars a-day." As if the clerk's pen could defy physics. As if mere human effort could balance an immense mass of bricks upon a cloud of paper.[86]

๛

Christmas Day dawned cold and bright in Boston, the latest moment of urban disorder to cap several days of near rioting in the city. On the twenty-second, Jefferson's opponents had marked *"twelve months degrading EMBARGO"* with bitter parodies. Seamen dragged a boat filled with stones through the streets to dramatize their sinking fortunes, "firing guns, & such things" along the way. In Marblehead a mob hanged Jefferson in effigy, while in Salem they inverted the American flag. Ironically, these protests coincided with Forefathers' Day, the region's annual commemoration of the English landing at Plymouth in 1620. Boston gentlemen celebrated with a feast at the

Exchange Coffee House, while outside that elegant banquet hall, the vaunted heroism of the Pilgrim fathers offered another excuse to turn the world upside down. The scene, William Bentley reported, "resembled the Juvenalia of Nero, when old men were licensed to act like children & crack their jokes on the best things & the best men." And now Christmas, another clamorous celebration—one Congregationalists dismissed as popery if not paganism. The lower sort made merry in the streets, while the Episcopalians—even those who stayed away from services the rest of the year—flocked to churches alive with music and decoration. (This in the heart of iconoclastic New England.) Perez and Sarah Morton, along with their daughter Charlotte and her new husband, Andrew Dexter, likely took their places that morning in the Morton family pew, at the head of the throng gathered in Trinity Church.[87]

But Andrew Dexter could not pause for long. He had paper to chase. Later that day, he wrote to William Colwell, rousting the Exchange Office's clerk, John Fullerton, from his Milk Street boardinghouse to carry the missive to Gloucester, Christmas or no. As usual, Dexter's letter bristled with instructions. Colwell should stop endorsing drafts on Dexter. He should send another fifty thousand dollars in the bank's notes to Boston forthwith, packing the bills "in a trunk or box in such manner as to prevent its being known or suspected what is contained," even by the courier. He should stay at his post. He should *not* come to see Dexter in Boston (as Colwell had proposed), lest his absence prove "very injurious" to the bank. Tucked among these urgent commands, Dexter included a rhetorical gift. As befitted the day, he offered Colwell a vision of peace on his little corner of the earth. Dexter proclaimed himself "morally certain" that the "difficulties" of the Farmers' Exchange Bank "will all be remedied." Praising Colwell's "zealous services," Dexter told him: "Be in good spirits, and I believe every thing will end well."[88]

Empty words, worth less than a Farmers' Exchange Bank note. As Colwell surely sensed, the final battle between bricks and paper loomed, its outcome all but inevitable. The problem was less the surge of barely legitimate banknotes—money that possessed "more of the levity of feathers than . . . the solidity of gold," as one Rhode Island writer put it—than the drag of the building. "Had the money . . . placed within his control, been employed judiciously," Appleton later mused, "it is difficult to say what might have been the result." Dexter's "consummate folly" was not the paper pyramid, but the masonry structure on Congress Street. Liquidity had made him. But then Dexter stopped the flow, sinking his groundless gains into "an enormous building, known by the name of the Boston Exchange." In a floating world the building was a giant brick wall: a vault in which capital was forever "locked up," a property "no human being believes will soon be converted into cash," the end of the line. Only in children's games did paper cover rock. On the ground, as Appleton warned, rock buried paper and everyone who held it.[89]

In the first weeks of the new year, Dexter managed to squeeze more money out of these tumbling stones. Some Boston merchants remained willing to do business with him, though the terms they demanded were justifiably harsh. From Jonathan Hastings, the postmaster who rented space in the Coffee House, Dexter begged a loan of $1,000, promising to repay the debt three days later.[90] On January 18, in a sign of true panic, he mortgaged the Coffee House and the land beneath it to the directors of the Berkshire Bank, to whom he already owed more than $200,000. With the Exchange as collateral, the Pittsfield money men loaned Dexter $24,000 for six months, during which they hoped he would turn his affairs around.[91] Through shameless cajoling, he managed to wheedle some more money out of Gloucester. "Be not alarmed, my good friend," Dexter wrote to Colwell on February 8, "and be assured, that we shall be able to manage in such way, as to prevent eventual difficulty." A laughable promise. Yet the next day, Colwell rewarded his boss's unaccustomed gentleness by forwarding what proved to be the final shipment of Farmers' Exchange notes, bringing the grand total Dexter had received from the bank to $760,265.[92]

By then, not even the most outlandish promises could keep the scheme aloft. Boston shopkeepers, alarmed by the relentless drumbeat of printed warnings and backstreet gossip imposed ever-steeper premiums on goods bought with notes from Dexter's banks. Like frantic players in the last round of a game of financial hot potato, ordinary folks caught holding the tainted monies paid these inflated prices, hoping to dump their notes before the music stopped. A few rapacious brokers smelled profit and hawked a "good chance to get rid of Suspicious Bills." But theirs, too, were false promises; good chances evaporated along with confidence in Dexter's empire. Soon the value of his paper was falling faster than the temperature in what was already shaping up to be an exceptionally snowy winter. By mid-February, the Gloucester notes traded for sixty cents on the dollar, or less. Shortly thereafter, a promoter announced his plan to launch a hot air balloon "embellished with the Portraits of the immortal WASH-INGTON, WARREN, &c.," from Boston Common. He asked for subscribers to defray the "Expense of the said Balloon." Before this fantastical creation ever took flight, Dexter's airy scheme had crashed to earth.[93]

First, Appleton's cartel had acted. Then, the broader community of buyers and sellers who constituted themselves as "the market" had its say. And now, as increasing numbers of people enjoined, the time had come for the state to step in. As far away as the nation's capital the hue and cry went up for banking reform. Unable to resist a play on Dexter's name (a temptation to which other writers would also soon succumb), one New York congressman proclaimed the economy of Massachusetts "UNHINGED through the dexterous influence" of unregulated banks. In Rhode Island, the large numbers of people holding large numbers of Farmers' Exchange Bills, combined with anxiety over the state's longstanding reputation for profligacy, gave calls "for Legislative attention" special urgency. "Surely our Legislature cannot be disposed to grant charters to companies for the purpose of enabling them to swindle with greater ease," one writer in Providence's *American* declared. Only punishing the true perpetrators—outsiders all—would "save the State from the ignominy that could otherwise attach to it." Neither the townspeople of Gloucester nor the merchants of Providence could stand to see "Rhode-Island left to bear alone the turpitude" of Dexter's "transcendent knavery."[94]

On the last Monday in February, as their charter prescribed, the stockholders of the Farmers' Exchange Bank convened to elect officers. Despite Dexter's attempt to pack the board by having Colwell "procure some persons to act as Directors," five men with enough gumption and enough shares and enough community support to elude his control stepped forward to win positions. Immediately, the new directors passed three resolutions. Their first official act compelled Andrew Dexter to return the ledgers and documents and banknotes he had carted off, with the assistance of Fairbanks, Harris, and Colwell, several days earlier. They then declared "a temporary suspension of the business of said Bank." Finally, they petitioned the General Assembly to "examine the affairs" of the institution, promising to turn over their books and papers and "certain steel types or dies" to the investigators.[95]

The next morning, the last day of the shortest month of 1809, the Farmers' Exchange became the first chartered bank in the United States to defy the conventional wisdom that such institutions could not fail. Those who rode down Gloucester's Main Street found the bank's doors closed, "probably never to be opened again for similar business," as one pressman opined. "The sign is taken down and the keys" handed over. Beneath the trapdoor just $86.48 in specie was left, along with the sheets of banknotes that Dexter had not wrestled out of Colwell. Empty, locked, shuttered, dead. All that remained, the observer noted, was for the "funeral of the late Farmers' Exchange Bank" to make its "way to the General Assembly at East-Greenwich." The mourners would not have to wait long. The six men the state commissioned to conduct the autopsy had already started their grim task.[96]

As the investigation began, Andrew Dexter made one last-ditch effort to keep his name out of the spring mud, one last demand on William Colwell's loyalty. On March 1, while the cashier waited to testify in the assembly's chambers in East Greenwich, yet another of

Dexter's clerks appeared, bearing yet another urgent request: Colwell should ignore Rhode Island's subpoena and head at once for Dexter's offices in Boston. Unless he came "immediately," bringing with him "all the papers respecting my business," Dexter wrote, the cashier would "entirely ruin yourself and friends, and *myself* in particular." Dexter begged: "Do come with the person who will hand you this letter. . . . PLEASE." He promised: "[I]f any damage should happen to you in consequence of coming here, I will fully indemnify you." He hectored: "I shall think you wholly unpardonable if you do not come instantly, and never shall forgive you if you don't." And he prevailed. In a final show of the deference that had undone him, Colwell walked out of the proceedings, "in Contempt of the General Assembly," as if Dexter's law trumped the state's.[97]

The cashier's gesture proved as futile as it was dramatic, and Dexter's pledge to protect him as empty as it was grandiose. Tipped off, perhaps, by his friends on the bench, Judge John Harris had escaped Rhode Island. Colwell was not so lucky. The sheriff of Kent County quickly remanded him and Dexter's messenger into custody, most likely before the pair left East Greenwich. Several days later, they released the Boston clerk and transferred Colwell to the Providence county jail, where he could be "safely kept" while the committee did its work. After two weeks in lockup, even Colwell had had enough. When they called him to account on March 15, he spared no details of Dexter's perfidy. His deposition runs to more than six closely printed pages. More witnesses would follow, but none as damaging as the clerk's tale. The postmortem of the Farmers' Exchange Bank had officially begun.[98]

Over the next month, the Rhode Island legislature laid bare the innermost workings of Dexter's shadowy empire. Carried on the winds of gossip, in letters, and in the papers, word of the scheme radiated outward from the chambers of the investigating committee in concentric circles. Ordinary farmers—the folks left holding the bills—packed the Town House in Providence to hear the committee's report to the legislature the last week of March. Six weeks later, the assembly's findings reached Detroit, where shopkeepers "discovered in one of the papers the Dessertion of the President [John Harris] and the Scheme Disclosed." From Rhode Island to Michigan the tale exceeded the wildest expectations of the most jaded hearers, whose faculties of "conjecture, rumour, calculation and . . . curiosity" had already been "wearied in their employment on this far-famed topick." In this case, even those "potent engines, whose usual tendency is to exaggerate and inflame," had "fallen far, very far short . . . of the truth."[99]

*Astonished* is the word that everywhere greeted the news. On the stand, Samuel Dexter proclaimed his *"astonishment"* that his brother's debts to the Exchange Bank topped a half million dollars. The editors of the *Rhode Island American* were likewise stunned. "Such a scene of dishonesty, dissimulation, turpitude and every thing that is iniquitous," they reported, "was never, we believe, before exhibited to an astonished publick." The *Providence Gazette,* too, deemed the "nefarious transactions" of the Gloucester bank "a matter of great astonishment." The publication of the state's proceedings as a dense forty-two-page pamphlet in late April provoked yet more amazement; the "astonished reader" of the *Report* saw "every principle of honour, probity and faith sported with like dice."[100]

*"Sported with like dice"*: with its obscure rules, its high stakes, and its sudden reversals, the money game had long made ordinary people feel like pawns in some cosmic game. By 1809, every American had at least one tale of fiscal turpitude to share by the fireside. And still Andrew Dexter's fall astonished. New Englanders were shocked at the brazenness and complexity of his scheme, by its enormity and its concealment in plain sight. They were shocked, most of all, to see a bank crumble like paper. However unwittingly, Dexter had destroyed one of the era's most comforting fictions: the "prevailing idea," as Appleton called it, "that a Bank cannot be *eventually insolvent,* as they must hold security for all their loans." What security? An act of incorporation, a set of bylaws, a vault full of promises: Dexter revealed them all to be just so many pieces of paper. It was, indeed, an astonishing bit of magic.[101]

But as Dexter knew better than most, paper had powers all its own.

By reprinting the letters they had found in the makeshift vault of the Farmers' Exchange Bank, along with the testimony of William Colwell and others, the Rhode Island legislature laid out the whole terrible scheme in black and white, indelibly. Which is why, no doubt, Dexter's allies were said to have purchased a thousand copies of the *Report* and "consigned them to the flames." But as the Morton family had discovered when they tried to suppress *The Power of Sympathy* two decades before, good stories could not be easily squelched. The *Report* survived, lifting the tattered veil of anonymity from Dexter's name. The pamplet turned the collapse of the Farmers' Exchange into a "Banking Drama" in which Andrew Dexter, his brother Samuel, William Colwell, and John Harris all starred as "the principle characters." The pamphlet made its way across the United States, crushing the man who had made himself out of paper beneath it.[102]

An "immense floating mass of . . . paper TRASH," as one Pittsfield writer styled it—a heap of worthless banknotes, unpaid mortgages, damning pamphlets, and vicious newspaper stories—hounded Andrew Dexter that spring. Worried that his "high station" might allow him to escape "proper vengeance," pressmen heaped scorn upon him. He should lose more than his good name, the Providence papers argued. A truly "ample justice" would cost Dexter not only his reputation and his wealth, "but even that smaller share of character that results from the possession of unclipped ears and an unbranded cheek."[103] The mockery only increased when Dexter proposed to redeem the Exchange Bank bills through a Tontine, a lottery that would allow investors the use of the Coffee House for thirty years, at which point the survivors would divide the accumulated profits.[104] Many found the plan darkly hilarious, a "DEXTEROUS project" worthy of "the most subtle financier in Europe, or in the world," a proposition "more shamefully extravagant and impudently fraudulent, if possible, than any thing which has emanated from the same quarter" before. How could "the privilege to drink coffee in a public or private room," or the right "to bath[e] amidst a throng of 4 or 500 persons" possibly compensate "the unfortunate individuals" stuck with the worthless notes of the Exchange Bank? Dexter ought to keep the bathing room for "his own exclusive use," one writer quipped, since it would take "an ocean of water" to "wash away *the impressions he has struck*." Signing himself "Justice," a Boston writer insisted that "the holders of Farmers' Exchange Bills had much better throw them into the fire."[105]

Unable to summon even a drop of confidence to float him along, Andrew Dexter—high priest of liquidity—liquidated. In March, he sold off the remaining pieces of the Exchange Coffee House lands. He sold the wharf that had carried construction materials to Congress Street. He sold his view, the passageway stretching east from the Exchange's main entrance. He sold his nine hundred shares in the Exchange Office. He sold his home on Round Lane, trading four short months of aspiring domesticity in south Boston for rented quarters in Charlestown. (The toll these reversals exacted on Charlotte Dexter can only be imagined. Several months pregnant with the couple's first child, she had suffered the death of her only brother the very day the Farmers' Exchange Bank failed.)[106]

Gone, everything gone, and the bottom not yet plumbed. In April, the Berkshire Bank called Dexter's enormous mortgages. Since what he owed them dwarfed his remaining assets, the Pittsfield gentlemen asked the Suffolk County sheriff to "take the Body of the said Andrew and him commit into our Goal in Boston . . . until he pay the full sums above mentioned." Choosing jail would mean facing a doubled shame: the sting of being locked in one of the third-floor apartments reserved for "liberty debtors," compounded by the presence in the building of so many of his own workers, those "respectable mechanics" ruined by the failure of the Exchange Bank.[107] And so, in the first days of May, Andrew Dexter chose the route of many once-wealthy bankrupts. He took his wife, his tarnished name, and whatever property he had left and fled, vanishing into the thin air from which his fortune had risen.[108]

starving, and my lady from nakedness." Still Flanagan refused to give up on Dexter. Twice that summer he wrote to him in Halifax, letters to which he "re^d no answers." For his boss's silence, as for everything else the man had done to him, Flanagan made excuses. Mr. D. *would* have written if he could have. But Nova Scotia, as a longtime friend of Dexter's had explained, suffered from "a considerable deficiency of paper."[6]

Dexter may have lacked a scrap to write on, but Boston was drowning in paper that summer, worthless, impossible, "imposing paper," as one editorialist called it. The "crisis is at length arrived," Nathan Appleton proclaimed in a long, self-serving editorial at the end of August. Flanagan would have agreed: *crisis* was not too strong a word for the wave of failures that swept outward from Gloucester. The notes of the defunct Farmers' Exchange Bank wreaked havoc on the accounts of everyone who held them, the more, the worse. Their coffers full of money-turned-wastepaper, each bank in Dexter's web pulled against the others. In November, the Boston Exchange Office closed shop, holding over $152,000 in depreciated bank bills and only $384 in coin, a liability to specie ratio of nearly 400 to 1. Over the next six months, most of the banks in Dexter's network—the Detroit Bank, the Berkshire, the Coos, the Penobscot—went under, failures begetting more failures. Some banks, wrongly swept up in the tide of rumors, managed quickly to right themselves. But faith in paper money remained at a low ebb. "Every day some bank is restored" and another "cried down," William Bentley noted in his diary. "We do not know what money to receive & what to reject."[7] The trust that had buoyed New England's banking system was unmasked as a shared delusion, a "paper mania." The hangover following the banking binge was "paperphobia": an acute loss of confidence not just in banknotes, but in confidence itself.[8]

People wondered aloud why they had ever "confided" in Dexter's bank bills—in *any* bank bills, for that matter. How blithely they had

## FOUR

# *BABEL*

*William Colwell was free:* sprung from jail, out from under the paper weight of the Farmers' Exchange Bank, cured at last of his stubborn, perilous loyalty to Andrew Dexter Jr. A thousand miles from Gloucester, the other clerk-William, William Flanagan, kept faith with the man who had brought him from his North End boardinghouse through the wilderness into the Michigan woods in May 1806. Flanagan had trusted Dexter then, and he kept on trusting him, even when the Boston partners left with the money that October, even after Congress nullified the Detroit Bank's charter the following March. In the summer of 1807, he had backed Dexter's plan to restart the bank as a private venture, and for two years since he had dutifully signed each and every promise the reincarnated Detroit Bank uttered. Flanagan believed in him still, as reports of the Exchange Bank's fate found their way to Detroit. Discount the gossip; ignore the newspapers; only Dexter knew the straight story. On May 15, 1809, William Flanagan and his wife, Sarah, locked up the bank building at the corner of Jefferson Avenue and Randolph Street, asking the mayor, Solomon Sibley, to keep the place "properly aired" until they returned. Then the Flanagans lit out for Boston, in search of whatever solace Andrew Dexter's explanation might offer them.[1]

Making the long journey east by way of Albany, the Flanagans reached their former home a month later. There on Congress Street,

steps from the Exchange Office where William had worked, they discovered what Flanagan (and everyone else in town) called an "immense
building": the Exchange Coffee House. No trace remained of the warren of tenements that had covered the block when the Flanagans went
west. In the intervening years, Dexter had bought up the neighborhood, and leveled the lots, and raised this astonishing tower, and
ruined everyone involved, from the investors at the top of the pyramid
right on down to the cellar diggers at the bottom. A day or two before
the Flanagans arrived in Boston, the Suffolk County sheriff held an
aptly named Coroner's Sale, auctioning off the building and the
ground beneath it in a vain attempt to satisfy Dexter's creditors.[2]

Bigger losers owned the building now, but that was fine. William
Flanagan wasn't after money so much as reliable intelligence, a commodity in nearly as short supply. As June wore into July, he set himself
up as a one-man fact-finding commission, charged "to look into the
affairs of the Detroit Bank" and report back to Michigan. His assignment must have taken him to the Changery, where he could inquire
of the gentlemen he had once served so faithfully. He and Sarah would
also have picked their way along the narrow streets of the sixth ward,
asking the carpenters and masons and boardinghouse keepers
who had been their neighbors about the fate of the man they called
"Mr. D."

They soon learned that Dexter was gone, "fled to Halifax for his
own security." Run out of town by more angry creditors than a lifetime's hard labor could satisfy, Dexter and his wife had taken
sanctuary with Charlotte's kin, Loyalists who had removed to Canada
during the Revolution. (For his fealty then, the Crown had rewarded
Sarah Morton's cousin with an appointment as lieutenant governor of
Nova Scotia, a post that allowed him to extend considerable largesse
to the Dexters.) Cast away in the tiny town of Windsor, Andrew and
Charlotte—"that amiable and afflicted lady," the papers called her—
awaited their first child, due in September. Hundreds of miles from
New England, a day's hard ride from Halifax (no stage line connected
the two till 1816), Dexter had slipped beyond the pale.[3]

So the ending—Dexter's ending—was clear enough. But the middle of the tale, like Dexter's accounts, was a tangle of "utmost
confusion." Despite his many contacts in town, William Flanagan
found it "impossible . . . to gain any satisfactory information." From
what he could piece together, Mr. D. had circulated "a large quantity
of paper money" from the Detroit, Berkshire, and Farmers' Exchange
banks in order to build the Coffee House. Using a lottery the complexity of which mirrored the building's own, Dexter planned to
redeem the baseless bills before they depreciated. "We may suppose
therefore, that he made his own calculations before he went to work,"
Flanagan explained. "But these calculations no dought were errone-
ous, and his whole business has been conducted without system."
Dexter finished the building. But the building had finished him first.
The bills were worthless; the lottery, hopeless. Nor did Flanagan see
another way to liquidate the brick giant, "because the property is not
worth, and will not fetch, one half its cost." "I am much afraid," he
told Sibley, "that it can never be set right."[4]

Everywhere he looked, Flanagan could see the fallout from Mr. D.'s
failure, a potent mix of fury and desperation. Merchants and masons,
schoolmistresses and serving women woke from Dexter's dream to
discover that "a cart load" of banknotes was "not worth a pinch of
snuff." As in the 1770s, when the despised *continental* money" fell
toward zero, the collapse weighed hardest upon "our labouring poor."
Workingmen who had risked their lives laying bricks a hundred feet
above the ground, carefully husbanding the banknotes they were tendered for their labors, found themselves unable to make rent or buy
bread. The municipal jail filled with once-respectable men, innocent
of wrongdoing but unable to pay off their debts.[5]

As the summer sweated on, Flanagan found himself among Dex-
ter's destitute. "It is a matter of doubt, how long I shall remain in
Boston," he told Sibley in August. "For from the time of my leaving
Detroit, to the present, I have been completely out of employment; and
I see no immediate prospect of meeting with any: but I am now
reduced to the necessity, of using all my exertions, to keep myself from

followed the "easy, consoling train of thought" running from goods to gold to the "paper which has assumed the rank of its *representative*." Not thinking twice, the worker took his pay in notes, thereby transforming them into a fair substitute for his toil and time. Without hesitation, the "industrious woman puts a bill in her pocket-book, and thinks on Saturday evening she can furnish her family with necessaries." Such tiny intuitive leaps, multiplied everyplace, every day, were the bedrock upon which the nation's entire monetary system rested (and rests): trust. Dexter had exposed the chinks in a foundation made of something thinner and more fragile than paper. Suddenly, as if roused from a "delirium," those "good easy men" who made up "the credulous part of the community" awoke to question the quaint "habit of receiving and passing *as money,* fine paper, with curious engravings and a *promise* thereon."9

*"What can be done?"* This became the "universal cry" throughout New England. Big thinkers proposed big changes to the political economy that had provided Dexter's cover. Federalists invoked the market to protect the creditor classes. The holders of country notes—"laborers and work-people of various kinds"—deserved pity but not recompense, they argued. Law could not resurrect dead paper. Republicans demanded legislative action to assist debtors. The state must make good on bad money, they insisted, and act to prevent the like catastrophe from happening again.10 Some called for the dismantling of the nation's banking system. Philadelphia pamphleteer Benjamin Davies argued that Dexter's fall embodied a larger truth: that "the issuing of Bank Notes is actually a public robbery," and banking itself "the highest species of gambling that was ever known." Such animus, though extreme, ultimately carried the day. Over the next two years, the antibanking tempest in New England would add fury to the storm over the First Bank of the United States, whose charter Congress allowed to expire in March 1811.11

While intellectuals debated the morality of banking, satirists proposed absurd new currencies to replace the discredited ones. In a letter to the *Palladium,* the notorious con man Stephen Burroughs—that

"Rogue for Life," the papers branded him—twitted Bostonians about founding a *"Pancake Exchange,"* and warned that *"buck-wheat pan-cakes* had been exactly counterfeited in *New Jersey."* (With his letter, Burroughs enclosed a caricature of a banknote bearing "a figure of an Ourang Outang, from whose mouth issues a label with the words *'Death or Botany Bay, ha, ha, ha!!'* ": the counterfeit of a counterfeit.) Under the headline GRAND CHANCE FOR SPECULATION!—OR, ANOTHER NEW BANK!!, another writer extolled the virtues of a *"Potatoe Bank,"* its capital to consist of a million and a half bushels of "good merchant-able potatoes," one of the few items that had so far "escaped the notice of the monopolist and speculator."[12]

The authors of such jokes took aim at once-trusting readers. But few could afford to laugh at their "fatal credulity." Poorer folks stuck with bags of Dexter's rags were too busy suffering the consequences of having invested their confidence in the "miserable stuff . . . ten-dered to them as money." Their question was not just what to do, but whom to punish. Calls for vengeance filled the papers, and doubtless the alleys, wharves, and grogshops as well.[13]

Blame the brokers, the runners, the exchange men; names too dig-nified for the "money-changers" who feasted like vultures "on the embarrassments of the circulating medium." Suddenly, it seemed, the town was awash in these bottom-feeders. "There are not so many money negotiators in the city of London in proportion to its popula-tion, as there are in Boston," one critic proclaimed. In August, currency brokers Samuel Gilbert and Thomas Dean got warning that a "for-midable phalanx" of angry note holders planned to "rob them of their hard earnings" (real money or more worthless rags?) and then run them out of Boston. One of the would-be mob was heard boasting that ten days hence, "the name of *Broker* shall not be heard in this town." But the plot was foiled, and the hope that "to kill the brokers would cure the evils arising from Bank Bills" shown to be misguided, or at least shortsighted. Others, too refined for the law of the streets, called for a return to the retributive justice of "our rigid fore fathers." Bring back the Puritans, men made of sterner stuff than their "charitable descendants." The swindlers deserved the pillory, not a comfortable prison cell.[14]

Blame the courts, the legislature, the governor. They had touched off the crisis by granting charters to unworthy applicants, whom they now failed to punish. "Have we no laws?" asked one editorialist. "Is there no such thing as *justice* in New-England?" Instead of tarring the brokers, he suggested, the aggrieved should mob the State House to demand "effectual laws" against bank fraud. Better still, throw the bastards out in the next election.[15]

Blame Dexter, the disaster's prime mover. Simon Larned, president of the imploding Berkshire Bank, knew that his own troubles stemmed from "placing too high confidence in A.D." He was not alone. As *Dexter* became a six-letter word, Dexter's onetime partners struggled to distance themselves from him. The Berkshire Bank declared itself Dexter's victim rather than his ally. The Exchange Office likewise embarked on a campaign to quash "unfounded conjectures and reports, that *Andrew Dexter,* jun. is still a large stockholder" in the enterprise. The "said *Dexter* does not own a share in the funds of said office," the trustees had insisted in May.[16] But by then there *were* no funds, not in the Exchange Office, or the Berkshire Bank, or anyplace else connected with Dexter. Scores of creditors—the merchants who had foolishly loaned Dexter money, the hatters and jewelers who outfitted him, the housewrights and bricklayers whose hard work built the Exchange, the lumber dealers who supplied them, the carvers and gilders who gave the building its luster, the upholsterers and chair makers and crockery sellers whose wares filled its lavish rooms—lined up to claim their due, only to find that neither the law of the streets nor that of the courts could wring blood from Exchange Coffee House stones. The border separating the United States from British Canada had placed Dexter beyond the reach of American courts in any case.[17]

In real terms, Dexter's flight from justice denied his creditors little enough. (He had few assets worth seizing.) Yet his exile offered a gift to American politicians on both sides of the nation's widening political divide. Democratic pressmen deemed it fitting that the Canadian province that had so eagerly welcomed Tories now gave asylum to infamous *"federal defaulters,"* and called Dexter's escape further proof of the secret "English influence" in Federalist politics. Federalist papers reminded their readers that "Andrew Dexter, the great *Banker,* is son-in-law of the great Democratic oracle Perez Morton, Esq.," from whom he had doubtless "learned his principles."[18]

Hot words offered cold comfort, but it was better than none at all. If they could not exact punishment, Dexter's dupes would make themselves heard. Shout him down, string him up, on the page if not in the streets. Brand him a failed climber who had ascended from "mediocrity" to "great ostensible wealth and splendor," only to fall faster than he had risen to lower than where he had started. In this version, his spectacular demise undercut the new national myth of the self-made man. Or label him, by contrast, a successful swindler, one who got away filthy rich and Scot-free. Some pictured Dexter cackling all the way to the bank. He was the smirking villain, the *"projector behind the curtain"* who "smiles with a *horrid grin,* to think how *dexterously* he has managed the business." (They hadn't seen Windsor.) One writer suggested that even the clerks who had abetted Dexter's "system of ROBBERY AND PLUNDER" were now "rioting in luxury."[19]

Hungry and jobless, William Flanagan must have been surprised to read of his ill-gotten fortune. Yet no matter how much he rued his situation, he could not bring himself to condemn Andrew Dexter. As Flanagan saw it, Dexter wasn't much better off than his victims. "You may think perhaps that he has taken a large sum—away with him," Flanagan told Sibley. And "such a thought is certainly very natural." But it was wrong. "I am informed by his best friends, indeed circumstances convince me, that he took with him a sum less than one thousand [dollars], and that he is without the means of bettering his condition from any former speculation, or from any speculation already made."

Despite all that had happened, Flanagan held fast to something stronger than trust: his charity. "I pity the man," he wrote, "because I think he intended well. That is to say, he never calculated that his speculations—would turn to the injury [of] any persons." No, Dexter simply hadn't calculated at all. "I am fully convinced that persons of more prudence than Mr. Dexter, never would have entered into such speculations." Not villainous, in Flanagan's eyes, Dexter was guilty only of a fatal combination of hubris and recklessness.[20]

That intoxicating blend was nowhere more visible than in the Exchange Coffee House itself. Too-solid residue of a broken bubble, the largely unoccupied building turned Dexter's failure into a monument that "almost intercepts the rays of the sun from the immensity of its elevation." "The astonished multitude gape at the edifice," one observer noted in May. As it stirred to life during the second half of 1809, the Coffee House took its place as Boston's tallest building and its largest metaphor. Right there on Congress Street rose a "NEW TOWER OF BABEL," a vertical colossus rising "out of a *nominal paper emission,* which . . . never had any foundation to support it." As they craned their necks to see the top of the Exchange, Bostonians didn't know whether this "modern Babel" would elevate their city or wind up, once again, "crush[ing] many of them beneath its ruins."[21]

⌒

How apt that the word *babel* has tangled roots. Scholars of ancient languages find in the term traces of the Akkadian *bab-ilu* ("gate of the god") and the Hebrew *babal* ("he has confounded"): the yearning for transcendence mingled with the fear of chaos. Peoples from many nations and religious traditions—Greeks and Aztecs, Confucians and Muslims—tell some version of the Babel story, a tale of ambition realized in bricks and punished by collapse. The version contained in Hebrew scripture, sketched in a few paragraphs of Genesis and amplified by Talmudic commentators and early Christian writers in the centuries thereafter, goes like this.[22]

On the plain of Shinar, part of that Fertile Crescent between the Tigris and Euphrates rivers, Nimrod (great-grandson of Noah, heir to memories of the flood) planted in his followers an age-old dream of earthly greatness. "Let us make us a name," they said, and let us write that name upon the land. Let us leave behind some testimony to our brief existence, "lest we be scattered abroad upon the face of the whole earth." Let us confront the next deluge—expect it, endure it, outclimb it. Let us breach God's dominion before he again destroys ours. *Let us rise above.* Armed with mud, straw, an ample supply of ingenuity, and a common language to give it voice, they declared: "Let us build us a city and a tower, whose top may reach unto heaven." They built fast and heedlessly and very, very high. When "the Lord came down to see the city and the tower, which the children of men builded," their achievement appalled him. Sensing that "now nothing will

The Tower of Babel, *from Athanasius Kircher, Turris Babel, 1679.*

be restrained from them, which they have imagined to do," God confounded their language and scattered their villages that humans might not thus conspire again. The tower left behind, he called Babel.[23]

The unfinished tower made a favored subject for medieval and Renaissance painters, who imagined buildings that spanned impossible heights. Scaled to the human figures on the scene, the version depicted in Athanasius Kircher's 1679 *Turris Babel* stands as tall as the Empire State Building. Tiers pile upon tiers, a surreal wedding cake. Levels emerge from half-built levels only to spiral back on themselves. The round tower includes doorways beyond number, yet possesses neither front nor back, entrance nor exit. For all its loftiness Babel remains unintelligible, literally impenetrable, a monument to hubris and its consequences. The story was ancient, yet its moral went unheeded, John Milton wrote in *Paradise Lost*. People "still with vain design / New Babels, had they wherewithal, would build."[24]

Beginning in the late sixteenth century, Europeans found in North America a fresh laboratory for thinking about Babel. The enormous variety of native languages convinced some colonial writers that they had discovered "the immediate descendants of Noah," peoples whose "strange diversity of incongruous tongues" gave the New World a biblical destiny.[25] The Revolution Americanized the story. Writers for and against the patriot cause accused one another of raising Babel anew. A few embraced the comparison. The work of "forming a perpetual union" from such diverse peoples resembled "the bold attempt to build the tower of Babel," declared one Fourth of July orator. More often, the legend of Babel stood for the danger of rising too far and too fast. One day, Thomas Paine mused in 1796, "the empire of America shall fall." He worried that scholars a thousand years hence would compare the lost nation to "a babel of invisible height." Beware unchecked pursuits of happiness: fitting lesson for a country aspired into being.[26]

❧

Leave the plains of Shinar for Boston Harbor, where the summer of 1809 is nearly over. Since March, when Jefferson lifted the despised Embargo Act in favor of more limited restrictions on international commerce, the port has struggled to wake from its long-forced slumber. As August's infernal heat dissipates, the frenzy of the country banking crisis also eases a bit. Slowly, haltingly, ordinary folks begin to recover their confidence in confidence.

Imagine yourself a young man on the make, son of a New England farmer from an enlightened village—the sort that boasts a bank, a social library, a historical society, an academy. Someplace like Woodstock, Vermont. Unlike Pittsfield or Gloucester, Woodstock has no direct ties to the now-infamous Andrew Dexter. But as aftershocks of his collapse ripple across the New England countryside, your town experiences its own banking troubles, contractions in the supply of money that make a farmer's rocky road harder still. You dream of trading the plow and the field for the pen and the ledger. You picture a paper life, a city life: Boston.[27]

After more than two days' travel by stage, you arrive on a sunny September morning, one of those crystalline days that finds the city at its best. The busy harbor, the vast Atlantic, the crisp sails of ships laden with the treasures of distant shores: all fairly glitter. The horizon beckons; Barbados, Java, and far-off Cathay lie within Boston's orbit.

Turn your back on the ocean and its riches to look west, toward the heart of the town. You notice the steeples of Boston's many churches stretching heavenward, their outlines sharp against the azure sky. Set in counterpoint with those spiky prominences two domes hover. "Two mighty emblems" of Boston's "wondrous *taste,*" a poet calls them. The pair embodies the town's Puritan virtues: the one gently mounded like "an *Indian Pudding*"; the other, with its peaked finial, looking for all the world like the pudding's "*Cover.*"[28] Though you've not seen it before, the yellow-painted cap of the new State House seems familiar. Commanding the town from the crest of Beacon Hill, the State House dome has become an icon, the signature of Boston, appearing in prints, in magazines, even on dishes. The second dome, rising from the flats

North-East View of the Exchange Coffee House,
*by Thomas Wightman, 1809.*

*Aerial view, east elevation of the Exchange Coffee House.*

much closer to the harbor, forms a plane equal to the base of the State House, so tall is the building it crowns.

This is the Exchange Coffee House. You can make out its upper stories from the quay side, just as a merchant peering through the telescope atop the building can watch his ships come into the harbor. The tower—there is nothing else to call a seven-story structure in a three-story town—stands nearly twice as high as the State House. Its dome, sheathed in polished tin, gleams in the September sun. Not on Beacon Hill, but a beacon nonetheless. A "proud Dome," as an anonymous poet noted in Philadelphia's *Port Folio* magazine last spring.[29]

Walk toward the Coffee House, past the warehouses lining the aptly named Long Wharf, continuing three more blocks along the broad straight spine of State Street, turning left onto Congress. The dome's shimmer draws you, but it is not only that. The building's reputation precedes it. Many come to town expressly to see it. "For the first time saw the Exchange": Salem minister William Bentley preserved the moment in his diary. By last March, so many novelty seekers had passed through its portals that the building's "master" announced with "regrets that he cannot, in future admit any person, not resident in the building, up stairs, without they previously apply at the bar." Twice more the proprietors repeat the warnings. "In future no strangers can be allowed to visit the interior of the House, unless attended by a waiter," they announce. A few months later, another reminder: "Orders have been recently given by the Directors, forbidding idle persons from entering the galleries or stair cases, and ranging over the Exchange building as heretofore." The idle strangers keep coming, undeterred by threats to bar the door.[30]

The Coffee House has been open (as open as the managers allow, anyway) for several months now. The plasterers and paperhangers, glaziers and gilders wrapped up their work last winter, officially completing the building. Finished does not mean full, however. A few long-term tenants have followed in the laborers' wake, but less than one-third of the building's offices are occupied. In April, the manager of the hotel department began renting rooms to travelers, though that practice has since been suspended. All told, the building attracts more tales than customers. Seven stories high, displaying the costliest materials in gross abundance: nothing that big sneaks into a city so compact without drawing attention. Neighbors began to vent their "prejudices against the structure" soon after workers broke ground on the project. It "was not built in the right spot," an onlooker complained. It "did not make so handsome an appearance from State-street as it ought," another argued. What's more, the merchants didn't *want* an indoor Exchange. They "would not frequent it," some said, "because they were accustomed to the street."[31]

Idle chatter compared to what followed. As the speculative scaffolding that propped up the hulking structure crumbled, the Exchange's celebrity turned to infamy. Damning stories about the building radiated outward from Congress Street, much as the spurious banknotes that financed the structure had done. At times, the building and the bank bills seemed to become one: both seen as the sort of "extraordinary novelty" destined "to excite wonder and gratify curiosity," both seemingly doomed. Imagine: a building novel enough—*alive* enough— to have enemies, far-flung, organized, mortal enemies. They scorned its cost, its height, its pretensions. They blackened the name of its projector. He was a fake, a villain, a wizard. And the Exchange was his castle, something out of the Arabian nights, conjured rather than built, a chimera. That age-old dream turned nightmare: here, once again, rose a monument to the enormity of human longing, "a Babel of *Brick* and *White Marble*."[32]

If height is the thing, this *could* pass for Babel. It is easily the tallest building you've ever seen. Only steeples and ships' masts might rival it. Immense, vast, lofty, even monstrous: writers have worn all of these adjectives thin trying to convey a sense of the place, yet none of their scribblings quite captures the tower's gargantuan hubris.[33]

Dexter's ambition has proven as costly as Nimrod's, it seems. Few descriptions fail to mention the price of building the Exchange, somewhere north of a half million dollars. (Your family still reckons in goods more often than in cash; you can't begin to compass this sum.

You could put the entire town of Woodstock on the auction block and not fetch anywhere near that much.) As they had in ancient Babylon, the workers wound up bearing much of this enormous cost. The papers report that scores, hundreds, even thousands of industrious men have been wiped out by the project. The tower is not just "extensive," as many say, but *over*extended. "[T]oo high and disproportioned," one writer calls it, using a phrase that could refer as easily to the scheme as to the building. Both stretched beyond limits, beyond reason, unto deformity. The Exchange fell even as it rose. It is falling still, at once palace and ruin.[34]

Like the Babel you know from Sunday sermons, the Exchange exudes confusion as well as ambition. You have never seen anything that looks quite like it. Or, rather, it looks like *many* things, some of them familiar to you from books. But never jumbled together as they are here. Like a blind man envisioning an elephant, you take in its mismatched parts: the dome of a London cathedral astride a Roman temple's frieze and pediment. The gracefully arched window of a Venetian palazzo above the stolid entryway of a bank. The eastern facade a catalog of classical embellishments, the north a curtain of masonry devoid of ornament. Writers can't seem to agree about some of the most basic contours of the place—about its size, for instance. One gives it four floors; another hedges his bets with "five or six stories"; a third, who damns the "huge ill constructed edifice," (correctly) counts "six stories in height and a basement" above grade and a cellar below. Wanting a more precise reckoning, you cross the road to get a better view. But Congress Street is only thirty feet wide, hardly the ideal vantage point for surveying a structure more than three times that high. With your back pressed against the building opposite the Exchange, you see only the expanse of gray granite and white marble that forms the tower's base.[35]

This is not the vista Andrew Dexter pictured. As one of the Exchange's few boosters explains, "[T]he ideas of the founder were grand and extensive." He believed the city fathers would "cut a handsome street" leading east from Congress. A corridor of mercantile

*Aerial view, north and east elevations of the
Exchange Coffee House.*

prosperity with the Coffee House at one end and the shops of Broad
Street at the other, the new street would "display this elegant front to
greatest advantage." But like many of Dexter's plans, this one had not
come to pass. Nor had he left you an unobstructed view of the building's north elevation. The alley connecting Congress Street to
Devonshire is so narrow that carriages can't travel it. Here Dexter
wanted to carve out "a spacious avenue" fifty feet wide, leading all the
way to State Street. In place of this clutch of tenements, he imagined
a pedestrian mall, its neat rows of shops and offices lining a covered
walkway that culminated in the Coffee House. Glimpsed from
beneath this colonnade, with an army of pillars drawing the eye forward, the Exchange might have found the "air of grandeur and
elegance" it was missing. But the avenue and the arcade became two
more links in a long chain of might-have-beens. Left behind was an

*North-East view of the Exchange Coffee House, street level.*

orphaned tower, completely "embosomed in other buildings," as one of its detractors noted. No prospect in sight. [36]

Unable to see the building whole, you find it difficult to figure out how to get inside. The architect, a country man like yourself, has left you more than a dozen entrances to choose from, none of them clearly the front. On the Congress Street side you find three doors. Two of them ferry tradesmen into the bowels of the building. Even the central entry on this side is relatively unadorned. A handful of steps leads from the street into an arched doorway, which feeds you into a warren of offices. Signs on the doors tell you that two brokers, an attorney, and a copyist work within. Any of them might have a place for an ambitious young apprentice. Still, not what you rode from Woodstock to see. Back through the archway, down the steps, and around to the right you walk, looking for a better way in.[37]

The south side of the Exchange, at almost 125 feet the building's

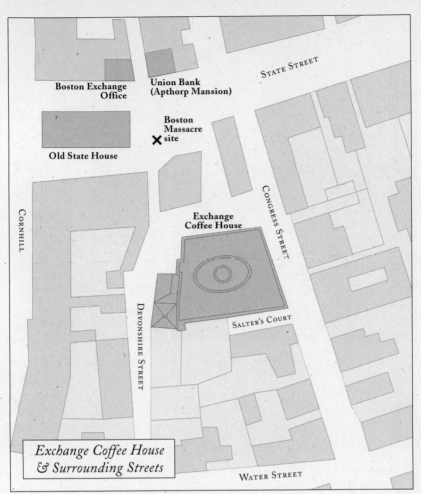

Boston Exchange Office

Union Bank (Apthorp Mansion)

STATE STREET

Boston Massacre ✗ site

Old State House

CORNHILL

CONGRESS STREET

Exchange Coffee House

DEVONSHIRE STREET

SALTER'S COURT

*Exchange Coffee House*
*& Surrounding Streets*

WATER STREET

longest wall, proves less inviting: a homely expanse of bricks broken by eleven bays of windows. Only an alleyway separates the tower from the Friends' meetinghouse and the old burying ground behind it. You count five doors on this side, two of them leading to offices (a clerk's, a hairdresser's) and three into the building itself. The most promising of these opens beneath a small portico. Sheltered from the elements and set back from the street, this entrance is retired, but not refined. The alley is busy with carters who bring wood and coal to the

*South elevation of the Exchange Coffee House, street level.*

Exchange's storehouses. Draymen ferry casks of wine, cider, beer, and stout down to cool storage. Washerwomen and cooks file past the colonnade as they head to the washroom and bake house on the cellar level, and the main kitchen, with its patented twelve-burner Rumford stove, one flight up. If this entrance isn't terribly private, it isn't public either. Keep going.[38]

As you continue along Salter's Court looking for a passage through to Devonshire Street, you walk past the building's wood house and its coal hole, around its well and cisterns. See (and smell) the Coffee House's enormous privy, a marvel in its own right. Four stories high, with windows on every floor, this outhouse is larger than many buildings in the neighborhood—than most in your hometown. Finding no way out of this back alley, you retrace your steps to Congress Street and walk all the way around the building to Devonshire. No front door there either. On its west side the Exchange is attached to a neat brick building four stories high. Here you see more trade entrances and a handful of shop doors, but nothing that conducts traffic directly into the Exchange.

Which leaves only the building's northern elevation. Its appearance is rather plain, a "naked front, without anything but its own surface," one visitor called it. Even so, this side of the Exchange makes a strong claim to being its public face. Men of commerce coming from State Street navigate a maze of shops and dwellings to reach the Coffee House's north door, up thirteen broad steps, beneath a covered porch supported by carved wooden columns.[39]

Smaller columns guide you across the threshold and into a grand foyer. Immediately to your right is Boston's main post office. No fear of being branded a "stranger" here, one of the first places to which any visitor would report. As stagecoaches arrive from distant towns, the room is packed with chattering men "waiting for the opening of the mails." Newspapers make up the bulk of postal business, and men on the make live for the information they bring.[40] The spacious apartment adjoining the post office is designated as the Exchange's Reading Room. Stocked with desks, tables, and chairs, the Reading Room offers the news-hungry gentleman a place to peruse the papers. In case his reading should spur him to writing, the managers keep a supply of paper, ink, and pens on hand as well. This is their intent, anyway. But with no money to support the endeavor, the Reading Room isn't up and running yet. For now, this corner of the Exchange remains more ambition than reality—another slice of Babel.[41]

Leaving the Reading Room you step into a large interior courtyard: the 'Change Floor that gives the building part of its name and much of its reason for being. Oblong like the dome that surmounts it, the sixty-by-forty-foot space looks vast, a room larger than many houses. Pillars frame the area, twenty on each floor, arranged so as to turn the rectangular space into an octagon. You notice that the capitals topping these columns grow more ornate story by story. The first two levels feature what the building's architect called "the grave solidity of the Doric," their strong lines and simple medallions evoking a manly steadfastness. As the atrium ascends toward the dome the carving becomes lighter, more feminine, a riot of acanthus leaves and flowers marking "the elegant delicacy of the Corinthian." Around the 'Change Floor, arches span the pillars, a gesture that reminds you of the blind arches set into the bricks on the Exchange's eastern elevation, and evokes in better-traveled patrons the arcades surrounding London's Royal Exchange. On the succeeding stories a railing keeps the overeager from tumbling onto the 'Change Floor as they regard the grand theater of commerce below. But you're looking up. And on a clear fall morning, with light pouring through the dome's lantern, the effect is dazzling: a tour through centuries of Greek and Roman history, a gaudy display of the carver's art.[42]

But the cavernous space is nearly empty. No desks, no stalls, no

*Looking up from the 'Change Floor.*

notices; few merchants and fewer customers. The covered plaza is indeed "a hollow square," as one observer has called it. Every day from noon to two, Dexter's 'Change Floor battles the town's ancient outdoor trading market. The building is losing. Boston's men of commerce continue "to parade themselves in dirty weather under the projections of buildings," even to "stand merely under the canopy of Heaven, exposed to any storms which may assail them." You don't know whether their choice reflects the pull of inertia or something more deliberate—a boycott of sorts. Either way, the traders hold fast to their habits. Backers of the Coffee House try their best to lure the merchants indoors. They praise the building as the equal of any such place in Europe, and far better than anything in New York. When their appeals to civic pride fail, the boosters try shame: Boston's outdoor 'Change is a "disgrace," they insist, and the Exchange Floor far "more honorable." All to no avail. As one editorialist points out, "until this institution is organized, and its contemplated arrangements completed, I am afraid the streets and insurance offices will still be occupied, notwithstanding the call to leave them." No meetings, no auctions, no sales, no *exchanges* are scheduled to take place on the 'Change Floor today, nor indeed any day this month.[43]

Your footsteps echo across the atrium. As you stroll past the servants' hall situated on the western edge of the 'Change Floor, notice the chambermaids who clean the hotel rooms, and the young men and boys who "attend on Table," all waiting to wait. Over the door more than fifty bells hang silent, ready to ring out the insistent demands of future patrons.

Continue walking, pausing to survey the bar tucked into the southwest corner of this principal story. How different from the servants' hall—a cozy, clubby, well-lit space where gentlemen can drain a glass or two in front of a roaring fire. But though the liquor closet is well stocked, the room is empty, and no hours of operation are posted.[44]

Next to the bar you discover the space that puts the *coffee* in the Exchange Coffee House. Along with the 'Change Floor, this Coffee

Room, which takes up much of the south wing of this story, is the building's professed reason for being. Measuring over fifty feet long and half that across, it's the largest room on the building's principal story, second only to the atrium itself. Late-morning sun streams through five large south-facing windows, while across the room an equal number of glass doors open onto the 'Change Floor. The flood of light from both directions sets off the room's vivid colors. The walls are painted a pale creamy purple. The furniture—the tables and chairs, the paneling on the bar, and the fourteen "boxes" that mark out private nooks for sitting and talking—is fashioned from imported mahogany buffed to a brilliant sheen. Drapes of crimson velvet adorn the bar and enclose each booth to "screen visitors from observation." (William Lemon, the upholsterer who sewed these curtains months ago, is still awaiting $210 in payment for his work.) A bell rope hangs beside each station, in case the gentlemen behind the curtains want refreshments. A large clock presides over the entire scene, reminding the coffee klatch that time is money. The overall effect is sumptuous, even regal. "Very few European Coffee Rooms are equal to this," another visitor notes. The aesthetic borrowed from England, the mahogany imported from the Amazon, the tables decked with silver from the Andes and porcelain from Canton, the cups awaiting a fill of coffee from the Caribbean or northern Africa or the East Indies: inside the Exchange's Coffee Room you stand astride the crossroads of empire.[45]

Such cosmopolitan ambiance seems well suited to coffee, a brew that conjures powerful, almost magical images. You've never so much as tasted the stuff. Though the quantity of raw beans coming into the United States has grown fiftyfold since the Revolution, coffee remains a luxury good, the province of genteel city folks. The embargo cut deeply into this relatively modest traffic in the crop. But if coffee is scarce, coffee *culture* is everywhere. Spreading north and west along the routes of the Levantine trade, the culture of coffee swept London in the mid-seventeenth century and found its way to British North

America within a generation. By the 1730s, places calling themselves coffeehouses had become the nerve centers of port towns from Boston to Charleston. And now, in the first decade of the new century, such establishments grace enlightened villages across New England. Like libraries and newspapers—indeed, like the growing number of *banks* popping up in towns like Woodstock—coffee houses help local elites imagine themselves as citizens of a world beyond the farm.[46]

You find it hard to see what distinguishes such places from taverns. Not the bill of fare; even the fanciest coffeehouse serves far more liquor than coffee. The Exchange's larder holds casks of Madeira and cider, kegs of beer and bitters, pipes of brandy, dozens of bottled wines, and only part of a bushel of coffee. Even so, coffeehouses, much more than taverns, claim an association with Enlightenment virtues: rationalism, pluralism, and liberality. Like their London counterparts, colonial coffeehouses had witnessed an increasingly broad and unregulated commerce in the fruits of empire, including, most centrally, information. Coffeehouses ran on and for stories, whether from around the corner or around the globe. So complete was coffee's identification with news that English critics said the drink tasted of print. Coffee was a "Syrrop of Soot, or Essence of old Shooes, / Dasht with Diurnals, and the Book of News." The first newspaper in North America, Boston's short-lived *Publick Occurrences,* was printed in the colonies' first café, the grandly titled London Coffee-House, which once stood just steps from Dexter's Exchange.[47]

Bursting with goods and chatter, coffeehouses both in Europe and the colonies earned a reputation as fiercely independent meeting spots— places outside the control of state and church, where all manner of men (if only men) might criticize their rulers. England's Charles II had tacitly endorsed this impression in 1675, when he closed the nation's coffeehouses, places where "tradesmen and others . . . mis-spend their time," resulting in the "spreading of false reports to the defamation of the Government and the disturbance of the peace of the realm."[48]

In the colonies, the imagined link between coffee and liberty grew stronger in the late eighteenth century. As the imperial policies of the 1760s transformed tea drinking from a symbol of beloved English liberty into one of despised British luxury, coffee came to seem American by comparison. "Drank Coffee at four," one Virginia diarist noted in 1774, for we "are now too patriotic to use tea." Coffee and the new nation's collective purpose seemed to go together. During the Revolution, Boston's British Coffee House became the American Coffee House. Dexter named his emporium the Boston Exchange Coffee House, not (as many earlier establishments had been called) the Royal Exchange Coffee House.[49]

Especially when pitted against the private, feminine preserve of the tea table, the label "coffeehouse" signaled the public world of public men, a realm where money was liquid and status, fluid. For over a century, writers on both sides of the Atlantic had alternately praised and damned the leveling tendencies of coffeehouses. "Old and Young, and Great and Small, / And Rich, and Poore, you'l[l] see" there: this was the mythology of the coffeehouse as penny university, where the price of a dish of coffee would turn any man into a citizen of the world. At Boston's Crown Coffee House (among the city's largest before the Revolution), one patron gushed, "all Conversation is built upon Equality: Title and Distinction must be laid aside" upon entering.[50]

The Exchange's Coffee Room doesn't strike you as a place where distinctions are ignored. For those within the scarlet-curtained booths to speak freely, others must remain outside the walls. Coffee culture is at once public and exclusive. One needn't be born to it; the refinement here is for sale. With well-tailored clothes (stop in at Brooks and Hooper, across from the post office) and well-practiced manners, you might buy your way into a mahogany box, no letter of introduction required. Least of all here, where the tables want for traffic.

But even this democratic brand of refinement defines itself against others: coffee versus tea, men versus women, the Exchange versus the street, the town versus the countryside. This Coffee Room is an urban sophisticate's fantasia upon the theme of the public sphere rather than the thing itself. Set back from the street, away from the offices, it occupies the least public corner of the building's most public floor—emphatically *not* the post office. You're reminded of a joke you've heard around Boston: a city gentleman "would be as much at a loss in a farm yard, as a countryman under the dome of the Exchange Coffee House." A Vermont Yankee in King Andrew's court, you feel more challenged than welcomed. Paper man, coffee man: the room gives shape to your aspirations by showing you what you are not.[51]

When it's open—no schedule is posted—the Coffee Room serves mostly drinks, from patented New York mineral waters to a bracing rum punch to the occasional cup of coffee. Tired and hungry, you head upstairs in search of a noonday dinner. The Coffee Room abuts the building's main stairway, a "grand spiral . . . lighted by an elegant skylight" cut into the roof. But it's something of an ordeal to reach the staircase from here. Designed to carry genteel patrons—women, especially—from the south entrance to the banquet and ballrooms on the third and fourth levels of the building, the staircase is walled off from the 'Change Floor, lest the ladies sully their gazes with commerce (and vice versa). The only inlet you find is from a large "withdrawing room" nestled in the Exchange's southeast corner, a bright, ample chamber that can be rented for private parties. Cross it quickly, gingerly, to reach the stairs. Marvel at the carver's art as the sinuous helix of banister unfurls beneath your hand.[52]

Exit one flight up, on the third level above the street. The "first gallery," the proprietors call it. On this genteel floor—nothing from which to shield feminine eyes—the spiral staircase opens on three sides. Step into a spacious room, its area of nearly two thousand square feet making it smaller than the 'Change Floor but half again as big as the Coffee Room underneath it. The larger number of windows—seven in all—compensates for the lower ceilings on this level, preserving an airy, open atmosphere. The Exchange's Dining Hall can seat three hundred. As in the Coffee Room, gentility reigns here. In the Dining Hall, as the *Port Folio* poet says, "high refinement's polished radiance glows." On a sunny day like this one, the crimson window shades cast "a transient blaze" on the room's soft green walls.

An enormous investment, these curtains; the cloth for the draperies, together with the acres of green baize that nap the tables, account for more than half the value of everything in the room. Do the drapes make the room as the clothes make the man?[53]

Not today. The sumptuous textiles, along with the mirrors and chairs and tables and sideboards arrayed along the walls, only make the room feel more deserted. Since the house opened last year, the proprietors have hosted a total of three dinners here: a commemoration of the landing of the Pilgrim fathers last December, a banquet in honor of the Spanish patriots in January, and a celebration for the state's congressional delegation in March. Earlier this month, the managers announced they would serve turtle soup on Tuesday and Thursday afternoons, a practice they plan to continue till March (or while the green turtles last). But this afternoon, like most others, the room is hushed. No posted "bill of fare" tells you "what the larder affords," when you might expect service, or at what price. It's not clear, in fact, whether the kitchen is open at all. Like much else in the building, meals here are not "conducted on a regular system."[54]

The remainder of this floor presents little worth gaping at. Pace the walkways that line its four sides. Lean over the railing to look down upon the 'Change Floor, still lifeless, below. Pass by a small private dining room (unoccupied), a large apartment leased to the hotel's managers (in hock), and the rooms rented by a law firm and a lottery ticket broker (plenty of customers willing to play at games of chance). Before heading upstairs, pause before the office in the northwest corner of the building, number 97. (The numbering system, too, lacks a clear logic; the adjacent door is labeled 81.) A curtain shields the doorway into a spartan room whose meager furnishings contrast sharply with the lavish appointments in the Dining Hall. Aside from a small drop-leaf table and a shovel and tongs for the fireplace, seventeen side chairs comprise the only items in number 97. But this is the busiest space on the floor. The commissioners of bankruptcy meet here to "receive and examine the claims" against Boston's insolvent debtors. While the region's economy slumps, the commissioners' business booms. Last spring, they moved from the fourth floor of the Exchange down to this space, more easily accessible to their many patrons. Count yourself lucky to have no business before them.[55]

Head up another flight, this time taking the utility staircase on the west side of the building. If the splendors of the Coffee Room made you feel like a bumbling rustic, you're truly out of your depth on this second gallery, four stories above the street. As the managers would be eager to explain, you have no business here. Indeed, there *is* no business here: no offices, no meeting rooms, no trade in anything but leisure. *Ladies'* leisure, for this floor is as feminine in purpose and decor as the principal story is masculine. You notice two card rooms outfitted with gaming tables, several well-appointed suites available for private parties, and, in the southeast corner, a large apartment reserved "solely for the use of the ladies." Crammed with plush gim-crackery—the ladies' lounge features a toilet table, a sofa, upholstered chairs, and a large "pier glass" in which women can preen between dances—these rooms project comfort, ease, retirement. Again, you think, the *Port Folio*'s anonymous poet got it right: if "busy Commerce holds her active reign" on the 'Change Floor, the second gallery is where "social Feeling calls the lounging train." Yet commerce is hardly banished. The beau monde of the Beacon Hill drawing room is transported to Congress Street for a price, by the hour, by the ticket, by the head.[56]

Nowhere does the intense concern for appearances figure more strongly than in the grand Ball Room that dominates the floor. Located above the Dining Hall, this assembly room is easily the most elegant space in the Exchange. One admirer pronounces it "one of the most tasteful splendid rooms on the continent." The Ball Room is also the Exchange building's largest; seventy-five feet long and thirty across, it nearly equals the area of the 'Change Floor. And in some ways, its design echoes that of the interior courtyard. Like the 'Change Floor, the Ball Room soars, with seventeen-foot ceilings that take up two stories of the building. As on the 'Change Floor, pillars ring the Ball Room, twelve of them in all, fashioned in the ornate Corinthian style rather than the stolid Doric. And the Ball Room also culminates in a domed ceiling, its three vaulted compartments hovering high overhead.[57]

There the resemblance between these two great spaces stops. On the 'Change Floor, *transparency* is the order of the day. Men of business need open sight lines and the clear light of day to assess each other's character and credit-worthiness, head to head and man to man. This passion for plain dealing had long recommended the sidewalks of State Street as the town's theater of exchange. But the outdoor 'Change was both exposed and disordered. A space that in theory promoted openness devolved in reality into a maze of obscure transactions carried out in semisecret locations—in the shadows beneath overhangs, behind closed doors in private countinghouses, in alcoves along the alleyways. The 'Change Floor, in contrast, marries transparency and exclusivity, imposing the orderliness of a classical building form on the

*'Change Floor.*

chaos of markets. The atrium confers credibility upon its patrons. It elevates commercial transactions, frames them, gives them shape and symmetry. The openness of the 'Change Floor draws your eye out-ward: across the faces of your customers, between the arches ringing the galleries, through the glass doors leading to the Coffee Room, toward the Reading Room, toward the post office, ultimately toward the harbor. The 'Change Floor allows no feints, no disguises.[58]

If the 'Change Floor is a fishbowl, the Ball Room is a hall of mir-rors. Above the large fireplaces at each end of the room the managers have mounted "superb" circular mirrors six feet across and framed by mirrored sconces. Smaller round glasses punctuate the Ball Room's long north wall, a solid partition that secludes the assembly from the atrium as if to shield Beauty from Commerce. Mirrors hang between the pillars, enlivening secret nooks for whispered confidences. High above the dance floor a pair of "mirror windows" frames the little bal-cony that holds the orchestra. Silvered glass everywhere you turn: you have never seen so many reflections of yourself. A mirror remains a costly item, difficult to produce and a status symbol to own. Even a tabletop model would claim a place of honor in a farmhouse. Here they hang in absurd profusion, reflecting the golden arrows above the drapes, the polished silver of the candlesticks, the general glitter of the surround. One might as well paper the walls with money, you think, and you're right: the Dancing Hall has the costliest furnishings in the building, and nearly half that value resides in its mirrors—four hun-dred dollars' worth—a year's wages for a skilled artisan.[59]

·  Where the 'Change Floor depends on daylight, the Ball Room comes alive in the evening, when mirrors and candles and crystal transfigure the darkness. During the long lazy days of June and July, dancers might take their places in the hall before sunset. But the rest of the year, the room's seven full-length windows go dark before eight. Then the patron of the Ball Room relies on artificial light—from the five "superb and costly chandeliers" hanging from the domed ceilings and the ten mirrored candelabras, called girandoles, that line the walls—to illuminate her "fair form" as she glides across the dance floor. Muted colors complement the room's soft lighting; buff-colored walls and curtains of yellow satin and purple silk bathe the dancers in "golden hues." The effect is veiled, romantic, a *"degree of light . . . adjusted with happy skill to suit"* the dancers' "complections," notes one belle of the balls. The mirrors, the fabrics, the alcoves, the candles, the palette: all conspire to ensure that nobody appears full face in the Ball Room. Every gaze is fractured, every move "reflecting and reflected." The space fosters the discrete "sidelong glances" and "whispering worship" of courting couples: private words exchanged in a public space designed to mirror the comforts of the most refined home.[60]

You sense, correctly, that the Coffee House has reached its pinnacle here in the Ball Room, yet three floors loom above it. Tour these quickly, worried that the management will brand you a stranger and ask you to leave. Head up and up and up again, still using the west staircase, to reach the Exchange's seventh and highest floor. Over two hundred stairs separate you from the street now. Across a little hallway you discover another thirteen steps, not much more than two feet wide, granting access to the roof: irresistible. Walk around the base of the gleaming dome, a "promenade" said to be "as salubrious as the mall" on Boston Common—and safer, perhaps, for strolling "ladies." Even this is not the Exchange's highest reach. You climb a ladder that follows the shallow curve of the dome into a railed box at its apex. Within the railing you find a "perspective glass" waiting. This truly *is* Babel, for you can glimpse the heavens. At night, the God's-eye view turns every amateur stargazer into "a NEWTON or a HERSCHEL." By day the glass offers an equally stunning vista of the harbor—every island, every ship in sharp relief. Even through the naked eye the scene amazes. Gaze above the rooftops, above the canopy of trees beginning to blush with fall color. To the south, only the steeple of the Old South Church reaches high enough to interrupt your field of vision. The other buildings—the wooden Quaker meetinghouse, a row of brick office buildings, a mansion or two—look like toys. The gentlemen in their top hats and carriages are so many ants. Looking west your eye traverses the Common, pausing at the State House before looking across the Charles to Cambridge and beyond. Facing north you see past the open-air 'Change on State Street (still crowded at two), past the enormous project raising new streets from the drained Mill Pond, out along the bridge to Charlestown. On all sides of the city but especially on the east you see glorious, shimmering water, the liquid source of the mercantile fortunes that fuel your own modest paper dreams.[61]

Descending from the roof feels like waking from an enchantment, especially since the building's seventh and sixth stories are its least spectacular. In the main they consist of hotel rooms, arranged in classic double-loaded fashion along the corridors. Those against the exterior of the building have views only slightly less spectacular than the ones outside the dome. Rooms on the opposite side of the hallway have windows facing into the atrium space. Numbering sixty in all, the bedchambers are furnished simply. The least among them—little berths for a manservant or a night watchman—make due with just a bed and a chamber pot. (No toilets above the fourth floor.) Most include only the basics: a bed, a washstand, a dressing glass, and a chair or two. The larger corner rooms boast more elaborate interiors: curtained bedsteads, carpets to cover the bed and the floor, a full-length mirror, an upholstered armchair, some extra bolsters, a Pembroke table for writing, matched drapes. But for the most part, the critic who called the lodging rooms "ill planned, dark, and inconvenient," was correct. On an overcast day, the interior rooms would be gloomy indeed. And many a traveler would consider it "inconvenient" to climb six or seven flights of stairs to reach his bed.[62]

Neither the gloom nor the climb nor even the expense of these rooms—a dollar a night—presents the chief obstacle to your staying here. The Exchange's proprietors aren't taking lodgers now. In fact, it's not entirely clear who the proprietors *are* at this point. Dexter had been the first, but he absconded before finding other investors to take over the quixotic venture. Barely five months since his hasty exit, and ownership of the building has already changed hands, twice. In June, the directors of the Berkshire Bank claimed the Coffee House and its lands as their spoils when the Suffolk County sheriff sold off Dexter's assets. The Pittsfield gentlemen then assigned the deed to two of their creditors, Samuel Gilbert and Thomas Dean, who held large quantities of Berkshire Bank bills. In mid-July, Gilbert and Dean tried to sell the whole pile—the main building, the attached block of stores on Devonshire Street, the "elegant and costly Furniture" filling both—offering five hundred shares at $500 a piece. The total price of $250,000 amounted to less than half the building's cost: a veritable fire sale. And still no takers.[63]

This month, in a last-ditch effort to make "a speedy settlement of their concerns, and to liquidate the demands of their creditors," Gilbert and Dean have lowered their sights, looking for only $200,000 in total, spread over four hundred investors. With their proposals for selling the building—an offer splashed about town on a handbill—the owners include a "Minute Estimate of the Yearly Income of said Property." The balance sheet reads like a wish-fulfillment dream. Every office has a tenant; the ballrooms and dining halls are booked four evenings a week in season; every hotel chamber is filled every night; a hundred merchants "take soup, beef steak, & c." after stopping on the 'Change Floor every day of the year save Sundays. If all that comes to pass, Gilbert and Dean reckon, the proprietors will clear $50,000 annually, "a net profit of 25 per cent. on the capital." Thus they find it "strange" when, once again, "no purchasers appear."

Having made their fortunes peddling long shots to credulous lottery ticket buyers, the pair faces the unhappy realization that they have now

> drawn a blank for themselves; the fickle goddess [Fortuna] having jilted them, at the moment when they were about to place her shrine in this new temple, where her worshippers might have more room, and her priests perform their functions with more grace.

The Exchange a temple of (mis)fortune, its owners spurned acolytes, their fate proof of "the instability of human affairs": cosmic morals drawn from an all-too-human failure.[64]

Having ruined countless tradesmen and two sets of owners, the Exchange is on its way to bankrupting its first manager as well. Last January, before he fled to Canada, Dexter enticed William Hamilton, a successful hotelier from that country, to come to Boston to run the building. Already Hamilton has begun referring the enterprise's bills to a lawyer; in February, he'll walk away from the establishment with five years remaining on his lease. As Hamilton drowns, the Exchange drifts, at once a mountain and a rudderless ship.[65]

Entering the grand staircase again, you trace a downward spiral that mirrors Hamilton's, Gilbert and Dean's, Dexter's: a series of dizzying turns that doesn't end till you hit the street. Taking a last look at the dome, you conclude that the Exchange is indeed a "modern Babel": an ambitious and confusing and extraordinarily costly failure. Few would disagree. The building counts few supporters, all of them self-interested. "Manto," the *Port Folio*'s pseudonymous poet, is clearly an intimate of Dexter's, one who knows his "world of woes" from the inside. (The gossips peg his mother-in-law, Sarah Morton, for the author.) Her lyric deems him a "struggling Genius" whose "high deeds" will in time overshadow the "pigmy soul" of the "insects" who gainsay him. If Manto wants to redeem the name of Dexter, the author of the lengthy and generally ecstatic description of the building in the *Omnium Gatherum* has a more practical aim. The illustrated eight-page encomium ends with a plea for investors to buy shares.[66]

The building's emptiness answers the boosters. The People—that amorphous civic body in whose name, with whose hands, and upon whose backs this public ornament was built—have voted with their feet. They will not bless the site of Andrew Dexter's disgrace with their livelihoods or their leisure. The Exchange's bewildered owners confess with "surprise, as well as regret" that the Coffee House "has not met the patronage so large an establishment requires." Through the fall of 1809, it remains an elaborate stage set in a dark theater. As you head back up Congress Street, you cannot know whether the orphaned Exchange awaits a happy ending or the apocalyptic fate of Babel.[67]

In the last dark days of New England's doleful year of 1809, the Exchange Coffee House found its rescuers, twelve merchant-apostles who incorporated as the building's governing body in late December. Ties of politics, blood, money, and sometimes all three linked many of them to Andrew Dexter. John T. Apthorp was Charlotte Morton's kinsman and one of the trustees of Dexter's bankrupt estate; Benjamin Weld shared the latter connection. William Payne, a broker with an office in the Exchange's basement, had ties to the Berkshire bankers. The merchant Cornelius Coolidge was thrice-bound to the project. He lived in Perez Morton's Dorchester mansion, which he had bought in July 1808, tendering Morton cash that likely found its way into the Coffee House. Coolidge was no Dexter ally; to the contrary he, like another of the new Exchange directors, had joined Nathan Appleton's syndicate to destroy Dexter's banks. Coolidge also represented Gilbert and Dean's creditors, a role shared by two more board members. Other proprietors may have been devoted to the building or its architect. Two worshipped at the West Boston Church that Asher Benjamin had designed. A third, builder and draftsman Thomas W. Sumner, belonged to the Society of Associated Housewrights, where Benjamin served as an officer. For their president, the Exchange's new board chose Harrison Gray Otis, a onetime political ally of Samuel Dexter's, and the town's master speculator.[68]

In their varied ways, then, each of the new directors held a stake in the fate of the Exchange. They planned to use its profits to pay off Dexter's myriad debts, to themselves and to others. Tearing the building down was simply unthinkable. Instead, for the next eight years, they and their successors struggled to fill it up: with tenants, boarders, dancers, and diners, with locals and strangers, with women of grace and men of capital. In the process, of course, they also hoped to line their own pockets. Optimists continued to insist that the building would bring its owners "a very great interest for their money," projecting returns of anywhere from 12 to 25 percent per year: visions of sugarplums to speculator and debtor alike.[69]

The building loomed. How to make it teem? *"Do not let us suffer the odium of possessing such a building to become indelible, by our refusing to make use of it."* So ran the owners' prayer for the town's "rich inhabitants" to step forward and "unanimously take possession" of the Exchange. Such pleas had failed. Now came the hard work: adapting the building to the desires and habits of its imagined clientele, and then teaching those liberal generous Bostonians to use a space they found disorienting if not odious.[70]

Organize time. Devise a "regular system," present "a plan." These were the first imperatives the directors confronted. In March 1810, Thomas Dean—the bankrupt third owner whom the directors rehabilitated as the Exchange's second manager—announced in the press "that said House was re-opened yesterday." The new proprietors, he promised, had taken numerous steps to earn the "patronage of the Merchants, the Stranger, and the Public generally." They had established regular hours. The Coffee Room and the promised Reading Room would stay open from sunrise until ten at night. They set mealtimes. At eleven in the morning a bell would call the hungry to soup ("mock" or "brown" every day, turtle when available) in the Coffee Room. In the Dining Hall at two, "discrete and obliging waiters" would serve dinner. The bar and Coffee Room would be "constantly supplied with the best Brandy, Spirit, Gin, Wines, Lemonade, Port, Ale, &c.," as well as "Tarts, Ice Creams, Custards," and other light refreshment. They posted a "regular bill of fare . . . with the prices annexed," meal tickets available at the bar. All according to schedule. The house was now "in complete order," the proprietors declared in June.[71]

Organize space. Straighten the building out, show it off, put it on the grid. With its numerous shops and apartments, the Exchange had something of "the appearance of a small city," as one critic wrote. But alas, the city the building initially resembled was the old Boston of the crooked and narrow streets. If the Coffee House overwhelmed visitors with its maze of routes and functions, the directors took up the charge to untangle it, outside and in.[72]

They gave it a true front door, a feat that required nothing less than redrawing the map. If the Exchange ever generated real traffic, the cramped north side would present a practical as well as an aesthetic challenge. Boston's selectmen, no fans of the building, acknowledged that this entrance was "exceedingly crowded & inconvenient, in consequence of the narrowness of the passages leading thereto." Through the summer of 1810, the Coffee House directors haggled with the town, the courts, and the owners of adjacent lots to create a new street running past the Exchange's north door, a plan far less grand than the arcade Dexter had imagined, yet far more sensible than what he had achieved. In late August, they committed the considerable sum of twenty thousand dollars to compensate their neighbors and indemnify the city. The town approved the project shortly thereafter, leaving just enough time to raze the extant buildings, level the site, and lay an avenue thirty feet wide before the ground froze. Given the Exchange's storied past, it can't have been easy to find laborers to sign on to the project. Nonetheless, by January carriages could travel from Congress Street to Devonshire with only the portico of the Exchange jutting into the lane to impede their progress. Come July 1811, the new passageway would be paved, even if it never earned a bona fide street name.[73]

Having transformed the north side into a viable commercial artery, the directors confronted the opposite challenge in the back of the building. There, ordering space meant making the approach *less* visible. Soon after the Exchange opened, Gilbert and Dean had expressed their desire to "purchase the estates on the opposite side of Salter's court" in order to create a more sheltered entrance for women on their way "to the balls, or assemblies." Until that happened, a makeshift screen of "Venetian blinds, or lattice work, between the pillars" of the little covered colonnade would help to "secure the ladies from impertinent observations."[74]

The campaign to shield female patrons of the Coffee House from the public gaze took much longer than the proprietors' efforts to reveal their male patrons to the public eye. Between 1813 and 1817, the

Exchange directors concluded nine separate agreements with the men and women whose lots bordered the building's south side, purchases that totaled over fifteen thousand dollars.[75] By the summer of 1817, they owned enough of the land below Salter's Court to set about transforming it into a refined court. They pulled down tenements and put up walls, separating what they grandiosely called the Exchange's "south piazza" from the building's own service functions, and from its neighbors. They finished the job by laying out an octagonal bed of grass leading back from Congress Street, a tiny railed green around which carriages could pivot after unloading passengers dressed for dancing.[76]

Organize profit. Inside the Exchange, the new owners ordered space according to financial as much as architectural logic. Make it clear, make it pay: these were their mandates. Each new manager offered new attractions and then asked new fees, transforming public space into private property in the process. The Reading Room, imagined in 1809 as the free and just reward of the postal customer with time on his hands, finally opened in April 1810 "for the use of Subscribers only." Thereafter, the privileges of the room—the papers, the chance to exchange information, the "right of introducing their friends who are strangers in town"—would belong to "Gentlemen" willing to commit five dollars annually to the enterprise, payable in advance. Or at least to those gentlemen whom the board found congenial; a clause in the manager's lease ensured "that no person shall be permitted to become a subscriber to said reading room who shall be disapproved of by said directors." Hundreds of the town's prominent merchants—including Dexter's onetime nemesis Nathan Appleton—signed up as members. To suit this elevated clientele, the room was made more exclusive. In July 1811, the proprietors moved it from its spot beside the post office to a new apartment in the back, beside the Coffee Room.[77]

In much the same spirit, the proprietors instituted a Marine Diary, a "registry of all kinds of Shipping Intelligence, which the Masters of Vessel, Supercargoes, and others, concerned in maritime business, are invited to fill up, with such advices as they may from time to time receive." Small boats with EXCHANGE COFFEE HOUSE emblazoned on their hulls cruised the harbor "constantly," gathering tales from sailors on the vessels moored along the wharves. The diary "keeper" posted the news he gleaned days before it hit the local papers, especially when winter weather kept seamen stranded in the harbor. To ensure that information-hungry readers could get at the volume readily, it was to be kept in the Coffee Room, an open book.[78]

The Exchange proprietors correctly imagined that strong "public interest" would attend this faster, more comprehensive, and direct compilation of commercial news. As soon as the diary opened in April 1810, gleanings from the Exchange Coffee House books began to appear in the newspapers. "There were about 50 vessels arrived at this port yesterday," one early digest ran, "and the Exchange Coffee House Books contain the names of upwards of 40." A tiny information revolution, the Marine Diaries carried the dispatches from the Napoleonic wars, reports of skirmishes in the West Indies and "French Spoilations" on the high seas, and rumors that dozens of Spanish priests had infiltrated New York. The Coffee House books told locals who had come to town from where, as well as when and at what cost they might leave Boston for distant ports.[79]

But once patrons of the Exchange came to depend on easy "public inspection" of the Marine Diaries, the proprietors announced that they couldn't continue to offer the service gratis. Keeping up the books cost money, they explained in July; a long-suffering copyist had "devoted his whole time and attention" to the project for three months without pay. Considerations of "*Policy*, as well as *justice*" now required them to charge for access to the book. Five dollars per year would grant "any gentleman" the right to peruse the diaries, as well as admission to a "room in the Exchange Coffee House, furnished with a telescope glass, commanding a full view of the harbor" from which he could espy his own shipping news. Ten dollars also purchased "the liberty of posting up advertisements in the Area." Nothing for free in *this* penny university.[80]

Despite the proprietors' best efforts, privatizing the free exchange of news and ideas promised by the name "Coffee House" proved difficult. The public persisted. Men who anteed up the requested fees complained about "the frequent difficulty of gaining access to the books," which were often monopolized by those who hadn't paid. A year after subscriptions opened, the Exchange's owners moved the diaries from the Coffee Room to the newly relocated Reading Room in order to "prevent non subscribers from intruding" on the privileges of paying customers. Two years later, manager John Jones (the building's third) announced further restrictions. Admittance to the "handsomely enlarged" Reading Room would "be regulated by Tickets, in order to ensure a regular system." According to Jones, the new policy would have the twin advantages of keeping freeloaders away from the Marine Diaries, and moving the diary traffic out of the Coffee Room, which would in turn seem "more retired for those wishing to take refreshments." Tickets and rosters, separate apartments and guarded doors, and still "the intruders" (somehow distinct from the desired "public") kept coming. In 1814, Jones declared that any who "visit the room, and have omitted to subscribe, will be considered as subscribers, and charged accordingly." Two years later, his successor felt compelled to reiterate the ultimatum.[81]

When the Exchange's rechristened News Room reopened in August 1816 after yet another extensive renovation, it was bigger and grander than ever. Since 1811, its size had roughly doubled; this members-only attraction now occupied twice the area of the ostensibly public Coffee Room out of which it was carved. A slate of seventeen "Rules and Regulations" accompanied the grand reopening, enumerating subscribers' perks and listing the categories of banned people and activities. No nonsubscribers, no minors, no unaccompanied strangers, no locals passed off as members' guests. No loud voices, no removing books or news sheets from the room, no soliciting. If rules generally indicate the presence of the behaviors they oppose, the Exchange's News Room remained more boisterous and public than the proprietors wished.[82]

The fate of the Reading Room and the Marine Diaries housed there is but one indication of the Exchange owners' broader struggle in the years between 1810 and 1818, as they pitted their business-class logic of novelty, order, and profit against the forces of habit, confusion, and debt at play within—and against—the building. Whether or not they prevailed in their battle depends on how you measure success.

The economic verdict is mixed at best. Tenants came and went, income waxing and waning with them. In 1809, the Exchange's first year in operation, only eleven of its three dozen offices filled. After that, the number of renters drifted up and down unpredictably, never rising past twenty-two and falling back to half that in 1816. Even in better years, more than a third of the shops and offices stood empty. Gilbert and Dean had projected that the annual income from rentals "exclusive of the Hotel" might reach $15,500. But with a vacancy rate of over 33 percent and rents of about $200 per year for the best offices, the proprietors never realized a quarter of that. Hotel rooms proved still less lucrative. Despite Dexter's original claim that the hotel was the "branch of the concern from which the greatest revenue is expected to arise," the income from short-term boarders was small and erratic. In the twelve months following July 1813 (the only period for which records remain), the Exchange's hotel department netted less than $2,500 for all the boarders it housed, the dinners it served, the liquor and coffee it poured, and the turtle soup it ladled out, combined. A profit, though a mere fraction of what Gilbert and Dean had imagined as a yearly income of over $40,000 from that part of the business.[83]

By leasing all but a few rooms in the building to a succession of managers—Hamilton in 1809, Jones from 1812 through 1816, and the New York hotelier David Barnum thereafter—the Exchange's owners replaced the inconsistent revenues generated by lodgers and diners with the steady tariff paid by a single tenant. But finding a manager willing to assume the risks of the enterprise wasn't easy, especially after Hamilton reneged on his lease in 1810. Despite an aggressive advertising campaign, a replacement for him didn't emerge for more than two years. Finally, in July 1812, Jones, a local wine seller, paid them $4,400 to rent the entire "hotel department"—including the Coffee Room, the Reading Room, the Ball Room, all the lodging chambers, and most of the Devonshire Street buildings—for the ensuing year. When Jones renewed his lease in 1813 and 1814, the proprietors accepted 10 percent less, suggesting that demand for the property had softened. Certainly Jones's own profits were modest. His second year managing the place he cleared $3,700: a respectable income for an innkeeper, but nothing like the riches Dexter once prophesied. Less, in fact, than Gilbert and Dean had imagined could be made on the sale of liquor alone.[84]

For a man of capital, the Exchange Coffee House proved a disappointing investment. Shares in the enterprise traded poorly, paid meager dividends, and declined in value over the years. In October 1814, Gilbert and Dean told their creditors that the "fall in value of the Exchange Coffee-House shares" was the chief cause of their becoming insolvent for the second time in a decade. Gilbert later recalled that the Exchange had cleaned him out, leaving him "with but five dollars in his pocket." Investing in a bank or an insurance concern made more sense. Even buying a lottery ticket might be a better, certainly a cheaper, bet. Financially speaking, the Exchange proved Nathan Appleton right. The building was "wholly inconvertible" into money. Creditors who clung to the hope that the Exchange's profits would make them whole had let Dexter's folly burn them a second time.[85]

But don't weigh the success or failure of the Exchange with the scales of an investor. Think instead like a socialite, a shopper, a flaneur who prizes the gossip-filled personal letter over the Marine Diary. Picture not a balance sheet, but a wash of images, an early-nineteenth-century version of the 1932 movie classic *Grand Hotel*. People come, people go, making each day unique and yet like every other.

Imagine the Exchange's brief life unfolding in the course of twenty-four hours.[86] Call it November 3, 1817, exactly a year before the building will fall to earth. The national horizon, like the brisk late-fall morning, is bright: Jefferson's embargo a distant memory, the unpopular War of 1812 won, the sectional chasm that had deepened in the 1810s slowly mending. New England cautiously anticipates the reign of peace and prosperity that James Monroe promised when he took the oath of office in March. The president's fifteen-week-long "tour of personal examination" through the region that so hotly opposed his Democrat-Republican Party reached Boston last July second, and he celebrated the forty-first anniversary of the nation's independence in the cradle of American liberty. The ceremony of reconciliation—which culminated in handshakes and speeches in the Exchange's atrium—had produced its desired effect. "All political distinctions were laid aside," the papers declared. A new "era of good feelings," pressmen called it, coining a phrase that would come to define (and later haunt) Monroe's administration.[87]

Like virtually every notable to pass through Boston in recent years, Monroe lodged in "superb apartments furnished for him at the Exchange Coffee House."[88] Nearly a decade after it opened, the Coffee House has finally embarked upon its own brief era of good feelings. The passions provoked by Dexter's name have cooled with time and distance, and the hard work of his successors has conquered some of the building's troubles. Last summer, David Barnum, who had earned a reputation for running "extensive establishments of the kind, in Philadelphia and New-York," became the building's fourth and ablest manager. He proclaimed the Exchange to be "in complete repair," praising extensive renovations that had splashed new furniture, paper, and paint everywhere. To these freshly face-lifted surfaces Barnum brings refinements of his own, a continental flair. As if Congress Street bordered the Seine, he calls the midday meal a table d'hôte. As if Boston were an English spa town, in the Exchange cellars he opens "BATHING-ROOMS fitted up in the handsomest manner, with suitable attendants and arrangements for the accommodation of *Ladies* and *Gentlemen*." Mrs. Barnum, who directs "the female department" of the hotel, insists on further luxuries: another two thousand yards of carpeting, another thirty sets of bed curtains. The Barnums' innovations—the latest of the many waves of "internal improvements" visited upon Benjamin's building—find a ready audience. After years of instruction about when and where and why to enter it, Bostonians have learned to live with the Exchange, if not always to love it.[89]

This morning, like every other save Sundays, begins at 3:00 a.m., with the sound of wheels grinding over cobblestones as the Enterprize Stage departs the building's east door on its two-day journey to New York. Up on the tower's sixth and seventh floors, lodgers ensconced in various degrees of splendor—from the lavish four-room suite numbered 147 to its bare-bones neighbor, room 119—slumber on beneath their counterpanes. In the cellars, cooks and bakers and scullery maids start in on their long days. Mrs. Barnum supervises a staff of "nearly thirty domestics," urging them always to go about their business "without noise, confusion, or waste." Indeed, the house's waste answers others' wants. In the relative quiet of these early hours, the girls wrap the "broken meats" left over from last night's elegant supper so the charitable ladies of Boston can distribute them to those less fortunate. (So "extensive an establishment" is the Exchange that its table scraps feed fifty poor families every day.) What fat and gristle they can't dispense as alms, they mix with lye to make the hotel's soap, their eyes stinging as they put up the week's ten barrels. Two flights up on the principal story, male attendants stir the embers of last night's fires in the Coffee and Reading rooms, readying them to open at dawn. But no sane merchant is afoot yet. In the early-morning hours, the Exchange is a theater of labor, not commerce or leisure.[90]

By eight, the enormous building shows signs of life. Male boarders breakfast in the Dining Hall "mess"; families eat in their rooms. The tenants who lease space on the lower floors of the building sweep the stoops in front of their shops and unlock the doors to their offices. In the hallway outside the post office knots of men await the newspapers. Others bring correspondence to place in letter bags labeled HAVANA or HALIFAX, LONDON or LIVERPOOL, SURINAM or BATAVIA.[91]

On the opposite side of the building, a few women, youngsters in tow, make their way from the secluded back entrance up the grand spiral staircase to one of the larger rooms on the third floor. There they pay an attendant twenty-five cents, half that for the children, to see the latest "panorama" touring the city. Depicting a battle from the late war, a sublime vista from the expanding West, or the skyline of a distant city, these epic canvases bring the nation's history and scope and purpose to life. The images are enormous and enveloping, sometimes thirty feet in length and half that in height. Few spaces *but* the larger rooms in the Exchange can show them to advantage. The painting goes on view at seven in the morning. After dark, the image will be "elegantly illuminated," the flickering candles adding an almost cinematic effect to the still life. Some evenings a band provides musical accompaniment. But daylight better suits the family crowd, and they come in small groups into the early afternoon.[92]

As the day wears on, the numbers and kinds of activity in the Exchange rise, the noise level mounting in tandem. At ten, the first scheduled meeting of the day comes to order. Members of the American Antiquarian Society, lately constituted to preserve the history and culture of the young nation, convene in a rented room on the sixth floor to celebrate the fifth anniversary of their founding. Down the hall, stockholders of the North American Insurance Company hear a special report.[93]

At eleven o'clock, a loud bell indicates that soup is ready in the Coffee Room. A bevy of men—black and white alike—wait table, serving a hearty brown broth to the businessmen milling about the place. Trading on the 'Change Floor begins at noon. Today two sales take place: bank shares—confidence restored, a popular investment again—are auctioned at noon, and several lots of Maine lands go on the block at one. Hardly a beehive of commerce, but more deals than most days see here. When the bell announces the start of table d'hôte at quarter past two, the traffic on the 'Change Floor disperses. The Dining Hall fills with businessmen and families passing through town. ( "[It] is a *very* common thing," one Boston attorney tells a friend, "for gentlemen with their wives & families to stop at the exchange Coffee House to dinner.") The house offers hearty plates of "surloin, saddle, or ham" for the man's "sound appetite," and lighter "luxuries" to suit ladies' "delicate palates."[94]

When dinner concludes, the Exchange slips into a postprandial silence that endures, with few interruptions, till sunset. Pockets of busyness defy the general hush. On the ground floor, one story below the central atrium, a dry goods merchant enters the offices of the Phoenix Fire Insurance Company to seek Joseph Otis's counsel about how best to protect his wares. Otis details the small premiums that will indemnify his business in the event of fire, a novel way to manage one of the biggest risks of living and working in a nineteenth-century city. On his way out of the building the merchant visits John Weiss's hairdressing shop, from which he emerges coifed "according to the latest London and Paris fashions," a pair of "excellent quality Spanish Cigarrs" in his pocket. Across the corridor a laborer ducks into Ralph Huntington's brokerage to purchase a lottery ticket, hoping that a dollar wagered today will yield a fortune when the wheel spins next week. Down the corridor a ship's master from Bristol seeks an audience with the British consulate, which has just moved to the Exchange.[95]

Four flights up, a dozen or so young women trickle into the sunny apartment fitted out as the Writing Room for their three o'clock course in penmanship. Following the suggestion of Mr. Wifford, the schoolmaster, they've taken the "winding Stair way at the south corner" of the building "directly to the room," thereby avoiding "any concern with the Public EXCHANGE." Later in the afternoon, a group of "young gentlemen" less vulnerable to the contagion of commerce, practice "*Plain simple Writing, Arithmetic, Book-Keeping*, and *Letter-Writing*": subjects that prepare them for the "*business of real life*." Some days the Writing Room doubles as "Mr. Fennell's School of Reading and Elocution," where pupils "of either sex" (never both together) train their voices rather than their hands for fifteen dollars per quarter.[96]

For all its variety, the building's daytime traffic is but an overture to the pageantry at night. Unlike its open-air namesake up on State

Street, this Exchange is a nocturnal creature. Its plumage shines after six, reflected in the artificial daylight of flame (candles, sconces, chandeliers) at play upon glass (windows, mirrors, crystal). Business meetings, penmanship classes, meal service, and the like: all of these continue into the evening. But at night, merchants and schoolboys and shareholders cross paths with men and women attending an almost endless variety of social events.

Grand balls, for one. Some of these "cotillions" are privately sponsored affairs for invited guests; others are announced in the papers, with tickets available for purchase at the bar. Swells gather. Even women who voice "hesitation about going to a public ball," as the seventeen-year-old Eliza Susan Quincy did, sometimes venture up the Exchange's back stairs into the Dancing Hall. One young belle pronounces tonight's assembly "the most brilliant collection of beauties that has appeared in publick for many years." The air heady with flowers, the "table cover'd with the luxuries of every clime": the scene mirrors their elegance. Just as the glow of the chandeliers shuts out the night, the bounty of the supper defies the season, as if "summer was robb'd its flowers, & its fruits to embellish this winter fete." Tables groan under plates heaped with "[f]ine peaches blushing with the Glow of September & a variety of melons . . . preserved with great care & expence" for the "gallant occasion." Even the plates—vivid blue transfer ware imported from Staffordshire, emblazoned with Neptune guiding his chariot through the waves—speak of maritime wealth. After the meal is cleared, a Turkish band in national costume plays for hours. The clock strikes two before the carriages line up to ferry the dancers home to Beacon Street. In an hour, the Enterprize Stage will leave for New York once again.[97]

Club meetings, for another. This is the dawn of what historians have dubbed "the era of association," and the Exchange's nightlife offers a case in point. Fraternal organizations of every stripe—groups of men linked by experience, politics, status, or an impulse toward charity—gather in the early evening to drink and dispute. The Boston Light Infantry, the Independent Company of Cadets, the New England Guards, the Sea Fencibles: all of these paramilitary organizations plan their training exercises over glasses of Madeira and port in the private dining rooms.[98] Harvard graduates hold reunions here, next door to the middling sorts who people the city's building trades. Last Wednesday, the housewrights, bakers, millers, and other artisans who comprise the Massachusetts Charitable Mechanics Association met to admit new members. (Many people connected with the Exchange, including former owners Samuel Gilbert and Thomas Dean, current board members Ebenezer Larkin and Thomas W. Sumner, as well as the building's head carpenter and its lead mason, belong to the organization.) The Masons were in session that night, too. Dressed in full regalia, members of the Grand Lodge processed into the hall they have renovated on the building's sixth and seventh floors, featuring double-height ceilings and a grand ceremonial altar napped in red and blue.[99]

Tonight the mechanics and the masons make way for the merchants who attend the monthly meeting of the Washington Benevolent Society, a Federalist association of which Nathan Appleton is a charter member. The Benevolents convene in room 110 to dream up new ways to honor the memory of "the illustrious patriot George Washington," under whose leadership "the commercial prosperity, the wealth and the power of the United States, were augmented to a degree without precedent, and beyond the most sanguine expectations." The nation's fortunes have been falling ever since, they believe, preyed upon by "ambitious men, who compass evil ends." Sworn "to oppose all encroachments of democracy, aristocracy, or despotism" upon the vulnerable Republic, they assemble each month to "deliberate upon the state of publick affairs, to enquire and to impart knowledge, and to increase the ardour of our patriotism by the warmth of our social attachments." In other words, they drink against Jefferson and his successors. These are dark days for Federalists. Long a self-consciously *exclusive* body—they fret about passwords to keep nonmembers from infiltrating their meetings—the Benevolents have seen their purpose questioned and their number diminished in this era of (Republican) good feelings. Their meeting is grim, despite the bounty laid out on the room's seven small dining tables.[100]

Washington is, quite literally, the patron saint of the Benevolents, with all the trappings of worship that implies. Some years back, one of the general's descendants sent the group his "ancient" gorget, the ornamental plate of armor that had encircled Washington's sacred neck when he fought "under General Braddock in the war of 1756." More than a half century later, the Benevolents venerate the keepsake as a "precious relic."[101]

Washington also serves more broadly as something of a patron saint for the Exchange, his name and image sanctifying many of its grandest events. A portrait of "our beloved WASHINGTON" presides over the Dancing Hall at all times. For banquets, the manager also trots out "an elegant triumphal arcade" supporting larger-than-life images of the Federalist trinity: Washington flanked by Alexander Hamilton and Massachusetts's own Fisher Ames. In the Masonic Hall, "a large marble urn, inscribed with a memento of Washington," forms the centerpiece of the eastern wall.[102] Many nights are consecrated to his memory. In March 1813, hundreds of the town's notables had attended the Washington and Naval Ball, a celebration of the general's birth and the young nation's halting progress in its second war against Britain—a war Washington had long forestalled and that New England strenuously opposed. In front of the building, a bust of Washington topped a pillar listing the name and heroic deeds of the war's most "gallant Commanders."[103]

The largest of these images are the sort called "transparencies," sheer curtains of cloth or treated paper upon which the founder's face is captured in translucent pigments. Enormous gauzy stage scrims, transparencies make easy prey for the flames that illuminate them, not to mention the ordinary wear and tear of moving and storage. The Exchange's transparencies of George Washington, painted in 1809, have become as frayed and tatty as Federalism itself. Washington may be the building's inspiration, but his acolytes alone can't pay the bills. An evening's offerings must extend beyond Federalists, beyond economic elites, beyond refinement. In the end, the Exchange is a business, not a temple. The entertainments mounted on any given night reflect the manager's commitment to profit above politics: anything for a buck.[104]

The main event typically begins at seven-thirty or eight o'clock, after the clubs conclude their suppers and the shareholders bring the gavel down on their meetings. In the Dancing Hall, when no balls are scheduled, there are plays and concerts of varied sorts. Shakespeare's works have been performed here on numerous occasions, as has a wide range of instrumental and vocal music, from Haydn symphonies to minstrel songs. The building's smaller assembly rooms feature experts lecturing on topics ranging from advances in natural philosophy to the evils of dueling. For such genteel and uplifting entertainments, gentlemen pay a dollar a ticket, escorting their ladies for free.[105]

In addition to this highbrow fare, the Exchange offers a variety of more popular entertainments. Not the bawdiest in town. Not the circus, for example, which plays outdoors in Haymarket Place. No animal curiosities, either; if you want to see a giant South American rodent, head to the Columbian Museum on Tremont Street.[106] Still, there's plenty to do in the Exchange even if you can't afford fine fashions and don't know the latest dance forms. In April, the Ball Room was made over as a "Dark Chamber" in which various optical illusions were projected and performed, including "Phantasmagoria, Spectreology," and the "Dancing of the Witches." (Witchcraft played for thrills just steps from gallows hill, where seventeenth-century Bostonians had hanged women convicted of that crime.) Earlier this month, a ventriloquist had dazzled the crowd by projecting his voice into a snuff box, a thimble, an oyster, and "a *Codfish*," from which he elicited "a tremendous noise, like that of a number of hogs." He brought down the house by causing "the voice of a Child *to be heard in a* TEA-POT" saying "*Let me out, let me out, or I shall smother.*" Next week, he plans to "cut off the head of a fowl, and afterwards reunite it as before." Just a few of the "*One Hundred Deceptions*" on view in the Ball Room, Tuesdays and Thursdays, fifty cents a head.[107]

All of these "delusions" are "new and surprising," as the promoters insist. But tonight's main attraction boasts feats "never performed by mortal man." The Ball Room is set with chairs for five hundred. Doors open at six, and at seven the show begins. Nepicos Box, a high-wire artist also known as the Little Devil, promises "to electrify the spectators." Perched upon his tightrope, he jumps through a small hoop seven times without faltering. He balances improbable objects, from "seven common Chairs, all at one time" to "100 full wine glasses." Still in midair, he plays the violin, juggles eggs, "catches a ball discharged from a gun," swallows "a number of knives & forks," and performs card tricks. Finally, he kneels upon the wire, ending a display of daring and agility that the audience rewards with loud cheering.[108]

Manager David Barnum is pleased at the evening's attendance. Five hundred tickets at fifty cents a piece, less the performer's small wage, makes for a respectable box office draw. At least for tonight. As he knows only too well, running the Exchange is itself a high-wire act. Every day he juggles the competing interests and tastes of many constituencies—men and women, elites and common folk, locals and strangers. Every month he labors to balance the books. Locals and strangers alike praise Barnum for at last giving the Exchange "a reputation which is not surpassed, if it be equalled by any similar establishment in the United States." Still, keeping the enormous building aloft always seems vaguely miraculous.[109]

Tonight the Dancing Hall rings with laughter and cheers. Yet tomorrow at midday, the 'Change Floor—the very heart of the building—will again be largely empty. Not from lack of trying. Andrew Dexter started exhorting on behalf of an indoor exchange more than a decade ago. Since then, every one of the building's managers has worked to people the atrium. Gilbert and Dean agitated with their fellow brokers in 1809 and 1810. In 1812, John Jones made the case yet again. He furnished the area "under the colonnade, on each side of the floor" with an array of "settees, desks, pens, ink, &c.," hoping these enticements would lure merchants "to meet on the floor of the Exchange, to transact business during 'Change hours." He promised that the "elegance of this Area, the shelter it affords from the summer's heat, and winter's cold; its proximity to the Reading Room, Post Office, Insurance Offices and Coffee Room are without a parallel in America." These improvements in place, the 'Change Floor was poised to become "the centre of mercantile transactions in this metropolis."[110]

Five years later, the 'Change Floor has not become a commercial center, nor Boston a metropolis. One guide to the town explains that the building's "principal floor was originally intended for a public Exchange, which design never was executed." The outdoor market has prevailed, "as the merchants from long habit, prefer to stand in the street, even during the inclement winter months." Unwilling for his establishment to lose out to a November day in New England, Barnum tries another tack. He places an "elegant pyramid Stove" in the 'Change area, pledging to make the atrium "so comfortable in the winter" that it "will undoubtedly be a resort for the transaction of business."[111]

The next twelve months prove Barnum wrong. Despite the roof and the warmth, despite the pens and the papers, business Boston continues to gather in the streets. At noon on the Exchange's last day, people throng State Street while the 'Change Floor remains desolate. The building wrapped around it is orderly now, Babel no more. But the atrium is less a bustling indoor plaza than an enormous, elegant chimney stretching a hundred feet into the air.[112]

# FIVE

# CONFLAGRATION

"*Like a fire bell in the night*": so great, Thomas Jefferson wrote in 1820, was his growing "terror" about what slavery would do to the fabric of the Union.[1] Whatever their positions on the so-called Missouri question, readers across the nation would have found Jefferson's metaphor of rude awakening as powerful as it was familiar. Bells tolled constantly, calling people to wake and to sleep, to vote and to pray, to celebrate and to mourn. Bells rang communities into being, marking their borders at the limits of earshot.[2] In this clanging world the fire bell carried particular horror. If you lived in the early 1800s, you knew the distinctive ring that transformed the church bell into a fire alarm. The peal for fire was rapid, even frantic. The "quickness of the strokes" upon the bell during a fire had been known to destroy an instrument.[3]

When sextons climbed to their belfries to give the alarm for fire, they swung their bells backward, inverting the usual order of tones so that low to high became high to low. How well the tocsin, as this upside-down melody was called, incarnated the ravages of fire, a "resistless element" that engendered "[s]udden reverses of fortune" wherever it touched. In a world obsessed with rising, fire felled more swiftly and surely and often than any other peril. Fire was "powerful and destructive," instantly depriving families "blessed with every comfort, every luxury of life" of "all they possessed on earth." Fire was "a thief in the night," stealing from the mighty and the humble alike, scattering "wealth to the winds." The fire bell sang of "the gain of a life . . . lost in a moment." So when you heard it, you felt (as Jefferson hinted) a terrible sinking in the pit of your stomach, a feeling of the purest existential dread. WHEN BACKWARDS RUNG WE TELL OF FIRE, ran the inscription on one ancient English bell, THINK HOW THE WORLD SHALL THUS EXPIRE. The fire bell translated apocalyptic nightmares into sound.[4]

Everyone in Jefferson's America knew the fire bell, but city dwellers knew it intimately. The fire bell belonged to the urban sound scape that accompanied the concentration of people and property in small spaces. Scripture acknowledged as much. "I will kindle a fire in his cities," warned the god of Jeremiah, "and it shall devour round about him."[5] Millennia later, the ancient prophecy still rang true. Especially in cold northern climates, where city dwellers heated with flame many months of the year. Especially in North America, where urban people had the cheap luxury of building with wood. Most especially in Boston, a veritable tinderbox since the first days of English settlement. As the town's fire wards—the officers appointed to oversee the prevention and fighting of fire—noted in 1802, Boston was "populous and extensive," its buildings "composed principally of combustible materials" and closely "crowded together," its narrow streets difficult to navigate quickly. Thus it was hardly "a cause of surprise, that the inhabitants are frequently summoned by the alarm of Fire."[6] Six Great Fires had leveled whole quarters of the fragile colonial town before 1700, all but pushing it into the sea. In the eighteenth century, sixteen major blazes joined what Alexander Townsend, the president of the Massachusetts Charitable Fire Society, called a "black register of destruction"; a half dozen more punctuated the first decade of the nineteenth. And these were just the large, multidwelling fires that earned the fearful label *conflagration*. Year in, year out, as Townsend noted, Bostonians lived through "innumerable others, deeply calamitous, though slashing less conspicuous from the dismal gloom" than

Great Fires did. The year 1816 brought fourteen such fires. The following year, there had been only six, all erupting during the colder months, most of them at night. In 1818, nine buildings had burned by the end of October. To live in Boston was to hear the fire bell hundreds of times over the course of your life, and to count yourself lucky indeed if it never tolled for you.[7]

So when the "bell rang for fire" around seven o'clock on the evening of November 3, 1818, a Tuesday, the frantic clanging can hardly have been surprising. Shocking, yes. Worrisome, certainly. But not surprising. Because Bostonians were old hands at fire. And because the knell, as they soon discovered, called them to a blaze on the topmost story of the Exchange Coffee House.[8]

Fire breaking out in the Exchange building was, in a word, overdetermined. The ground upon which the enormous building stood had burned in living memory, the whole of it in the Great Fire of 1760, a corner once again in 1767. And if the city had again and again proved itself flammable, the building—so tall, so extensive—appeared more so. Before the tower's doors had opened, Andrew Dexter's enemies had warned potential investors about the "risk of fire." Events had proven the Cassandras right. On the day after Christmas in 1813, a room in the building's north corner "took fire," and the eruption was quickly put out.[9]

Five years later, the Exchange remained "a monument of combustible materials," as one critic noted on November 11, 1818. The writer, a longtime enemy of the building and its backers, relished the clarity of hindsight. But it was hard to deny his point. When "the bells proclaimed the distressing catastrophe," the Exchange was stuffed—overstuffed—with wood and velvet and paper. And, of course, with domesticated flame.

November in New England: before the month was out, the ice would be thick enough to skate on. The night was cold, the building drafty. Fire brought warmth. At day's end, the Exchange's patrons were famished. Fire meant food. The sun set at four-thirty; the moon, a waxing crescent, wouldn't rise for hours. Fire made light. Well before the alarm bell rang, scores of fires were carefully, deliberately set throughout the building. Wood blazed in its thirty-two fireplaces, twenty heating stoves, five subterranean ovens, and beneath its twelve-burner cooking stove. Oil and candles flickered in the "multiplicity of lamps" that lit its rooms. Cigars and pipes by the dozen punctuated the conversation around the tables. The embers of the previous day's burnings smoldered in the ash hole beneath the cellar floor. Just like any other evening.[10]

Those were the real fires; never mind the Exchange's inflammatory history. Some of those most closely connected with the project had been baptized by fire. The press had branded Samuel Dexter an arsonist during the suspicious "bonfires" in the War and Treasury buildings at the end of the previous century. Samuel Gilbert and Thomas Dean had lost everything to fire in 1804, before they lost everything to the Exchange a decade later. They were not alone. Everyone caught holding the residue of Andrew Dexter's empire of paper had been burned. When the bell rang, some wondered *why?* And others, *What took so long?*[11]

❧

That the Exchange's death by fire was foreseeable—and foreseen—does not mean that patrons expected the conflagration on the evening of November third. The only bells ringing at six o'clock signaled the everyday happenings of the house: servants beckoned, meetings called to order, supper served. As it often did, the 'Change Floor stood empty. The Dancing Hall, too, was dark, since no grand public event was scheduled. (There had been none all month.) But as usual, the Reading Room was packed with men of commerce hunkered over the Marine Diary and the latest newspapers. And in the many rooms for rent upstairs, "a large number of citizens" convened in their "various societies." One of the Exchange's smaller assembly rooms housed members of the Boston Marine Society as they went about the ordinary business of their annual meeting: dispensing charity to the families of needy seamen, expelling three of their number for the nonpayment of dues, electing two others to serve as officers for the coming year. On the sixth floor, in the spectacular two-story theater they had built for themselves the year before, seventy or eighty of the Masons who comprised the Columbian Lodge awaited a visit from the Right Worshipful Thomas Power, Grand Master of another local chapter. As the brethren filed into the galleries projecting from three sides of the room, Joseph Jenkins, the Columbian's Grand Master as well as the architect of the great space, mounted the throne in the middle of the "superb altar" at the front.[12]

Three flights down in the Dining Hall, hotel guests gathered for supper. During the previous two years, under David Barnum's able stewardship, many of the "eminent characters" who passed through Boston had stayed at the Exchange. Tonight was no exception. Henry Clay, the Kentucky congressman serving as the Speaker of the House of Representatives, had taken rooms in the hotel for the duration of his visit to Boston. Clay had spent the afternoon in Salem and returned to the Exchange in time for supper. The men arrayed at nearby tables must have strained to overhear the famed orator. Around them swirled a constant rush of waiters, black and white, ferrying soups and roasts and wines from the cellar larders up the narrow stairs to table. A wholly ordinary night, in short, during which no one anticipated "what the next hour would bring forth." For none had yet sensed the fire "kindling . . . within the walls."[13]

Near seven o'clock—accounts of the exact time vary—the too-familiar smell of something burning drifted through the house. Someone—a Mason dashing up from the sixth floor? a servant carrying slops down from the seventh?—traced its source to the southwest corner of the topmost story: the Billiard Room, a gambling den whose presence in the Exchange was itself incendiary. By the time the long-simmering fire revealed itself, the room had "filled full of smoke." Flames danced between "fissures in the walls" and licked along the ceiling. Shouts of "Fire!" echoed throughout the building and onto the streets. A watchman walking his route—perhaps William Brooks, the constable who lived on Devonshire Street just south of the

Exchange—picked up the cry and rang the alarm on his handbell as he sped to the cupola of the Old State House. From there the tocsin announcing the Exchange's distress passed from belfry to belfry, moving outward in concentric circles. First the steeples of King's Chapel and the Brattle Square meetinghouse and the bell tower atop Faneuil Hall pealed the alarm. (The sexton of the church nearest the fire, the Old South, forbade the watchman from ringing its bell, a display of "officiousness" that would prove "ill-timed.") Then the Federal Street Church and the Holy Cross Cathedral and the New South and Park Street meetinghouses joined the choir, and on and on around Boston's twenty-odd houses of worship, until at last the sextons climbed the steeples of Asher Benjamin's West Church and Charles Street meetinghouses to ring out the news at the edges of the city.[14]

As the chorus of bells swelled into what one who heard them called a "general alarm," the scores of men who comprised Boston's fourteen engine companies—a mixture of artisans and laborers—ran to their firehouses. With a swiftness honed in monthly drills, they donned heavy leather hats and brass badges bearing the numbers of their companies, insignia that the town fathers believed promoted "order & other good effects at Fires" by distinguishing leaders from looters. They threaded long wooden poles through the handles of the dozen "painted & marked" buckets that the selectmen required each fire squad to maintain. They gathered the axes and saws and hooks and picks they might need to demolish a burning building, killing the patient in order to save it. Captains took the speaking trumpets through which they would bark orders over the din of the crowd and the bells.[15]

Most of all they readied their engines. Jacob Perkins, the Newbury-port inventor whose counterfeit-proof bank bills Andrew Dexter used to such effect, had patented a stronger, smaller engine pump in 1801, and its local manufacturer guaranteed that the new technology produced "engines . . . superior to any others ever made either in Europe or America." Boston owned one of these, as well as several others of recent vintage. Though the improved engines may indeed have been easier to use and less likely to freeze, as their promoters claimed, they remained essentially variants on a century-old design: wheeled wooden carts topped with a tub to hold water and a pump to expel it.[16]

The engines, old and new alike, relied on hand power at every turn. Harnessed like oxen, the members of a fire company dragged their machine from its storehouse to the fire. They rolled out spools of treated canvas hose, screwed them together to reach the desired length, and attached the base to the engine. Then some men pumped the long handles, or "brakes," at either end of the cart to speed water through the apparatus, while their brethren emptied buckets into its reservoir. The work was backbreaking and slow, the results uncertain. But despite their limits, these crude engines were better than none, and their captains gave them names that testified to their importance. Some—the Hancock, the Washington, and the Congress—recalled Revolutionary idols and ideals. Others immortalized the firefighters themselves. *Hero-Comes*, fire company number 6 named the engine they kept in west Boston. At major fires, Hero-Comes might stand beside Extinguisher, Endeavor, Eagle, Rapid, or Dispatch: fond labels that summoned hope against hope.[17]

*Hunneman Engine Number 39 ("Dexter"), ca. 1815.*

In addition to calling the municipal engine companies, the tocsin alerted members of the town's private fire clubs to the danger on Congress Street. Such groups had flourished in Boston since the mid-eighteenth century, with more founded each decade; by 1818, the town counted over a dozen. With names like Alert, Amicable, Attentive, and Vigilant, these associations promoted mutual aid among their elected dues-paying members. Unlike those who staffed the municipal fire companies, fire club members tended to be persons of parts, men who had amassed sufficient estates to make their safekeeping a priority. Until his creditors ran him out of Boston, Andrew Dexter had been a member of the Massachusetts Charitable Fire Society. Many of the Coffee House's current proprietors, including board chair Harrison Gray Otis, belonged to similar groups whose members would have vowed to defend the Exchange.[18]

Theirs was at once a civic and a self-interested obligation. As the Attentive Fire Society's 1810 constitution put it, the subscribers felt both "a sense of social duty, and the natural motive, self-preservation." Thus they pledged, in the event of fire, to protect property—*each other's* property, and only that. The Attentive, like most Boston fire clubs, convened quarterly in a tavern, where members strove "to blend *conviviality* with *duty*." Liberal applications of rum and stout took care of the former. Their "duties" included memorizing the best routes to one another's homes and businesses, inspecting the bags and buckets every clubman was required to maintain, electing new brethren (the Attentive insisted on a unanimous ballot), and reciting the "*watch-word* whereby we may know each other." When the clerk called on him, each member had to whisper the closely guarded password. Those who forgot it paid a penalty of twenty-five cents; those who shared it promiscuously were assessed twice as much. Amid the chaos of a fire scene, the watchword distinguished a member's "best endeavours" to save his fellow's goods from the "embezzlement of the same" by the opportunists who flocked to fires hoping to turn someone else's bad fortune into their good own luck.[19]

Flock they did. Before the firemen towed their engines to the scene, before the clubmen arrived with buckets in hand, hundreds of ordinary Bostonians heard the bells or spied the fire from their windows and "made all haste into State Street." Some came to help, others to gaze at the "flames bursting frightfully from the upper windows" of the Exchange. The tide of merchants and clerks surging into the plaza in front of the Old State House created an eerie nighttime parody of the noonday bustle on 'Change. John Gallison, a young lawyer who had just walked the three blocks from the Exchange's Dining Hall to his Court Square office only to go running back when he heard the bells and spotted the flames, called it a "great crowd."[20]

Despite the mounting excitement in the streets, the mood inside the building remained surprisingly calm. The first cries of distress had produced "confusion among the various boarders, visitors, and citizens in the several apartments." But their panic quickly turned to purpose, and by the time the frenzied ringing began, they had already started to beat back the fire.[21]

Those working to save the Exchange had much in their favor. Water was plentiful. For two centuries Bostonians had depended on the vagaries of the tides to battle fires. But in recent years, workers had fashioned at great cost a rudimentary system of underground wooden pipes and sluices linking Jamaica Pond to thirsty Boston. (The Aqueduct Corporation, chartered in 1796 to raise the funds and organize the labor for the immense public works project, made its headquarters in the Exchange's basement.) The fifteen-mile network extended from Dorchester all the way to Congress Street, stopping just south of the Exchange. From there the building's own "house aqueduct" put "a full supply of water within ten feet" of the fire. In addition, the Proprietors had seen to it that "numerous buckets were at hand" in the building, a sensible precaution for such an immense structure, one the city required for schools and some other public places.[22]

The Exchange had happy coincidences on its side as well. Lucky timing, for one. At seven o'clock, the fire caught nobody in bed, giving those inside the building every hope of escape and the engine men an excellent chance at a speedy arrival. Reasonably lucky weather, too.

No rain (which aided firemen more than the most powerful engine could), but not much wind (fire's most faithful ally). And lucky, especially, in the personnel on the scene. Scattered among the clubmen in the building that night were several of Boston's twenty-four fire wards. Like the members of private fire clubs, the fire wards typically had significant standing in the community. These were "prudent persons of known fidelity," as the law creating the post had put it back in 1711. In practical terms, this meant that they were merchants and skilled artisans, men more used to giving orders than to following them. Bolting from their tables, these experienced firefighters "immediately assembled on the spot" to direct the effort. Within minutes—"instantly," according to one of the first reports—they organized the denizens of the buildings into bucket brigades. Following centuries-old custom, rows of men faced one another, passing full buckets up one side of the line and sending empties back down the other. The queue must have snaked from the suction pump in the Exchange's basement all the way up the western staircase to the seventh floor. According to the newspapers, no one skirted his duty; Henry Clay himself "stood in the ranks to hand water" from man to man to man till at last it reached the flames.[23]

However efficiently Clay and the others moved the heavy leather buckets up and down the line, they knew that water tossed by hand was only a stopgap. But almost immediately the engines began to arrive, those stationed closest coming first, mimicking the order of the bells. And here, too, the Exchange was in luck. Housed two blocks south on Milk Street, engine number 14, the aptly named Cataract, held more water than any other in Boston. The directors of the Union Fire and Marine Insurance Company had imported this "large & valuable Fire-Engine" from England "at a considerable expense" in 1800, a generous gift to the city as well as a wonderful calling card for the insurance business, still in its infancy. Cataract's company was the largest in town as well. The treadles that primed its pump—side-mounted in the style favored in England and New York—were so long and cumbersome that the engine required forty-one men to operate it: twenty stationed at each side, plus one to direct the plume rushing through its water cannon. No sooner was the engine "drawn into the area" than they filled its reservoir and leveled the spray at the building's fifth story, much higher than water could reach without such a powerful pump, if still not quite high enough.[24]

The brigades formed, the engines manned, the water flowing, the hoses trained: no wonder the fire wards nursed "confident hopes . . . that small limits would be put to the destruction." And for a time, perhaps twenty minutes after the alarm first sounded, their confidence seemed warranted. A thorough drenching from the buckets snuffed the fire in the Billiard Room, prompting a "cheering cry of *all out*" that calmed the crowd outside. The tongues of flame licking at the roof died, and soon there was "no fire to be seen" from the street. "Many went away," Gallison wrote in his diary later that night, "supposing that danger past." The fire wards pronounced the blaze "not very alarming" and called off the alert. As quickly as they had started their chorus, "the bells ceased ringing." Much of the audience shuffled home, feeling the mixture of relief and disappointment that greets the spectacle denied.[25]

But those who lingered, as Gallison did, soon realized the show was just beginning. During the lull in the sound and the lights, the fire had continued quietly "working behind the partition walls, and round the cornices, in places beyond reach." Smoke thickened. The walls grew hotter, until the chambers bordering the Billiard Room alit. Flames burst from the rooms along the west wing of the attic story into the gallery overlooking the 'Change Floor a hundred feet below. Once the fire entered the atrium, it found all the fuel it wanted. Bright "columns of flame" incinerated delicate columns of wood. Soon the ferocity of the blaze drove those who had stayed to fight it from the seventh floor. Willard's grand spiral staircase echoed with frantic footfalls as people fled the upper stories ahead of the flames.[26]

From his post on State Street, Gallison sensed "much bustle within the house," and saw people "in difft parts" of the Exchange throwing open their windows "to avoid smothering," a sure sign that fire was spreading downward. He noticed "flashes of light, which seemed to come from the roof," evidence the fire was trending upward as well. Then flames everywhere at once, their "progress . . . inconceivably rapid." On the roof a "flash of light," followed by a "cloud of black thick smoke," revealed that the cheap mixture of tar, gravel, and paper that surrounded the dome had ignited. On the seventh floor flames suddenly "burst again with great fury from the windows." Then the sixth story was engulfed. And then "almost every part of the building," as discrete tongues of fire merged into "one sheet of the most vivid flame which we ever beheld."[27]

Not yet half an hour after the bells stopped ringing, the resurgent blaze had turned so violent and the smoke "so suffocatingly dense" that those assembled outside and those remaining within reached the same conclusion: "The building could not be saved." Heroic efforts to contain the damage had fallen short of their mark—literally so. The blaze had started in the Exchange's most "elevated spot," well "out of the capacity of fire-engines aided by mere human exertions to reach with effect." So with regret and resignation, the engine men declared human exertion futile and consigned the pile to the pyre. Thomas English, the bank clerk who served as the secretary of the Boston Marine Society, noted the moment in the club's minutes. "The House being on fire & no expectation of extinguishing it," he wrote, "the meeting is adjourned." Not yet eight o'clock, the second collapse of the Exchange Coffee House had become a foregone conclusion.[28]

The death of the fleeting hope that the Exchange would withstand the blaze only increased the frenzy surrounding it. The bells resumed their tocsin, their "peals of sonorous solemnity" now audible in nearby towns. ("When I got on deck," one midshipman aboard the U.S.S. *Independence* in the Charlestown navy yard told his brother, "my ears were saluted by the damndest noise, The Bells ringing, &c. &c.") Light from the conflagration traveled farther and faster than sound could reach. "The whole town of Cambridge was one blaze of light," wrote a young woman who recalled walking through the Exchange only a few days earlier, sure the "magnificent" building would endure for years. People in New Hampshire, Connecticut, and Maine—up to one hundred miles from the scene—detected a strange lightness in the dark November sky. From nearer towns, the fire's brilliance made it appear as if "the whole city was . . . involved in a general conflagration." One man visiting a sick friend on Poplar Street stayed put when he heard the bells, having been "frequently alarmed by trifles" before. But the strange "appearance of the light" convinced him there was indeed a fire, a big one, and he "hastened out" to find it. On Congress Street, "indeed almost throughout the town," Gallison wrote, the glare was blinding. One witness called it "unspeakable brilliancy." The thrill seeker who ran from his darkened room to witness the spectacle "could not but be startled for a moment at the unnatural day, into which he seemed to enter."[29]

Such reversals—backward-ringing bells, night turned "light as the brightest day," the heights of the Exchange brought low—mimicked the upside-down atmosphere in the streets. Spectators thronged the rooftops and windows of buildings close enough to offer a view of the action but far enough away to provide safe shelter. The crowd surrounding the building swelled into the thousands, a mixture of "every class of citizens": the curious and the purposeful, the young and the old, the rich and the poor, all packed side by side.[30]

Engine companies arrived from every ward of the city and beyond, streaming across the bridges and up the Neck, running and riding from Charlestown, Cambridge, Roxbury, Dorchester, and several other towns. (So many engines came from such great distance, the *Repertory* noted the Saturday after the fire, that "we cannot enumerate them at present without the hazard of error.") Military men stationed in the area showed up to lend a hand. Lieutenant William M. Hunter, a naval officer who lived on Belknap Street, brought the sailors who served under him aboard the *Constitution* to help keep the peace.[31]

Some armed themselves with spyglasses, the better to watch a fire they couldn't extinguish. Others prepared to memorialize the drama. Abel Bowen, an engraver with a shop next to the Exchange, brought either his sketchbook or a keen visual memory; the next morning, he printed a broadside bearing a woodblock "Representation of the Exchange Coffee-House in Flames." A member of the Columbian Lodge, the painter John Ritto Penniman, probably took a turn in the bucket brigade when flames broke out down the hall. As the gravity of the situation became clearer, he may next have helped to rescue his own large canvas, a landscape incorporating Masonic emblems that hung on the rear wall of the lodge. Once the painting was safe, Penniman trained his practiced eye on the burning building, cataloging colors and impressions for the renditions he would paint of the scene a year hence. Though many doubted the ability of words to capture the raw power of the spectacle, writers from the newspaper offices that ringed the Exchange brought their pencils, jotting notes for the reports they would run in their next editions.[32]

What the chroniclers witnessed was a frantic and courageous effort, the point of which was no longer to save the Exchange, but to spare the treasures within it from the furnace. People tarried in the building "as long as it was possible to remain," Gallison wrote, "even long after the hazard had become considerable from the falling of burning pillars." Working alone and in teams, they lugged mirrors and carpets and mattresses and boxes and pillows and chairs and washstands and the baggage that fleeing lodgers had abandoned. Using a bed key, the small iron hand tool that every firefighter kept at the ready, they dismantled the hotel's valuable bed steads and dragged the pieces outside. They rolled casks of liquor upstairs from the cellars. They stuffed their salvage bags—linen drawstring sacks a yard and a half long and nearly as wide—with crockery and clothing and bottled wines and glasses and decanters and whatever else would fit. They pried loose parts of the building itself; "even the glass doors & windows were taken out & removed," Gallison recalled. And then they passed these items, large and small, intact and damaged alike, from hand to hand through the crowd to be spirited off around the city for safekeeping. Bostonians practiced the steps of this salvage dance more often than they would have liked. Even so, the size of the Exchange and the opulence of its

"Fire on State Street Near Old State House,"
*detail from Massachusetts Fire and Marine
Insurance Company Policy, ca. 1804.*

contents made the occasion extraordinary, a film of the building's construction and furnishing run backward at high speed, projected against the November night.[33]

While the parade of singed furniture crept through the streets, the flames raged, feeding on the Exchange's ornate woodwork until "the greater part of the 210 halls, rooms, chambers, &c. comprized in the building, exhibited a mass of intense fire seldom witnessed." After the fire devoured the supports for the building's galleries, the collapse began in earnest. About nine o'clock—not two hours after the first plumes of smoke had been detected in the Billiard Room, just an hour after the building had been given up for lost—the roof caved in. The Exchange's "noble dome," the signature gesture that had transformed the city skyline, the subject of poetry and song, was reduced to a mass of burning plaster and white-hot metal. The fragments plummeted five stories before breaking through the 'Change Floor "with a frightful crash." Theophilus Parsons, a young lawyer who had stayed in the building with a handful of others all this time, was standing beneath the colonnade on the principal story when the dome came down. He told his friend Gallison "that the spectacle was truly sublime, the whole area being immediately filled with white flame." A college student outside the building recalled, even sixty years later, the way the shudder moved through the crowd. One Vermont farmer in the throng laughed ruefully. Nine years before, he had sold some cattle for Farmers' Exchange Bank bills, only to discover that the paper was worth less than magic beans. Over the din of the dome's crash, people heard him clap and shout, "There goes a fine pair of three year old steers!"[34]

As the Exchange's lower floors blazed, the last workers and witnesses quit the building to join the battle outside, no longer a battle to save property, but to save the neighborhood. The dome's collapse had removed the last barrier between the burning Exchange and the close-packed streets around it. Its roof and interior walls incinerated, the brick shell blazed like a "burning glowing furnace," Gallison wrote. Flame "poured out" from doors and windows and the gaping hole where the dome lately stood, giving the hollow tower "the elevation and brilliancy of a volcano." The breeze from the southwest picked up, sending a cloud of burning debris toward the water. To the *Galaxy*'s correspondent, these flaming cinders looked like "horizontal rockets," a nightmare image for a city that had feared destruction during the War of 1812. Homes and shops and warehouses along State Street, ships docked in Charlestown, even the city's powder store on Noddle's Island were bombarded with flakes of burning tar paper and chunks of the wooden balustrade that had ringed the Exchange's roof. Here and there—on a tarp covering a ship moored at a wharf in the North End, on roofs made of the same cheap "composition" material as the Exchange's had been—sparks "took fire," and were quickly snuffed out by vigilant owners.[35]

But the hazard of airborne debris was nothing compared to the threat looming on Congress Street, where the force of the dome's cave-in and the intensity of the fire made the collapse of the wounded giant all but inevitable. The Exchange's exterior walls were colossal, "immense double walls" of solid brick, over four feet thick at their base. The least of them, the building's northern elevation, spanned ninety-four feet along the street line. All four stood more than ninety feet high, at least three times as tall as the surrounding streets were wide. Suddenly the Exchange's longstanding design problem—the too-tall building on the too-small lot—spelled mortal peril.[36]

The walls quivered, "shaken to their foundations by the strength of the ravaging element which they appeared to confine." Fatally weakened, the building's northern and southern faces toppled simultaneously, bending, groaning, and then tumbling outward, away from the blazing core. Gallison missed the moment, "having gone to my office to dry myself" after becoming "wet in handing water" to the engine men. But he must have felt the vibration on Court Street: a "thundering crash upon the earth," as one newspaperman reported, that made the whole neighborhood tremble. Bricks and flaming beams pummeled the office buildings to the north of the Exchange, but most of the debris "crumbled down" into the lane between the Coffee House and its neighbors. "It is wonderful that it did not crush the building[s] it fell upon," Gallison noted. Pieces of the disintegrating southern wall staved in part of the tiny Friends Meeting House across Salter's Court. To the west the Exchange chiefly injured itself, flattening the attached row of stores along Devonshire Street to rubble.[37]

For a moment after the walls came down, smoke and dust cloaked the flames. But then the cloud parted, and "the illumination flashed wider and farther than before," revealing a startling sight. Though entirely "unsupported," as the *Boston Intelligencer* put it, the Exchange's eastern facade had survived nearly intact. This was the elevation Benjamin and Dexter had ornamented most elaborately, decorating the brickwork with a sextet of highly attenuated marble pilasters and a two-story Venetian window, capping the whole with a pediment that raised the wall's profile still higher above Congress Street. Silly architectural theatrics, many thought, especially when performed on such a narrow street. Now, for better or worse, those embellishments kept the wall aloft, marble bones holding up a sagging skin of brick. Unmoored, the wall vibrated, setting off tremors that the multitude gathered before it could feel in their feet. It buckled and swayed. The upper stories leaned a foot or more into Congress Street, tons of mortar and granite and marble virtually levitating. A concrete echo of Dexter's own downfall: how long could bricks stay afloat?[38]

By ten o'clock, all that remained of the Exchange was that wavering wall. But on all four sides of the former tower, fire continued "stealing along." The terror this situation would normally have inspired was further increased by the extraordinary value—and flammability—of the neighboring properties. The "riches of Congress, State, and Kilby-streets," as one reporter put it, seemed destined for the ash heap. *Paper riches*. As Andrew Dexter had known when he paid dear for the real estate beneath the Exchange back in 1806, this was Boston's paper district, a favored location for a coffeehouse. Every bank and insurance office in Boston lay "within a stone's throw" of the flames, one writer noted. As the fire raged, bank directors crated specie and notes to be carried out into the chaos. The town's printers and bookbinders, along with almost all of its newspapers, also adjoined the Exchange. The *Daily Advertiser,* the *Palladium,* the *Columbian Centinel,* the *Gazette,* the *Repertory,* the *Weekly Messenger,* the *Intelligencer,* the *Recorder,* the *Weekly Magazine:* all leased space on the east side of Congress Street, right in front of the swaying east wall. The *Patriot* and the *Chronicle* published from the Rogers Building, already damaged by the collapse of the northern elevation. It was easier to list the news organs that *weren't* at risk. "The offices of the Yankee and Galaxy were the only ones which escaped uninjured," wrote the reporter from the *Independent Chronicle,* whose own paper had not proven so lucky.[39]

On the east side of Congress Street a block of stores burned off and on for the next two hours. Some thought the "danger . . . too great to encounter," and declined to charge into the print shops and binderies. But despite the buildings' exceptionally flammable contents—reams of dry paper, stacks of urine-soaked sheepskins for cleaning type, vats of resin-based ink, cans of oil to lubricate the presses—and the added menace of the swaying wall, several fire companies working in tandem managed to preserve the entire row. To save the building that housed the *Palladium*'s offices, firemen ran a hose into the fourth story on the north side, and dragged another up a tree on the south. All the while, the *Gazette* later reported, courageous men "kept their stand in the garret," dumping bucket after bucket. (A full week later, the *Palladium* would be able to print its Tuesday edition "without other wetting than what it received during the efforts to extinguish the fire.")[40]

Next door, a flaming fragment of the Exchange wall set the Suffolk Insurance Building ablaze. For its rescue, Gallison credited "the intrepidity & perseverance" of an engine company from Charlestown, whose captain had made sure that his men "kept their ground." Gallison marveled at the men's courage, there at the foot of the "tottering wall that . . . seemed every instant about to crush them." But the Harvard-trained lawyer expected nothing less of these artisans and laborers. "Regardless of danger," he noted, "they are trained to work, & finally saved these buildings." Nearly fifty years later, one of the men who had battled the Exchange fire would recall this as "the hardest night's work of his life."[41]

Not all of the firefighters were as diligent. The Harvard College Fire Department, also on the scene, used their "'horrible and grotesque' regalia"—beat-up hats and ancient coats—as a disguise for the sort of "frolic which is so delightful to unregenerate man when youthful blood bubbles within his veins." Young Josiah Quincy, a member of the Harvard squad and the son of the man who would soon become Boston's first mayor, could not "remember that we ever rendered the slightest assistance in extinguishing a fire." Often, the college boys found "so many good reasons for stopping on the way" to a blaze that they "arrived after it was out." The Exchange burned long and fiercely enough that Harvard's "little tub" of an engine got there in time. But as Quincy admitted, the company only added to the "tumult and confusion of the night" before returning to the engine house in Cambridge to relive their exploits over mugs of the potent rum-and-molasses mixture known as black strap.[42]

It was not just among college boys that chaos trumped order. Local newspapers emphasized displays of vigor and valor that reflected "the highest honor of our citizens." But not everyone in the crowd behaved in quite so intrepid a fashion. As at every major fire, Boston's streets—too narrow to begin with—were clogged with people "led thither by no other motive than curiosity." The fire wards vented their "vexation" and "disgust" at gawkers whose "idle example" demonstrated "cold indifference" to their neighbors' cries and "mortifying disregard" of the city dweller's burden of mutual aid.[43]

No wonder the "streets exhibited one complete scene of confusion" that night, as an anonymous letter to the *New York Evening Post* held. "[H]undreds were running in all directions," their arms and wagons heaped up with "rich furniture, half demolished." The frenzy made it difficult to distinguish rescue from riot. Printers watched their presses "literally torn asunder," and their drawers of iron type—the largest fonts weighing 400 pounds or more—"carried into the streets in cases, galleys, forms, pages, &c." (The presses themselves, too heavy to move, were left to withstand the flames.) Ezra Lincoln, a printer burned out of one of the buildings that adjoined the Exchange on Devonshire Street, "lost a great part of materials, not only by the fire, but the mismanagement of those who attempted to save them." A stationer in the Suffolk Building saw his whole inventory carted off: bound and unbound books, sheet music, game boards, and chess pieces all scattered into the night. And as everyone knew, not all property landed back with its owners.[44]

In the end, the Exchange conflagration shared the antic quality of early-modern spectacles from hangings to elections to parades, rites of inversion during which social order was at once suspended and affirmed.[45] At moments, the assembled masses may well have resembled the idealized image with which the city of New York decorated the certificates appointing its firemen. In this exemplary scene the

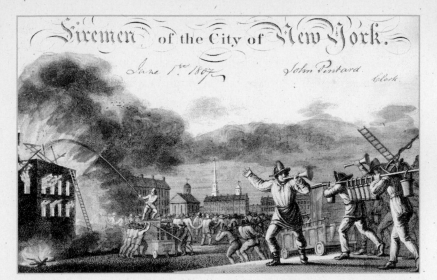

*Detail, certificate of membership,*
*"Firemen of the City of New York," 1807.*

crowd arranges itself in straight lines, a grid of humanity within a gridded city. Engine companies man their pumps with the precision of a corps de ballet. The arc of water projecting from their hose follows the incline of the tall-enough ladder, parallel lines running onward and upward to save property. Honest men stand face-to-face and hand in hand, feeding water to the engines. Closest to the viewer, the captain is plainly visible, his orders clearly heard through his speaking trumpet and carefully obeyed down the ranks. Even the buckets hang in lockstep, soldiers at the ready.

But at other points the spectacle looked more like the fire scene William Hogarth satirized in his 1762 political cartoon "The Times." The crowd gathers in knots. Civic leaders kneel and fawn. Bucket toters collide with looters. Water cannons cross streams, spraying firefighters, the ground, each other: everything but the fire. A dandy in cocked hat fiddles while the block burns. Bellows in hand, a man on stilts fans the flames. A beggar sleeps in the fire's warmth with her child, while a

The Times, *by William Hogarth, 1762.*

pickpocket ogles the easy mark. A look of grim determination on his face, a brawny man scuttling away with a wheelbarrow full of "rescued" papers becomes the most purposeful figure in the frame.[46]

In whatever blend the two moods coexisted on Congress Street, both the heroics and the festivities drew to a close around midnight. Five hours, start to finish, when the last of the flames burned out. The brightness of the "unnatural day" doused, night fell again, darker for the smoke that hung over the area. The half-light of torches and street lamps revealed the immense east wall, scarred and smoking. Otherwise, as Gallison wrote, "nothing was left of the Coffee House." The spectacle of the Exchange—a show that began in 1807—was over.[47]

∽

The sun didn't rise much before six-thirty, just ten hours of cold northern light separating gray dawn from inky night. Best set to it. At daybreak on Wednesday, the men and women of the neighborhood tackled the long work of "overcoming misfortune and effacing its traces" with the same gritty "resolution" they had used to fight the conflagration the night before. Draymen began the unbuilding, hauling away the heaps of rubble that now choked off Congress Street completely. (The bricks piled so high that men were still carting them off on Saturday.) A clear approach was needed for the day's most urgent task: pulling down that looming wall before it fell on its own.[48]

Dismantling the eastern facade was a "work of great difficulty and danger," the *Messenger* said. The selectmen entrusted the operation to a trio of skilled craftsmen: the housewright Ephraim Marsh teamed up with the younger and elder William McClennens, a father-son pair of boat riggers. Trained to outfit brigs and schooners, the McClennens applied their craft to the hulk of a giant land-ship, while Marsh brought years of practice in building a tight structure to the grim work of destroying one. Working with a large crew of laborers, they braced long wooden beams between the curb and the midpoint of the hulking wall, and then encircled the section above it with a lattice of cables and pulleys to catch falling debris and ease it to the ground. Coming after a day's suspended animation, the wall's long-delayed fall, around four that afternoon, was spectacular. Borrowing an apocalyptic image from Joseph Addison's *Cato,* the *Centinel* called it a "sublime 'wreck of matter.'" The following day, Marsh and the McClennens took down fragments of the north, south, and west faces of the building, all without injury to life or property.[49]

Which is remarkable, considering just how many people were milling about the area. As Wednesday wore on, the previous night's crowd reconstituted itself, its numbers in the thousands. The selectmen posted "peace officers" around the perimeter of the rubble pit to keep the masses at bay. Though the concern for public safety was surely warranted, this was hardly an idle mob. Taking stock and telling stories, they, too, were engaged in the work of recovery.[50]

At first it was *only* through word of mouth that Bostonians began to make sense of the calamity. Three newspapers normally published on Wednesday mornings, but their presses had been dismantled during the fire. (Even local papers printed later in the week show the extent of the disruption in an unusual number of misspelled words, inverted letters, and fonts out of sort.) In the absence of the press, people reverted to older and still powerful ways of spreading news: writing letters, posting broadsides, and telling tales. "Nobody did anything but talk about the fire and view the ruins," the painter Ethan Greenwood noted in his diary. When the papers resumed printing, their accounts followed the path of rumor. "*It is said . . . ,*" many articles began, adopting an Old Testament cadence well suited to the disaster.[51]

How had the fire begun? The blaze left behind nothing to betray its origins. In the absence of evidence, stories multiplied.

*It is said:* Gallison heard "many conjectures, as to the manner, in which this fire took." The "most probable," he decided, blamed "a defect in the kitchen chimney near the roof," where fire had erupted before. Others claimed that a lamp hanging in the room had ignited the curtains, or that a live coal tumbling from the heating stove had burned the carpet, which in turn kindled the room, and then the building, and then the block.[52]

*It is said:* Some accounts placed human bumblers on the scene. Writing anonymously, one Bostonian told the editors of New York's *Evening Post* that he'd heard "that a woman set the curtains of a bed on fire, and ran off and left it." He didn't *believe* the report, the correspondent stressed, preferring the version that faulted the kitchen chimney. Nonetheless he repeated the tale. Another letter printed in a Philadelphia paper offered a more troubling version. The conflagration began, the writer said, when a "man threw a glass of brandy into the fire." The liquor's vapors "blazed out" and ignited "some paper hangings in the room." Frightened, the "fools ran out, left the door *open,*" allowing fire to enter the corridor.[53] These were taller tales, and it can be no accident that they appeared far from Boston. The first was unlikely; all other observers agreed on the Billiard Room as the fire's point of origin, and the Billiard Room had not contained a bed. The second was demonstrably false; the Billiard Room had no fireplace. Neither was especially threatening. The stories blamed hapless serving women and drunken billiard players: hardly the incendiaries who had menaced Boston at various points in its history.[54]

*It is said:* It is easy to picture some of those who gaped at the ruins wondering aloud about arson. Writings that collected the rumors passing through the crowd offer tantalizing hints. Many remarked on the speed and intensity of the blaze. "The rapidity of the fire, under such peculiar circumstances," was nearly without parallel, the *Palladium* stated. A New York editor had heard that "the building and property were insured to an immense amount," enough to ruin the underwriter. Boston pressmen quickly countered the allegation, lest readers imagine that someone had burned the Exchange for profit. "The only insurance on the Exchange Coffee House," the *Gazette* insisted, was the ten-thousand-dollar policy a proprietor had taken with the Phoenix Fire Insurance Office. Others forcefully dismissed the possibility that the fire had been set. *"The fire, we are satisfied, was accidental,"* the *Centinel* maintained, setting the line in italics near the top of their story. When news of the blaze reached western New York State two weeks later, the *Palmyra Register* noted the competing accounts of "the mode in which it caught," adding that "no one, however, attributes it to design." If arson was whispered, it was not written.[55]

Where some came to gawk and many to gossip, others looked for ways to profit from the previous night's destruction. Part of the salvage operation was officially sanctioned, a business. Within days, the Exchange proprietors sold off the bricks that once formed the building's walls. Within the week, the *Palladium* reported, "numerous labourers were busy preparing them for use again." The owners also put the doors and windows "saved from the flames" up for auction, hoping for a small windfall to counter their huge costs.[56] Sometimes salvage lapsed into theft. Levi Merriam and Levi Brigham, owners of the wine cellar beneath the Suffolk Building, sought the person who had broken into their desk as it sat in the middle of State Street. They assured the thief that the five-dollar note he had lifted was a counterfeit and offered him "a good bill, with a little advice on how to dispose of it," if he returned the fake and their large Bible.[57]

Some of those sifting the debris were neither looters nor property owners, but scavengers hunting for anything they might use or sell. In nineteenth-century Boston as in all early-modern cities, poor families counted what they picked from the streets as a regular part of the household economy. Scavenging was traditionally a child's job. Boys as young as six or seven daily combed the alleys and docks in search of useful scraps. Seen through their eyes, the ruined Exchange was a treasure trove, more the glittering palace than it had been while it stood. Now the opulent materials had come down in the world to the point where they had a purpose, or at least a price. Iron mongers would buy old nails; coppersmiths would take bits of heat-twisted piping; glass manufacturers would pay for window and pot shards; scorched linens could be bundled for sale to paper makers. Chunks of the elegant woodwork that had ornamented the ballroom might now keep a poor family warm through the New England winter. Even ashes—there were plenty of those—had uses in the making of gunpowder and glass. In addition to their promise of cash, the ruins held small delights. The scattered contents of the various printing offices offered those combing the streets "a perfect harvest" of letter forms. Schoolboys made themselves "little printing offices," one writer remembered, using the dies they salvaged to strike off handbills saying whatever they could spell from their purloined "waifs" of type.[58]

Such childish joys notwithstanding, scavenging was a nasty and sometimes dangerous business. On Wednesday morning, twelve-year-old John Quilty was making his way along Devonshire Street, working at what the papers called "the very common but hazardous practice of picking up fragments of the ruins," when the rubble shifted beneath him. Pitched into the burned-out cellar of the building attached to the northwest corner of the Exchange, he landed chest deep in a barrel of beer that had been stored there. The beer, still boiling from the fire, scalded Quilty so badly that he died within hours. A "promising lad," the *Centinel* called the doomed boy.[59]

John Quilty's ghastly death gave the newspaper something useful, for melodrama featured death as well as destruction. At points, the news writers appear hungry for human tragedy. "That some personal injury has been sustained by individuals we think almost certain," the *Yankee* opined two days after the blaze, "for the exposure of hundreds was apparent." In this respect, the Exchange fire fell short. As the papers began to distill fact from rumor, it became clear that young Quilty was the fire's only fatality, and an indirect one at that. "It was said"—that familiar formula again—"that one man perished who was asleep in his room" in the Exchange, a Boston gentleman told the New York papers on November 4. But this proved untrue, as did tales that many had been "buried in the mass of the falling walls." Several papers strained to link the demise of the sixty-four-year-old Judge William Hammatt to the calamity. "He was at the fire on Tuesday evening, returned home, and was a corpse before the Exchange was burnt down," the *Centinel* reported, turning coincidence into cause. As if plucked from the pages of sentimental fiction, the boy ragpicker's horrible ending lent a welcome romantic flourish to an otherwise bloodless catastrophe.[60]

If lost lives were scarce, lost goods abounded. With the immediate danger past—the flames out, the walls leveled, the crowd again scattered—attention turned to missing objects. Wednesday's dawn broke over streets clogged with "deranged property," in the *Palladium*'s evocative phrase. Every yard and alley for blocks around was "filled with torn and broken furniture—bales, books, casks, papers, &c. a strange mixture." One correspondent saw "thousands of dejected countenances" as men picked their way through the muddle. The hunt took the searchers well beyond Congress Street. David Barnum, the Exchange's manager, discovered a few of his belongings nearly a mile away.[61]

Men who had exhausted themselves fighting the fire prepared for the next one by rounding up the equipment they had abandoned in the chaos. Lemuel Blake, an auctioneer with a shop across the street from the Exchange, sought the bucket bearing his initials. C. F. Knupfer, a member of the engine company stationed on Middle Street, had raced to the fire pulling the redoubtable Old North, and returned home without the salvage bag bearing his name and the logo NO. 1. The West India goods merchant Calvin Haven was missing both his bucket and his monogrammed bag, which he had last seen filled with rescued goods. Another man hoped to find the elegant frock coat of blue broadcloth and black silk, its "sleeves lined with bright olive," that he had stripped off in the heat of the blaze.[62]

Travelers boarding in the building when the fire broke wanted happy reunions with their luggage. Some knew just where they had stashed their property and found it quickly. By midmorning on Wednesday, Commodore Lewis, the Exchange lodger with whom John Gallison was visiting before the fire broke out, had recovered his trunks and sent them on to Hannah Delano's Beacon Street boardinghouse. Others were less fortunate. Two weeks later, Barnum had yet to identify the owners of four trunks he had pulled from the flames, one "a hair covered, square trunk, about two feet in length and breadth, iron bound—another is covered with black leather, and bound with iron—another covered with red hair and trimmed with brass nails—the fourth small and hair covered." Given Barnum's own considerable losses, the temptation to keep the boxes and their contents must have been powerful.[63]

People whose shops and homes had been stripped clean during the disaster searched for the articles they needed to resume their trades and their lives. George Manners, Britain's consul in Boston, had to recover diplomatic papers. Nathan Sawyer, a bookbinder whose Congress Street shop had been emptied, was missing "21 of Murray's Sequel, 2 Blair's Lectures, 1 Atala, and 20 Haydn's Creation, in an unfinished state," along with "a number of Backgammon Frames, containing several sets of Chequer Men." The men who printed the *Intelligencer* hunted for drawers containing the "upper and lower cases of Double-pica *Italic"* type, while the *Patriot's* editors had lost a collection of reference books. Humbler folk found themselves once again lacking some of the most basic materials of life. A young woman who boarded near the Exchange sought a bundle that may well have contained all her worldly possessions: her "Wearing Apparel, and one piece of Pellisse Cloth." Another family—one of many who continued to keep domestic animals in the heart of the growing city—wondered after the whereabouts of a small white pig that had taken advantage of the chaos surrounding the fire to wander off into the night.[64]

In a town encompassing tens of thousands of people but relatively few sources of fast, reliable information, it was difficult to match salvaged goods with their distraught owners. Some newspapers ran notices of lost or rescued property free of charge. Municipal officials tried to help, too. On the Saturday after the blaze, the fire wards called for "all persons that have taken charge of Goods of any kind" to bring them to Faneuil Hall, where their owners could find them easily. Still the process of recovery inched along. More than a month after the fire, Henry Fleury had not found the owners of the "2 pair Bellows— 3 Mahogany Framed Looking Glasses—1 piece Carpet—2 Band Boxes, containing a few articles, [and] 1 Glass Door" that had been dumped in his confectionery shop while the Exchange burned. Those still missing property worried, too. "Should any of the articles alluded to be offered for sale," one displaced printer urged readers of the *Independent Chronicle,* the would-be buyer should "detain" both goods and seller "and give due notice thereof." Just below numerous notices of thanks from people whose property had been saved from the flames, the *Gazette* printed a reminder of the "law relative to Fires in Boston": anybody who "takes charge of goods supposed to be in danger at such times, and does not report the same within two days" would be prosecuted as a felon. Finders should not appoint themselves keepers.[65]

As fall edged toward winter, it became ever clearer that much of what disappeared during the conflagration would never be recovered. Looters had kept some of the spoils for themselves, and fenced other goods into the black market that had flourished in the town since before the Revolution. But fire had claimed the great bulk of what was lost that night, a tally Bostonians continued to refine.

For the first time since 1809, reckoning the Exchange's accounts became public sport. Estimates ranged widely and changed often. Manager David Barnum was widely seen as the night's "great loser," having seen "all his expectations blasted in a moment." Little of the elegant furniture he had purchased for the house survived, a loss amounting to perhaps $16,000. Between $5,000 and $8,000 worth of wines and other provisions for the larder had been consumed, some by the flames and some, no doubt, by the crowd. A New York newspaper alleged that Barnum's cash box, stuffed with $4,000, had gone missing as well. But Boston news sheets disputed that, and also dismissed reports that he "had effected an insurance on part of his property": details that could make a cynical reader suspect that Barnum had somehow used the fire to cover illicit gain.[66] The Masonic brethren—including some of the housewrights and bricklayers who had built the Exchange—saw their fortunes devoured by the building for the second time. Along with Penniman's painting, the lodges had preserved their "jewels, regalia and records," but fire took the master's chair and much else of value, property worth roughly $3,000.[67] And so on around the building; every office destroyed, every tenant suffering. "Nine tenths of every thing taken from the house was ruined," one witness told New York's *Evening Post*. Boston pressmen deemed this an exaggeration, but not an outright lie. The rescue effort had been "ardent and persevering," but ultimately "not so successful," the *Gazette* conceded. So many and splendored were the "valuable articles" housed in the Exchange that the *Centinel* deemed it "impossible to estimate the extent of the loss." But when the ledgers were totaled, the balance would clearly be negative.[68]

In the end, most of the recovery work consisted not of discovering profits, but of counting losses, a process that neatly mirrored the history of the Coffee House. Barnum had lost both his job and his home, as had the scores of "domestics" who worked and lived at the Exchange. The fire left others hungry; as many as fifty poor families lived on what the Coffee House threw away, their tables piled daily with what Mrs. Barnum and her staff reclaimed from the trash pile. The list of individual victims reached into the hundreds.[69]

The most glaring deficit was the sudden absence of the Exchange itself, as much an insult to the town's psyche as to its skyline. Struggling to evoke the drama of the change, the *Yankee*'s correspondent cribbed from Prospero's soliloquy near the end of Shakespeare's *Tempest*. "Those 'cloud capt towers' which were yesterday the pride of our town," he wrote, "and which seemed as permanent as the foundations on which they stood, have disappeared like the enchantment of a dream." A decade earlier, Nathan Appleton had used the passage to warn that Andrew Dexter's "airy stuff" would soon "vanish like the 'baseless fabric of a vision.'" Now bricks had followed Dexter's paper into thin air.[70]

The Exchange was irreplaceable, the *Yankee*'s reporter lamented. "Never again will Boston contain a building of such much general utility and of so great ornament. The profits . . . would afford too little inducement to re-invest the capital." As surely they would. In fact, given the building's limited success, some wondered exactly what had been lost, especially when they remembered the flimsy foundation upon which it had risen. The costs of the fire would ultimately be reckoned in ethical as well as in economic terms. The defunct Exchange would serve as a potent reminder that markets and morals were never far apart.[71]

⁕

For months after the fire, the "melancholy pile of ruins" that had lately been the Exchange Coffee House continued to draw "crowds of spectators," especially during the enforced idleness of Boston Sundays. There was not much to see: a pit roughly a third of an acre across and two stories deep, choked with rubbish not worth selling for scrap. A "wide and silent space of dessolation," the *Intelligencer* called it, a "tomb" filled with "relicks," yet offering no hint of resurrection. And still people came in droves, behaving not unlike the "large flock of pigeons belonging to the establishment . . . yet seen whirling around the ruin."[72]

A simple homing instinct moved the pigeons, which had once been kept in a dovecote atop the fourth story of the Coffee House's privy. Rudely displaced, the birds knew no other roost and so proved "unwilling to forget the place in which they enjoyed so much plenty."[73] What fascination the charred plot of ground held for the good people of the town is more complex. Certainly *they* were not homing. Few of them had patronized the Exchange while it stood. Most could not, in any real sense, actually miss it. Instead, they were thinking through the ruins. As the *Gazette*'s correspondent noted, the imploded Exchange contained "many hints for the consideration of the public." The detritus on Congress Street amounted to a gigantic memento mori: a place to ponder the fleeting nature of existence and to learn more pressing lessons as well. And so crowds continued to gather at the edges of the pit, hoping to add its wisdom to their own.[74]

To the practical-minded, the ruined building and its wrecked contents testified to the need for better crowd control. The chaos around the burning Exchange offered proof positive that more must be done "to preserve order among the idle spectators" who flocked to disasters. The *Gazette* suggested that not only ordinary constables, but their superiors—the superintendent of police and his deputy—be "required to attend" such occasions, holding aloft staffs of office to indicate their power to enforce the law. A board of auxiliary fire wards might be created as well, and charged with supervising "all property removed from places on fire or in danger."[75]

The destruction on Congress Street also demonstrated that Boston needed more fire wards—half again as many, some argued. (Eventually the selectmen settled on a total of thirty, an increase of 25 percent.) And its engines needed longer, better hoses. One of the first engine men to reach the Exchange fire remarked that "had it been possible for him to have obtained a *hose* ten or twelve feet longer than the one he made use of, the flames would have been extinguished with ease." At the very least, hose couplings should be standardized so that shorter pieces might be readily linked. "Had this method been adopted," the *Gazette* opined, "the magnificent pile which now forms a melancholy heap of ruins, would have still remained the pride and ornament of our capital."

The town acted quickly on these proposals. Meeting the week after the blaze, the fire wards directed the engine builder Ephraim Thayer to inspect the hoses and screws at every firehouse in the city, and to report back about "how many of the same are not constructed to connect." The selectmen also provided each fire company with ninety feet of hose, lines far longer than those used against the Exchange fire.[76]

Longer, but not long enough. Not even ninety feet of hose could have reached the heights of the former tower. Others beholding the ruins concluded, quite reasonably, that the fault rested less with too-short hoses than with too-tall buildings. The most profound lesson to be gleaned on Congress Street was a history lesson, one less banal than Wordsworthian reveries (*"How vain are the works of man!"* and all the other *sic transit glorias* circulating in the press), and less urgent than patching the gaps in Boston's infrastructure. Those who read backward from the building's violent death, through its brief, tenuous life, to its inglorious beginnings found morals as old as the Greeks and as relevant as the day's news: morals about ascent and its price.[77]

For a time, the losses sustained in the fire made drawing attention to what the *Gazette* called "the origin and early difficulties which occurred in this establishment" seem churlish. But the building's shocking disappearance could not long obscure the plain fact that many in Boston had despised the Exchange, and for good reason: they had paid the price of its first implosion long before they witnessed its second. "The erection of this hotel was the unsuccessful project of an individual," the *Intelligencer* noted four days after the fire. By the time the scheme failed, the building had cost the projector—"and through him the public"—over a half million dollars. Styling himself "Caution," another writer insisted that compassion for the "unfortunate sufferers" in the blaze should not keep people from reading the ruins—which might, after all, have been far more extensive. Had it broken out after midnight, or had the November winds fanned the flames, the conflagration might have been "as destructive in its ravages, as an eruption from Mount Vesuvius." If Boston were to avoid the fate of Pompeii, the town should not trust fickle fortune a second time.[78]

Caution argued for stricter building codes. Henceforth the town should not permit "such huge elevated edifices to be erected," he proclaimed. But the Exchange's collapse should prompt Bostonians to reexamine their *moral* codes as well. *Elevated*—Caution used the word five times in his commentary—meant tall, of course, a building high enough to crush its too-close neighbors. Elevated also meant grandiose, decadent. A "modern Babel," he labeled the building, as others had called it a decade before. Elevated meant unmoored, floating, meant *baseless*, to use Prospero's word. The Exchange had been "founded on injustice," not solid ground, Caution recalled. The tons of brick and marble entombed on Congress Street "arose on the ruins of many industrious citizens." Elevated meant *inflated,* puffed up, aching to fall. The Exchange "at first cost upwards of 600,000 dollars," he wrote, but the "rapid depreciation" of its paper foundation had reduced its worth by two-thirds before the building opened. Between the cost of bricks and the worth of paper lay illusion. The bank bills that had paid for the place had "less value . . . than the rubbish now lying in the cellar of the building." The wreckage heaped ruin upon ruin. The higher they rise, the harder they fall.[79]

Look and remember, Caution cautioned. But many of the pilgrims who flocked to the ruins could not recall the Exchange's first demise. Boston had changed so much in the intervening decade, weathering lean times during Mr. Jefferson's embargo and Mr. Madison's war (as the Federalists who clung to control of the town's shifting politics called those events) before regaining a tenuous prosperity after 1815. As it revived economically, the city had grown physically. Bostonians continued to raise new land from the tidal flats and to raise new structures upon the acres it stole from the sea. A number of imposing public buildings—many of them designed by Bulfinch—had gone up since the Exchange had simultaneously risen and fallen back in 1809, and now loomed high above the ruins. These new monuments to God, Mammon, and the state eschewed the delicate tracery of the Federal style. Made of granite rather than brick, their exteriors appeared weighty, fortresslike: austere surfaces that projected power and, not incidentally, a determination to withstand the urban plague of fire.[80]

The city was filled with new faces as well as new buildings. Between 1810 and 1820, Boston's population had increased almost as rapidly as New York's and Baltimore's. The town counted fewer than thirty thousand inhabitants when the Exchange rose; over forty thousand lived in the city that watched it burn. Thousands who called Boston home in November 1818 hadn't yet arrived there in 1809; just as many who knew Dexter's Boston were long gone by the night of the fire. Some had moved out to the burgeoning "suburbs" of Brookline, Cambridge, and Somerville. Others, tired of being poor and crowded and cold, had bet on easier lives and cheaper lands in the West. Still others, of course, had since died.[81]

But don't exaggerate the impact of the years. Like the Vermont farmer with his dark, self-deprecating joke, many who contemplated the rubble-strewn pit on Congress Street clung to what Hanover's *Dartmouth Gazette* called "*Farmers' Exchange Bank* memory": they still felt, in more and less tangible ways, the crush of that moment in March 1809 when the monumental building had dissolved into a mountain of paper. That legacy didn't breed charity—to the contrary. "Awful as was the catastrophe," one Boston editor recalled in 1872, "there were many others amongst us who richly enjoyed it."[82]

For the artisans and laborers who had worked on the Exchange, the ruins inspired less melancholy than Schadenfreude. As the *Chronicle*'s Caution proclaimed, some "credulous tradesmen" still held the "fallacious promises" foisted upon them a decade before. Carpenters and masons would never recover the time and skill they had exchanged for wisps of worthless paper. "If ever the Exchange Coffee House should get fire," a prescient mechanic had mused before the conflagration, "rather than take a hand to save it, I'd take a pair of bellows and blow the flames." Some of them might have done so.[83]

The brokers Samuel Gilbert and Thomas Dean, who had swapped good bills for bad back then, felt fortunate to be off the hook this time. The *Gazette* called the pair "the greatest sufferers" of the building's difficult early years. In the spring of 1815, broken by the debts they had incurred owning and managing the Exchange, Gilbert and Dean had sold their interest and moved their offices into the Old State House. Luckily—and these lottery ticket sellers still trafficked in luck—they now held no interest in the defunct Exchange, "beyond that of good wishes." Near enough to have watched it burn, the two must have viewed the ruins many times, marveling at their late, happy turn on fortune's merry wheel. One of Samuel Gilbert's sons felt less charitable. After the fire, he was heard to remark, "I am glad that building is down. I have never been able to bear the sight of it."[84]

The sight of the Exchange standing proud inspired more mixed feelings in Nathan Appleton. He had loathed the building's paper double; his enmity for Dexter's banking empire was largely responsible for the building's first collapse, back in 1809. The tower, too, he labeled a "consummate folly": a ludicrously *fixed* ending for a dream of endless circulation. Yet Appleton couldn't help but find the building useful. He paid the five-dollar annual tariff that admitted gentlemen to the Reading Room. Information was a form of currency to the merchant, and the Reading Room offered more of it, in more timely fashion, than anyplace else. Plus, Appleton could easily afford the fee. He had dealt fairly, invested with care, and earned a reputation for unwavering honesty that was itself a sort of capital. He had been canny, but also lucky, managing by accidents of timing to prosper in trade even when the economic tides ran against him. By the time the Exchange burned, he had amassed what he called "a moderate property": over two hundred thousand dollars, enough to vault him into the town's richest decile.[85]

Appleton deemed this moderate fortune sufficient to his equally "moderate desires" and prepared "to retire altogether from business," following a script now generations old. That he had stayed in the game, and ultimately "gone further," was, he later said, "altogether accidental." But accident profited him again. After the War of 1812, he joined forces with a small group of New Englanders bent on making rather than importing cloth. When the Exchange caught fire, Appleton was well on his way to reinventing himself as an industrialist. The cotton milled by his manufactories in Waltham and Lowell was heavy stuff, less refined than the delicate lawns that came from India, but much more durable. Sturdier, too, than the "baseless fabric" of paper money, toward whose reform Appleton continued to work. In 1818, he became one of the largest shareholders of Boston's new Suffolk Bank, which met initially in the Exchange Coffee House. The directors soon appointed him to a committee to consider the still-urgent question of country paper. The resulting "Suffolk System" of deposits and exchanges smoothed out the inequities among New England's various currencies over the next thirty years. But it did not rationalize the system to Appleton's satisfaction. Common wisdom held that "the banks are all tied together, like a pile of bricks, and that the strong ones must hold up the weak ones," he wrote in 1856. The analogy was all too apt, he pointed out; banks "may as easily *fall* as a pile of bricks."[86]

Appleton didn't watch the pile of bricks fall on Congress Street that November night. (An accident the previous month had left him temporarily unable to walk.) Still, he rode occasionally to his store, and the route from his Beacon Street mansion led him past the ruins every time he did so. Later in his life, Appleton wrote a great deal about currency and banking, and he remembered his early battles over the Exchange. He memorialized his little war against the country banks twice, in a pamphlet he published in the 1830s and again in the notes toward an autobiography he wrote shortly before his death. But aside from a fleeting mention that Dexter's "enormous pile" had since been "destroyed by fire," Appleton didn't make much of the building's passing. Whether his former enemy's second great fall delighted or saddened him, or whether Appleton had grown simply too rich to care, is anybody's guess.[87]

Fortune had lately been crueler to Asher Benjamin, the building's architect. He, too, lived in Boston when it fell, a couple blocks and a world away from the Appleton mansion he had built in 1808. Benjamin was thirty-six when the Exchange opened, which would turn out to be both the halfway point and the high-water mark of a long and strenuous life. The tower was his most ambitious building when it went up in 1809, and remained so when he died, close to his Connecticut Valley birthplace, in 1845. Yet the grand commission seems only to have reduced Benjamin's stature as an architect.

The before-Exchange half of Benjamin's professional life traced a steep and mostly linear ascent. He arrived in Boston around 1802, possessed of little capital and trailing an equally modest reputation. By 1809, he had planned eleven of the town's buildings, including mansions for prominent merchants and four churches as well as the Exchange itself. After completing the Exchange, Benjamin never again designed a public building in Boston, neither did he build so much as a house there until 1821. Before the Exchange, his small, carefully husbanded fortune climbed steadily, more than quadrupling between 1803 and 1809. After the Exchange, his net worth stagnated. When the building burned, he owned roughly what he had when it opened. Six years later, he was destitute.[88]

Asher Benjamin didn't go broke for lack of scrambling. After the Exchange, Bostonians knew him as a supplier to the building trades more than a practitioner of them. A year after Dexter absconded, Benjamin opened a paint store on Broad Street, just across the road from Nathan Appleton's countinghouse. For the next decade and a half, he ran the business alone, eking out a modest living selling pigments, brushes, and glass, and working odd jobs for his wealthy landlord. Like Andrew Dexter, Benjamin continued to make paper his métier even while he abandoned bricks. After 1809, Benjamin added five successful builders' guides to the two he had published before. Carpenter to architect, artisan to gentleman: that had been Benjamin's path before the Exchange. Author, shopkeeper, handyman, bankrupt: Benjamin became in the years thereafter a jack-of-all-trades more than a master of one.[89]

Imagine, then, the depth and complexity of his feelings when the building burned. Seven o'clock on a Tuesday evening: just past the end of a storekeeper's working day. Benjamin would have been closing up shop two blocks east of the Exchange when the bells started. That was close enough not only to hear the alarm and see the light in the night sky—people for miles around did that—but also to *feel* the fire, to gag on the smoke and dust, to sense the earth shake when the dome caved in. As flaming debris drifted across Broad Street, Benjamin must have regretted the loss of his grandest creation on Congress Street. But surely he was more concerned with keeping his modest paint store safe from the Exchange. He would not be burned by Dexter's folly again.

Two weeks after the fire, the town asked Benjamin to play an official role in the building's deconstruction. Deeming Marsh and the McClennens' charges for pulling down the walls "unreasonably high," the selectmen appointed Benjamin to a committee of three charged with arbitrating the matter. The rigger and the mason—who had put forth the initial list of a dozen names from which the selectmen chose their troika—may have assumed that Benjamin's affinity with their trades, not to mention his own long experience with the Exchange building, would help their case. (None knew better how thick those walls had been, or how formidable the task of dismantling them.) But if they hoped Benjamin would support their account of the job's value, he disappointed them. The committee knocked down Marsh's fee by ten dollars, the younger McClennen's by twenty dollars, and charged both for materials they had billed to the town. Even the cost of getting rid of the Exchange, Benjamin seemed to think, proved inflated.[90]

Benjamin Austin's feelings about the building were anything but mixed. He loathed the place. He hated its politics with a vehemence that only an old-school republican—a man who still proudly sported his three-cornered hat nearly fifty years after the Revolution—could bring to this temple of the "high flying federalists." He hated its economics, both its origins in the kind of rapacious speculation against which he fulminated often, and the scenes of "Exchange Alley traffic" that daily unfolded within it. And he hated the building personally as well, as the embodiment of the Dexter family. Once they had fought on the same side, the Dexters and "Old South" (with "Honestus," one of Austin's favorite self-congratulatory pseudonyms). In 1793, Samuel Dexter had represented Austin in a lawsuit against the Federalist printer Benjamin Russell, who had spit in his face one day on 'Change. (People had strong reactions to Austin.) Dexter had prevailed, but the price the court attached to Austin's wounded honor was so low that he might have been better off losing. Ever since, Austin had hounded Dexter though the pages of the *Chronicle,* casting him as "a wicked and abandoned man" who "prostitut[ed] his professional powers" on behalf of murderers like the man who slew Austin's son at high noon upon 'Change in 1806, and "defrauders of the public revenue," like Dexter's nephew Andrew.[91]

Austin was sixty-six when the Exchange took fire. But the debilities of age didn't prevent him from scaling the heights to watch the building burn. Amid the tumult outside the Exchange, Austin met a friend who rented an office in the Old State House and kept a key to that building's roof door. Deciding they "could be of no service to the sufferers"—a doubtful proposition—the two men headed off. They walked up the Old State House's hallowed front stairs and climbed 123 steps into its windowed cupola, and then out onto the walkway around the tower's topmost level to get "an uninterrupted view of the . . . . grand and awful scene." The "heat was so intense," Austin's friend wrote, "that occasionally we were obliged to turn from it." Austin would not turn from what he saw as the evening's stern moral. The building had been "conceived in sin," he remarked, and "brought forth in iniquity, but it is now purified by fire." Like those who had called for a dose of Puritan rigor when Dexter's paper empire collapsed, Austin saw the fire as more than an earthly comeuppance. This was retribution on a cosmic scale: a republican god's verdict against the *"wild goose chase"* of unfettered capitalism.[92]

Let the romantics wax rhapsodic about the departed building. Benjamin Austin, Asher Benjamin, Nathan Appleton, Samuel Gilbert and Thomas Dean, and many others who gathered around the pit on Congress Street knew otherwise. To stare into the abyss the Exchange left behind was to witness a double negative: the loss of loss.

# SIX

# PROMETHEUS

*In one of the* small mercies of an otherwise bleak middle age, fate spared Andrew Dexter the sight of the Exchange Coffee House in flames. His family surely saw the wreckage. About a year before the conflagration, Charlotte Morton Dexter and the couple's three children—Alfred (aged nine in the fall of 1818), Sophia (six), and young Samuel (just three)—had returned from their long exile to the Morton family home in Dorchester. There Charlotte enjoyed the "kind protection & hospitable roof" of her "dear Parents" while she waited for her husband to send word that the wilderness where he had lived since August 1817 was sufficiently civilized for women and children. If she wrote to Andrew with news of the calamity on Congress Street—no correspondence between them survives—it would have taken her letter months to reach him. When the Exchange burned, Andrew Dexter was hard at work carving out a new life on a high red bluff above the eastern bank of the Alabama River.[1]

The route from New England into the heart of the burgeoning southwest ran over twelve hundred miles, a "long & arduous Journey," as Charlotte Dexter noted when at last she embarked upon it herself. It had proven especially so for Andrew Dexter, whose path southward began in Canada. Run out of Boston during the banking debacle of 1809, the family spent three years in Nova Scotia, going from small town to small town a step ahead of creditors searching for "the notorious Andrew Dexter, jun." By early 1811, they had moved across the Minas Basin from Windsor to River Philip, a tiny inland hamlet without a single public building. There Dexter tried his hand at refining one of the only commodities the harsh land brought forth in abundance: gypsum, a soft mineral used for fertilizer and plaster making. Richard Cunningham, the new husband of Charlotte's sister Sarah, grew rich quarrying Nova Scotia gypsum, and likely brought his brother-in-law into the trade. But Dexter lacked the capital to make a go of it, and soon added another small failure to his earlier spectacular one.[2]

In the summer of 1812, with Britain and the United States once again at war, the Dexters quietly made their way to Athens, New York, the village where Andrew's father, his brother Simon Newton, and a cousin, one of his uncle Samuel's sons, had recently settled. About thirty miles south of Albany, Athens was an Indian community turned Yankee river town. Its native inhabitants had favored the pathway that traversed the land from north to south across its hilly middle, but the Anglo-Americans who began colonizing the region in large numbers in the late eighteenth century turned their energies toward the Hudson, which bordered the town along its eastern edge. (Just across the river lay Hudson City, from whose quarries Andrew Dexter had procured some of the white marble that ornamented the Exchange Coffee House.) Founded during the land boom of the 1790s, the town had originally been called Esperanza, a hopeful name that suited its ambitious denizens. When Andrew and Charlotte and their growing family arrived—their daughter, Charlotte Sophia, was born there in late October—the little village was booming. Nearly a thousand townsfolk packed themselves into the 150 or so houses that comprised the newly rechristened Athens, which also boasted three schools, several manufactories, and a thriving dockside.[3]

In this small pond, the Dexter family had established themselves as big fish. Simon Newton Dexter owned some three hundred acres in the village when his brother Andrew got to town. Their father, the elder Andrew Dexter, laid claim to more than five hundred acres of this fertile Hudson Valley land, a country estate worthy of a gentle-man farmer. Surrounded by the trappings of a modest luxury—a chaise that bore him regally through town, some silver tea equipage that allowed him to serve visitors in refined style, and an enslaved black child who did some of the work of the estate while embodying his owner's alleged mastery—Andrew Sr. spent his days like a would-be biblical patriarch, fretting over his flocks and herds and bondsman.[4]

Andrew Sr. fretted as well over his fallen namesake. Several times in the years after 1812, the prosperous father staked his eldest son to a new start. Following the dictates of New York's 1811 insolvency law, he auctioned his son's goods and disbursed the proceeds among the many people with claims against Andrew Jr. Beyond the right to redeem ornaments Dexter had commissioned but not paid for at marble quarries around New England, there was little of value to dispose of. Those who attended the first sale of Andrew Jr.'s property, held at Andrew Sr.'s home in September 1812, pored over the tattered remnants of a genteel life: a few bits of furniture, some clothing, a watch and watch fob, a necklace and earrings, a "painting box," and some empty trunks. Even the family Bible went on the block. At a second auction eighteen months later, the offerings were meager. Some clothes and a desk, two blankets and a plated tea set, a crowbar and an ax: the sale can't have raised much. The elder Dexter must have helped the younger to acquire the eighty acres he held in Athens, enough for a modest homestead. And despite the son's reputation for paper profligacy, his father loaned him money as well, more than $1,280 by 1816.[5]

During those years, Andrew Jr. worked tirelessly—with "restless activity," as one memorialist later put it—to recover his brief early prosperity. On his father's land, he cut the old-growth white pines that commanded great value as ships' masts. He farmed, partly as a gentle-man interested in the ennobling effects of rural pursuits, partly as a poor debtor interested in eating. Ever the champion of building materials, he invested in limestone quarries in New York State. With Charlotte, he founded an academy, a private secondary school that opened a doorway to ambition for the uncultivated youth of Greene County, New York.[6]

Only the last of these many short-lived enterprises leaves even a trace in the archives, thanks to the faithful, pleading correspondence of the long-suffering Charlotte Dexter. Like many young women of her day—though relatively few of her class—she taught in the school, likely driven by the couple's continuing financial pressures to take up employment that few genteel mothers would have sought. To her "dear Pupils" she imparted the usual lessons for young ladies of distinction, including instruction in religion, belles lettres, and dancing. Refinement wasn't easy to come by this far up the Hudson. "We have a great difficulty in procuring a dancing or french master," Charlotte told her sister in 1815, wishing that a "*first rate* dancing master" might be found in Boston and shipped north. For the urbane, sensitive Charlotte, Athens was a wooded exile made bearable only by letters and visits from Boston. "I have been much disappointed at not having received a reply to my last letter," she chided her "dear Mama." Since "it constitutes so great a share of my happiness to have constant communications from home," she went on, "I cannot feel otherwise than anxious, at such repeated disappointments." Although she told her sister Frances that village life was "pleasant," Boston remained "home," and Charlotte mourned "the friends of whose society I am deprived." For solace she turned to religion, "preparing for another world" since she had learned that "no object in this world . . . can afford lasting happiness." She conveyed the same message to her students, invoking "the unfortunate situation into which I have been called to act" when she urged them to focus their sights on "*the world to come.*"[7]

Despite all the capital she brought to her marriage—her great beauty and high birth and fine education—*this* world had not been kind to Charlotte Dexter. Alongside her husband she scrambled, working with her parents to help him pay off his creditors. "Andrew says his affairs cannot be settled without the Vermont Land papers," she told her mother in 1813. "His assignees are anxious to procure the[m] & he would thank you to send them by Newton."[8]

Year upon year, such attempts to free Andrew Dexter from the hole he had dug for himself came up short. His father loaned him what and when he could, but the years took their toll on the old man. In early 1816, Athens town fathers declared the sixty-seven-year-old Andrew Sr. non compos mentis and appointed a "Committee of Lunacy" to supervise his affairs. Young Andrew's erstwhile Boston lending network couldn't do much on his behalf, either. Perez Morton had money troubles of his own, largely thanks to his son-in-law. And partisan warfare consumed ever more of Samuel Dexter's time after he broke with the Federalists by supporting the War of 1812. As always, Andrew Jr. struggled to help himself. But as one of his descendants later reflected, "fortune continued to frown upon his efforts and to withhold that golden crown which is seldom awarded unless as the meed of perseverance in a single pursuit."[9]

On the last day of April 1816, with spring finally warming New England, Samuel Dexter took the steamboat up the Hudson to attend the wedding of his son, and to visit his nephews and console his suffering older brother. No sooner had he arrived in Athens than he fell ill with scarlet fever. He died within the week, too fast, too healthy, and too young to have made a will. At his death, Samuel Dexter owned a house in Boston and a farm in Westborough, more than two hundred law books and nearly as many Merino sheep, along with other worldly goods whose total worth came to nearly $44,000. The most valuable single item in his ample estate was a sheaf of paper: $24,742.20 in "Mississippi Stock," the certificates that the federal government awarded to the Yazoo claimants in 1814, after nearly twenty years of litigation.[10]

Andrew Dexter Sr. died that November, barely six months after his younger, richer, more famous brother. He, too, left an estate made of paper. Over 90 percent of his personal property consisted of notes of hand, shares of stock, and other securities. Among them were "about three thousand dollars" in Mississippi stock, shares his brother's widow probably doled out to him the summer before. Andrew Sr. had drawn up a will before madness robbed him of reason. In it he took care to protect his oldest son and namesake from the always-hovering creditors, cloaking Andrew Jr.'s portion under the names of Charlotte, Simon Newton, and Andrew's children. It was they who decided what Andrew Jr. would receive. They gave him the Yazoo scrip.[11]

The certificates Congress created with its 1814 Yazoo compensation law entitled their bearers to purchase government lands in the Mississippi Territory. They were also merchantable securities, a form of money. Andrew could have cashed them in, making earth into paper, much as Samuel Dexter and Perez Morton and William Hull had tried to do in 1795. He did not. Perhaps he longed to escape his creditors. Or maybe he was sick of the paper chase. Certainly nothing held him in Athens, neither could he ever return to Boston. So he embraced the middling man's Western fantasy, a dream of land rather than its derivatives. After his father's estate cleared probate in June 1817, Andrew Dexter dispatched his wife and children to his in-laws' home in Dorchester, packed up his Yazoo stock, along with what remained of his Revolutionary ideals, and lit out for the territories. Perhaps he brought his father's young slave along as well; an anomaly in most of the north by now, chattel slavery was the life's blood of his destination.

That summer, Dexter joined thousands of land-hungry families from every corner of the nation, traveling on horseback and on wagon and on foot into the region west of Georgia and east of Mississippi that Congress had recently designated the Alabama Territory. Since 1814, when Andrew Jackson forced the Creek to cede these lands in order to end their war with the United States, the Alabama had become legendary. It would be "the garden of America ere many years," one traveler predicted. Soaring prices for cotton, the crop that planters called white gold, only heightened the attraction. When Dexter left Athens, the entire country was said to be in the grips of "Alabama Fever." South of Virginia, he would have found the roads thick with all manner of humanity—northern merchants and southern planters, poor whites fleeing crowded port cities and enslaved blacks driven in chains from the Carolina tobacco fields, squatters and speculators and would-be settlers—all hoping to stake a claim in the Alabama. Since April, *Niles' Weekly Register* cautioned, the number of fortune seekers had so thoroughly overwhelmed local stores of food that travelers risked "absolute starvation unless they are shortly relieved by supplies from other parts." The main pathways across the southeast looked as if they had been beset by an occupying army. Between 1817 and 1820, the nonnative population of the territory (and then state) would soar from 35,000 to 127,000.[12]

Not just people, but paper flooded into the Alabama, feeding the booming land markets much as the territory's abundant rain nourished its fertile soil. The federal government required minimal capital from would-be purchasers, who typically put down a quarter of the price of their parcels. Still, the quantity and quality of lands on offer made the demand for money insatiable. Yazoo scrip satisfied some of it, but hardly enough. Merchants with cash to spare grew rich loaning it at usurious rates. State legislatures throughout the nation's south and west chartered scores of new banks in 1817 and 1818. "Banks have sprung up like mushrooms," wrote one North Carolina newspaperman the following year. "There is no state, which has not been cursed by them, as Egypt was by her locusts." In 1820, even after the bubble had burst, half again as much bank money per capita flowed through Mississippi as through New England.[13]

Thanks to his father and his uncle, Andrew Dexter had paper of his own. When he reached Milledgeville, Georgia, sales at the regional land office had risen to a frenzied pitch. On August 13, the first significant portion of the Creek Cession went on the auction block: thirty-one townships near the headwaters of the Alabama River, bottom lands whose rich silty soils planters coveted. The bidding was heated as the Georgia summer. Blocks put up at two dollars per acre fetched fifteen times that before the gavel came down. In the township labeled Sixteen North, Range Eighteen East, forty-eight parcels totaling more than seventy-five hundred acres changed hands that afternoon. The luckiest buyers—the richest, at any rate—snapped up a thousand acres and came back for more later in the month. Dexter had nowhere near that kind of capital, but he made his play nonetheless. Using his Yazoo inheritance as a down payment of 5 percent, he bought two plats in the southern half of section seven, a purchase of just over 320 acres. Like many speculators before and since, Dexter bought the land sight unseen. Unlike the Yazoo men of the 1790s, however, he meant to live there. Shortly after the auction, he set out to see what he owned, accompanied by a wealthy speculator from Georgia.[14]

Only two hundred miles separated Milledgeville from Dexter's purchase, almost exactly the distance between Boston and New York. But where a mail stage barreling down the Post Road from Boston could reach New York in forty-eight hours, here ten miles a day counted as good progress. For most of the way the travelers followed the Federal Road, a grand name for the narrow track of rutted dirt that connected the eastern United States with its southwestern territories. The government had commandeered this old trading path from the Creeks in 1805, slowly widening the trail to accommodate horses and rolling vehicles. The route crossed invisible boundaries, winding from Georgia through what was left of the Creek Confederacy before crossing into the Alabama Territory. To Anglo-Americans used to bustling port cities, the country appeared desolate. You could ride for days without glimpsing a farmstead. Having gone twenty miles without seeing a soul, a merchant who made the journey several months after Dexter said it was "a real joy to see Christians once more." Food was harder to come by than company, comfort scarcer than either. Travelers berthed in forts abandoned after the Creek war, or camped with the Indians, or begged a bed from backwoods traders and their mixed-race families. If night fell with none of these in sight, they might "resort to the 'Earth under the waggon.'"[15]

Despite the hardships, this was "good land," as the speculators said, fertile and well watered. The travelers forded rivers, wading the smaller ones, canoeing across the largest, and traversing those in between by climbing along great felled pines. The trees loomed, taller than any in southern New England had seen in over a century. The Federal Road led through forests of chestnut and hickory and live oak where feral hogs foraged, and across canebrakes and cypress swamps where the mosquitoes rose in clouds. Especially during the steamy summer months, this was pestilential country. What people of the day called "the Billious fever"—probably typhus—raged between July and October. In 1817, the epidemic proved "more violent . . . than I ever knew it," one surveyor accustomed to the country noted. By the time Dexter's party neared Fort Jackson, three weeks after setting out from Milledgeville, both men had contracted the disease. Despite the ministrations of an "eminent physician" who had recently come into the Alabama from Virginia, Dexter's traveling companion died of the disease. Dexter recovered and continued down river toward the still-nameless township Sixteen.[16]

In the final miles of the journey, he at last saw evidence of American dominion over the land. Denton's ferry landing on the bank of Line Creek (as the little waterway separating Indian country from U.S. territory was called), Abraham Mordecai's cotton gin, Meigs and Mitchell's trading post, James Powers's grocery store: these were the "improvements" made by the early pioneers, a handful of white citizens and black slaves living off the red earth. Good signs, however small and scattered. Dexter declared himself "much flattered with the prospect of its advantages for a town site." This was his plan, then: to carve not just a homestead, but an entire town out of his purchases.[17]

Town founding was a popular game along the east bank of the Alabama that summer, and those who would win it had to act fast. Villages bloomed amid the forests like so many wildflowers, but only those nourished by settlers and commerce survived. Within days of the Milledgeville sales, the Georgia planters who had bought parcels adjacent to Dexter's began advertising the "commercial advantages" of a town they called simply "Alabama."[18]

The promoters of Alabama Town had a stake in several other new villages in the territory. Dexter had enough money to place only one bet, and he had to work quickly to best his richer rivals. Through the beastly summer and into the mild southern fall, he employed survey-ors to lay out some eight hundred house lots near the trading post that the Creek called Econchate, or "Red Ground," and that Dexter rechristened New Philadelphia. To entice settlers, he offered the only thing he had: cheap land. The incentive worked. By the new year, lots were selling well, fetching $50 to $150 each. A score or so of log houses had gone up, "laid out on the plan of Phil. in Pennsylvania," observed Peter Remsen, a New York merchant who visited Dexter in January 1818. Taking advantage of the fast-moving streams crossing his land, Dexter built grist and sawmills nearby, amenities that would help the little settlement to grow. Though "yet a wilderness," Remsen thought, the town had "a high pleasant situation and bids fair to flourish."[19]

In August 1818, a year after Andrew Dexter made his way into Alabama, the *Richmond Enquirer* marveled at the "astonishing rage . . . for the establishment of new towns." Such mania ought to inspire wariness, the writer argued. "We lay it down as a rule, that where this spirit for speculation rages, some persons are to be benefited and others are to be bit." But some situations truly were fortuitous for the "man of enterprise. . . . Happy is he, that owns a bend between two rivers!"[20]

When the Exchange burned in Boston that November, Dexter numbered among those happy few. He owned the rich bottom lands below the confluence of the Coosa and the Tallapoosa, directly oppo-site the Alabama River's fabled "big bend," which encircled the most valuable stretch of cotton land in the southwest.[21]

Here at last was a new beginning for a prodigal son. Damn the embers on Congress Street. He would rise from the ashes yet.

❧

Back in Boston, the wreckage of Andrew Dexter's first ascent was slow to cool. One bitter morning in January 1819, a cart man hauling rubbish from the pit on Congress Street paused to warm his hands on a hot brick he had found in the ashes. Two months later, a ship's captain who had sailed for Liverpool just after the conflagration returned to discover that the Exchange's "smouldering flame had not been extinguished by all the snows of the Winter." Maps printed that year and the next labeled THE RUINS OF THE LATE EXCHANGE COFFEE HOUSE, the better to guide gawkers to what had become one of the signposts by which people navigated their city, and themselves.[22]

If she could not quite see the monument to her husband's fall from her parents' home in Dorchester, Charlotte Morton Dexter lived too close by to escape the urban-disaster pilgrims and their sad souvenirs of ruin. So it was with decidedly mixed feelings that she quit Massachusetts for the second and last time in April 1819, bound on what she called a "long & arduous Journey to a remote & uncultivated Country." "It is impossible, my dear Parents, to express to you all I feel at *parting*," she wrote. For all his failings, Charlotte explained, her husband retained "the *first* claim upon my *duty*," and sparked "sentiments of affection, which so powerfully draw me to him." She had hoped, "beyond utterance," that Andrew would honor his pledge to "come to us, & give us his protection" on the trip to Alabama. But this was yet another promise he hadn't managed to keep. She would make the journey alone, bringing her two smaller children, Samuel (nearly four) and Sophia (not yet seven), along with her. Alfred, almost ten, stayed on with his grandparents. Charlotte Dexter strained to imagine a happy ending to their odyssey. Surely it was not "impossible that the Almighty may in his wisdom, see fit to try me with Prosperity," she wrote. Perhaps her husband yet had it "in his power to prove that he is upright and good." Perhaps Alabama's rich soil would set them all to right: Perez and Sarah Morton once again "independant and unencumbered," their grandchildren healthy and thriving, their prodigal son-in-law tendered "the credit due to the amiable qualities he possesses." These, at least, were the wishes of a devoted wife and daughter as she headed into the woods.[23]

Halifax and Athens: those had been distant ports as well. But they had always been part of Charlotte's network of ken and kin. The Alabama Territory was outlandish by comparison. *New Philadelphia:* the town's very name must have seemed a cruel joke to the Morton family. What homage could this frontier outpost possibly pay the nation's birthplace and one-time capital, the refined city where Sarah Morton had sat for Gilbert Stuart in the first years of the century? Even those who lived in Dexter's frontier village—mostly Georgians—mocked the name. "Yankee Town," they called it, deriding the founder's origins if not his pretensions.[24]

Travel between Boston and the "old" Philadelphia was now routine, a week's trip by turnpike, less under sail. No simple route led to this New Philadelphia. The most direct course headed southwest from Baltimore to Georgia, traversing dense backcountry and narrow mountain passes. The "most infernal Roads that we ever saw," said a farmer who made the trip late in 1818. A slower, kinder itinerary hugged the coast and afforded stopping points in Richmond, Raleigh, Columbia, and Augusta before meeting the Federal Road west from Milledgeville. Despite the reassuring name of that highway, it threaded through Creek Nation, *not* federal territory and hardly secure. The war between the Creeks and the United States had ended five years before, but periodic skirmishes continued. Perhaps Charlotte Dexter had heard of the incident in February 1818, when native warriors attacked a party of travelers near the Georgia line, killing one man and gravely wounding a woman and her infant. Now American soldiers patrolled the route. But however numerous the infantrymen, the "hostiles" were more so. "They are so scattered & their forests & places of retreat so extensive that the effects of any victory of them will be only partial," a federal agent noted that spring. Whatever the map said, this remained "new settled frontier," a vast country under uncertain authority.[25]

The water routes—by sea around the Florida peninsula, or by river, down the Ohio from Pittsburgh, continuing south on the Mississippi until it emptied into the Gulf—were certainly longer than either of the main pathways overland. But the travel was easier, especially for a woman with small children in tow. When he sent for his son Alfred in 1820, Andrew Dexter asked his Boston kin to send the boy by boat, under the protection of a particular captain; he likely gave Charlotte, Sophia, and Samuel similar instructions.[26]

As with overland travel to central Alabama, the final leg of the journey was the most arduous. New Philadelphia lay more than four hundred miles upriver from Blakeley or Mobile, the two small ports competing to link the Gulf to the territory's booming interior. Sluggish and shallow, the Alabama River frustrated commercial boatmen. Schooners could make it as far as Claiborne, about a quarter of the way to Dexter's town. From there rough-hewn barges—little more than log rafts—carried most of the produce upon which New Philadelphia depended. Powered by men wielding long poles, these unwieldy craft inched along, barely exceeding walking speed when the river was low. It could take as long as three months to conquer those last four hundred miles.[27]

Andrew Dexter's young family spent fifteen weeks in transit, finally arriving in New Philadelphia on August 5. The endpoint of their ordeal could scarcely have been more different from where they had started. The land teemed in the tropical heat. Moss hung from canopies of live oak. But if the "vegetation was . . . exceedingly luxuriant," as one traveler noted, the streetscape was anything but. By comparison to Boston—even to Milledgeville—New Philadelphia barely merited the label of town. Fewer than four hundred people, nearly half of them enslaved, navigated its muddy alleyways and two principal streets, Market and Main. (At 140 feet across, the former outstripped New York's Broadway, carving the magnitude of Dexter's ambition into damp earth.) In the two years since Dexter and his partners had laid claim to the place, some forty-four buildings had gone up, outbuildings and slave quarters excepted. Most were basic log cabins. Only the five loftiest structures in the village boasted a second story; perhaps Dexter's homestead was one of them. Though the town counted a tavern, a post office, and two cemeteries, not a single brick building would grace it for another seven years, neither did it yet have a school, a church, a courthouse, a marketplace, a jail, a library, a bookseller, or a printer.[28]

These crude surroundings served as the stage for a variety of activities that a refined northern woman like Charlotte Dexter can only have considered appalling. Peddlers hawked all manner of goods. Buskers performed acrobatic feats and "sleight[s] of hand." Horses ran match races through the village. The town's freeholders—roughly three score property-owning white men of voting age—fretted over "the practice of shooting in the Streets," which they proclaimed "dangerous to the citizens & others visiting said town." They also worried about "riotous or obstinate . . . negros" who strolled New Philadelphia with dogs or with firearms, hardly the sort of promenade that graced Boston Common.[29]

About the only thing the "infant establishment" had in abundance was water. Flowing springs turned the junction of Market and Main streets into a mudhole. Water pooled in the declivities along the river. All manner of garbage—rotting trees, human and animal waste, heaps of putrefying cottonseed, construction debris—collected in the swamps and ponds. Mosquitoes bred in the filthy water, swarming thickly from July through September. Village leaders linked the noisome "miasmas" from rotting garbage to the spread of disease, and regularly ordered the ponds drained. But the water outran them. Malaria dogged New Philadelphia, and epidemics of yellow fever ravaged it intermittently. One traveler who came through the place several years later wondered whether such a "young town, whose situation, at least in summer, is unhealthy," could ever attain "a fixed character," let alone "a high degree of cultivation." Charlotte Dexter must have asked herself the same.[30]

She would not wonder for long. On August 17, Charlotte Morton Dexter died, having spent exactly twelve days of her thirty-two years in New Philadelphia. In a town without a newspaper, let alone a board of health, the cause of her death went unrecorded. Yellow fever is the likely culprit. The mosquito-borne virus raged that summer in

Blakeley and Mobile, where she may have picked it up en route. The disease fells quickly enough—incubating for three to six days and proving fatal to up to two-thirds of its sufferers within a week—that she could also have contracted it in New Philadelphia. Or she may have fallen prey to malaria, or typhus, or any of the other myriad "agues" that plagued the American south. In Charlotte's day, people understood these physical causes to be inseparable from the deep melancholy that attended her journey from Boston. Recalling this daughter who "perished in the morning of her days," Sarah Morton described Charlotte as a casualty "of cares, and of climate . . . the affectionate victim of conjugal duty."[31]

Whatever claimed Charlotte Dexter's life, the loss was profound. When the news reached Boston weeks later, Sarah Morton poured out her grief in rhyme. Andrew Dexter's feelings can only be imagined. Back in 1817, when he donated five acres of land to the town for a burying ground, he could not have guessed that his wife would be among the first interred there. Their young son and daughter would have flanked him at her funeral, a humble affair. Baptized and married amid the pomp of Boston's Trinity Church, Charlotte Dexter was consigned to the grave after a few words preached in a makeshift meetinghouse, probably the front room of James Vickers's tavern. The Reverend James King, an itinerant Methodist passing through the territory, delivered the eulogy. The cemetery was equally haphazard; without plan or sexton, burial plots were chosen at random. Despite these modest circumstances, her mourners covered her in all the glory they could muster, beneath a tombstone that recalled a woman

> In virtue's brightest robes attired,
> With grace and beauty rarely given,
> In her no change could be required
> To make her welcome into Heaven.

Standing beside a gash cut into the red earth of New Philadelphia on that stifling August day, heaven seemed impossibly remote. What grace, what beauty for a forty-year-old widower and his two small children here, in this raw country? Not the ending Charlotte Dexter dreamed when she set out from Boston. No trial by prosperity, this, not by any means.[32]

❧

Thanks to its topography more than the genius of its founders, New Philadelphia did prosper. Merchants, planters, and widows, artisans, innkeepers, and slaves: people of various sorts trickled into the little town. Some with the freedom to choose their destination came "for the purpose of amassing property," as one traveler noted. Many came *as* property. Still others were "driven . . . by the prostration of their fortunes, in their old residence!" Whether they were fleeing the past or betting on the future, emigrants favored the village on high ground over the adjacent plantations vying to become the trading center of this new cotton kingdom.[33]

In December 1819, less than four months after his wife's death, Andrew Dexter's village absorbed its neighbors. The proprietors of the three rival towns bickered over what to name the settlement, which combined New Philadelphia with Alabama Town and East Alabama Town. The southern-born speculators who owned Alabama Town argued that it would "never do to call it 'New Philadelphia,' nor 'Yankee Town,'" since both of those carried a "scent too strong for 'Georgy.'" The factions agreed instead on "Montgomery," chosen in homage to the hero of the Battle of Quebec whose long-moldering remains had come home to New York with great fanfare in 1818. *Montgomery:* here was a name above section and party, a "name . . . equally dear to every American throughout the land," as one local merchant held.[34]

Did Dexter recall that he had invoked General Richard Montgomery twenty years earlier, when he addressed his classmates graduating from Rhode Island College in 1798? Then just nineteen, bursting with ambition verging on arrogance, he had implored the "indignant shades of WARREN and MONTGOMERY" to "start from their tombs, point at the wounds of their country, and cry aloud, revenge for our injured rights!" How far this Montgomery lay from that one, how many wounds since endured.[35]

The panic of 1819, the convulsive beginning of a prolonged nation-wide depression, was fast becoming another such injury, nowhere more debilitating than in the booming southwest. Cotton prices—the fuel that stoked Alabama fever—fell to less than half the giddy highs they had reached in 1817. Credit shrank in tandem with profits. The Bank of the United States called loans and hoarded specie. State-chartered banks felt the pinch of deflation and passed the pain along to their customers. Speculators who had bought their slices of Alabama on margin scrambled to pay their debts. Many failed, the most highly leveraged falling first, and hardest. Some blamed the banks for their reversals; others faulted themselves. If the banks "have led us into temptation," scolded one writer in the *Carolina Centinel,* "it must be confessed we have easily fallen into it." "We wanted to take short cuts to fortune," the writer who called himself Economicus lamented. Now they paid the price of their greed. A "deeper gloom hangs over us, than ever was witnessed by the oldest man," he said. The darkest days of the War of 1812 looked like "sunshine, compared with these times."[36]

As hard times overspread the new state, many Alabama boomtowns disappeared from the map. Speculators and traders who failed to turn a profit quickly moved on to the next new thing, leaving their stores and houses to rot along muddy not-quite-streets that weeds reclaimed in a season. Yet as Dexter had once prophesied of the martyred general's bones, his latter-day Montgomery managed a tenuous resurrection. The town weathered the panic, and survived the "sickly seasons" of the mid-1820s—though such plague years, as the *Alabama Journal* quipped, tended to "give a dog a bad name" that was "hard to get quit of." Its unhealthy reputation deterred some would-be settlers, but many ignored the warnings. In the decade following its incorporation in 1819, the population nearly quadrupled. By 1830, Montgomery counted some fifteen hundred residents, barely a village's worth by New England standards, but enough to qualify as "a considerable place" by the lights of the southern backcountry. And if, as one English visitor maintained, its inhabitants looked to be "exclusively of the poorer order," appearances deceived. The typical Montgomery freeman that year held property worth more than seven hundred dollars, which put him well ahead of the average U.S. citizen. The richest in the county owned one hundred times that.[37]

The town's wealth came from these planters, whose fortunes rested on the unholy trinity of cotton, slavery, and a navigable river. Each year between September and January, wagons carrying thousands of pounds of ginned cotton rumbled over Montgomery's wharves, bound for sale in Mobile, New Orleans, New York, and Liverpool. When the rush to market subsided, planters plowed what profit remained back into more lands and more "hands," as they called the human chattel in whom so much of their capital congealed. In the off-season, Montgomery's market house—built at a cost of eighty dollars in the spring of 1821—was crowded with men trafficking in fields and town lots and slaves.[38]

During those years, the town's free citizens—just over half the total—founded the institutions that had been so lacking in the early days. By the mid 1830s, the town boasted schools, churches, hotels, and theaters. It published two newspapers and sponsored numerous associations, from Masonic lodges to tract societies to horse racing clubs. As it did across the nation in those years, transportation to and from Montgomery improved. Though locals continued to complain that there was "not a good road leading to our town, from any part of the country," the overland route from Milledgeville was certainly better than it had been when Dexter first traveled it. Beginning in 1826, a mail stage "furnished with good substantial carriages, and a supply of excellent horses" made the trip three times each week, shrinking the distance between the two towns from three weeks to four days.[39]

The Alabama River was more fickle than the Federal Road, alternatively nourishing Montgomery's commerce and destroying it. After 1822, steamboats plied the river between Montgomery and Mobile, carrying cotton to the Gulf and returning to the interior laden with cloth, groceries, and other finished goods. In the dry season—which stretched for six months some years—the water level sank so low that boats couldn't pass. The prices of household goods spiked, and newspapers published erratically, hamstrung by a lack of paper from Mobile. But if the summer brought too little water, heavy rains made the river treacherous in spring. In three days during February 1828, the Alabama rose more than thirty feet. And then there were the steamers themselves, primitive creatures prone to run aground or explode. Montgomery lost ten boats—about four hundred thousand dollars' worth of property—before the town's first decade was out. But when the Alabama ran deep and swift and true, the riverboats offered a lifeline, and the passage that had lasted three months when Charlotte Dexter made it could take as little as three days.[40]

As they built the infrastructure of community, the free people of Montgomery also tightened the chains of chattel slavery, the labor system on which the wealth of the town, the state, the region, and indeed the entire nation depended. Creating slave patrols numbered among the town's first official acts. Enforcing the state's increasingly restrictive slave laws, patrollers administered lashes, confiscated firearms, and even "kell[ed] all dogs owned or kept by negroes." Despite or because of such draconian measures, every issue of the town's weekly newspaper featured notices from owners seeking to recover men and women who had stolen themselves by running away.[41]

Decades hence, such pressures would force the slave system to crack, and then to crumble. But in the 1820s, from the planter's perspective, runaway slaves were part of the cost of doing business. And by mid-decade the cotton business was booming once again. A German traveler passing through central Alabama in 1826 saw the "signs of cultivation everywhere": the "cotton fields . . . in beautiful order," the "gins and presses . . . at work" around the clock, and "negroes, wagons, horses, and cattle" streaming into the Alabama countryside. Montgomery remained a fledgling venture, he stressed, "so new, that the original forest still stands between the houses." But those buildings were "tolerably good," the streets "very broad," and the riverbanks alive with commerce. All told, he concluded, the town had "already a very lively appearance" for a "place . . . first laid out about five years ago."[42]

In the coming years, Montgomery made good on its early promise, becoming the capital of Alabama in 1846, and the first capital of the Confederate nation in 1861. For transforming the frontier trading post into a leading southern city, some credited Dexter's vision and perseverance. In 1884, the town fathers changed the name of Market Street to Dexter Avenue in his honor. Sixty years later, the Sophie Bibb Chapter of the United Daughters of the Confederacy put up a granite monument there, to celebrate Dixie, Jefferson Davis, and Andrew Dexter. It stands there still.[43]

✇

Andrew Dexter's family hoped their kinsman's fortunes would mirror Montgomery's. In what he called a "sing song kind of letter" posted

*Dexter Avenue Memorial,*
*Montgomery, Alabama.*

to Alabama in the summer of 1821, Andrew's younger brother Samuel passed along good news. He had been elected speaker of Rhode Island's House of Representatives, "that body that we both of us at one time so justly reprobated." Though the Farmer's Exchange Bank debacle in the spring of 1809 nearly ruined him, Samuel Dexter had righted himself. "Things have turned around strangely in ten years," he mused. "I find all those who were then in our stories are dead, and myself who was then persecuted, standing in the plase of the highest of them." Bottom to top: he had recovered the path of a rising man in a rising nation.

Now he awaited word that Andrew, too, had rebounded. He had heard that the young widower was soon to remarry, a choice he applauded. "[Y]ou ought not to live single with your domestick character," Samuel counseled, for "it would be a miserable life." Perhaps public life would reward his brother as it had himself. "I expect soon to hear that you also are advancing yourself in political life," Samuel continued. "I know you are worthy of it both as to talents & character." But "above all," he closed, "I hope you will be prosperous & happy."[44]

Andrew Dexter was neither. Where Samuel Dexter's life "turned around" decisively, Andrew's fortunes continued to swirl and eddy. From time to time, he reported that his spiral was at last poised to rise. "I am happy to understand the bright Prospects which are opening upon you," Sarah Morton wrote after receiving one such letter, in the fall of 1825. But almost inevitably, bright prospects dimmed, and the mill wheel of Andrew Dexter's life turned full around again.[45]

His privations weighed heavily on the man and, in turn, on the historical record. Neil Blue, a long-lived Montgomery merchant who knew Dexter well, recalled an embittered man who boasted of his early success and "was frequently heard to lament, when worried for debts, the inferior position he occupied, notwithstanding the advantages of high family connection." Though he may have romanticized his high birth and inflated his youthful achievements—bragging that he had attended Dartmouth (not Brown) and had bested Daniel Webster in debate there—Dexter did not exaggerate his "inferior position" in Montgomery, where he left few ripples. A journalist who set out to write an "extended sketch" of Dexter's life in the late nineteenth century complained that "scanty materials exist for the purpose." Given "his mental culture and literary acquirements," the memorialist noted, Dexter "could have left ample materials in an excellent form[,] but the cares and vicissitudes of his busy and unsuccessful life were too exacting on his time." No letters or journals survive from the two decades Andrew Dexter spent in the south. Indeed, not even a census entry remains to document where he lived and with whom—or whether, like so many of his neighbors, he bought and sold people as well as real estate.[46]

The fragments in the archives reveal that Dexter's business dealings in Alabama followed the pattern he had set in Boston and perfected in Canada and New York. Big gambles yielded but fleeting gains. Much as he had on Congress Street, he mortgaged his Alabama landholdings, and then sold them off piecemeal when feeling cash poor, land hungry, or both. Having borrowed 95 percent of the price of his initial stake in the territory from the federal land office, he came into the country in hock. The loans came due quickly, some within forty days of the purchase. Almost immediately, Dexter signed over the deed that established his claim as the town's founder to another merchant. In addition to his frantic speculation in town lots—dozens of transactions some years—Dexter "resumed the practice of LAW," as he announced in Montgomery's new weekly paper, the *Republican,* in 1821. Despite the heavy demand for legal services in a place that was rising upon a mountain of contracts, he found little success as one of the three attorneys in Montgomery. Throughout the 1820s, he seldom had enough cash on hand to pay his tax bill. As a local historian explained in 1871, Dexter's "calculations on paper were splendid and convincing to him[,] but he could not manage to realize them in practice": words that evoked the Exchange Coffee House all over again.[47]

Nor did political life reward Andrew Dexter, as his brother hoped it might. His education, his legal and business experience, and his family connections made him one of the eminent men in tiny Montgomery, if not in all Alabama. Yet his neighbors never stood him for the state legislature, and only once appointed him to a position of modest local power. In 1828, Dexter became Montgomery's tax assessor, an ironic office for one who was so often in arrears himself.[48]

If newspapers can be trusted to reflect the town's civic life, Dexter rarely voiced his sentiments publicly. But that same year, he boldly entered the debate over one of the most contentious issues of the day: the role of the federal government in removing the Creek population from what remained of their Alabama lands. Like tariffs and slavery and internal improvements, Indian removal was a partisan rallying cry in the deep south. With a presidential election to be held that fall, most Montgomery voters were Andrew Jackson's men: determined believers in states' rights, and vocal opponents of President John Quincy Adams and the so-called corrupt bargain that had put him in office four years earlier. Everything about Adams, whose "American system" favored a strong Union governed by a strong national bureaucracy, infuriated Alabamans. Living as they did on the borders of the nation, they found the administration's Indian policies especially galling. On a sweltering August Saturday, Montgomery's free white men thronged the courthouse to discuss the matter. They condemned what they saw as the nation's crimes against the sovereignty of Alabama, and agreed "to plant themselves as barriers to the encroachment of unconstitutional power." To that end they organized a "Committee of Correspondence," a little band of brothers pledged to fight the tyranny of the "General Government," as their forebears had done during the Revolution.[49]

Andrew Dexter, by contrast, remained as ardent a nationalist as he had been when this Adams's father was president. In a set of competing resolutions submitted to that meeting, and in a series of lengthy articles published in the town's only newspaper over the following weeks, Dexter laid out his contrary view. That the "Indians should be removed from our limits," he conceded. But he and his opponents agreed on little else about the reasons, methods, or ultimate authority for their removal.[50]

Like many northern romantics, Dexter believed that the colonial experience had "enfeebled" once-proud natives, *noble savages,* as eastern intellectuals were beginning to style them. He invoked a primeval past when "the Indian roamed unrestrained over boundless regions; and while he admired the wonders of nature, listened to the foaming cataract, or trembled at the thunders of Heaven," bowing to "no superior but the Great Spirit." Then came the settlers, in ever-increasing numbers. The "unmeasured forests, entangled swamps, and ever green and blooming prairies": all these riches natives had been "obliged to abandon to the white man." Of course Dexter himself was one of those who had covered the wilderness with "cultivated fields and populous towns." Still, he saw tragedy as well as triumph in the improved landscape, and in the reduction of a once-autonomous people to clients of the United States. Victims not just of history, but of bad bargains, the Creeks had exchanged their lands, lives, and labor for false promises and "liquid poisons." In the process they had "lost all the virtues of the Indian, and acquired only the vices of the white man." Now it was both the right and the duty of the government that served as their "parent and guardian" to move them west of the Mississippi, where they could live safe and sovereign, as the Americans had pledged in treaty after treaty after treaty.[51]

Dexter's logic, as he took pains to point out, represented the best interests of his fellow citizens. Removing the Creeks would help to preserve the fragile peace in a volatile slave state, he emphasized. "In case of an insurrection, by joining the blacks, they might, if possible, darken the horrors of a St. Domingo massacre, by adding all the terrors and cruelties of Indian warfare." If the nightmare vision of a joint uprising by Indians and slaves failed to frighten his opponents into agreeing with him, Dexter held out happier prospects. The Creeks held about a quarter of the best land in Alabama. White homesteaders would use those fields and rivers to "increase our agricultural products," but the natives, by contrast, "constitute what Adam Smith calls an unprofitable class, which are always injurious in proportion to their numbers." Their speedy removal would free up eight million acres, which the land office could sell as quickly and cheaply as it had disposed of the last Creek cession, including Montgomery itself. The resulting influx of "industrious planters" would then add "still more . . . to the great capital stock of our common country."[52]

But ineluctably Dexter's argument drifted from "capital stock" to moral stock, from the hard fiscal logic of Adam Smith toward the humanitarian impulses of Montaigne. Were not the Americans, as much as the Creeks, guilty of barbarism? Dexter lamented the day when former colonials began to use their hard-won independence to "take away the rights and liberties of the Indian *nations*." "Are things then, in these times, altogether reversed," he wondered, "and are Republics instead of monarchs become entitled, by some inherent and divine right, to oppress their fellow men?" Did only might matter? Dexter concluded his four-part series with a long counterfactual, in which he imagined the *Creeks* rather than the Americans asserting that power was "the only criterion of right":

> If so, these Indians, when their country was first invaded by the fathers of those who now treat them with so much ingratitude, might have been fully justified in subjecting them to the Indian government and laws; answering their complaints by upbraiding them with their weakness and want of power to resist; and tomahawking those who refused to submit. In that case, it would have been only the lawful possessors of the soil attempting to rule over its invaders; but in ours, it is the invaders themselves, or their descendants, depriving the natives of the rights of their birth, the rights of nature herself.

However "the wise, good, and great men of our country" ultimately resolved the issue, Dexter urged that their course remain "consistent with justice and our own honour." A good gospel message from a member of Montgomery's new Bible Society: it would not profit a nation to gain the world but lose its soul.[53]

So much ink spilled so suddenly by a man who otherwise maintained a deep public silence. What compelled Dexter to speak out on this vexed question? Certainly he hoped to benefit from the land sales, and thought the federal government would conduct them most favorably. But greed, while a necessary motive, seems an insufficient one. The passionate argumentation of the essays suggests *affinity* as much as self-interest. It is easy to imagine that Dexter saw his own small story reflected in the epic tragedy of the Creeks. He, too, had been born near the centers of power, only to find himself driven (by ambition, by circumstance, by bad exchanges) to the peripheries, reduced and finally removed. Now he, too, was an exile, his dominion shrunken and himself brought low. As a young man, Dexter had yearned for the day when the "hatchet of industry, wielded by the strong arm of freedom, shall resound from the shores of the Atlantic to the banks of the Mississippi." He had since wielded that hatchet, and fallen to it. The path of American progress he outlined in 1828 was more muted than the martial cry of 1798. In the interim, the United States had become "a great and powerful nation"—at least by comparison to its Indian rivals. But Dexter had not become a great and powerful man. Not even in Montgomery.[54]

Dexter's arguments on the Creek question failed to move his fellow townsfolk, except in the contrary direction. The few men who had originally supported his resolutions quickly abandoned him. Come November, Jackson's Democrats easily won Alabama, and the state legislature resoundingly approved a bill extending its jurisdiction over the Creeks. The heaviest support for Jackson and states' rights came from counties like Montgomery, which bordered Creek Nation. By the summer of 1829, the Creeks were on the march, with government "escorts," bound "for their destination beyond the Mississippi." Andrew Dexter, who had resumed his customary silence and obscurity in Montgomery's small public sphere, would soon follow them.[55]

Despite what his brother Samuel had lauded as his "domestick character," Andrew Dexter's family life offered the same slender rewards as commerce and politics. His rumored second marriage never came to pass, and the widower father found it near impossible to make much of a life for his children in a small Alabama town. The older two, Alfred and Sophia, spent their youth shuttling between Montgomery and New England, where they boarded with whichever relatives would shoulder the cost of raising them. For two years after his mother's death, Alfred stayed on with her family in Dorchester; Sarah Cunningham, Charlotte Dexter's only married sister, served as his guardian. But when she returned to Nova Scotia in 1821, her husband declared himself "unable to support Alfred any longer," and refused "to take him on again." Believing that Andrew wouldn't want his son to become "burthensome to his friends," Samuel Dexter brought Alfred to live with him in Providence. The boy, effectively orphaned twice, was not quite twelve.[56]

By the time he turned sixteen, the duty of caring for Alfred Dexter had passed to his father's youngest brother, Simon Newton Dexter, who lived in Whitestone, New York. Simon Newton, whose own children were still toddlers, schooled his nephew in his chosen trade of civil engineering. Perhaps it was Simon Newton's influence that helped Alfred to make the striking "personal, & mental Improvement" that his maternal grandmother noted in the fall of 1825. She congratulated her son-in-law on the transformation, calling her grandson "a Gentleman, in Looks, in Deportment, & in Sentiments." Given the young man's accomplishments, Sarah Morton marveled at the nameless critics whose "wicked & hardened . . . Hearts" made them "capable of vilifying such praise-worthy, & excellent Children." She felt no need to elaborate what these carping tongues had said about the boy and his sister; Andrew Dexter must have known the rumors too well.[57]

While Sarah Morton fretted over her grandson's reputation, Alfred Dexter worried about his father. In the summer of 1827, Alfred was working for his uncle in Summit Bridge, Delaware, helping to survey the Chesapeake and Delaware Canal, when he received a plea from his father in Montgomery: would Alfred ask Simon Newton for one hundred dollars? Andrew Dexter promised his son that he would head north as soon as he received the cash. Knowing that a letter from Delaware would reach his father more quickly than one from New York, Alfred sent the money directly. "You may not esteem it very delicate in me to Do that without yr consent," he told his uncle. But he knew Simon Newton shared his "anxious solicitude to hasten my Dear father from a land of misfortune and suffering to one in which he may be happy with his friends & relations." Still two months shy of his eighteenth birthday, the boy was father to the man.[58]

Alfred's brother, Samuel, also took up his father's burdens. Of the three Dexter children, Samuel, the youngest, left the faintest record of his life. His maternal kin rarely mention him in their correspondence with his siblings, which suggests that he had the dubious blessing of being reared by his father in Alabama. About the only thing that can be gleaned of his life there is that he had schooling enough to acquire a steady hand. His fine penmanship served him well when he began to act as his father's proxy in land dealings in the mid-1830s, work that brought him more peril than reward. In January 1836, the twenty-one-year-old Samuel penned a long letter to his sister, Sophia, promising to send her funds shortly, "as I know you must be in want of money." The family disease: Samuel was hard up as well, forced to use $150 he had set aside for his sister "to make a Payment." But he hoped that some recent luck in "selling a good deal of Property" would soon allow him and Alfred "to pay the debts we assumed for Father." With Andrew Dexter, Samuel shared the gambler's creed: the earnest belief that the next hand would be a royal flush. This faith proved misguided, as it so often does. Before the next year was out, Samuel lay dead in Texas, where he had gone to service his father's real estate interests.[59]

Sophia Dexter experienced neither her brothers' entanglement in their father's failures nor their chances to reverse his course. Even a poor boy could learn a trade and earn a future. The girl born to modest circumstances faced slimmer prospects of a good marriage and a respectable life.

Andrew Dexter must have decided that his daughter's best chance lay in Boston, for he packed her off to the Mortons' before she turned thirteen. Her grandmother took the charge as a gift, telling Andrew that "the dear Child" had become "the Glory, & Comfort of my Existence." A bright, tractable young woman, Sophia resembled her late mother "in all Things appertaining to Mind, Morals, and Manners," Sarah Morton announced—though "certainly not in her extraordinary beauty." But however much they loved the girl, her mother's family lacked the wherewithal to "do all & every Thing, which her fine Capacities and excellent Principles require, & deserve." Ever since Andrew Dexter had shared his failure with them in 1809, the Mortons, too, had struggled to make ends meet. They could not afford to purchase the portrait of their dear departed Charlotte which had lain, unfinished, in Gilbert Stuart's studio for nearly two decades, let alone to guide Charlotte's daughter into refined womanhood. For her part, Sophia talked only "of residing with her Father, & Brothers, provided they are prosperous."[60]

They were not, and she did not. Bouncing from her grandmother's to her uncle's home in Providence to boardinghouses in Alabama and South Carolina, Sophia, like her brothers, got less than she needed. With neither beauty nor property nor accomplishment to recommend her, she remained unmarried long past the expected age. Her choice to live single in the south—as a governess, perhaps—mystified her Yankee kin. Why did she not "remain in Boston & get a situation as teacher in some respectable Academy," her grandmother wondered. "You must know Dear Sophia that in this world we must accommodate ourselves to circumstances," instructed her mother's sister Louisa, herself a spinster of modest means. "[W]hether a place is agreeable, or otherwise we must submit to remain in it if mostly for our honor, and respectability. Poverty is no disgrace." Disgrace or no, poverty was her lot. Sophia was every bit as "weak & suffering" and discontented as he was, Alfred Dexter said, maybe even more so. Through her thirties she remained in the household of her uncle Samuel, the maiden niece paying, after a woman's own fashion, for her father's debts.[61]

Those debts only mounted, until the myriad small upsets that had plagued Andrew Dexter since his arrival in the south finally drove him from Alabama. The proximate cause was the failure of yet another ill-starred capital-intensive project. In November 1827, Dexter struck a bargain with Samuel Moniac, an elderly trader—half Creek, half Dutch—who had served as an interpreter for American generals from George Washington through Andrew Jackson. According to a military man who had known Moniac for years, he "was always looked upon as being one of the most intelligent half-breeds in the [Creek] Nation." Yet Dexter—despite the idealized portrait of Indian virtues he would publish in the papers several months later—swindled Moniac, paying him a total of four hundred dollars for 320 choice acres along the Alabama, far less than the going rate. Among the parcels Dexter bought was Moniac's Island, a small cay near the mouth of Catoma Creek, a tributary of the Alabama. Moniac, who spoke many languages but signed his name with a mark, may have thought he was granting Dexter lifetime use of the property; the words *during my life* have been carefully excised from the deed. Instead, he signed away ownership to "Dexter his heirs and assigns for ever."[62]

For decades, the island had served Moniac's kin as a refuge in time of war. Dexter apparently saw in it strategic value of a different sort. Betting on the demand for lumber in a booming region, he began another large-scale building project: a series of mills that would draw power from the rushing waters of Catoma Creek. The "disastrous enterprise," one early-twentieth-century commentator noted, was "attended with a heavy outlay" of money and labor. But as it had so often in the past, luck ran against Dexter. No sooner were the mills running than a flash flood swept the whole works away. Perhaps the scene was something like the "Great Freshet" of August 1831, when the river swelled more than an inch an hour, not cresting until it had covered the wharves and the bluffs and surged on through the city. When the water receded, Dexter moved on, defeated by the loss and drawn west again by the next big gamble.[63]

He spent the next several years tumbling through the borderlands between Mexico and the United States, a region that Mexicans called

Coahuila and that American settlers called Texas. He touched down in Nacogdoches, where the Red River crossed the old road heading west to San Antonio, El Camino Real. Nacogdoches was smaller than Montgomery, yet its social geography was infinitely more complex. Throughout the eighteenth century, the Caddo and other native groups had struggled for control against the Spanish, and then the French, and then the Spanish once again. Since the Adams-Onis Treaty of 1821, the land had formally belonged to Mexico. But signatures on paper didn't stop American settlers, Dexter included, from flooding into the region. When he got there, he found a village comprised of Mexican officials; planters of English, French, American, and Spanish origin; slaves of varied African descent; and the surviving members of many native groups, including those making the forced march west from Alabama. Buying, as always, on credit, he quickly amassed what his son Samuel called "*immense interests,* in that Country." As Dexter knew from his Yazoo inheritance, political instability often favored the speculator, who would scoop up clouded titles cheaply.[64]

If the paper value of the country attracted the opportunist in Dexter, the romantic in him would have been drawn by its uncanny beauty. In the summer of 1832, just after a bloody battle between American homesteaders and the Mexican *alcalde,* he wrote a letter about his life in Nacogdoches, which a Montgomery newspaper reprinted. Neither the letter nor the newspaper survives. But the description likely resembled the one his son Samuel penned four years later, when he journeyed into Texas for the first time on his father's errands. It was, he told his sister, "a Country as beautifull as the *Sun ever shone upon*." Flowers "of almost every variety of hue" carpeted the prairies, game birds darkened the skies, and deer and wild cattle ranged across the meadows. The rivers ran so deep and fast and clear—so unlike the brackish Alabama—that to see them was to "conceive of the beauty of the River of Paradise." Texas was a wonder, a "*Fairy Land*" worthy of "comparison with the *Garden of Eden*." A decade and a half away from

Boston, five hundred miles even from Montgomery, Andrew Dexter again believed he had found his promised land.[65]

❦

Nathan Negus, an aspiring painter, spent the last week of October 1819 slaving away in his master's studio on the aptly named Warren Street, a densely packed neighborhood south of Boston Common, the "*wooden* part of the town," as one writer called it. Like all craft worlds in the early Republic, the business of art was both fiercely competitive and steeply hierarchical. Negus, who turned eighteen that year, clung to a place on its bottom rungs. Since age twelve he had served John Ritto Penniman, washing brushes and grinding pigments and painting base coats and doing whatever else his master asked of him besides, much as Penniman had done for Gilbert Stuart a decade earlier. It was hard work, for scant credit. But at least Negus *had* work, a skill, a roof: all these when many around him were suffering.[66]

"*Hard Times*": the phrase resounded from the wharves to the workrooms. In Boston as across the nation, the economy veered from panic toward depression, a replay of the 1807 embargo without Jefferson to blame. This time, the business cycle itself was the culprit, and the remedy was equally obscure. Prices and incomes fell; boardinghouses emptied; jails and almshouses filled. "Every where we hear the murmurs of discontent," ran a story in the *Massachusetts Spy,* headlined, like so many others, HARD TIMES. Every walk around the city revealed "new objects and exhibitions of misery—dishonoured credits, deserted dwellings, inactive streets, declining commerce, and exhausted coffers." Penniman could be a taskmaster, but Nathan Negus was among the lucky ones.[67]

Perhaps Negus reminded himself of his relative good fortune as he and the other boys in the shop rushed to complete a large transparency, rendered on treated paper or loosely woven cloth and spanning fifteen feet on each side. Penniman had taken the commission and sketched the outline. The apprentices did the rest, filling sections of the freestanding mural with sheer washes of color. The trick—and the transparency *was* a trick, a visual deception—was to use enough paint to bring the scene to life, while applying it so thinly that light would pass through it. When the work was mounted, and the candles and lanterns strategically placed behind it, and the audience admitted to the show, the image must shimmer and move. Luminescence was key to any transparency's success as entertainment, and would be especially so for the one Negus and his fellows were completing: a re-creation of "the burning of the Exchange, with the view of Congress Street."[68]

From Monday through Saturday Penniman's boys—the "Pennimanic Society," they called themselves jokingly—worked at the project without interruption. Sunday they rested, as both the Bible and the law required. The next day, November 1, they put the final touches on their creation before carefully taking it across town to Ethan Greenwood's New England Museum and Gallery of Fine Arts on Court Street, where it would appear alongside a collection of Copley engravings and the skin of an eight-legged calf. Then it was the impresario's turn. While Negus and the rest of Penniman's crew tidied the Warren Street studio, Greenwood "[t]ried the lights with the great transparency," preparing for its unveiling Wednesday night.[69]

*FIRE! FIRE!! FIRE!!!* Again the cry went up in Boston on November third. But what a difference a year made. This time it was not a watchman's alarm, but a hawker's pitch: *Come see it all once more.* For twenty-five cents, members of the public could "witness" the "Splendid Transparent Painting . . . just executed by PENNIMAN" (no credit, as usual, to Negus and his fellow toilers), "representing the conflagration of the *Exchange Coffee-House.*" Save for the lack of danger, toil, and cold, the gallery owner promised, the transparency offered a "wonderfull imitation of the reality." The *Centinel* agreed. "Having seen the Painting," a reporter noted, "we can assure all who saw the calamity, that all the occurrences of it will be forcibly brought to the recollection." Those who had missed "the reality near the spot" could now take in "the most perfectly correct representation of a conflagra-

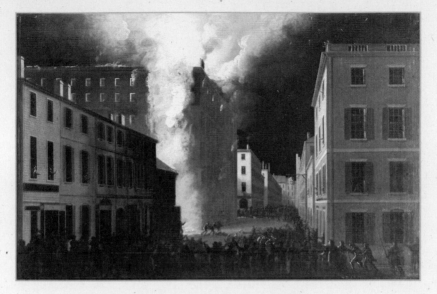

Conflagration of the Exchange Coffee House,
*by John Ritto Penniman, 1824.*

tion, considered one of the most awfully magnificent that ever occurred in this country." All told, a fitting "commemoration of the event" on this, "the anniversary of the destruction."[70]

One year after its second collapse, the Exchange Coffee House burned to the ground again. The transparency's debut, Negus noted proudly, garnered "great applause." Critics deemed it "the sublimest specimen of perspective Painting, ever seen in New-England"—"another wreath of additional brilliancy" to crown the "ingenious artist." Ordinary people voted with their feet. Every night for a week, men and women braved the same crisp late fall darkness that had enveloped them the night of the fire to watch the spectacle unfold in miniature. Those coming from the east side of town could file past the Exchange's ruins on their way to the gallery. They may have talked of where they were when the great building fell, or remarked on the irony of seeing such a painting *of* the Coffee House rather than *in* it. Perhaps some mentioned Andrew Dexter, whose wife's untimely death the papers had announced six weeks before. The transparency—which simulated fire much as the banknotes of 1809 had impersonated money—offered multiple reasons to remember him.[71]

The crowd's size so gratified Ethan Greenwood that he held the exhibition over for an additional week. The following month, the rival Boston Museum commissioned its own version. On Christmas Day, Nathan Negus once again "commenced painting [a] transparency of the burning of the Exchange." The second transparency attracted such a "numerous and respectable" audience when it opened on Tremont Street in January that the museum owners decided to keep it on view permanently. Or until interest ran out. Or, as often happened with these flammable scrims, until the image of the conflagration itself caught fire.[72]

The transparencies Penniman's studio produced were not the first

*Staffordshire teacup with a prospect of the
Exchange Coffee House, ca. 1819.*

commodities inspired by the Exchange fire, nor would they be the last. Less than two weeks after the building burned—while the city still smelled of smoke and "the late conflagration" remained "fresh in the memory of every citizen," as the newspapers held—the *Boston Weekly Magazine* issued a keepsake engraving of the "magnificent edifice . . . as it once stood." Those who wanted literally to drink in the memory could soon purchase a Staffordshire tea set emblazoned with a view of the building. And in July 1819, when the hotel's former manager David Barnum left Boston for a new situation in Baltimore, he sold off "the Household Furniture saved from the ruins." Mourners not content with manufactured souvenirs could now buy genuine relics of the Exchange, including, richly, some of the *"Fire Sets"* that once tended its many hearths.[73]

That people bought such prints and trinkets should not surprise us. Then as now, calamity made a popular subject. Fires, battles, murders, hangings: nearly every sort of deadly mayhem promised visual—not to mention commercial—riches. As John Penniman had done in his transparencies (and the smaller framed version he painted in 1824), those who crafted such images worked hard to capture disaster in action, or to evoke its immediate aftermath. After a deadly fire in Virginia in 1811—a blaze to which the Exchange's demise was compared—printmakers sold engravings of the Richmond Theater in flames in which burning children could be seen tumbling from the windows. Three years later, Washington's Capitol was depicted in its wrecked glory, silent and smoldering after the British invasion of the city. Other artists asked viewers to imagine an extant building—the Bank of England, for example—not as the fortress it was in life, but as the ruin it must one day become.[74]

Most depictions of the Exchange inverted these ways of seeing. Penniman's paintings were virtually the *only* images to show the Exchange falling or vanquished. Instead, people paid to remember the building as they had (or hadn't) seen it during its brief existence, in images that cloaked its checkered life and violent death in a gauzy, timeless pastoralism. This sort of portrait was traditional, too; tea drinkers and

*"Boston Exchange Coffee House, Burnt 1818."*

print buyers could choose among views of a seemingly infinite number of the era's public buildings transferred onto paper, china, and
linens. Yet Dexter's tower was different. People wanted to picture it
"as it stood" only when it no longer did. But for one engraving that had
appeared in an obscure, short-lived Boston magazine in 1809—
the same image that graced the Coffee House's worthless stock
certificates—portraits of the Exchange circulated only after its
death.[75]

Traffic in these once-upon-a-time images of the Exchange continued into the 1830s, and the trade in stories about the place would last
much longer. But in important ways, the first anniversary of the conflagration marked a turning point in the Exchange's short life and
sudden death and long afterlife: a moment of simultaneous reliving
and reburying, "closure" for a world without grief counselors. Six
weeks after Ethan Greenwood pulled back the curtains to reveal Penniman's dazzling transparency, a crew of surveyors got to work on

Congress Street, "*lotting* off" the ground upon which the Coffee House had stood. They leveled the site, clearing away whatever debris the scavengers and wrecking crews had left behind, and filling in the remains of the cellars. Then they measured and divided it, parceling the land into a dozen plots averaging 1,150 square feet each. A new L-shaped street, to be called Congress Square, bisected the remade neighborhood. Leading west from Congress Street and turning north

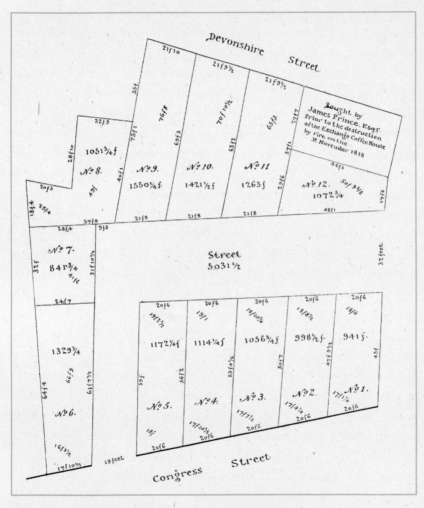

*Lots for sale on the Exchange Coffee House lands, December 1819.*

toward State, the avenue would enhance the value of the lots for retailers, improving traffic flow and giving each potential store two street fronts.[76]

On December 28, while Nathan Negus painted in the second "Conflagration" transparency, the owners of the vanquished building put the lots up for sale. Three buyers stepped forward. James Prince, whose store adjoining the Exchange had been crushed when the Coffee House caved in, safeguarded his property by buying the neighboring plot. Merchant John Parker bought one of the smaller parcels facing Congress Street, a good site for a shop or small warehouse. Neatly reversing the past two decades, the remaining lots went to Edward H. Robbins Jr., the son and namesake of the man who had owned most of the block in 1798, back before Dexter had bought it and mortgaged it and razed it and elevated it and lost it all.[77]

Reclaiming his family's old land was no sentimental gesture for the younger Robbins, a well-to-do physician who was also, as a newspaperman later put it, a "large operator." A speculator with holdings in Boston and its suburbs, Robbins was known as "a very sagacious judge of real estate," and the price was right. The choicest piece, a corner with frontage on three sides, commanded $5.25 per square foot; the least of the lots, tucked in the back, fetched barely a quarter of that. For all ten lots Robbins paid $26,952, just $840 more than this section of the property had cost Dexter in 1806. A good bargain for Robbins was a poor showing for the Exchange's beleaguered owners, who had taken in just $33,396 when the auctioneer lowered his gavel for the last time. They loaned Robbins $20,000 toward his purchases, leaving a net profit of $13,396: the grand total wrung from land for which Dexter had paid more than $100,000, a building that had cost over a half million dollars to put up, and a business that had struggled for a decade. For the next several months, the proprietors collected from their debtors and paid their creditors. On May 9, 1820, they reckoned the balance and dissolved the corporation. Equity holders surrendered their stock certificates to the treasurer, receiving exactly "twenty-two dollars and six and two thirds cents" per share in exchange.[78]

Considering that shares in the Coffee House had once been offered at $500 a piece, this was a meager return. But it marked an ending at least, one the proprietors had been trying to write since the fire eighteen months before. A week after that calamity, they had gathered at the Manufacturers and Mechanics Bank on State Street, within sight of the smoking ruins, and resolved to "sell the land and materials saved, and to close the concern." They formed a committee to oversee the liquidation and invited "proposals from any person or persons for the purchase of all said land, with their right in the act of incorporation."[79] The call generated a flurry of responses in the press, all of them beseeching investors to resurrect the Exchange in some form. Debate centered less on *whether* the Coffee House should be rebuilt than on how— or rather, *which one*. Dexter's tower had tried—and failed—to combine so many functions: civic and commercial, popular and genteel, male and female. To succeed, its replacement must choose among them.[80]

The "former building . . . was misnamed when it was called an Exchange," wrote one merchant. "It was an Hotel, or an eating house; not one for the transaction of business." A new version should be truer to its title, with space for "Insurance Offices, Consuls, Notaries, Ship, Money, and Merchandize Brokers, and a spacious Area for an Exchange": enough services to pull the merchants out of the streets and at long last impart some "system" and "regularity" to the town's "singular . . . manner of doing business." Others called for the construction of a "grand town Hotel" that would "secure the applause of every stranger who may visit the metropolis of Massachusetts," even if it disappointed Boston businessmen.[81] Some wanted to build both a hotel and an exchange, and more. The most ambitious plans outdid Dexter's, seeking funds to purchase the blocks surrounding the ruins to create an "elegant square" stretching from State Street to Water Street. One promoter envisioned a "Magnificent Exchange" rising from "streets of sixty feet wide," flanked by "ranges of uniform buildings for business and genteel dwellings" instead of "dirty back yards, filthy avenues, narrow lanes and worn out buildings." As Dexter had proven time and again, grandeur had its appeal.[82]

But most agreed that less would be more if fantasy were to "ripen into a plan." A new Exchange building must not loom. One merchant argued that "two or three stories in height would be quite sufficient"; another thought four or five floors adequate. *Not seven.* If the Coffee House were to rise again, it must make dollars and sense. Only a building radically "differing in architecture," the *Weekly Messenger* argued, could "render the undertaking a profitable investment of property."[83]

"Shall the stranger's hope and the pride of Boston, the late magnificent coffee house, lay in ruins without an exertion to repair its loss?" Unwilling to let hope lie in ruins, or potential profits slip through their fingers, a group of investors arrived at a modest goal. They would begin by constructing "an orderly and well kept Hotel," siting it to allow "a more extended suite of buildings" to be added at some later date. On the last day of 1818, they appointed fifteen gentlemen to study the feasibility of the project. Two weeks later, the committee reported that the land might be acquired and the building erected for roughly $150,000, which they proposed to raise through an offering of 1,500 shares. But when subscription books opened on January 23, 1819, it became apparent that the town that had endorsed the project "with one voice" would not, could not pay for it. As the economic downturn deepened, talk of rebuilding the Exchange ceased. Winter, spring, summer, fall: the ruins endured. By the anniversary of the fire, the proprietors had reason to fear that the Exchange had been consigned to art. Come December 1819, they must have thought themselves lucky to find buyers for the ruined land at any price.[84]

Soon after the sales, Edward Robbins set to work improving the block, beginning with the parcels for which he had paid the most—the lots facing Congress Street. Before breaking ground, he petitioned the selectmen to enlarge that street, whose narrowness had cramped the old Exchange. The board agreed that a wider Congress Street "would be of public utility," and pledged to undertake the work and to compensate the landowners. This concession secured, Robbins hired on masons and carpenters. The prevailing depression made labor cheap and plentiful. Either because the job was too small to require it, or because help was so readily available, Robbins did not advertise. During the spring and summer, his crews put up a row of plain brick warehouses, three stories high. Until tenants hung signs hawking their wares and services, the large display windows on the ground floor constituted the buildings' only adornments.[85]

In September 1820, less than seven months after the town had approved the street-widening project, tenants began to move in. The Massachusetts branch of the Bank of the United States, which took the southernmost store, was among the first. A diverse array of other concerns—among them a clothing warehouse, a hairdresser's shop, the Swedish consulate, a barroom, and two print shops—leased space in the row soon thereafter. By the end of 1821, some twenty businesses had crowded into the little buildings, including at least two—the Phoenix Fire Office and the Aqueduct Corporation—that had made their offices in the old Exchange.[86]

The rents from these stores and offices helped Robbins offset the cost of developing the remainder of the property, the back lots. Again he bid out the work privately, not feeling the need to post a call in the newspapers. Perhaps he used the crews that had put up the Congress Street row. Like those warehouses, this construction job—the erection of a moderate-size hotel—was straightforward. The concern would be called the Exchange Coffee House, less in imitation of that building than in recognition that it rose on hallowed ground. Despite the associations conjured by its name, the design of this Exchange was basic enough that Robbins had no need to hire one of the few Boston builders who called himself an architect. An honest housewright would suffice.

When the hotel opened for business in January 1822, its first keeper, Dudley Bradstreet, assured potential customers that this second Exchange Coffee House followed "a more appropriate and convenient plan than that of the former building." This was an understatement. In many ways, the new building negated the old. Where the first

*The second Exchange Coffee House, ca. 1825–1835.*

Exchange had been brazen, courting public men with its heavily orna-mented facades fronting Congress and State streets, this one was "retired" (as its trade cards said), turned inward on the cobble-stone courtyard that was Congress Square. More decorous than its predecessor, Robbins's building was also shrunken and stooped by comparison. Following the property lines of the cheaper lots on which he built it, the second Exchange comprised two parts: a main building running north to south, with its back toward Devonshire Street, and a smaller wing jogging east along Salter's Court. Together these two simple boxes covered 6,126 square feet, less than half the footprint of the first Exchange. The main building stood roughly sixty feet tall, squat where its namesake was soaring. A shallow cellar, a first floor of granite, several more of brick (four in the main building, three in the wing), and a sloping roof. A portico over the front door to shield patrons from the worst of the weather, and wooden shutters to keep out the sun. That was the whole of it. If buildings speak, this one said: *Enough.* [87]

The second Exchange Coffee House did not lack ambition; it bounded it. Where the old Exchange aspired to embody the multifac-

eted public life of a first-rate city, the new one was content to do one
thing well. Where Dexter's Exchange took the nation, Europe, or
indeed the world for its audience, the second Exchange had a decidedly regional orbit. Travelers would find its accommodations
"decidedly superior to any house of publick entertainment in the New
England States," Bradstreet pronounced, a claim limited enough to be
true. The hotel contained fifty sleeping chambers, ten fewer than Benjamin's building had and more than any other public house in Boston.
In addition, it counted a dozen parlors and private dining rooms suitable for families, a Coffee Room for gentlemen, and an "Assembly
Room 75 feet long and 28 wide": almost exactly as large as the first
Exchange's Dancing Hall, if not nearly as elegant. But Bradstreet did
not promise opulence. In addition to a well-stocked larder, guests
would find "order and quiet," "respectability." Perhaps the most grandiose statement the manager made was his boast that the furniture
was "all new, and of the very best quality": reassurance, perhaps, to
those who wondered whether this Exchange's bedding had been
pulled from the rubble of the last.[88]

The new Exchange gained a reputation consistent with its aspirations. For a while, it served as the hotel of choice for dignitaries
stopping in Boston. The papers proudly announced when military
heroes, visiting heads of state, and assorted politicians—including
President John Quincy Adams himself—took rooms there. In those
flush times, the hotel and its patrons were prosperous enough to attract
thieves. In 1824, Boston's police court charged Ho Sam, a Chinese man
employed as a servant in the Coffee House, with stealing watches and
silver from wealthy boarders there. Several years later a con man—
"an *apparent* gentleman"—booked a room in the Exchange under an
assumed name, and was caught rifling through the trunks of his
neighbors. The flow of well-heeled traffic through the building—the
hotel's combination of affluence and anonymity—provided the ideal
cover for such crimes. Local businessmen, club members, and politicians convened in its meeting spaces and flocked to the dining room
at noontime. At night, the assembly room filled with audiences eager

for a variety of entertainments, from displays of ventriloquy to the occasional ball. Demand for space in the Exchange Coffee House seems to have remained steady, and the costs of the enterprise modest. The new Exchange didn't make its owner rich, but neither did it bankrupt him.[89]

If the modesty of the second Exchange Coffee House afforded it a measure of success, it also ensured that buildings with grander ambition would soon transcend it. A bigger hotel went up on nearby Bromfield Street within a year of the Exchange's opening, and the Tremont House, an ornate 180-room hotel designed by the architect Isaiah Rogers, displaced the Exchange upon its completion in 1829. The Coffee House's owners responded with renovations to enhance their establishment's "usefulness and elegance," but the Tremont handily won the contest to become the city's first resort. Nor could the Exchange long hang on to second place. By 1838, a travel guide that gave the Exchange a respectful six lines of text devoted a long paragraph to the American House—"the second hotel in size and importance in the city"—and three illustrated pages to the Tremont. Not even the Tremont could rest easy. That same year, the new City Hotel dwarfed Rogers's palace, and in 1839, the 400-room United States Hotel surpassed the City. So it went (and so it goes), with each new biggest and best outshining the last, if only for a moment.[90]

By the 1840s, the second Exchange Coffee House had also given up its claim to be a center of business. In 1842, the city's first dedicated Merchants Exchange opened at 55 State Street. Rising on the footprint of buildings that had been gravely damaged by the burning of the old Coffee House, this Exchange displayed the ideas and technologies of a new generation. Like virtually every important Boston building from the 1810s on—the Tremont and the City hotels included—it was sheathed in white granite, making its pale, smooth face appear stronger and fresher than either the first or the second Exchange Coffee House, with their humble skins of Charlestown brick. Six massive columns—squat and squared in the idiom of the Greek revival—guarded the main entrance. Among them nestled an enormous globe with an American eagle astride it, testament to the reach Boston men imagined for their money. This was no overgrown coffeehouse, with that label's now-quaint evocation of Restoration London. The Merchants Exchange was a commercial fortress worthy of a leading city in an emerging industrial nation. Its architect, Isaiah Rogers, secured this stronghold with a fireproof design, making the staircases out of stone and the roof out of iron.[91]

The brick town had become a granite city. But Boston's skyline at midcentury hovered only slightly higher than it had in 1809: roofs three to five stories above the street, their uniformity punctuated only by steeples, masts, and the State House dome. The Tremont House had wings of three and four stories in height; the United States Hotel topped out at five. The Merchants Exchange featured soaring interior spaces and a tall telegraph antenna, but it rose only seventy feet to the base of its narrow cupola. As befitted a world without steam-powered fire engines or elevators, the public buildings of the new city stretched horizontally. The old Exchange Coffee House would have towered above them all, even still.[92]

Not the second Exchange, of course. As bigger and better establishments rose, the profile of the new Coffee House inched lower in comparison. By 1850, the year Edward H. Robbins Jr. died, "rich at last" after enduring "many ups and downs," the establishment that had once declared itself to be the best in New England bid for the attention of only commercial travelers, to whom it promised "comfort and convenience" at competitive rates. At times even these modest ambitions seemed beyond reach. As the hotel aged, a writer for the *Boston Herald* mocked the pretensions of the place, claiming he'd seen two diners "from the rural districts" polish off the liquor left behind by a table of gentlemen. Smacking their lips as they banged their glasses down, one rube supposedly said to the other, "This is a first rate *boarding house,* ain't it?" Yet if the hotel had ceased to draw the better sort of patrons, neither was it a magnet for disaster. Five times during the 1840s, small blazes broke out in the Coffee House, and some combination of luck and firefighting acumen and self-effacing architecture allowed it to survive each one. It sagged. But it did not fall.[93]

In 1851, its thirtieth year of life, the second Exchange Coffee House was one of the cheaper among Boston's ninety-three hotels. Its nightly tariff of one dollar—reduced in recent years—was now half what the best houses charged. When Nathaniel Dearborn published his lavishly illustrated "New & Complete Map of the City of Boston" that year, he did not think to include it among the three-score buildings he portrayed in the margins. By then, it seemed, the only thing noteworthy about the second Coffee House was the still-lingering ghost of the first. "Exchange Coffee House, Congress Square, on the site of the old Exchange, built in 1808, and burnt in 1818": thus read the hotel's entry in the *New Guide to the City of Boston*.[94]

Memory did not pay. In January 1854, the Coffee House's owners decided that its earnings no longer justified the price of its existence. Having wrung the last bit of commercial utility out of the business, they closed the hotel and gutted the building to create a block of stores and offices. "Many old citizens deplored its demolition," a reporter for the *Boston Budget* later recalled. But this time, there was nothing spectacular in the Exchange's death. No fire, no moral, no mourning, no *tale,* save for what was becoming the American story: the gospel of progress. Just the quiet removal of a quiet building at the end of what moneymen defined as its natural life. Just the obsolete giving way to the new.[95]

❧

Flush with the promise of the new, new West and as usual, pressed for cash, Andrew Dexter returned to Montgomery in the spring of 1833. Once again he tried churning earth into paper. Lot by lot he traded away his claims to the town he had helped to plant. Between May and November, he signed thirty-one deeds, selling land to pay loans, taking out mortgages to be paid off by future windfalls, exchanging what small solidity he had achieved for the liquidity he craved. In exchange for a dollar, he granted a section of twenty lots to the Catholic bishop of Alabama, instructing him to build there an academy "for the education of young ladies of all Christian denominations." An extravagant gesture from a barely solvent man, the gift honored both his dead wife and his struggling daughter. Such benevolence suggests that Dexter was settling the kinds of accounts that don't reside in ledger books.[96]

Dexter also tended his legacy (and wasted his pocketbook) on another venture during those hectic last months in Montgomery. In May, he sat for a portrait, the second and last image he left of himself. The painter this time was Joseph Thoits Moore, an itinerant New England artist who had made his way West to Chillicothe, Ohio, in the 1820s. Beginning in the winter of 1828 to 1829, Moore came to Montgomery once or twice a year, setting up a shop for a few weeks at a time and inviting "those who wish[ed] to obtain a correct likeness" to call on him. That first winter, Moore painted forty-nine portraits in Montgomery, enough to encourage him to make it his home base beginning in 1830. He opened a "Gallery of Paintings," where he took commissions and offered lessons in drawing. Most years thereafter he found at least thirty sitters in Montgomery, more than in any of the other Alabama towns on his circuit.[97]

As he made his way through Montgomery's tiny commercial district to the workroom on the top floor of Moore's home, Dexter could not help but recall the portraits Gilbert Stuart had done of his brash younger self and his beautiful bride-to-be on the eve of their wedding. Those portraits had been taken—begun, anyway—by the nation's very best, an artist whose fame was reflected in his prices. The cost seemed reasonable to the rising gentleman who commissioned them. But the Fall had come so suddenly, and Dexter could not afford them in the end. Charlotte died before he could redeem hers from Stuart, who was dead now as well. Of the three in the studio in Boston that April, a quarter century later only Andrew Dexter remained.[98]

Capturing the mature Dexter on canvas was no easy task. His biography traced such an uneven shape, all soaring heights and plunging

depths, no easy middle ground. Others—his brother, for example—
had failed and restored themselves. *"Things turned around,"* in Samuel
Dexter's phrase. But Andrew Dexter had resisted mere stability.
Whenever solid competence lay within his reach, he chased airy
dreams instead. So his fortunes *kept* turning, rags to not-quite-riches,
and back to rags again.

How to put a face to a tale in which triumph and tragedy forever
stalk each other, with no clear victor? This was Moore's challenge,
and Moore was no Stuart. Stuart had studied under Benjamin West
in London. Born in North Yarmouth, Maine, Moore was self-taught,
an apprentice chair maker who took up house painting before moving on to signs and miniatures and finally to portraits. But he was the
best Montgomery had to offer. His likenesses garnered praise in the
local papers, which noted that frontier living seemed to generate a special hunger for mementos. "As life is so precarious, and as it is
consoling to our friends to look ever upon the features of those who
were near and dear to them while living," the *Journal* opined, readers
should seize the chance to have "a correct portrait taken." "[F]ew such
opportunities are offered in this section of the country," the writer—
perhaps Moore himself—continued. A painted likeness was a hedge
against the moment "when oblivion's mantle might otherwise have
shrouded us in forgetfulness." Moore conjured the ghost of Hamlet's
father in Montgomery: *Remember me.*[99]

Moore's Dexter is less skillful than Stuart's—less luminous and
moody, less *painterly,* as art historians like to say. But the likenesses fit
their subjects, Moore's as perfectly suited to the careworn fifty-four-
year-old widower of 1833 as Stuart's had been to the arrogant young
bridegroom of 1808. If Moore's folkloric portrait is a comedown
from Stuart's high style, Dexter's life had come down as well, from a
gleaming dome one hundred feet above Boston's Congress Street to
J. T. Moore's workshop in Montgomery. Who had Andrew Dexter
become? The paintings speak. Where Stuart's Dexter—taut and
defiant—dares the viewer, Moore's—slack, undefended—projects
resignation. The flatness of Moore's planes, the somberness of his

palette, the attention to surfaces over soulfulness: all these choices jibe well with the aging Dexter.

Moore had enough experience to follow one of the central conventions of European portraiture, posing subjects with props that embody their accomplishments and desires. Nineteenth-century American men often appear surrounded by the sources of their mastery: lands and ships, buildings and pens and Bibles. Dexter poses with paper, object of his making and unmaking. Seated at a baize-covered desk, he points to a plan of Montgomery, a gesture that identifies him with the city and vice versa. (*La ville, c'est moi:* the statement becomes less true each day, as Dexter pawns his patrimony.) Dexter's right index finger marks the intersection of Market and Main streets, the two impossibly broad avenues that had shown the founder's faith in the

Andrew Dexter, *by Joseph Thoits Moore, 1833.*

town when the place was still forest and swamp. His hand follows Main Street northeast toward the Alabama's "big bend," source of the town's cotton-based wealth. From the viewer's perspective, Main Street rises. But not from Dexter's. If he paused in Moore's studio to look at the map in front of him, he saw a path descending steep and straight toward a vortex. Knowing the man's history, it is hard not to see his lifeline there.

Dexter clearly thought Moore got his likeness right, for in September, he commissioned a copy, as well as a portrait of his son Samuel, who had just turned eighteen. More luxuries he could ill afford—and to what end? Perhaps he gave one of his own portraits to each of his sons and sent Samuel's to his daughter. Or maybe he left a picture of himself for posterity in Montgomery—to grace the new courthouse at the intersection of Market and Main—and took the other canvases west that winter, where the image of Samuel could serve as an aide to memory, and the one of himself as a way to stake a new claim.[100]

⁓

Andrew Dexter came to rest in Mobile, Alabama, a place that had much in common with the other entrepôts he had favored over the years. Like the Detroit of 1806, Mobile in 1834 was a replacement city that had sprung, all at once, from the rubble of a fire. After the great conflagration of 1827, merchants and shopkeepers substituted neat brick buildings for burned out log huts. The new city's streets, made from crushed shells and gulf sand, fairly gleamed. From the ashes Mobile had "risen in all the vigor and beauty of a phoenix," the *Mobile Register* bragged in 1833, just before Dexter got there.[101]

This glittering streetscape mirrored Mobile's new economy. Cotton had turned the onetime garrison into a frontier boomtown. The year Dexter arrived, one hundred fifty thousand bales of white gold passed through the port. By 1837, that number had more than doubled. Between 1830 and 1840, Mobile's population grew fourfold, from just over three thousand to just under thirteen, making it one of the fastest-growing places in the fast-growing United States. As in the rest of

Alabama, roughly half the town's inhabitants were slaves of African and Creole descent. These African Americans and the whites who held them in bondage made up the majority of the population, but there were other groups as well. Free blacks and Frenchmen and Brits and Spaniards all did business along the town's bustling quays, their accents a reminder of the empires that had battled over the port since colonial days. Only in 1813 had the United States won the territory, making Mobile barely more American than Nacogdoches. These succeeding waves of national dominion added to the social complexity of the city, and they also confounded the transmission of property there. Fluid and fast and moneyed and remote, Mobile in the mid-1830s was yet another speculator's dream.[102]

Deputizing his son Samuel as his attorney, Andrew Dexter continued to sell off his holdings in Montgomery in order to build his portfolio in Mobile. With a douser's knack for finding land that, as one Montgomery pressman later put it, "had been overlooked by our government," he began to raise another paper fortune. Once again, he dreamed building dreams, leveraging Mobile town lots as fast as he could buy them to fund the construction of an immense sawmill on the outskirts of the city. He bought the land—3,000 acres held under Spanish title—on credit, putting down less than a quarter of its $7,000 price. He spent $15,000 erecting the works. Several years later, Alfred Dexter redeemed the whole parcel—land and mills together—for $400.[103]

The culprit this time was neither flood nor fire, but a more general paper collapse. In the spring of 1837, Dexter's bubble burst for the last time, imploding along with the speculative economies of the city, the region, the nation, and beyond. As in 1819, a bumper cotton crop led to a fall in prices that prompted a tightening of credit across the Atlantic, a shock the highly leveraged economy couldn't withstand. Banks shuttered, firms folded, and fortunes evaporated, especially in the Southwest. For the second time in a generation, "panic" engulfed the country. Reeling from the scores of failures New Orleans had experienced within a period of weeks, one correspondent suspected that the "fire . . . now raging in our mercantile community will not slacken so long as there is fuel to feed it."[104]

In Mobile, the speculative run-up of the 1830s provided fuel aplenty. A mood of hopelessness infected the city, the "countermania," as one correspondent in the *Mobile Register* said, of the confidence that had earlier prevailed. Between 1837 and 1838, the value of taxable property in the city fell by nearly 30 percent. Real estate was especially hard hit, and soon was worth less than half what it had been before the panic. Lenders grew anxious, speculators, desperate. By July, Andrew Dexter's promissory notes were being returned for nonpayment, and his creditors were circling once again.[105]

They would not have a chance to collect. That October yellow fever stalked Mobile, another threat to a shaken town at the end of a miserable year. The plague came later than usual, aided by unseasonably warm temperatures. By midmonth, the board of health estimated that the "malignant fever" was claiming fifty lives a week. The halls of the city hospital filled with the dying, and sextons wearied from the strain of burials. At month's end came the first sign of relief. FROST AT LAST, the *Register* proclaimed, hopeful that a hard freeze would "dissipate any remains of malignant disease." On November 3, the board of health confirmed that only two new cases of the fever had emerged during the previous week.[106]

By then it was too late for Andrew Dexter. In the last days of October, as the epidemic eased, he caught the disease that had likely claimed his wife eighteen years before. There is no reliable account of his final days. Memorializing this "founder of Montgomery" in 1871, the Alabama journalist Wallace W. Screws claimed that Dexter had been in custody when he took sick, confined for one of his many debts. A generation later, another Montgomery newspaperman floated a different story. Dexter was on the upswing, "gradually returning to that sphere which was his true position," Michael Woods argued. He might have stayed away at his "healthful" country seat eight miles out of town, but he came to the pestilential city to do business at his office on Royal Street, two blocks away from the Bank. Ever the "victim of his benevolent and charitable impulses," Dexter fell ill, Woods said, while paying a sick call on an acquaintance dying from the fever. Whether Dexter was free or under house arrest when he caught it, the disease followed its swift, relentless course: a week, maybe less, from mild chills and aches to high fever, kidney failure, hemorrhaging, and convulsions. On November 2 he died.[107]

A death for its time and place: in a city reeling from failure, Dexter embodied reversal to the last. Even by the boom-and-bust standards of the day, his life had been marked by what the *Mobile Advertiser* labeled "extreme fluctuation in worldly circumstances." "Fame once was busy in heralding his name," the obituary noted. But he died obscure. "Once he was a rich banker in the North." He died a pauper on the southern frontier. Once he had "owned an entire bank, and with it broke almost every other bank in the State, before he got broke himself." He died owning almost nothing. Once he had surveyed his domain from the heights of "the celebrated great Exchange in Boston." He "died in a little ten by twelve office, in this city, with scarcely the necessaries of life furnished him . . . but five or six persons followed his remains to the grave!" With no will and no assets to pay for his funeral, Andrew Dexter was probably consigned to a potter's field. In later years, when Montgomery's city fathers decided to raise a monument to his memory, they tried to recover his remains. The appointed committee "could never find the exact spot where he was buried."[108]

Here is what he left behind: two children still weeping over the grave of the third. Two brothers struggling to care for their niece and nephew as well as their own families. A work ox and an enslaved man named Dick, both soon sold in the futile attempt to settle the bankrupt estate. Piles upon piles of paper: worthless banknotes, mortgaged titles, unpaid loans. No fame, no fortune, no building, not even a stone to mark his passing. A legacy of debts, and dreams.[109]

Both halves of this doubled inheritance weighed heavily on Alfred Dexter in the coming years. After the state of Alabama auctioned his father's lands, Alfred told his uncle and mentor that there was "nothing of any consequence to divide." Although his father's many unsatisfied creditors had no claim against him personally, Alfred wanted to pay off as many of them as he could, just to leave *"no possibility* of trouble hereafter in case I make something handsome, by my trouble & expense."[110]

Like his father, Alfred Dexter believed in the handsome future that awaited the businessman who, as Freeman Hunt's popular *Merchants' Magazine* said, "ascends the ladder of fortune with a quick, lithe, and easy step," getting "a firm grasp upon each round . . . as he fearlessly and rapidly advances in the upward way of fortune." Alfred's father offered him a powerful counterexample. He was not the sort of failure Hunt's magazine sketched, a man of halting thoughts, "self-made doubts and supposed contingencies," one "who is always attempting to climb and never gets beyond the first round or two of the ascent . . . always standing at the bottom looking upward." No, Andrew Dexter climbed too far, too fast, and then lost his footing, only to do it all again. A victim of his father's mistakes, Alfred became in time their custodian, working in the 1840s on a memoir of the man whose life he wanted to document, but not to repeat.[111]

Alfred tried on different lives—surveying railroads, planting cotton, trading Texas lands—always certain he was about to "make something handsome." He sometimes glimpsed the easy upward way that Hunt and so many others said could be gained merely by striving. But he never quite reached it.

Lacking his father's daring and lightness, Alfred Dexter did not soar as high as Andrew had. But if he remained earthbound, he made of his torments something momentous. "Here I am tied as Prometheus was to the rock," he told his sister in 1844, comparing himself to the brave Titan's son whose quest to better humanity's lot the gods had answered with eternal torment. "I am sinking, sinking," Alfred continued. "All the best part of my nature—all the mother in me—is crushed down." In place of Charlotte Dexter's placid, accepting nature, he had inherited his father's "constitutional defect," a fatal combination of hope and hunger and heedlessness. Lack of contentment: this "family failing," this "horrible calamity," was his patrimony. "Nothing

can satisfy," he lamented. Fortune's ladder was as cruel as it was irresistible. The "present is always a mere step to the future—but so
narrow so sharp & unsteady that we rest upon it with pain—tottering,
ready & fearing every moment to fall backwards into irretrievable
ruin. . . . Hard doom!"

Hard doom indeed, to live with the "mountain in sight, never to be
gained!" The Dexters' enduring nightmare, the underside of an
American dream.[112]

# RELICS

*August 1848*, nearly seventy years after Andrew Dexter's birth. The worlds he inherited, imagined, and made have largely vanished. In February, the treaty ending the Mexican war pushed the western boundary of the United States—which had just surged past the Alleghenies in 1798—all the way to the Pacific. Their "Manifest Destiny," some white Americans call this continental nation; the Mexicans, the Indians, the slaves on whose backs it is built see it differently.

Like the ever-expanding country it still claims to inspire, Boston bears but faint traces of its former selves. The town that had fewer than twenty-five thousand inhabitants when Dexter arrived there is now a teeming city nearly five times that size. The early years of the present decade were hard times here, as everywhere. But now, fed by the toil and energy of thousands of new immigrants, nourished by a veritable renaissance in literature and art, embattled by the great question of slavery dividing the country, the city is stirring to life again.

As it shakes off the long depression that followed the last and deepest of the century's many busts, Boston has embarked upon its most ambitious public works project to date: the construction of a massive system of conduits and pipes to send the waters of Long Pond (rechristened Lake Cochituate to suggest an aboriginal purity) twenty miles east into the heart of the city. The cost will top four million dollars. For two years, teams of masons and diggers have worked in shifts

around the clock, resting only on Sundays. These tireless "labors of
the hammer and spade," as Boston's mayor puts it, have created a
brick aqueduct fourteen miles long, ending at a new reservoir capable
of holding a hundred million gallons. In recent months, the pipe fitters have led the effort, laying cast-iron mains and lead branch lines
from the reservoir in Brookline, nearly eighty miles of pipe branching
beneath two miles of ground. As the network advances into down-
town Boston, crowds gather to marvel at the scale and complexity of
the job.[1]

During the last week of August, the project reaches Congress
Square, where the second Exchange Coffee House, long past its prime,
continues to do a decent business. The workmen cutting trenches for
the water pipes peel back years. Cobbles and curbstones yield to dark
earth, and then to pale ash. Shards of a long-buried past begin to
emerge. Working in the steamy late-summer heat with picks and
spades, the ditchdiggers unearth broken bricks and charred timbers,
twisted ironwork and chunks of carved marble, broken plates and
melted bottles. Similar fragments turn up on Congress Street, and
along Devonshire. The discoveries, as one writer will later recall, pro-
voke "great wonder and curiosity."

For several days, the work site becomes something grander, a public works project elevated to the status of an archaeological dig, the
debris turned back into ruins. Many in the audience puzzle over these
scraps, the "remains of a destruction, which they knew not of." Older
members of the crowd solve the mystery. The specimens belonged to
the old Exchange Coffee House, once "the most prominent public
building in the whole country," now thirty years gone.[2]

"Relics," the papers call these bits and pieces, and the term fits.[3] Congress Square is a tomb, and the fragments buried beneath it belong to
a former world. Nearly everyone who shaped and was shaped by the
Exchange is gone: its architect, the scores of carpenters and masons
who erected it, the farmers and shopkeepers bankrupted by the place,
the firefighters who exhausted themselves trying to save it.

The moneymen are dead now as well, some of them (Samuel

Dexter, Crowell Hatch, Samuel Brown) long since. Andrew Dexter died in 1837, two weeks after Perez Morton, his father-in-law and a key member of his lending network. Both went to their graves more or less ruined by the building. Sarah Morton lasted till the spring of 1846, when she died at the age of eighty-seven. To her descendants she too left relics, shabby vestiges of a once-glittering life: monogrammed silver mugs that had descended through the Apthorp family, a "small silver box containing four gold ducats" that a brother had given her, some mourning apparel. (Despite her proper widowhood, in the next world she would be an Apthorp, not a Morton; she directed her survivors to bury her in the family crypt at King's Chapel, and to move the remains of her children there as well.) She died holding Yazoo paper, too—$33,384.32½ worth, according to its face. The probate court assigned it a value of zero.[4]

The avowed enemy of the enormous building and its paper double survives to see its remains unearthed nearly four decades later. Born during the war that created the United States, Nathan Appleton will live to see the one that divides it. He is sixty-nine years old now, the same age Dexter would have been. Hardly the same sort of man, though. Appleton is quick to point out the differences between the honest trader and the slippery speculator, and Dexter cannot contradict him. Neither can anyone else. Nathan Appleton has triumphed at what the day's business manuals refer to as "the great game of life." Winner takes all, including the right to tell the story: Appleton the conqueror.[5]

Appleton the conqueror is also Appleton the gambler. But unlike Dexter's, his bets—even long shots like the hunch that cloth could be manufactured in New England on a grand scale—have paid off. He has endured every economic insult the century has thrown at him: the embargo, the regional banking collapse of 1809, the national panics of 1819 and 1837, and the long years of depression thereafter. And he has profited by them all. From humble origins, he has reached great heights. By 1848, his assets, of over a million dollars, make him the seventh richest person in Boston: one of "our *first men*," as a listing of the town's ultrawealthy—part biographical dictionary, part lifestyle pornography—puts it.

"We are told and taught that all men are *born* equal; yet they do not long stay so," the pamphlet's author observes. "When we look around us, we see a very great inequality existing: this man in a hovel—that man in a palace . . . surrounded with every luxury that wealth can afford." Nathan Appleton is one of the latter, a member of the new "Boston aristocracy." He lives in splendor befitting a merchant prince, on Beacon Street, in a "mansion house" stuffed parlor to attic with reflections of his good fortune and his good taste. He owns enough silver to serve dozens. Works of art cover every wall. Ten canvases, two Brueghels among them, share the drawing room with a marble bust of Byron, a bronze statue of Demosthenes, and a mosaic depicting a duck hunt, the antebellum equivalent of "Dogs Playing Poker."[6]

In the manner of venerable old men before him and since, Nathan Appleton thinks a great deal about his pedigree and his legacy. In the 1830s, he became consumed with history and heraldry, tracing his family and its coat of arms back to the fourteenth century. To the future he leaves an image of himself. Two years ago he sat—or rather, stood—for a mature portrait, as Andrew Dexter had done in Montgomery in 1833. For the task Appleton selected an artist worthy of his commission: a Boston-born, Paris-schooled painter of growing international renown. George Peter Alexander Healy is near kin to Gilbert Stuart, having trained with Stuart's daughter Jane before abandoning the provinces for the École des Beaux-Arts. He has painted crowned heads and diplomats; Appleton is one of America's cotton kings. Just as Joseph Thoits Moore posed Dexter with a map of Montgomery, Healy places Appleton in front of a calico printing machine, wellspring of his fortune. Dressed in striped trousers, spotless linens, and a double-breasted waistcoat, Appleton holds a gleaming fur top hat in one hand and a fine walking stick in the other. His proud bearing accentuates a prosperous paunch. The quizzical look that marked his 1808 portrait by Stuart is gone, replaced by the imperious gaze of a

Nathan Appleton and the
Calico Printing Machine,
*by George Peter Alexander
Healy, 1846.*

monarch surveying his domain. Appleton's children jokingly call the
portrait "The Great Manufacturer."[7]

Appleton often meditates on his success, and he does not laugh
about it. "Wealth is power," he wrote in 1844. "Its possessor is the
object of envy and flattery." Certainly this is true in his case. As he
ages, people court him for his wisdom, and his money, hoping to be
first in line when the Great Manufacturer becomes a Great Benefactor. That same year, Harvard awarded the man who had once taken
a mercantile apprenticeship over a place at Dartmouth an honorary
Master of Arts. A decade hence, they will make him a Doctor of Law.
The American Academy of Arts and Sciences, the American Antiquarian Society, even the Archaeological Institute of Suffolk County,
England, have all elected him to their august ranks as well. They heap
him with laurels and extend their empty hands. The attention flatters
him, but he does not want people to suppose him "peculiarly devoted
to money-making." His spectacular and sustained rise makes this "a

natural inference," Appleton knows. "Yet nothing is more untrue. . . . That has never been a passion with me, or ever a subject of concern. Accident, and not effort, has made me a rich man."[8]

Like the eighteenth-century merchants from whom Andrew Dexter descended, Nathan Appleton cannot bear to be considered a treasure seeker. His contemporaries feed his anxiety on this score, flattering the rich while derogating the single-minded pursuit of profit. "It will be well to remind them," the otherwise-fawning author of *Our First Men* says of his title characters, that the

> money which so puffs them up, and makes them feel so big, came to them through toil and labor, and close shaving, and tight economy; and now and then, perhaps, a little cheating; sometimes by business not very creditable; and that, in the same way, it may come, and is every day coming to others, who are willing to use similar means.

Appleton admires toil. ("Human labor is the only source of wealth," he writes, imagining his own deliberate efforts more than those of the women who work his power looms, much less the slaves who grow the cotton they mill.) Despite their pinched quality, he might also applaud "close shaving" and "tight economy," ancient Yankee virtues, if not especially liberal ones. But he will not own shady dealings, and he abhors cheating. Nathan Appleton believes that the great game of life is fundamentally fair, and that he has played it skillfully. To deny chasing wealth is not to pronounce himself unworthy of it. Accident is not caprice. Nathan Appleton deserves what he has gotten. He would say the same of Andrew Dexter.[9]

Appleton's private library runs to nearly two thousand volumes, including numerous titles in French, the language he taught himself at night while clerking in his brother's shop. In addition to prizing the classics that feed his cultivated mind, he fills his shelves with books that confirm what Alexis de Tocqueville called the "desire to rise" that "gnaws at every American." He collects Freeman Hunt's *Merchants' Magazine,* carefully binding every volume since it began its run in 1839.

Like Appleton, *Hunt's* insists that virtue begets affluence. *Worth and Wealth,* its editor titles a collection of his favorite merchants' maxims. Nathan Appleton wholeheartedly believes that these two travel together, a fallacy his age shares with our own. Strength of character breeds success, Hunt argues, and failure blooms in its absence. The "Good Merchant," Appleton reads, is the "Saint of the nineteenth century . . . he is wisdom for the foolish, strength for the weak, warning to the wicked, and a blessing to all. Build him a shrine in Bank and Church, in the Market and the Exchange, or built it not: no Saint stands higher than this Saint of Trade."[10]

It is easy to picture Appleton nodding in smug recognition and thinking about the man who once built such a shrine to Mammon, the inglorious remnants of which now emerge from a ditch beneath Congress Street, a hole much like the one Andrew Dexter dug for himself. The "Literature of Commerce," as Hunt calls his genre, understands such rogues, men he deems neither wholly wicked nor wholly blameless. Hunt offers Appleton a parable, a contemporary version of the tortoise and the hare, in which those who resort to fraud are men with abundant daring but little patience. They "attempt to grow rich rapidly by financiering, rather than by diligence in business." Financiering is a "deep game," he explains, one that substitutes manipulation for *making.* A paper man, the financier forsakes "honest toil" for "calculations of chance." He climbs high, but not steadily. And then, "on the brink of the precipice," he panics. Instead of saying, " 'Here gentlemen, are my books, here is my statement, such and such causes have brought me here,' and commencing anew," he leaps headlong "into the vortex, and, having lost the confidence of [his] fellow men, find[s] it impossible to rise again."[11]

The brave climb, the terrifying drop, the irretrievable depths: there is empathy in this explanation. In this vertiginous world, even such plunges as Dexter's no longer seem *astonishing,* as so many people had found his collapse in 1809. "All men are liable to the ups and downs of business," *Worth and Wealth* explains. More than "seventy-five per cent of those engaged in trade, fail in the course of their career." *There but for the grace of God,* Hunt seems to suggest, while holding out the post-Calvinist promise that grace shines most brightly upon the good. Perhaps Nathan Appleton shares this view as well. He can afford to extend a small measure of charity to his former adversary, and soon he will need to. The Appleton and Dexter families, twinned for decades, will formally unite in 1851, when Franklin G. Dexter, a distant cousin of Andrew's, marries Nathan's cousin Harriet Cutler Appleton.[12]

Several years later, when the Great Manufacturer writes the fragments of an autobiography, he will devote several pages to Andrew Dexter and his "tremendous speculation." The last of several versions of those events Appleton has written, this account is as self-serving as the others. Appleton and his allies ride on white chargers; he gives their syndicate full credit for effecting "a correction of public opinion in relation to bank circulation." But aside from damning the "barefaced fraud" that doomed the Farmers' Exchange Bank, Appleton tells the tale without rancor. There is wonder, even, in his definition of Dexter's "consummate folly": sinking the paper circulation so boldly cornered into the "enormous building, known by the name of the Boston Exchange."[13]

Few recall the grand old Coffee House as clearly as Appleton does. Most of those who lived in Boston while the building stood were children then; the masses who have come to the city since 1818 never knew it at all. For them it belongs to the perpetual past, one of those Boston bygones like the Massacre, the Tea Party, and the vanquished hills. The hunks of debris that the diggers disinter are thus relics in another sense: venerable as well as old, mementos of another way of being in the world.

After the bricks and the ash are cleared away, after the pipes are soldered and the pavement replaced, after the second Exchange is razed and its successor built, after Andrew Dexter's children have died, and their children, too, the story endures. In the 1870s, the *Boston Commercial Bulletin* will publish more than sixty installments—nearly five thousand column inches of print—of a series called "Reminiscences of the Old Exchange Coffee House." On the anniversary of the fire in the first year of the new century, the Boston *Herald* will devote its front page to an account of the "First Sky-Scraper: Boston's Original High Building." Into the 1920s, the third of November will be marked as one of the "Red Letter Days in New England History." In each retelling the narrative of the Exchange is cast as an Icarus tale, a Babel tale. Part romance, part seduction, part comeuppance: the story admits the lure of the sun as it points out the danger of reaching for it. And then, when it becomes threadbare, its moral too quaint for a people who find no peril in unbounded ambition, the tale will also vanish, like the bricks and the ashes and the relics, into thin air. Just as Prospero foretold.[14]

✍

March 2007, nearly two hundred years after workingmen broke ground on the Exchange Coffee House. Although this twenty-first-century city lives on its history the way the Federalist-era town lived on maritime trade, no one alive in 1807 would recognize Boston today, least of all the old Eighth Ward. Congress Square itself is gone. The first Exchange Coffee House, and the second, have been reburied many times over.

Towers of steel and glass surround the site now, as tall as they are banal. One of them, standing nearly five hundred feet high, is called Exchange Place. At this writing it is Boston's thirteenth tallest building, a minor behemoth, three hundred feet shorter than one metric for the minimum height of a skyscraper. Even so, it and its faceless neighbors cast the lot upon which the Exchange Coffee House rose in shadow for most of the day. Which is no terrible shame. A soot-blackened eight-story office building, a copy shop, a littered alley: nothing of consequence stands there now. In this city of tourists and trails, monuments and markers, there is no plaque to note that anything ever did.

The bricks leave no trace, but the paper endures. "Money is something substantial," the author of *Our First Men* wrote in 1846. The claim seemed laughable even then. But in his own curious way, Andrew Dexter has proven it right. The banknotes that his scheme (his plan, his plot) rendered worthless in 1809 survive in great number, almost two centuries after the fact. These fragile slips of a paper so thin it's almost translucent have lasted for a number of reasons. They exist because Dexter printed so many of them, which in turn made them cease to function as a medium of exchange before hands and pockets could wear them out. They survive because they were too densely printed to write on, and not substantial enough to make decent kindling, or even toilet paper. Perhaps they last for sentimental reasons, as well: because they were hand signed, evidence of human intention that makes them hard to throw away. Or because they were talismans: rosary beads of early capitalism, tracing powerful mysteries of loss and deception, and maybe of resurrection as well. Or maybe not. But thinkingly or unthinkingly, generations of ordinary men and women hung on to their Dexter Dollars. Today you can find them through Internet auction sites or obsolete coin dealers.[15]

You might wonder what they're worth. The easy answer is nothing. I can't buy so much as a cup of coffee with my two-dollar bill from the Farmers' Exchange Bank, any more than Christopher Gore (its first bearer) could use it to pay for two nights' lodging at the Exchange Coffee House after the bank failed in March 1809. The notes have no *exchange* value, then. But the bills have market values, set by numismatists and ratified by their customers. (A price, as my husband, who makes his living as a "value investor," is fond of reminding me, represents not the worth of a thing, but what somebody—read: a sucker like me—is willing to pay for it.) By this calculus, their worth varies, largely according to scarcity. Farmers' Exchange Bank notes are among the most common of all "obsoletes," and thus among the cheapest. I bought my two-dollar bill for only sixty-four dollars, tax, shipping, and handling included. I found it on the Web and used PayPal to wire the money from my Visa account: a promise rooted in plastic and realized through pixels. Collectors value Detroit Bank bills rather more. Those from Dexter's private reincarnation of the bank, especially the ones routed through branch offices, are as rare as hen's teeth, and priced accordingly. A five-dollar note payable in Providence in July 1807 recently sold for five hundred dollars.[16]

What would Andrew Dexter make of this latter-day market in the paper he made and unmade, and which made and unmade him in turn? He would cackle at the prices, certainly. Yet the ongoing traffic in these strange hybrids of the worthless and the precious would tickle him as much as their seeming appreciation. That I've framed some of them—glued them down—might please him considerably less.

One type of Dexter Dollar retains both its face value and the collector's market value. In 1863, tired of the dizzying proliferation of competing notes from the nation's fifteen-hundred-plus banks, and clear of the roadblocks regularly put up by southern legislators, the United States Congress created a national paper money, the bills popularly known as "greenbacks." The widespread shortage of silver that followed the Civil War prompted the government to experiment with "fractional" notes as well, greenbacks in denominations of less than a dollar. In June 1873, a new issue of the fifty-cent note—this one allegedly more difficult to counterfeit than the prior three—honored onetime secretary of the Treasury Samuel Dexter. For roughly six months, until January 1874, his face was money.[17]

My Samuel Dexter fifty-cent note is the best in my collection, bearing a grade of "AU" or "almost uncirculated," in the argot of coin dealers. It is a lovely little thing, measuring barely two inches by four, printed in green and black ink on watermarked paper flecked with pink and blue fibers to prevent duplication. It looks and acts like modern money. But don't let its appearance deceive you; it is the philosophical descendant of the stuff Samuel Dexter's nephew Andrew tried to foist upon New Englanders in the first decade of the nineteenth century. Which is to say, the Samuel Dexter fifty-cent note does not represent a promise to pay anything but itself. THIS NOTE IS EXCHANGEABLE FOR UNITED STATES NOTES, the bill's or-

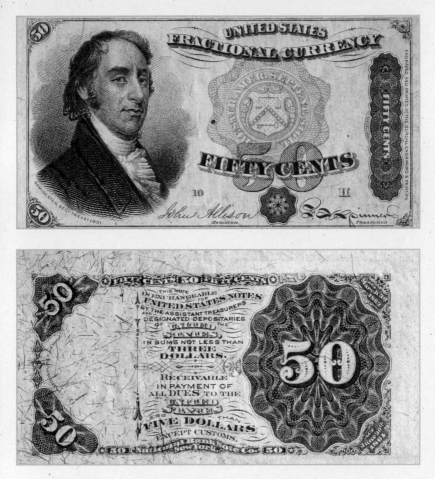

*Samuel Dexter fifty-cent note, ca. June 1873–January 1874.*

nately engraved back explains. No vault of gold stands behind it, not even a dry well beneath a trapdoor in the woods of Rhode Island. Only the full faith and credit of the United States transmutes this little ticket bearing Samuel Dexter's slightly distorted likeness into a half dollar.

I paid seventy-seven dollars for mine, a pretty good deal, I am told. My husband questions this. I explain that this one still counts as money. My local bank doesn't recognize it, so I need to send it to the Office of Currency Standards, a division of the Bureau of Printing and Engraving, which is a section of the United States Department of the Treasury. There, the person staffing the desk marked CUR-RENCY RESIDUE REQUEST will give me two quarters for it, more than enough to cover the cost of my first-class stamp: a dexterous exchange after all.[18]

# A NOTE ON THE DRAWINGS

*In the fall* of 2004, I presented this project to the Charles Warren Center's workshop on the history of the built environment in North America. In addition to the usual suspects—assorted historians— the audience that afternoon included architects, urban planners, and others engaged in the study and creation of buildings and their surround. I showed them the surviving images of the Exchange Coffee House: a handful of exterior elevations and portraits created while the building stood or soon after it burned, a period map or two, and a comprehensive set of floor plans drawn after a renovation in 1817, most likely for insurance. To a historian who had written a first book on seventeenth-century New England, Andrew Dexter's world seemed positively awash in images. Yet my listeners that day saw this record as visually impoverished. The vanished building was hard for them to *see,* and seeing was their way of knowing.

What surprised me more than their disappointment was their suggestion that I improve upon the traces in the archives. What chance had left behind was a beginning. Architecture students could take those floor plans and elevations, redraw them with CAD (computer-assisted design), and then use a rendering program like Rhino or Maya to bring the building back to life. Virtually, if not actually, I could experience the Exchange in three dimensions. I could see it from the south and the west, elevations nobody at the time cared to depict. I could see the interiors, never otherwise represented but in words (worth exactly one one-thousandth of a picture a piece). I could feel what it was like to peer down from the uppermost galleries toward the 'Change floor, or to look up at the dome's occulus from a hundred feet below. If I threw enough talent at the problem, I could "walk" the space, see it in the morning or at night, on a brilliant summer afternoon or under lowering April skies. I could sense how high it stood in relation to its neighbors, and learn how little of it a pedestrian could see from the ground. All this virtual seeing would lead me to ask new questions, and maybe suggest new answers as well.

Historians have feet of clay. So these promises that the invented would outdo the actual struck me as puzzling, if not downright sinister. Nonetheless, with Margaret Crawford's help, I commissioned the images. Using a combination of surviving images and textual evidence I assembled from travelers' accounts, newspapers, diaries, and letters, Elliott Hodges drafted plans, sections, and elevations. Ana Pinto da Silva added textures and lighting effects. The three of us went back and forth for months. Which bricks mapped onto the virtual Coffee House to give a truer red—Faneuil Hall's or the West Boston Church's? What defects in the historical images could we correct some two centuries later? What *was* right . . . and what *felt* right? You see the combined results of our research and guess work and interpretations in Chapter Four.

Scholars will ask what we are to do with this kind of latter-day documentation, which does not, in any conventional sense, qualify as *evidence*. Yet Elliott's and Ana's art is more lifelike—and yes, in some ways, more *real*—than the engravings and woodcuts and paintings that survive from the first quarter of the nineteenth century. Their conjectural renderings are more dimensionally accurate and more perspectivally nuanced than the technologies of the early 1800s allowed even the finest draftsmen of the day. And their images are sharp-edged and technicolored: precisely as the past looked to people in the past. Age has warmed their paper to ivory and faded their iron-gall inks to brown. But the denizens of Federalist-era Boston did not live in a sepia-toned world.

Had Asher Benjamin, the architect of the Exchange, the vocabulary to describe these images, he might say the drawings feel too vinyl, too anodyne: hyperreal. Just as likely, I think, he would recognize in them something of the sublimity of the Exchange, the looming bulk of a too-tall building in a too-small city on a sunny morning early in 1809, just before the Fall.

# ACKNOWLEDGMENTS

*What would Dexter do?*

This is a question I ask myself often, about a character with whom I've grown to empathize, if not quite to admire. He might tell you that writing a book is a bit like building a building. You start with an idea, gather around it a heap of raw materials, and draw upon the skill of many people to assemble them, brick by brick, into something more or less coherent. Doing this takes time. And time, as Andrew Dexter well knew, is money. He would admit that this writing business is a highly leveraged enterprise, with debts incurred every step of the way. He would describe those debts, trying to pay them off with compliments and promises. But they would remain essentially uncompensated when the roof went on. As, alas, do mine.

A number of generous grantors underwrote this project. A University Teachers Fellowship from the National Endowment for the Humanities, together with a fellowship from the Charles Warren Center for Studies in American History at Harvard University, provided a year's leave from teaching, during which much of the first draft was written. A grant from the Graham Foundation for Advanced Studies in the Fine Arts helped defray the cost of illustrations. The last bits of finish carpentry took place at the Radcliffe Institute for Advanced Studies. I am truly grateful for these indispensable gifts of money, and especially of time.

I drew on the expertise and sometimes taxed the patience of archivists scattered across Andrew Dexter's America. I owe special thanks to Norwood Kerr and Bob Cason at the Alabama Department of Archives and History in Montgomery, and to David Poremba at the Burton Historical Collection of the Detroit Public Library, as well as to dedicated staff members at the American Antiquarian Society, the Boston Athenaeum, the Bostonian Society, the Rare Books Department of the Boston Public Library, and the Massachusetts Historical Society.

I have been lucky to employ a number of brilliant Brandeis graduate students who helped me find and cull and make sense of the materials in these and many other far-flung collections. Benjamin Irvin worked with me when this was to be another book entirely, and helped me to discover what it was not. In addition to spending hours poring over dusty deeds in Dedham, Jason Opal served as a patient tutor in the literatures of the early American Republic. Rob Heinrich and Jennifer Lindsay (of the University of South Alabama) turned up valuable nuggets of "Dexteriana" in Montgomery and Mobile. Emily Straus and Lindsay Silver stuck (or *were* stuck) with the project longest and best, bringing a combination of insight, perseverance, meticulousness, and good humor that enlivens their own historical work, and added immeasurably to mine. To Lindsay, in particular, my debt is large and happily acknowledged, though hardly discharged. Elliott Hodges and Ana Pinto da Silva of Harvard's Graduate School of Design offered an entirely different kind of research support. Their technical skills and visual imaginations turned the spare surviving images of the Exchange Coffee House into a three-dimensional, navigable, virtual world. (See "A Note on the Drawings.")

Scholars like to speak of intellectual community, an oxymoron if ever there was one. But if our work is essentially solitary, we learn a great deal in conversation. This is especially true in Brandeis University's Graduate Program in American History, for many years my working home. I have benefited enormously from trading ideas with David Engerman, pages with Jackie Jones and Michael Willrich, from David Fischer's passionate commitment to the craft of writing history, and from the richly imagined community that our graduate students create and renew year upon year.

I have shared pieces of this work at meetings of the Society for

Historians of the Early American Republic, the Organization of American Historians, and the Omohundro Institute of Early American History and Culture, and at seminars, lectures, and workshops hosted by the American Antiquarian Society, Boston University, the Bostonian Society, Colby College, Johns Hopkins University, the McNeil Center for Early American Studies at the University of Pennsylvania, Oregon State University, the University of Georgia, and Yale University. I thank the audience members who caught me flat-footed with tough, smart questions, some of which I hope I've at long last managed to answer herein. Under the enlightened direction of Lizabeth Cohen and Margaret Crawford, the Charles Warren Center's yearlong workshop on the history of the built environment in North America was the liveliest intellectual community I have yet known, or expect to. For their extraordinary camaraderie, their fine minds, and their hollow legs, I thank that splendid cohort of fellows, especially Danny Abramson, Eric Avila, Alice Friedman, and Martha McNamara.

Numerous patient souls generously shared their own unpublished work, and took time to answer my endless questions about architecture, money, and politics. I thank Peter Benes, Abbott Lowell Cummings, Matt Hale, Bernie Herman, Jeff Pasley, Bob St. George, and Joe Torre for putting up with me. Ed Balleisen, Ed Gray, and Cathy Matson read early chapters and offered crucial lessons on early American political economy in exchange. I am fortunate to belong to a monthly writing group, among the oldest established permanent floating crap games in Cambridge, consisting always of Steve Biel, Jona Hansen, and Michael Willrich, and sometimes of Stephen Mihm, Steve Nelson, Mark Peterson, Jennifer Roberts, Seth Rockman, and Conevery Valencius. Together they read much of the book and helped to refine it in more ways than I can count. Jona in particular attacked the pages with a winning mixture of energy, affection, and admonition. So I inflicted the entire manuscript on him, and on Elise Broach, Dick Brown, John Demos, Jackie Jones, and Jill Lepore, who responded in different ways and from different perspectives, all sharing a combination of critical acumen and basic human kindness that makes their colleague-hood and friendship a treasure.

Tina Bennett at Janklow & Nesbit had faith in this project before there was anything to read at all. Her labors put me in the path of perhaps the world's most discerning, hardest working, and least forgiving editor: Wendy Wolf at Viking. Her keen ear, relentlessly logical mind, and sharp humor have improved every sentence. Had Andrew Dexter a Wendy in his corner shouting encouragement from the rafters while probing the holes in his business plan (an anachronism she would *never* permit him to use), the story of the Exchange Coffee House might have turned out very differently indeed.

I own my personal debts last, and they are profound and ongoing. This book began in conversation with John Demos, on a walk through the forest in the Berkshires one sunny day in May 2001. But for that shining moment on the hill, I would have abandoned a book about coffee, rather than written one about Andrew Dexter and his monstrous coffeehouse. I thank John for his inspiration that day, and the many before it and since. Elise Broach and Jill Lepore invented the "writing retreat," a magical sort of parallel play that has nurtured several books among us. They write faster than I do, even if they walk slower. So I'm delighted to have this effort join theirs on a shelf in Woodstock, Vermont. Much belated gratitude goes to Lorrie Kamensky for all the support I didn't let her give me on the last go-round. Dennis Scannell has endured my company for more than two decades now, twice as long as Dexter's Exchange stood on Congress Street. Every day gives me new reason to marvel at his fortitude and my fortune, and to revel in his partnership.

No animals were harmed in the writing of this book, but a pair of little boys suffered now and then along the way. Calvin and Malcolm Scannell have grown up alongside Andrew Dexter, a dead guy with whom they are on a first-name basis. Sometimes they like him, and sometimes they don't. (Tacked to the wall in my office is a sign Calvin carefully lettered in rainbow pencil that reads YOU ARE NEVER GOING TO WORK AGAIN, a memento of the family vacation I spent hunkered over my laptop with Andrew.) When I have ears to listen, they remind me of what matters. In meager compensation for making life count, I dedicate this book to them.

Cambridge, Massachusetts

# NOTES

### Newspapers

BG   *Boston Gazette*
BP   *Boston Patriot*
CC   *Columbian Centinel* (Boston)
CD   *Columbian Detector* (Boston)
IC   *Independent Chronicle* (Boston)
NEP   *New-England Palladium* (Boston)
PG   *Providence Gazette* (Providence, RI)
PS   *Pittsfield Sun* (Pittsfield, MA)

### Libraries and Repositories

ADAH   Alabama Department of Archives and History, Montgomery, Alabama
BHC-DPL   Burton Historical Collection, Detroit Public Library
BPL   Boston Public Library, Rare Books and Manuscripts Department
MHS   Massachusetts Historical Society, Boston
MArch   Massachusetts Archives, Boston
NEHGS   New England Historic Genealogical Society, Boston
RIHS   Rhode Island Historical Society, Providence, Rhode Island
SD   Suffolk County Deeds, Massachusetts Archives, Boston

## PROLOGUE: RUINS

1. This synopsis is drawn from many accounts of the fire in newspapers and personal documents, but see especially *Boston Intelligencer & Evening Gazette* 7 November 1818, *Boston Weekly Messenger,* 5 November 1818; and entries for 3, 4 November 1818, John Gallison, "Journal, Volume K," Boston Athenaeum, 85–96. Reports that live coals were still burning in the rubble pit surfaced in January and February; see [Natchez] *Mississippi Republican,* 9 February 1819; Gallison, "Journal," 134; and Curtis Guild, "Reminiscences of Old Boston or The Exchange Coffee House," bound clippings from the *Commercial Bulletin,* BPL, Rare Books Department (ca. 1872), 2: 90.

2. "Fire!—Exchange Coffee-House," *Yankee,* 5 November 1818. (Compare to *The Tempest* act 4, scene 1, lines 150–58.) The article appears anonymously in the *Yankee,* and over J. Hooper's signature in the [New York] *Commercial Advertiser;* see "Extensive and Melancholy Conflagration," 6 November 1818.

3. John A. Carr to Dabney S. Carr, 6 November 1818, in Carr-Cary Family Papers, 1785–1839 MSS 1231 Tracy W. McGregor Library of American History, Special Collections, University of Virginia, box 1. Two signed letters were written by S[amuel] Topliff (running first in [Philadelphia] *Poulson's American Daily Advertiser* 9 November 1818), and J. Hooper (appearing signed for the first time in the [New York] *Commercial Advertiser,* 6 November 1818). Three additional letter-versions are distinguished as follows: an unsigned letter beginning "Presuming that you feel" (first appearance in the *New York Evening Post,* 7 November 1818); a second unsigned letter beginning "The entire destruction," which ran first in *New York Mercantile Advertiser,* 7 November 1818; and the last beginning "The Exchange Coffee House took fire last night" (first in *Poulson's Daily Advertiser,* 9 November 1818).

4. For FÜRCHTERLICHES FEUER! see [Pennsylvania] *Readlinger Adler,* 17 November 1818; reprinted in [Sudbury, Penn.] *Nordwestliche Poste,* 11 December 1818. See also "The Late Fire at Boston," [London] *The New Times,* 2 December 1818; "Fires," [London] *The Times,* 1 December 1818; "The Old Exchange," *Mississippi Republican,* 9 February 1818.

5. Terrifying spectacle safely watched is a central ingredient of the sublime as Edmund Burke defined it; see Edmund Burke, *A Philosophical Enquiry Into the Origin of Our Ideas of the Sublime and Beautiful* (2nd ed., 1759), ed. James T. Boulton (Notre Dame, Ind.: University of Notre Dame Press, 1968), 47–48, 57, 63, 72, 76–77; and Neil Hertz, *The End of the Line: Essays on Psychoanalysis and the Sublime* (New York: Columbia University Press, 1985), 21–39.

6. "Appropriate Reflections," by Caution [pseud.], *IC,* 11 November 1818; "Fire!—Exchange Coffee-House," *Yankee,* 5 November 1818; "Destructive Fire," *CC,* 7 November 1818.

7. "Be Up and Doing!" *NEP,* 25 July 1806; Nathan Appleton travel journal, 18 July 1802, Appleton Family Papers, 1539–1910, MHS, box 23, folder 13. On Appleton's early life, see Frances W. Gregory, *Nathan Appleton, Merchant and Entrepreneur, 1779–1861* (Charlottesville: University Press of Virginia, 1975); and Robert C. Winthrop, ed., "Memoir of Hon. Nathan Appleton," *Proceedings of the Massachusetts Historical Society* 5 (October 1861): 252–60.

8. [Charles Jared Ingersoll], *Inchiquin, the Jesuit's Letters, During a Late Residence in the United States of America* (New York: I. Riley, 1810), 110, 113, 123. On cultures of ambition in the wake of the Revolution, see Jason M. Opal, "Beyond the Farm: Ambition and the Transformation of Rural New England, 1770s–1820s," (Ph.D. dissertation, Brandeis University, 2004); J.M. Opal, "Exciting Emulation: Academies and the Transformation of the Rural North, 1780s–1820s," *Journal of American History* 91, no. 2 (September 2004): 445–70; and Joyce Appleby, *Inheriting the Revolution: The First Generation of Americans* (Cambridge, Mass.: Harvard University Press, 2000).

9. On the spatial imagination in the early Republic, see Drew R. McCoy, *The Elusive Republic: Political Economy in Jeffersonian America* (Chapel Hill: University of North Carolina Press, 1980); and John Demos, *Circles and Lines: The Shape of Life in Early America* (Cambridge, Mass.: Harvard University Press, 2004).

10. Andrew Dexter, *An Oration, on the Importance of Science and Religion, Particularly to American Youth* (Providence, R.I., 1798), 6.

11. For populations of American ports recorded by the decennial federal census of 1800, see http://www.census.gov/population/documentation/twps0027/tab03.txt.

12. "Local Communication: Public Works," *BG*, 1 January 1807. The Dexter family's place on the map of Providence, ca. 1792–1798, is established by Providence Deeds, 23: 90, 203; RIHS miscellaneous manuscripts 14: 255, 287; and Henry R. Chace, *Owners and Occupants of the Lots, Houses and Shops in the Town of Providence Rhode Island in 1798* (Providence, R.I.: Livermore & Knight, 1914), plate 3. On the Providence Exchange Coffee House, see ibid., 13; and Clarkson A. Collins, ed., "Pictures of Providence in the Past, 1790–1820: The Reminiscences of Walter R. Danforth," *Rhode Island History* 10:1–11:2 (January 1951–April 1952), 93–96.

13. "Public Works," *BG*, 1 January, 5 January 1807.

14. John Lambert, *Travels Through Canada, and the United States of North America, in the Years 1806, 1807, and 1808: To Which Are Added Biographical Notices and Anecdotes of Some of the Leading Characters in the United States* (London: C. Cradock and A. Joy, 1816), 334; Milton Halsey Thomas, ed., *Elias Boudinot's Journey to Boston in 1809* (Princeton, N.J.: Princeton University Press, 1955), 80; "Banks—Banks—&c. &c.," by Justice [pseud.], *CD* 9 May 1809.

15. "The Exchange Coffee-House," *Intelligencer,* 7 November 1818.

16. Thomas A. P. van Leeuwen, *The Skyward Trend of Thought: The Metaphysics of the American Skyscraper* (Cambridge, Mass.: MIT Press, 1988), 9, quoting Louis Sullivan, ca. 1923.

17. Adam Smith, *An Inquiry Into the Nature and Causes of the Wealth of Nations*, ed. Edwin Cannan (New York: Random House/Modern Library, 1994), 349. (Orig. pub. 1776.)

18. Ibid., 349–50.

19. Letter to the editor, by "P," *BG,* 1 December 1808. On paper money as a kind of alchemy, see Hans Christoph Binswanger, *Money and Magic: A Critique of the Modern Economy in the Light of Goethe's Faust,* trans. J. E. Harrison (Chicago: University of Chicago Press, 1994).

20. *Report of the Committee Appointed by the General Assembly of the State of Rhode-Island . . . to Inquire Into the Situation of the Farmers' Exchange Bank in Glocester* [hereafter *RICA*] ([Providence, R.I.]: n.p., March 1809), 10.

21. "Gloucester Bills," *PS,* 1 April 1809.

22. "A Subject to Serious to Joke With," by Anti-Speculation and Fraud [pseud.], *CD,* 9 May 1809; and "Farmer Bank Bills," by Fair Play [pseud.], *CD,* 18 April 1809.

23. "Banks—Banks—&c. &c.," by Justice [pseud.], *CD,* 9 May 1809.

24. "Farmer's Bank Bills . . . Again, and Again," *CD,* 11 April 1809.

25. Scott A. Sandage, *Born Losers: A History of Failure in America* (Cambridge, Mass.: Harvard University Press, 2005), 7; and Bruce H. Mann, *Republic of Debtors: Bankruptcy in the Age of American Independence* (Cambridge, Mass.: Harvard University Press, 2002), 36. On the history of failure in early national America, see also Toby L. Ditz, "Shipwrecked; or, Masculinity Imperiled: Mercantile Representations of Failure and the Gendered Self in Eighteenth-Century Philadelphia," *Journal of American History* 81, no. 1 (June 1994): 51–80; and Edward J. Balleisen, *Navigating Failure: Bankruptcy and Commercial Society in Antebellum America* (Chapel Hill: University of North Carolina Press, 2001).

26. Letter, signed "N," *NEP,* 30 December 1808.

27. Nathaniel Dearborn, *Boston Notions; Being an Authentic and Concise Account of 'That Village,' from 1630 to 1847* (Boston: W. D. Ticknor, 1848), 211 ("brought forth . . . purified"); "Appropriate Reflections," by Caution [pseud.], *IC,* 11 November 1818. The remarks (and possibly the editorial) came from Benjamin Austin.

28. On the vogue for Shakespeare in nineteenth-century America, see Lawrence W. Levine's classic essay, "William Shakespeare and the American People: A Study in Cultural Transformation," *American Historical Review* 89, no. 1 (February 1984): 34–66. For uses of Prospero's soliloquy from *The Tempest,* act 5, scene 1, to refer to architectural and financial ruin, see Sir John Soane, "Lecture I" (1809), in David Watkin, *Sir John Soane: Enlightenment Thought and the Royal Academy Lectures* (Cambridge: Cambridge University Press, 1996), 496; Richard Price, *Observations on the Nature of Civil Liberty, the Principles of Government, and the Justice and Policy of the War with America* (London: T. Cadell, 1776); quoted in James Sullivan, *The Path to Riches: An Inquiry Into the Origin and Use of Money* (Boston: P. Edes, 1792; 2nd ed., 1809), 33–34; and Letter, signed "P," *BG,* 1 December 1808.

29. "The Bankrupt's Soliloquy, After Going Through the Mill," *PS,* 31 March 1806.

## CHAPTER ONE: PROMISES

1. Matthew Carey [Colbert Jr., pseud.] *The Age of Paper, or, an Essay on Banks and Banking* (London, 1795). Carey's own career as printer, publisher, and political economist made him accutely aware of the manifold importance of paper; see James N. Green, *Mathew Carey, Publisher and Patriot* (Philadelphia: Library Company of Philadelphia, 1985).

2. Useful primers on the meaning and history of money include Glyn Davies, *A History of Money from Ancient Times to the Present Day* (Cardiff, Wales: University of Wales Press, 1994), 27–64, 455–85; John Kenneth Galbraith, *Money: Whence It Came, Where It Went* (Boston: Houghton Mifflin, 1975), 7–17, 45–57; and Robert E. Wright and David Cowen, "An Historiographical Overview of Early U.S. Finance (1784–1836): Institutions, Markets, Players, and Politics" (unpublished paper for the National Park Service, 1999). The notes of chartered state banks dominated the U.S. money supply until the Civil War; see Robert E. Wright, *The First Wall Street: Chestnut Street, Philadelphia, and the Birth of American Finance* (Chicago: University of Chicago Press, 2005), 56.

3. On early banknote design and printing, see Virginia Hewitt, ed., *The Banker's Art: Studies in Paper Money* (London: British Museum Press, 1995). On the depersonalization of credit relations in the early-modern period, see Craig Muldrew, *The Economy of Obligation: The Culture of Credit and Social Relations in Early Modern England* (New York: St. Martin's Press, 1998); Bruce H. Mann, *Republic of Debtors: Bankruptcy in the Age of American Independence* (Cambridge, Mass.: Harvard University Press, 2002), Chap. 1; and Jose R. Torre, "The Political Economy of Sentiment: Money and Emotions in the Early Republic" (Ph.D. dissertation, SUNY Binghamton, 2002).

4. Article I, section 10. On the debate over paper money during the Constitutional

Convention, see Bray Hammond, *Banks and Politics in America from the Revolution to the Civil War* (Princeton, N.J.: Princeton University Press, 1957), 89–113; and Janet A. Riesman, "Money, Credit, and Federalist Political Economy," in *Beyond Confederation: Origins of the Constitution and American National Identity,* eds. Richard Beeman, Stephen Botein, and Edward C. Carter II (Chapel Hill: University of North Carolina Press, 1987), 128–161. On the character of banknotes see Robert E. Wright and David Cowen, "Historiographical Overview of Early U.S. Finance," 8, 23–25; R. E. Wright, *The First Wall Street,* 52–54; Naomi R. Lamoreaux, *Insider Lending: Banks, Personal Connections, and Economic Development in Industrial New England* (New York: Cambridge University Press, 1994), 2–3.

5. Thomas Willing (Philadelphia) to William Phillips et al. (Boston), 6 January 1784, in N. S. B. Gras, *The Massachusetts First National Bank of Boston, 1784–1934* (Cambridge, Mass.: Harvard University Press, 1937), 209–12, quotation at 210. On these pioneering experiments in colonial banking, see Margaret E. Newell, "A Revolution in Economic Thought: Currency and Development in Eighteenth-Century Massachusetts," in *Entrepreneurs: The Boston Business Community, 1700–1850,* eds. Conrad Edick Wright and Katheryn P. Viens (Boston: Massachusetts Historical Society/Northeastern University Press, 1997), 1–22; Margaret Ellen Newell, *From Dependency to Independence: Economic Revolution in Colonial New England* (Ithaca, N.Y.: Cornell University Press, 1998); Janet Ann Riesman, "The Origins of American Political Economy, 1690–1781" (Ph.D. dissertation, Brown University, 1983). For the early years of banking after the Revolution, see Gras, *Massachusetts Bank,* 3–15; Fritz Redlich, *The Molding of American Banking: Men and Ideas* (New York: Hafner Publishing, 1951), 1: 5–42.

6. J. Van Fenstermaker, *The Development of American Commercial Banking, 1782–1837* (Kent, Ohio: Kent State University/Bureau of Economic and Business Research, 1965), 111, 139–40.

7. Rules for reducing currencies were a standard feature of annuals from the late 1790s; these examples from *The Massachusetts Register and United States Calendar; For the Year of Our Lord 1807* (Boston: John West, 1806), 179–80. On the skill of reading money see David M. Henkin, *City Reading: Written Words and Public Spaces in Antebellum New York* (New York: Columbia University Press, 1998), 137–66.

8. Mercator [pseud.], "The Subject of Banks Considered," *BG,* 26 January 1804. On counterfeiting in the nineteenth-century United States, see Stephen A. Mihm, "Making Money, Creating Confidence: Counterfeiting and Capitalism in the United States, 1789–1877" (Ph.D. dissertation, New York University, 2003); and Alan Taylor, "The Early Republic's Supernatural Economy: Treasure Seeking in the American Northeast, 1780–1830," *American Quarterly* 38, no. 1 (Spring 1986): 6–34. On the broader issue of fraud in this first age of mechanical deception, see Karen Halttunen, *Confidence Men and Painted Women: A Study of Middle-Class Culture in America, 1830–1870* (New Haven, Conn.: Yale University Press, 1982); and James W. Cook, *The Arts of Deception: Playing with Fraud in the Age of Barnum* (Cambridge, Mass.: Harvard University Press, 2001).

9. "Bank Bills," *PG,* 14 April 1804; *BG,* 20 February 1804, 25 December 1806. Descriptions of circulating counterfeits from *The Massachusetts Register and United States Calendar for . . . 1807,* 181–85. Advertisements for Gilbert and Dean's pamphlet

(*The Only Sure Guide to Bank Bills*) began appearing in early 1806; see *CC*, 15, 19 February; 25 June 1806. No copies of the original *Only Sure Guide* survive, but the genre proved popular through the Civil War. The great benefit to printers, of course, was that counterfeits kept evolving, requiring continual updates and postscripts; see *CC* 16 August, 15 October 1806, e.g. On counterfeit detectors, see Henkin, *City Reading*, 146–57.

10. *BG*, 3 January, 14 February 1803; Phillip Ammidon to A. Wood, 14 December 1804, in Philip Ammidon Letterbook, August 1803 to July 1805, MHS. On Ammidon's bankruptcy, see Suffolk County (MA) Deeds, lib. 207: 27–30, MArch; *IC*, 25 August 1803; *CC*, 24 September 1803. Since Ammidon had ties to Providence and to Mendon, Massachusetts (where Andrew Dexter's father eventually settled), it seems likely that Dexter was a party to what Bruce Mann calls a "collusive" bankruptcy; see Mann, *Republic of Debtors*, 223, 227.

11. Orrando Perry Dexter, Henry L. Mills, and John Haven Dexter, *Dexter Genealogy, 1642–1904; Being a History of the Descendants of Richard Dexter of Malden, Massachusetts, from the Notes of John Haven Dexter and Original Researches* (New York: J. J. Little, 1904), 20–43.

12. Samuel Dexter diary quoted in Dexter, Mills, and Dexter, *Dexter Genealogy, 38*, see also 33; Samuel Dexter, *Our Fathers God the Hope for Posterity* (Boston: Thomas Fleet, 1796), appendix, 49. See also Clifford K. Shipton, *Sibley's Harvard Graduates*, vol. 6, *1713–1721* (Boston: Massachusetts Historical Society, 1942): 376–80; and Carlton Albert Staples, *Samuel Dexter, 1726–1810: A Paper Read Before the Dedham Historical Society, February 3, 1892* (Dedham, Mass., 1892), 5–6.

13. [Samuel Dexter (1761–1816)], "Biographical Notice of the Late Hon. Samuel Dexter [1726–1810]," *Monthly Anthology and Boston Review* IX (July 1810): 3–4; *Boston Evening Post* 5 February 1750, 21 October 1751, among many others. See also Staples, *Samuel Dexter, 1726–1810*; Dexter, Mills, and Dexter, *Dexter Genealogy, 53–58*; and William Pencak, "Dexter, Samuel," *American National Biography Online*, http://www.anb.org/articles/01/01-00217.html.

14. John Colman, *The Distressed State of the Town of Boston Once More Considered* (Boston, 1720), reprinted in Andrew McFarland Davis, ed., *Colonial Currency Reprints, 1682–1751*, 4 vols. (New York: Burt Franklin, 1964), 2: 65–95, quotation at 88 (Orig. pub. 1910–1911.); [William Douglass], *An Essay, Concerning Silver and Paper Currencies, More Especially with Regard to the British Colonies in New-England* (Boston: S. Kneeland and T. Green, 1738), 1, 2, 5, 7. On the intricacies of these debates see Elizabeth E. Dunn, " 'Grasping at the Shadow': The Massachusetts Currency Debate, 1690–1751," *New England Quarterly* 71, no. 1 (March 1998): 54–76; Margaret E. Newell, "A Revolution in Economic Thought"; Margaret Ellen Newell, *From Dependency to Independence*; Roger W. Weiss, "The Issue of Paper Money in the American Colonies, 1720–1774," *Journal of Economic History* 30, no. 4 (December 1970): 770–84; and E. James Ferguson, *The Power of the Purse: A History of American Public Finance, 1776–1790* (Chapel Hill: University of North Carolina Press, 1961), 3–24.

15. [Samuel Dexter (1761–1816)], "Biographical Notice of Hon. Samuel Dexter," 4, 5; Clarence Winthrop Bowen, *The History of Woodstock, Connecticut* (Norwood, Mass.: Plimpton Press, 1926), 183–85; Samuel Kendal, *A Discourse, Delivered at Mendon . . . at the Interment of the Honorable Samuel Dexter, Esq.* (Boston: John Eliot, 1810), 4–5.

In 1767, the colony's governor named Dexter and two other men "Commissioners for settling the Land Bank affairs"; see *Boston Evening Post,* 23 March 1767, and Clarence Winthrop Bowen, "Samuel Dexter, Councilor, and His Son, Hon. Samuel Dexter, Secretary of War, and Secretary of the Treasury," *Proceedings of the American Antiquarian Society* 35, no. 1 (April 1925): 23.

16. Obituary in [Hudson, N.Y.] *Northern Whig,* 19 November 1816; advertisements in *Boston Weekly News-Letter,* 21 May 1772; *BG,* 17 May, 27 December 1773. See also Dexter, Mills, and Dexter, *Dexter Genealogy,* 82–84.

17. John Andrews, August 1774, quoted in Ralph V. Harlow, "Economic Conditions in Massachusetts During the American Revolution," *Publications of the Colonial Society of Massachusetts* XX (1920): 164.

18. [Worcester] *Massachusetts Spy,* 10 November 1774. On Samuel Dexter's wartime roles, see Staples, *Samuel Dexter, 1726–1810,* 6–9.

19. Richard Frothingham Jr., *History of the Siege of Boston, and of the Battles of Lexington, Concord, and Bunker Hill* (Boston: Little, Brown, 1849); Jacqueline Barbara Carr, *After the Siege: A Social History of Boston, 1775–1800* (Boston: Northeastern University Press, 2005), 13–42.

20. Bowen, *History of Woodstock,* 182. Ephraim Ward, Andrew Dexter's brother-in-law, became pastor of Brookfield's First Church in 1771. Lyman Whiting, *A Bi-Centennial Oration . . . of the Settlement of the Town of West Brookfield* (West Brookfield: Thomas Morey, 1869), 46–60; Dexter, Mills, and Dexter, *Dexter Genealogy,* 54, 65–66, 82–84.

21. John Adams to James Warren (Philadelphia), 23 July 1775, in Paul H. Smith, ed., *Letters of Delegates to Congress, 1774–1789,* 26 vols. (Washington, D.C.: Library of Congress, 1976–2000), 1: 650. For Samuel Dexter's signature on the "King Philip Bond," see Udo Hielscher, *Financing the American Revolution* (New York: Museum of American Finance, 2003), 4 (fig. 2). For Continental note issues, see Ferguson, *Power of the Purse,* 25–47; Benjamin H. Irvin, "Benjamin Franklin's 'Enriching Virtues': Continental Currency and the Creation of a Revolutionary Republic," *Common-Place* 6, no. 3 (April 2006): http://www.common-place.org/vol-06/no-03/irvin/; and Ralph Volney Harlow, "Aspects of Revolutionary Finance, 1775–1783," *American Historical Review* 35, no. 1 (October 1929): 46–68.

22. Samuel Dexter to Caleb Davis, Autumn 1775, quoted in Bowen, *History of Woodstock,* 183; Abigail Adams to John Adams, 1 August 1781; Samuel Dexter to Governor James Bowdoin, 26 January 1779, *Proceedings of the Massachusetts Historical Society* 6 (1862–1863): 359–60; see also [Samuel Dexter (1761–1816)], "Biographical Notice of Hon. Samuel Dexter," 6. A *pistareen* represented a quarter of a Spanish milled silver dollar, or two *reales.* On Revolutionary hyperinflation, see Cathy Matson, "The Revolution, the Constitution, and the New Nation," in *The Cambridge Economic History of the United States,* eds. Stanley Engerman and Robert E. Gallman (New York: Cambridge University Press, 1996), 1: 366–69; and Galbraith, *Money: Whence It Came, Where It Went,* 58–61.

23. Baptismal records from the Hollis Street Church put the Dexters in Boston on 15 July 1781; see Dexter, Mills, and Dexter, *Dexter Genealogy,* 83. For Mary Newton Dexter's family home, see her father's advertisements in the *Newport Mercury,* especially the description of their home on 30 November 1772. On the destruction of city

property during the siege, see Frothingham, *History of the Siege of Boston,* 281–82, 287, 289, 293, 327–28. On the state of post-Revolutionary Boston, see *Boston Selectmen's Minutes from 1776 Through 1786,* Records Relating to the Early History of Boston (1894), 135–36, 139; Harold Kirker and James Kirker, *Bulfinch's Boston, 1787–1817* (New York: Oxford University Press, 1964), chap. 1; Lisa Beth Lubow, "Artisans in Transition: Early Capitalist Development and the Carpenters of Boston, 1787–1837" (Ph.D. dissertation, UCLA, 1987), 33–35; Evelyn Marie Walsh, "The Effects of the Revolution Upon the Town of Boston: Social, Economic, and Cultural" (Ph.D. dissertation, Brown University, 1964), 355–56; and Jacqueline Barbara Carr, "A Change 'as Remarkable as the Revolution Itself': Boston's Demographics, 1780–1800," *New England Quarterly* 73, no. 4 (December 2000): 583–602. For the Hollis Street Church, see Walter Muir Whitehill and Lawrence W. Kennedy, *Boston: A Topographical History,* 3d ed., 2000 (Cambridge, Mass.: Harvard University Press, 1959), 39–40, 50–51.

24. For wounded infantrymen and shoe drives, see advertisements in the *BG,* 9, 16 July 1781; and *Boston Town Records, 1778 to 1783,* Records Relating to the Early History of Boston (1895), 159, 187, 189, 194, 201, 204–5, 209, 217, 242 (quoted), 244, 250–51, 269. See also Carr, *After the Siege,* 118–24; Gary B. Nash, *The Unknown American Revolution: The Unruly Birth of Democracy and the Struggle to Create America* (New York: Viking, 2005), 232–38.

25. James Warren to John Adams, 13 June 1779, *Warren-Adams Letters: Being Chiefly a Correspondence Among John Adams, Samuel Adams, and James Warren* (Boston: Massachusetts Historical Society, 1925), 2: 105. On the economic upheaval of the 1780s, see Ralph V. Harlow, "Economic Conditions in Massachusetts During the American Revolution"; John J. McCusker and Russell R. Menard, *The Economy of British America, 1607–1789* (Chapel Hill: University of North Carolina Press, 1985), 351–77; and Drew R. McCoy, *The Elusive Republic: Political Economy in Jeffersonian America* (Chapel Hill: University of North Carolina Press, 1980), 105–19.

26. I have found no traces in Boston newspapers or land records of the Dexters' post-1781 sojourn. Nor is it clear exactly when the Dexters left for Rhode Island. Samuel Dexter advertised to recover a parcel of boys' clothing lost "On the Road to Providence, between Gay's and Daggets," in July 1783; *BG,* 21 July 1783. The first certain record documenting their residence in Providence is an agreement signed by Andrew Dexter Sr. on 14 May 1784; Peck Collection, vol. 3, item 43, RIHS. A letter addressed to Andrew Dexter Sr. remained in the Boston post office in September 1784, suggesting either continued business contacts there, or a relatively recent removal; see [Boston] *Continental Journal,* 2 September 1784.

27. See *Extract of a Letter to a Gentleman . . . Concerning the New Notes of Hand* (Boston: 1734), in *Andrew McFarland Davis, CCR,* 3: 3–19; see also Margaret Ellen Newell, *From Dependency to Independence,* 199–203; Hammond, *Banks and Politics in America,* 17–23.

28. M. Randolph Flather, "Four Hundred Dollars for a Hat: When Inflation Raged in Rhode Island," *Rhode Island History* 1, no. 4 (October 1942): 134.

29. Thomas Allen, "Landed Versus Paper Property in Rhode Island, 1781–1790," *Rhode Island History* 53, no. 1 (February 1995): 3–17; Daniel P. Jones, *The Economic and Social Transformation of Rural Rhode Island, 1780–1850* (Boston: Northeastern University Press, 1992); Irwin H. Polishook, *Rhode Island and the Union, 1774–1795*

(Evanston, Ill.: Northwestern University Press, 1969), 6–8, 46–51, 105–62; and Hillman Metcalf Bishop, "Why Rhode Island Opposed the Federal Constitution: The Paper Money Era," *Rhode Island History* 8, no. 2 (April 1949): 33–44. The depreciation of the bills between July 1786 and October 1789 is detailed in *PG*, 16 January 1790.

30. J. P. Brissot de Warville, *New Travels in the United States of America, 1788*, ed. Durand Echeverria, trans. Mara Socenu Vamos, (Cambridge, Mass.: Harvard University Press, 1964), 128 (Orig. pub. 1792.); Luther G. Riggs, ed., *The Anarchiad: A New England Poem (1786–1787), Written in Concert by David Humphreys, Joel Barlow, John Trumbull, and Dr. Lemuel Hopkins* (Gainesville, Fla.: Scholars' Facsimiles & Reprints, 1967), 15, 17.

31. The first mention I have found of the Cheap Shop appears in *PG*, 14 December 1793. The Dexter family's place on the map of Providence, ca. 1792–1798, is established by Providence Deeds, book 23: lib. 90, 203; RIHS miscellaneous mss., 14:255, 287; and Henry R. Chace, *Owners and Occupants of the Lots, Houses and Shops in the Town of Providence Rhode Island in 1798* (Providence, R.I.: Livermore & Knight, 1914), plate 3. For other land transactions, see Providence Deeds, 12:506; 13:160; 21:477; 22:333, 386, 393; 23:11, 90, 203, 366; 24:327, 366; 25: 274, 557; 26: 11; 27: 60; 30: 236; 32:332; 34:212; and 39: 462; all at NEHGS.

32. David Wilkinson, "Interesting Reminiscences . . . The Beginning of the Cotton Manufacture in This Country," *Scientific American* 7 (26 July 1862): 59; George S. White, *Memoir of Samuel Slater, the Father of American Manufactures* (1836; reprinted in New York: Augustus M. Kelley, 1967), 62–63, 65–67; Lawrence A. Peskin, *Manufacturing Revolution: The Intellectual Origins of Early American Industry* (Baltimore: Johns Hopkins University Press, 2003), 62–64, 133–46. On the "rotten row," see Walter R. Danforth, "Pictures of Providence in the Past, 1790–1820: The Reminiscences of Walter R. Danforth," ed. Clarkson A. Collins, *Rhode Island History* 10 and 11, no. 10:1–11:2 (January 1951–April 1952): 17–19, 54–55.

33. [Providence] *United States Chronicle,* 1 July, 26 August, 2 September 1790; 23 June 1791; *PG*, 6 November 1790. For the Providence Bank see Hope F. Kane and W.G. Roelker, "The Founding of the Providence Bank, (October 3, 1791)," Rhode Island Historical Society Collections 34, no. 4 (October 1941): 113–28; and *PG*, 1, 10, 24 September 1791; 8 October 1791. The listing of the bank's directors is clearly not alphabetical and thus likely reflects the number of votes for each man. For Dexter as town auditor, see *PG*, 10 June 1797.

34. "Selling Off," *PG*, 10 January 1798. A letter places Andrew Dexter Jr. at Brown in August 1796; see Andrew Dexter Jr. to William E. Green, in *Memories of Brown: Traditions and Recollections Gathered from Many Sources,* Robert Perkins Brown et al., eds. (Providence, R.I.: Brown Alumni Magazine Company, 1909), 23–24. For the future occupations of Dexter's classmates, see *Historical Catalogue of Brown University, 1764–1894* (Providence, R.I.: The University, 1905), 85–87. On the college's early history, see Walter C. Bronson, *The History of Brown University, 1764–1914* (Providence, R.I.: Merrymount Press/Brown University, 1914). For the confidence of Dexter's class in their voice in national affairs, see their Address to John Adams, 24 April 1798, Theodore Foster Papers, RIHS, vols. 3–4: 151. The students' address to Adams, signed by a committee of six including Andrew Dexter Jr. was reprinted in the *PG*, 19 May 1798, along with Adams's response. See also Thomas M. Ray, "'Not

One Cent for Tribute': The Public Addresses and American Popular Reaction to the XYZ Affair, 1798–1799," *Journal of the Early Republic* 3, no. 4 (Winter 1983): 389–412.

35. Jonathan Maxcy, *An Address, Delivered to the Graduates of Rhode-Island College . . . September 5, A.D. 1798* (Providence, R. I.: Carter and Wilkinson, 1798), 5, 10, 11.

36. Andrew Dexter, *An Oration, on the Importance of Science and Religion, Particularly to American Youth* (Providence, R.I., 1798), 3, 7; *PG,* 15 September 1798. The description of Dexter is based on his April 1808 portrait by Gilbert Stuart. On ambition in eighteenth-century Anglo-America, see Jason M. Opal, "Beyond the Farm: Ambition and the Transformation of Rural New England, 1770s–1820s" (Ph.D. dissertation, Brandeis University, 2004), chap. 1. The nation's "unborn millions" figured as a popular trope in early national civic texts; see François Furstenberg, *In the Name of the Father: Washington's Legacy, Slavery, and the Making of a Nation* (New York: Penguin, 2006), 37–39.

37. John Brown to Moses Brown, Providence, 14 August 1791, quoted in Kane and Roelker, "Founding of the Providence Bank," 117.

38. *IC,* 24 July 1800; James Frothingham Hunnewell, *A Century of Town Life: A History of Charlestown, Massachusetts, 1775–1887* (Boston: Little, Brown, 1888), 93. Compare to the description of Andrew Dexter Sr.'s house in "Selling Off," *PG,* 10 January 1798. See also valuations for Dexter's house and lands, ca. 1 October 1798, Federal Direct Tax of 1798, Middlesex County, Schedule C, 9: 413, NEHGS. The British had burned Charlestown to the ground in 1775; see Brissot de Warville, *New Travels in the United States,* 106.

Placing Andrew Dexter Jr. in his uncle's household between 1798 and 1800 requires detective work and intuition. No personal papers of either figure survive from those years. As a nonhead of household in 1800, Andrew doesn't appear by name in the federal census. Still, there are tantalizing hints in city records to back up the genealogist's contention that he followed his uncle to Charlestown to read law. In 1798, the Charlestown tax assessor's entry for Samuel Dexter's household notes, "enquire about poll"—that is, an additional taxable household member, a wage earner. The 1799 Charlestown tax list notes "Saml. Dexters 2 polls," likely indicating the addition of Andrew Jr. to the household. (Samuel Dexter's children, then aged six, seven, and ten, would not have qualified as ratable polls by 1799, and there is no evidence he took on a servant that year.) "Charlestown Assessors Rate and Tax Books," Msf Box xc6.2, BPL. The manuscript schedules of the federal census confirm that Samuel Dexter's Charlestown household included one free male between ages sixteen and twenty-six in 1800, when Andrew Jr. was twenty-one; see Middlesex County schedules, reel M32-17, 83.

39. Brissot de Warville, *New Travels in the United States,* 84–85; John Lambert, *Travels Through Canada, and the United States of North America, in the Years 1806, 1807, and 1808: To Which Are Added Biographical Notices and Anecdotes of Some of the Leading Characters in the United States* (London: C. Cradock and A. Joy, 1816), 333–34; see also Thomas Pemberton, "A Topographical and Historical Description of Boston, 1794," *Massachusetts Historical Society Collections* 3 (1794): 286–87. On Boston's economy in the 1790s, see John D. Forbes, "European Wars and Boston Trade, 1783–1815,"

*New England Quarterly* 11, no. 4 (December 1938): 714–20; Lubow, "Artisans in Transition," 42–46; Timothy Pitkin, *A Statistical View of the Commerce of the United States* (Hartford: Charles Hosmer, 1816), 51–55; and David T. Gilchrist, ed., *The Growth of the Seaport Cities, 1790–1825,* Proceedings of a conference sponsored by the Eleutherian Mills-Hagley Foundation, March 17–19, 1966 (Charlottesville: University Press of Virginia, 1967), 56.

40. *PG,* 10 January 1798, 27 July 1799.

41. [Samuel Dexter], *The Progress of Science: A Poem Delivered at Harvard College* ([Boston], 1780), 3; "To the Hon. Samuel Dexter," by Camillus [pseud.], *BG,* 14 March 1816 (paraphrasing *Julius Caesar* act 2, scene 1, line 22); *BG,* 30 July 1781; "The Great-the Important Question. Who Shall Be Our Govenor?" *CC,* 20 March 1816; Letter signed "Q," [Philadelphia] *Poulson's American Daily Advertiser,* 22 March 1814; see also "50,000 Dollars! A Plot Wanted Immediately," *New Bedford Mercury,* 1 April 1814. Samuel Dexter's biography is well summarized in Joseph Prentice, *A Sermon, Delivered in Trinity Church, Athens, on the Sunday Following the Interment of the Late Hon. Samuel Dexter of Boston* (Hudson, N.Y.: Ashbel Stoddard, 1816); Joseph Story, *Sketch of the Life of Samuel Dexter* (Boston: J. Eliot, 1816); and Lucius M. Sargent, *Reminiscences of Samuel Dexter: Originally Written for the Boston Evening Transcript* (Boston: Dutton, 1857), works whose edginess belie their purpose as eulogies and fond remembrances. Dexter was admitted to the bar in Worcester County in 1784; his first appearance in the spotty records of the Suffolk County bar comes in July 1789; George Dexter, "Record-Book of the Suffolk Bar," *Proceedings of the Massachusetts Historical Society* 19 (December 1881): 163.

42. Fisher Ames to Christopher Gore, 5 October 1802, Fisher Ames and Seth Ames, eds., *Works of Fisher Ames, with a Selection from His Speeches* (Boston: Little, Brown, 1854), 300; [Samuel Dexter (1761–1816)], "Biographical Notice of Hon. Samuel Dexter," 6; *The Glass; or Speculation: A Poem* (New York: printed for the author, 1791), 3.

43. Adam Smith, *An Inquiry Into the Nature and Causes of the Wealth of Nations,* ed. Edwin Cannan, reprint (New York: Random House/ Modern Library, 1994), 131. (Orig. pub. 1776.) For the changing meanings of *speculat[or],* see *Oxford English Dictionary,* 2nd ed. Smith, writing at the precise time of this transition, also uses the noun in its earlier sense of "philosopher"; see ibid., 11.

44. Adam Smith, *Wealth of Nations,* 131; "Proposals for . . . Paper Money," by Belhphegor Copperplate [pseud.], *New-Haven Gazette,* 12 October 1786; *The Glass*. For the opposition of artful speculators to honest, industrious dupes, see "Of Georgia Lands—Cautionary," *CC,* 16 March 1796.

45. William Priest, *Travels in the United States of America; Commencing in the Year 1793 and Ending in 1797* (London, 1802), quoted Charles H. Haskins, "The Yazoo Land Companies," *Papers of the American Historical Association* 5 (October 1891): 61. For a decidedly celebratory interpretation of these complex characters, see Robert E. Wright and David J. Cowen, *Financial Founding Fathers: The Men Who Made America Rich* (Chicago: University of Chicago Press, 2006). For more nuanced assessments of the post-Revolutionary speculative economy, see Mann, *Republic of Debtors*; and Cathy Matson, "Public Vices, Private Benefit: William Duer and His Circle, 1776–1792," in *New York and the Rise of American Capitalism: Economic Development and the Social*

*and Political History of an American State,* eds. William Pencak and Conrad Edick Wright (New York: New-York Historical Society, 1989), 73–123; and Ferguson, *Power of the Purse,* 251–86.

46. On the first Bank of the United States (1791–1811), see James O. Wettereau, "New Light on the First Bank of the United States," *Pennsylvania Magazine of History and Biography* 6, no. 3 (July 1937): 266 n.14, 273–77; Joseph Stancliffe Davis, "William Duer, Entrepreneur, 1747–99," in *Essays in the Earlier History of American Corporations,* Harvard Economic Studies, vol. 16 (Cambridge, Mass.: Harvard University Press, 1917), 202–4.

47. "Land Speculations!" by No Speculator [pseud.], *CC,* 16 March 1796; "Poetic," [Boston] *Federal Orrery,* 18 January 1796; Timothy Dwight, *Travels in New England and New York,* ed. Barbara Miller Solomon (Cambridge, Mass.: Harvard University Press, 1969), 1: 160 (Orig. pub. 1821). On land speculation in the 1780s and 1790s see Malcolm J. Rohrbough, *The Land Office Business: The Settlement and Administration of American Public Lands, 1789–1837* (New York: Oxford University Press, 1968); and Alan Taylor, *William Cooper's Town: Power and Persuasion on the Frontier of the Early American Republic* (New York: Alfred A. Knopf, 1995).

48. Dwight, *Travels in New England and New York* 1: 160. See also C. Peter Magrath, *Yazoo: Law and Politics in the New Republic* (Providence, R.I.: Brown University Press, 1966), 3–19; Haskins, "The Yazoo Land Companies," 87–88.

49. For the Georgia Company's agents in Boston, see *Articles of Association and Agreement, Constituting the New-England Mississippi Land Company* ([Boston], [1797?]), 1; [New England Mississippi Land Company], *To the President of the United States* ([Boston], [1798?]), 3; [Gideon Granger and Perez Morton], *Memorial of the Agents of the New England Mississippi Land Company to Congress, with a Vindication of Their Title at Law Annexed* (Washington: A & G Way, 1804), 91. For Dexter's holdings, see "Evidences of Title Derived from the State of Georgia," 14 February 1805, *American State Papers: Public Lands* 1: 201–28; and Magrath, *Yazoo,* 15, 38. Rhode Island occupies 1,045 square miles and 1 million acres equals 1,562 square miles.

50. "For the *Independent Chronicle,*" *IC,* 6 December 1798. Most purchasers paid partly in cash and partly in notes; see Haskins, "The Yazoo Land Companies," 87–88; and "Law Intelligence: Georgia Lands," *CC,* 9 October 1799. Dexter certainly did not have cash equal to the price of his Yazoo shares. His Charlestown estate, his largest real asset, was worth about $2,000; see Federal Direct Tax of 1798, Middlesex County, Schedule C, 9: 413, NEHGS.

51. "And Now a Bubble Bursts...," *Federal Orrery,* 7 March 1796; "For the *Independent Chronicle,*" *IC,* 3 December 1798. See also "By the Last Mails," *CC,* 24 February 1796; "Georgia Lands" and "Georgia Land Speculation," *CC,* 2 March 1796; "Of Georgia Lands—Cautionary," *CC,* 16 March 1796. On share prices in Boston, see Magrath, *Yazoo,* 17.

52. For Samuel Dexter's purchases of NEMLC shares after March 1796, see *American State Papers: Public Lands* 1: 203, 205, 209. For the opening chapters of the Yazoo land claims, see: "Georgia Lands—Important Decision," *CC,* 17 November 1798; [New England Mississippi Land Company], *To the President of the United States;* [Gideon Granger and Perez Morton], *Memorial of the Agents of the NEMLC;* and "New England Mississippi Land Company Records," mss. 945, Hargrett Library, Uni-

versity of Georgia. Chief Justice John Marshall upheld the Yazoo claimants in March 1810; Congress passed a bill compensating them in March 1814.

53. For Andrew Dexter's apprenticeship in law, see George Dexter, "Record-Book of the Suffolk Bar," 144; William T. Davis, *History of the Bench and Bar,* vol. 1 of *Professional and Industrial History of Suffolk County Massachusetts* (Boston: Boston History Company, 1894). Samuel Dexter's law office is listed in *The Boston Directory* for 1800, compiled in 1799. On the walking time from State Street to Dexter's Charlestown seat, see *CC,* 26 July 1800. For Samuel Dexter's law library, see "Inventory and Appraisement of the Estate of Samuel Dexter," 24 June 1816, Suffolk Probate Record Books, case 24936, 114: 437–438, MArch.

54. On the habits of 'Change, see Samuel Eliot Morison, *Harrison Gray Otis, 1765–1848: The Urbane Federalist* (Boston: Houghton Mifflin, 1969), 209. On the overlap of financial and social networks in the early Republic and antebellum period, see Lamoreaux, *Insider Lending.*

55. Samuel Dexter's political enemies used his lack of service against him; see "Who Shall Be Our Governour," by A Federalist of the Old School [pseud.], [Worcester] *Massachusetts Spy,* 27 March 1816.

On William Hull see Samuel C. Clarke, "William Hull," *NEHGR* 47 (1893): 141–53, 305–15; and William B. Skelton, "Hull, William"; *American National Biography Online,* February 2000, http://www.anb.org/articles/03/03-00228.html. For Hull's involvement in the Yazoo speculation see *NEMLC Articles of Association;* and "New England Mississippi Land Company Records." For Samuel Dexter's land transactions with Hull, see Middlesex Deeds 152:351–52, 157:386–87.

56. Information on Brown comes from his death notice in the *Newport Mercury* 4 June 1825; *Proceedings of the Massachusetts Historical Society* 13 (1873–1875): 206–7; *NEHGR* 80 (1926): 175; Paul Goodman, *The Democratic-Republicans of Massachusetts: Politics in a Young Republic* (Cambridge, Mass.: Harvard University Press, 1964), 97–98; Frederic W. Howay, *Voyages of the* Columbia *to the Northwest Coast, 1787–1790 and 1790–1793* (Boston: Massachusetts Historical Society, 1941). For his town offices, see *Minutes of the Selectmen's Meetings, 1776–1786,* 61, 84, 142, 146, 261–78; "Samuel Brown Papers, 1799–1805," MHS; [Trustees of the Boston Theater], "To All People . . . " (Boston, 1794). For Brown's involvement in the Yazoo purchases, see the receipts contained in folder 1 of "New England Mississippi Land Company Records"; and *American State Papers: Public Lands* 1: 201–28, esp. 203. On the Boston theater controversy of the 1790s, see T. A. Milford, "Boston's Theater Controversy and Liberal Notions of Advantage," *New England Quarterly* 72, no. 1 (March 1999): 61–88.

57. "Among of Certificates of Georgia Lands held by me . . . " and other pages of tabulation, "New England Mississippi Land Company Records," folder 2. For other non-Yazoo connections between Dexter and Morton, see George Dexter, "Record-Book of the Suffolk Bar," 163, 164.

58. For Morton's biography, see John Noble, "Some Massachusetts Tories," *Publications of the Colonial Society of Massachusetts* 5 (March 1898): 282–93; and *Sibley's Harvard Graduates* 17: 555–61. For his tendency to stick out his chin, see the satiric "Song of Liberty and Equality," *Federal Orrery,* 28 September 1795. On the man of feeling as a Revolutionary type, see Sarah Knott, "Sensibility and the American War for Independence," *American Historical Review* 109, no. 1 (February 2004): 19–40.

59. Letter from Abigail Adams to John Adams, 7–11 April 1776, *Adams Family Papers: An Electronic Archive* (MHS), http://www.masshist.org/digitaladams/. See also [New York] *Constitutional Gazette,* 24 April 1776; *New-England Chronicle,* 2 May 1776; *Newport Mercury* 13 May 1776; *New-York Journal,* 16 May 1776; *Pennsylvania Packet,* 20 May 1776. For the influence of Morton's address on Dexter's, compare Perez Morton, *An Oration, Delivered at the King's Chapel in Boston, April the Eighth, 1776, on the Re-Interment of the Remains of . . . Joseph Warren* (Boston: J. Holt, 1776), 5; to Andrew Dexter, *On the Importance of Science and Religion,* 7.

60. For "the Orator," see "On the Trial," *BG,* 26 January 1778; and Letter from Justice, *BG,* 9 February 1778. The anonymous verse is reprinted in James Spear Loring, *The Hundred Boston Orators Appointed by the Municipal Authorities and Other Public Bodies, from 1770 to 1852* (Boston: John P. Jewett, 1852), 130; on charges of privateering, see also *Sibley's Harvard Graduates* 17:557.

61. Sarah Wentworth Morton, "Lines to the Mansion of My Ancestors, on Seeing It Occupied as a Banking Establishment," in Sarah Wentworth Morton, *My Mind and Its Thoughts, in Sketches, Fragments, and Essays,* reprint, 1823 (Delmar, N.Y.: Scholars' Facsimiles & Reprints, 1975), 30–31, 271n. The description of the Apthorp mansion comes from *The Statistics of the United States' Direct Tax of 1798, as Assessed on Boston,* Records Relating to the Early History of Boston (1890), 296; and James Brown Marston's painting *The Old State House,* oil on panel, 1801, MHS. On the sale to Morton, see Emily Pendleton and Milton Ellis, *Philenia; the Life and Works of Sarah Wentworth Morton, 1759–1846,* University of Maine Studies, 2nd series (Orono, Me.: University of Maine Press, 1931), 25; and David Clapp, "The Old Morton and Taylor Estates in Dorchester," *New England Historic and Genealogical Register* 46 (1892): 83.

62. Letter to "Messieurs Edes," *BG,* 24 January 1785; [William Hill Brown], *The Better Sort: Or, The Girl of Spirit* (Boston: Isaiah Thomas, 1789), 10; *Sans Souci, Alias Free and Easy: Or an Evening's Peep Into a Polite Society* (Boston: Warden and Russell, 1785), 10, 19. See also Charles Warren, "Samuel Adams and the Sans Souci Club in 1785," *Proceedings of the Massachusetts Historical Society* 40 (1927): 318–44; Pendleton and Ellis, *Philenia,* 29–31.

63. Joseph Dennie to Jeremiah Mason, 6 August, 25 August 1797, in Laura Green Pedder, ed., *The Letters of Joseph Dennie, 1768–1812,* University of Maine Studies, 2nd series (Orono, Maine: University of Maine Press, 1936), 161–64.

64. Sarah Morton, "Stanzas, To a Recently United Husband," Sarah Wentworth Morton, *My Mind and Its Thoughts,* 182–83; *Occurrences of the Times. Or, the Transactions of Four Days . . . a Farce in Two Acts* ([Boston], 1789), frontispiece, 20, 11; Frances T. Apthorp, letters of 20–27 August 1788, Miscellaneous Bound Manuscripts, MHS. The fullest account of these events appears in Pendleton and Ellis, *Philenia,* 32–40; see also Sarah Swedberg, "The Popular Culture of Depression in the Early American Republic," *Journal of American and Comparative Cultures* 23, no. 3 (Fall 2000): 46; and Arthur W. Brayley, "The Real Author of 'The Power of Sympathy,'" *The Bostonian* 1 (1894–1895): 231–32.

65. *Occurrences of the Times,* 11. For newspapers discussing the scandal, see *Massachusetts Centinel,* 27 September, 8 October 1788; *Herald of Freedom,* 9, 13, 16 October 1788. On the publishing history of *The Power of Sympathy,* see Cathy N. Davidson,

*Revolution and the Word: The Rise of the Novel in America* (New York: Oxford University Press, 1986), 83–109.

66. *Herald of Freedom,* 7 May 1790; [Robert Treat Paine], "Song of Liberty and Equality," *Federal Orrery,* 28 September 1795.

67. Sarah Morton, "To the Mansion of My Ancestors," in Sarah Wentworth Morton, *My Mind and Its Thoughts,* 30, see also 271n.

68. Abraham Bishop, *Georgia Speculation Unveiled* (Hartford: Elisha Babcock, 1797), 139, 38; "Georgia Lands!!!" *IC,* 8 March 1798. On Bishop's politics, see Gordon Wood, *The Radicalism of the American Revolution* (New York: Alfred A. Knopf, 1991), 271–75. For his ownership of Yazoo securities, see *American State Papers: Finance* 3:282.

69. Abraham Bishop, *Georgia Speculation Unveiled,* 38–39; J. Hector St. John de Crèvecoeur, *Letters from an American Farmer* (Philadelphia: Mathew Carey, 1793), letter 3, 46–47.

70. [Gideon Granger and Perez Morton], *Memorial of the Agents of the NEMLC,* 31; compare to Alexander Pope, *Essay on Man* (London, 1732), first epistle, stanza x, line 394. On the diverse membership of the Yazoo "tribe," see Magrath, *Yazoo,* 38.

71. Ebenezer Mattoon to Thomas Dwight, 2 March 1801, quoted in Catherine Allgor, *Parlor Politics: In Which the Ladies of Washington Help Build a City and a Government* (Charlottesville: University Press of Virginia, 2000), 4–5. On real estate speculation in Washington, see Bob Arnebeck, *Through a Fiery Trial: Building Washington, 1790–1800* (Lanham, Md.: Madison Books, 1990). For the city's early years more broadly, see also Barbara G. Carson, *Ambitious Appetites: Dining, Behavior, and Patterns of Consumption in Federal Washington* (Washington, D.C.: American Institute of Architects Press, 1990); Cynthia Diane Earman, "Boardinghouses, Parties and the Creation of a Political Society: Washington City, 1800–1830" (unpublished M.A. thesis, Louisiana State University, 1992); both correctives to James Sterling Young in *The Washington Community, 1800–1828* (New York: Columbia University Press, 1966). For Samuel Dexter's move to Washington, see Samuel Dexter to John Adams, 13 May 1800, Adams Family Papers, MHS, reel 397; *CC,* 21, 28 May; 4, 7 June; 26 July; 29 October 1800. For Andew Dexter in Washington, see Dexter, Mills, and Dexter, *Dexter Genealogy,* 122–28; *National Intelligencer,* 6 April 1801.

72. For the Dexters' residence in Washington, see *National Intelligencer,* 7 April 1802. For editor William Duane's campaign against Samuel Dexter, see *CC,* 25 June 1800; [Philadelphia] *Aurora,* 12, 13, 17 November 1800; 2, 8, 24, 26, 27, 28, 31 January 1801; 2, 3, 4, 6, 10, 13, 19 February 1801, 17 March 1801. For Federalist counternarratives, see *Washington Federalist,* 21, 23 January 1801; 4, 12 February 1801. Congress cleared Dexter of responsibility for the fires in the War and Treasury departments; see [Washington] *National Intelligencer* 30 January 1801; 25 February, 4 March, 3, 6 April 1801; and "Causes of the Late Fires in the War and Treasury Departments," 28 February 1801, in *American State Papers: Miscellaneous* I: 247–52. See also George Gibbs, *Memoirs of the Administrations of Washington and John Adams, Edited from the Papers of Oliver Wolcott* (New York: W. Van Norden, 1846) 2: 478–84. On Duane, see Jeffrey L. Pasley, *"The Tyranny of Printers": Newspaper Politics in the Early American Republic* (Charlottesville: University Press of Virginia, 2001), 79–104, 176–95.

73. "Political Miscellany, from the *Aurora*," [New London, Conn.] *Bee*, 17 September 1800.

74. Boston Assessors' Records (BPL), 1803, tax books 8: 6; transfer books 8:7; and taking books, 8:6. The date of Andrew Dexter Jr.'s admission to the Bar is unclear; compare William T. Davis, *History of the Bench and Bar*, 623; to George Dexter, "Record-Book of the Suffolk Bar," 178. Andrew Dexter Jr. is not listed as an attorney in the *Massachusetts Register and United States Calendar for . . . 1803* (Boston: Manning and Loring, [1802]), but appears in that capacity in the *Massachusetts Register and United States Calendar for . . . 1804* (Boston: Manning and Loring, [1803]), 74. Taken together, these fragments place the beginning of the younger Dexter's legal career between October 1802 (after the tax assessments for that year) and September 1803 (before the assessments for the following year).

For traces of Dexter's early legal career, see, e.g., the advertisements he placed as an assignee in two bankruptcy cases (*CC*, 24 September 1803, 11 January 1804). In 1803, he was an attorney at the Suffolk County Court of Common Pleas; by 1804, he had become an attorney to the Supreme Judicial Court. See *Massachusetts Register and United States Calendar for . . . 1804* (Boston: Manning and Loring, [1803]), 74; *Massachusetts Register and United States Calendar for . . . 1805* (Boston: Manning and Loring, [1804]), 78.

75. Susan Apthorp Bulfinch to Dr. Apthorp, ca. 1804, in Ellen Susan Bulfinch, ed., *The Life and Letters of Charles Bulfinch Architect, with Other Family Papers* (New York: Burt Franklin, 1973), 150–51. On the links between the Bulfinch and Apthorp genealogies, see Kirker and Kirker, *Bulfinch's Boston, 1787–1817*, 26–28; and "Genealogical List for Madam Apthorp," 23 September 1794, box 3, Bulfinch Family Papers, MHS.

76. Annie Haven Thwing, *The Crooked and Narrow Streets of the Town of Boston, 1630–1822* (Boston: Marshall Jones Company, 1920); Whitehill and Kennedy, *Boston: A Topographical History*.

77. Bulfinch, *Life and Letters of Charles Bulfinch*, 155, 150, 159. For the dismantling of the fortification walls, see *Minutes of the Selectmen's Meetings, 1776–1786*, 136, 139, 181, 195; see also Pemberton, "Topographical and Historical Description of Boston."

78. Carr, "Change as Remarkable as the Revolution Itself."

79. Robert C. Winthrop, ed., "Memoir of Hon. Nathan Appleton," *Proceedings of the Massachusetts Historical Society* 5 (October 1861): 304; Frances W. Gregory, *Nathan Appleton, Merchant and Entrepreneur, 1779–1861* (Charlottesville: University Press of Virginia, 1975), 1–10.

80. Winthrop, "Memoir of Hon. Nathan Appleton," 255, 256–57. The bundle of possessions was a trope; compare the recollections of Nathan Appleton's cousin William: Chandler Robbins, *Memoir of Hon. William Appleton* (Boston: John Wilson, 1863), 7.

81. Winthrop, "Memoir of Hon. Nathan Appleton," 304–305; Robbins, *Memoir of Hon. William Appleton*, 20, 19. On the mercantile ethos of prosperity without avarice, see Paul Goodman, "Ethics and Enterprise: The Values of a Boston Elite, 1800–1860," *American Quarterly* 18, no. 3 (Autumn 1966): 437–451. For Appleton's first decade in Boston, see Gregory, *Nathan Appleton*, 13–30; *Boston Directory* for 1805, 8, 12; Boston Assessors' Records, 1804, tax books 10:1; transfer books 7:1–2.

82. William Bentley, *The Diary of William Bentley, D.D., Pastor of the East Church, Salem, Massachusetts* (Gloucester Mass.: Peter Smith, 1962) 3:14; "The Adventures of a Bank Note," by Five Dollars, *NEP,* 1 January 1805. For the Appleton's scales, see Gregory, *Nathan Appleton,* 9, 15, 15 n.10. For Massachusetts bank charters, see Fenstermaker, *The Development of American Commercial Banking,* 139–40.

83. For the argument that financial institutions led rather than reflected the economic dynamism of the early United States, see Peter L. Rousseau and Richard Sylla, "Emerging Financial Markets and Early U.S. Growth," *Explorations in Economic History* 42, no. 1 (January 2005): 1–26; Lamoreaux, *Insider Lending*; and R. E. Wright, *The First Wall Street*. On the imbalance of trade in early national seaports, see Redlich, *The Molding of American Banking* 1:66.

84. "Banks," *NEP,* 20 January 1804; "The Subject of Banks Considered," *BG,* 26 January 1804. See also "Banks,"*NEP,* 21 February 1804.

85. "Banks," *NEP,* 21 February, 24 January 1804. For the theory that bad money crowds out good, see "The Subject of Banks Considered," by Mercator [pseud.], *BG,* 26 January 1804, a classic statement of what nineteenth-century economists knew as "Gresham's Law." Modern economists generally discredit this assumption; see Arthur J. Rolnick and Warren E. Weber, "Gresham's Law or Gresham's Fallacy?" *Journal of Political Economy* 94, no.1 (February 1986): 185–199; Robert L. Greenfield and Hugh Rockoff, "Gresham's Law in Nineteenth-Century America," *Journal of Money, Credit and Banking* 27:4.1 (November 1995): 1086–98.

86. Gras, *Massachusetts Bank,* 73–74, 368–89; and *NEP,* 24 January 1804.

87. "Truly Alarming," by Aristides, *IC* 3 May 1804; "The Examiner, No. XXIV," *IC,* 26 March 1804; "For the Boston Gazette," by A Friend to Banks [pseud.], *BG,* 26 January 1804; "To the Members of the Hon. Legislature of Massachusetts," by Justice [pseud.], *CC,* 5 February 1803.

88. "A Misapprehension. . . ," *BG,* 26 January 1804; "Banks," by A Merchant [pseud.], *BG,* 31 January 1805 (emphasis mine); see also Nathan Appleton, *An Examination of the Banking System of Massachusetts, in Reference to the Renewal of the Bank Charters* (Boston: Stimpson and Clapp, 1831), 9–12.

89. "Local Miscellany: Exchange Office," *IC,* 31 May, 14 May, 17 May 1804; "Exchange Office," *CC,* 18 April 1804. The Office's petition was submitted to the Massachusetts General Court on 14 February 1804, and held over for discussion until the next legislative session in June; MArch. Articles defending the plan began running in May, in anticipation of the court's spring session; see *IC,* 14, 17, 24, 28 May, 31 May, and 7 June 1804. A brief "Prospectus" of the operation ran on 11 June 1804.

The Exchange Office proposed a primitive version of the regional clearing-and-redemption fund that the Suffolk Bank System would institute in 1824, and that the nation's Federal Reserve banks perform today. See D. R. Whitney, *The Suffolk Bank* (Cambridge, Mass.: Riverside Press, 1878); Howard Bodenhorn, *State Banking in Early America: A New Economic History* (New York: Oxford University Press, 2003), 95–122.

90. "Exchange Office," *CC,* 18 April 1804; "Exchange Office," *IC,* 14, 24, 17 May 1804; "Prospectus of the Boston Exchange Office," *IC,* 11 June 1804; Perspective [Thomas Odiorne], *The Changery, an Allegoric Memoir, of the Boston Exchange Office: Or, the Pernicious Progress of Bank Speculation Unveiled* (Boston: n. p., 1805), 9, 24; *An*

*Act, to Incorporate the President, Trustees & Associates of the Boston Exchange Office, or Association Fund* (Boston: Young and Minns, 1804), 9 (sect. 6).

91. "Exchange Office," *IC,* 31 May, 24 May 1804; "Exchange Office," *CC,* 18 April 1804; see also Perspective [Thomas Odiorne], *The Changery,* 30–31.

92. Perspective [Thomas Odiorne], *The Changery,* 14, 11–12. Part satire of the office and part polemic on its behalf, this pamphlet paraphrases debates about the proposed Exchange Office that unfolded before the Massachusetts legislature. While the author clearly takes literary license with the material, his proximity to the Exchange Office— of which both he and his brother were trustees—makes it safe to assume that the conversations he describes echoed actual discussions about the organization. I am grateful to Richard D. Brown for suggesting the label "romantic capitalism."

93. Using various genealogical sources, I have found birth dates for twelve of the twenty men who led the Exchange Office in its first two years. Ten of those twelve— Dudley S. Bradstreet (b. 1773), David S. Eaton (b. 1776), Crowell Hatch (b. ca. 1760s), George Odiorne (b. 1770), Thomas Odiorne (b. 1769), Nathaniel Parker (b. 1771), William Ritchie (b. ca. 1770s), Beza Tucker (b. 1772), Phineas Upham (b. 1776), and Eliphalet Williams (b. ca. 1775)—were born in the late 1760s or 1770s. See Robert J. Dunkle and Ann Smith Lainhard, compilers, *John Haven Dexter's Memoranda of the Town of Boston in the 18th and 19th Centuries* (Boston: New England Historic Genealogical Society, 1997).

94. Perspective [Thomas Odiorne], *The Changery,* 9 ("ordinary walks"). For exchange men born in the New England countryside, see Thomas Minns, "The Detroit Bank, the First Bank in the Territory of Michigan," *MHS Proceedings,* 2nd ser., 20 (December 1906): 522; J. C. Odiorne, *Genealogy of the Odiorne Family,* 74–83. (Thomas Odiorne *did* attend college, graduating from Dartmouth in 1791.) For their work, see David S. Eaton receipts dated 10 May, 27 May 1803 in Samuel Brown Papers, MHS; Samuel Clap receipt dated 18 February 1799, David S. Greenough Papers, box 19, MHS. Other occupations and business locations are documented in the *Boston Directories* for 1803, 1805, and 1806.

95. "Middling Interest," *IC,* 4 April 1803 ("India Nabobs"). For Dexter's assessed worth in 1804, see Boston Assessors' Records, 1804, tax books 8:6. These figures, drawn from the Boston Assessors' Records of 1802, are found in Torre, "The Political Economy of Sentiment," 262–63:

| Bank | Avg. Directors' Total Estate, 1802 |
|---|---|
| Massachusetts | $47,388 |
| BUS | 37,575 |
| Boston Bank | 25,485 |
| Union Bank | 22,439 |
| Exchange Office | 6,222 |

The Exchange Office leadership overlapped significantly with that of the proposed Town and Country Bank, project of the self-styled "Middling Interest" whose charter the General Court rejected in the spring of 1803; see *IC,* 4 April, 9 May 1803; *CC,* 28

May, 18 June 1803; and Torre, "The Political Economy of Sentiment," 233–36. I have not found the original Town and Country Bank petition with its 1,152 signatures, and thus do not know whether Andrew Dexter was among them.

96. Perspective [Thomas Odiorne], *The Changery*, 12, 8, 9, 13. On Bradstreet, see *Essex Antiquarian*, 4 (June 1900). For Crowell Hatch as an owner of the *Columbia*, see Howay, *Voyages of the* Columbia, 145, 162, 211, 363, 465. Hatch had donated some of the curiosities collected on the voyages to the Massachusetts Historical Society; MHS *Proceedings* 1: 26; 11: 299. In addition to writing *The Changery*, Thomas Odiorne published an epic poem, *The Progress of Refinement* (Boston: Young and Etheridge, 1792). An example of Samuel Sumner's manuscript poetry, "Restored Health" (1808), is preserved in Miscellaneous Bound Manuscript, 1808–1812, MHS. On John West's stocks of books, see Dale Warren, "John West—Bookseller," *New England Quarterly* 6, no. 3 (September 1933): 613–19.

97. *BG*, 5 November 1804; "Journal of the Massachusetts Senate, May 1804 to March 1805," MArch, 162–63, 175; Perspective [Thomas Ordione], *The Changery*, 16; *An Act, to Incorporate . . . the Boston Exchange Office*, 11. For steps to make the Exchange operational, see *CC*, 11 July, 1, 8 August 1804; *BG*, 30 July, 2, 9 August, 3 September 1804; *NEP*, 21 August 1804. For the Exchange Office's location, see *CC*, 8 August 1804; Boston Assessors' Records for 1805, tax books 8:13; taking books 8: 4; transfer books 8:10. For Samuel Dexter as a previous tenant, see Boston Assessors' Records for 1802, transfer books 8:16, and the advertisement for painter N. Hancock, *IC*, 3 January 1803. For the Exchange Office's business and discount hours, see *NEP*, 28 August 1804; *IC*, 11 October 1804; *BG*, 10, 17, 24 September 1804.

For the names and addresses of the first Exchange Office clerks, see *Boston Directory for 1805*, 34, 65, 127; *Massachusetts Register for 1805*, 59; *Boston Directory for 1806*, 50 (Flanagan). For Flanagan's estate in 1805, see Boston Assessors' Records, taking books, 7:28; tax books 7:28.

98. Phillip Ammidon to N&W Smith, Esqs., 26 December 1804, Phillip Ammidon Letterbook, MHS; Perspective [Thomas Odiorne], *The Changery*, 31, 9. "Blank Checks" on the Exchange Office were advertised in *BG*, 20 August 1804. Ads for goods sold for EO-approved notes appear in *IC*, 29 October 1804 (brandy); *BG*, 18 October 1804 (broadcloth); 12 November 1804 ("American Gin"); 15, 19 November 1804 (brandy); 22 November, 6 December 1804 (fur muffs and tippets); 20 December 1804 (cloth); 24 January 1805 (plated wares, tobacco). For payment of the Exchange Office's capital, see *IC*, 28 November 1804; share prices are specified in *An Act, to Incorporate . . . the Boston Exchange Office*, 5 (sec. 3). The publication of *The Changery* was announced in *BG*, 17, 31 January 1805.

99. For a March 1805 joint meeting of all the Boston banks save the Exchange Office see Gras, *Massachusetts Bank*, 388n.1. On the Exchange Office's attempts to gain the right to issue small bills, see *NEP*, 25, 29 January 1805. Their petition was approved by 67 to 42 in the House, but "non-concurred" by a vote of 12 to 18 in the state Senate; *NEP*, 1 March 1805. The Changery pressed the case again in March and again failed: *NEP*, 8, 12, 15 March 1805. On the small bills controversy more generally, see *IC*, 28 January, 25 February 1805; *NEP*, 26 February, 12, 19 March, 18 June 1805.

100. *A Correct Abstract of All the Statements Which Have Been Made According to Law by the Incorporated Banks in This Commonwealth, from 1803 to January, 1807*

([Boston], 1807); *True Abstracts of the Statements of the Several Banks in the Commonwealth of Massachusetts Rendered in January, 1808* ([Boston], 1808). For politicians seeking support from the "friends of the *Exchange Bank,*" see *BG,* 5 November 1804; "The Middling Interest," *BG,* 1 April 1805; and Torre, "The Political Economy of Sentiment," 238–39. For dividends and secondary share sales see *CC,* 30 January, 2 February 1805; *NEP,* 22 January 1805, 18 June 1805; *BG* 24 January 1805; and *IC,* 24 January 1805, 16 January 1806. Liability-to-specie ratios in other Boston banks ca. June 1805 ranged from 2.13 (Boston Bank) to 5.98 (Union Bank); Torre, "The Political Economy of Sentiment," 254, table 3.

101. Petition of the President and Trustees of the Boston Exchange Office or Association Fund, 1 June 1805, MArch, signature page. Andrew Dexter's election as an Exchange Office officer was reported in *IC,* 12 August 1805; see also *BG,* 26 August, 21 October 1805; *Massachusetts Register . . . for 1806,* 54. For Dexter's acquaintances among the Exchange Office founders see Suffolk Deeds 207:27–30 (David Tilden); and Boston Assessors' Records for 1803, transfer books 8:7 (Exchange Office president Samuel Clap).

102. Appleton, *Examination of the Banking System,* 12; see also Hammond, *Banks and Politics in America,* 173.

103. Perspective [Thomas Odiorne], *The Changery,* 33. For this shift in policy on the part of other Boston banks, see Gras, *Massachusetts Bank,* 387–90; Perspective, *The Changery,* 32–43; and Torre, "The Political Economy of Sentiment," 260, table 5.

104. Andrew Dexter to John Harris and William Colwell, 10 December 1808, in *RICR,* 35; Winthrop, "Memoir of Hon. Nathan Appleton," 284; Appleton, *Examination of the Banking System,* 12.

105. *PS,* 3 March 1806; "An Act to Incorporate Simon Larned and Others, by the Name . . . of the Berkshire Bank [Mass. 1805: 44]," in *Laws of the Commonwealth of Massachusetts Passed at Several Sessions of the General Court Holden in Boston . . . February 1806* (Boston: Young & Minns, 1806), 48–53. To compare capitalizations and liability-to-specie ratios in banks across Massachusetts, see *A Correct Abstract . . . to January 1807.* On early Pittsfield and the Berkshire bank's founders, see Thomas Allen, *An Historical Sketch of the County of Berkshire, and Town of Pittsfield. Written in May 1808* (Boston: Belcher and Armstrong, 1808); David D. Field, *A History of the Town of Pittsfield, in Berkshire County, Mass.* (Hartford, Conn.: Case, Tiffany and Burnham, 1844), 40, 55, 59, 63–64, 73; Thomas Lawrence Davis, "Aristocrats and Jacobins in Country Towns: Party Formation in Berkshire County, Massachusetts (1775–1816)," (Ph.D. dissertation, Boston University, 1975), 128–30, 158, 372–73, 369–70, 373–75, and appendix X; and J.E.A. Smith, *The History of Pittsfield, Massachusetts, from the Year 1800 to the Year 1876* (Springfield, Mass.: C. W. Bryan, 1876), 2: 181–84.

106. "Report," *PS,* 21 March 1810; see also J. E. A. Smith, *History of Pittsfield, Massachusetts,* 2: 181–83; *PS,* 3, 10, 24 May, 5 July 1806; *BG,* 4 August 1806; *Boston Directory . . . for 1807,* 28. For Goodwin, see "Direct tax list of 1798 for Massachusetts and Maine, 1798," NEHGS, vol. 20, 493, 514. Appleton married Maria Theresa Gold, daughter of Pittsfield merchant Thomas Gold, in April 1806; see Gregory, *Nathan Appleton,* 43–44.

107. "Report," *PS,* 21 March 1810. The Berkshire Bank had less than $75,000 in specie on hand when it issued the notes to Dexter; its charter permitted it to issue notes

totaling twice its specie capital. See *A Correct Abstract . . . to January 1807;* "Act to Incorporate the Berkshire Bank," 50–51 (sec. 3).

108. Advertisement for lost traveling trunk, *CC,* 10 September 1806. For the Berkshire Bank building, see J. E. A. Smith, *History of Pittsfield, Massachusetts,* 2:184; advertisement for Michael Bird, "Ladies and Gentlemen's Hair Dresser," *PS* 3, December 1808.

For the Exchange Office's involvement with the Penobscot Bank of Bucksport, Maine (over 225 miles from Boston), the Hallowell and Augusta Bank of Augusta, Maine (160 miles from Boston), the Lincoln and Kennebec Bank of Wiscasset, Maine (150 miles from Boston), the Coos Bank of Haverhill, New Hampshire (145 miles from Boston), and the Cheshire Bank of Keene, New Hampshire (115 miles from Boston), see "Bank Thermometer," *CC* 11 March 1807; Walter W. Chadbourne, *A History of Banking in Maine, 1799–1930,* University of Maine Studies (Orono: University Press of Maine, 1936), 15–19, 23–24; *Report of the Committee Relative to the Penobscot Bank* ([Boston?], 1811); *Reports of the Committees, Appointed in June, 1810, to Investigate the Situation of the Coos, Cheshire and Hillsborough Banks* (Concord, N.H., 1811); Andrew Dexter Jr. to William King, 6 December 1806, William King Papers, Maine Historical Society, Portland, box 6; and *President and Directors of the Coos Bank vs. Andrew Dexter Jr.* (Appeal), Record Book of the Suffolk County Court of Common Pleas, July 1808, 193–94, MArch. Dexter did not become a director of any of these banks, nor does he seem to have become a majority shareholder.

109. "Bank Thermometer," *CC,* 9 December 1807.

110. "Legislative," *CC,* 13 March 1805. On the early history of Detroit, see Charles Moore, "The Beginnings of Territorial Government in Michigan," *Collections of the Pioneere and Historical Society of the State of Michigan* [hereafter *MPHS Collections*] 31 (1902): 510–22; and F. Clever Bald, *Detroit's First American Decade, 1796 to 1805* (Ann Arbor: University of Michigan Press, 1948).

111. "Detroit in Ashes!," *CC,* 25 June 1805. See also Henry Dearborn to William Hull, 23 July 1805, in Edwin Clarence Carter, ed., *The Territory of Michigan, 1805–1820,* vol. 10 of *The Territorial Papers of the United States* [hereafter TPUS] (Washington, D.C.: U.S. Government Printing Office, 1942), 23–24; Moore, "Beginnings of Territorial Government," 510–18; and *Documents Relating to Detroit and Vicinity, 1805–1813,* vol. 40 of *Michigan Historical Collections* (1929), 56–59.

112. William Hull to James Madison, 30 April 1806, *MPHS Collections* 31 (1902): 559–60; *Annals of Congress,* House of Representatives, 9th Cong., 1st sess., 921. On the Yazoo claims in Congress in 1804 and 1805, see also ibid., 433–34, 487–88, 905–21; "Georgia Land Claims," *American State Papers: Public Lands* 1:145–46; Haskins, "The Yazoo Land Companies," 93–98; *Report, from the Committee of Claims . . . Under the Georgia Company, of the Agents for Persons Composing the New England Land Company* (Washington City: William Duane, 1805); *Facts, in Reply to the Agents of the New England Land Company* (Washington City: William Duane, 1805). For the allegation that Hull would not have returned to Michigan but for the denial of the Yazoo claims, see [John Gentle?] to William Duane, 16 October 1806, reprinted in Worthington C. Ford, ed., "Letters of William Duane," *MHS Proceedings,* 2nd ser., 20 (May 1906): 289.

113. Hull to Augustus B. Woodward, 1 April 1806, in Carter, *TPUS: Michigan,* 47–48; see also Woodward to the Senate, 15 April 1806, *American State Papers: Miscellaneous*

1: 461–63. For Woodward's biography, see William L. Jenks, "Augustus Elias Brevoort Woodward," *Michigan History Magazine* 9, no. 4 (October 1925): 515–46; and Eric W. Rise, "Woodward, Augustus Brevoort," *American National Biography Online*, February 2000, http://www.anb.org/articles/11/11–00931.html. An overview of the Detroit Bank's history, accurate in most particulars, is found in William L. Jenks, "The First Bank in Michigan," *Michigan History Magazine* 1, no. 1 (July 1917): 41–62. For the list of Detroit Bank petitioners and investors, see "Petition for a Bank . . . Dated, March 31, 1806"; and "Bond for William Flanagan," 27 May 1806, *MPHS Collections* 8 (1886): 571–73. In addition to Flanagan, Dudley S. Bradstreet, David S. Eaton, George Odiorne, Nathaniel Parker, and Eliphalet Williams were leaders in the Exchange Office. Russell Sturgis had pioneered the failed Town & Country Bank that anticipated the Changery; he sold his share in the Michigan venture to Andrew Dexter Jr. before the Detroit Bank was organized.

114. [John Gentle], "On the Evils Which Have Proved Fatal to Republics . . . History of the Government of Michigan Territory, from Its Commencement, in June 1805, Till Nov. 1806," no. 19 [Pittsburgh] *Commonwealth,* 10 February 1808; [John Gentle?] to William Duane, 16 October 1806, in Ford, "Letters of William Duane," 289; Stanley Griswold (Detroit) to Elijah Boardman (New Milford, Conn.), 10 October 1806, Stanley Griswold Papers, BHC-DPL. Griswold concurred with Gentle that "Nearly the whole [bank] is owned by *Yazoo men* at *Boston,* and elsewhere." For Gentle's property, claim see "Allotment of Lands after the Detroit Fire of 1805," *MPHS Collections* 31 (1902): 582. For the value of Michigan manufactures ca. 1810, see *American State Papers: Finance* 2: 712, 713. For Detroit lots, see *MPHS Collections,* 36 (1908): 114–15.

115. "Petition for a Bank . . . Dated, March 31, 1806," *MPHS Collections* 8 (1886): 571–72; Hull to Woodward, 1 April 1806, Carter, *TPUS: Michigan,* 48.

116. Bond for William Flanagan, 27 May 1806, *MPHS Collections* 8 (1886): 572–73; [John Gentle], "On the Evils," no. 6 *(Commonwealth,* 19 August 1807). For the contents of the bank building, see also *Joseph Emerson v. Andrew Dexter Jr., 1810,* in William Wirt Blume, ed., *Transactions of the Supreme Court of the Territory of Michigan, 1805–1814* (Ann Arbor: University of Michigan Press, 1935), 1: 203, 544; Silas Farmer, *The History of Detroit and Michigan of the Metropolis Illustrated* (Detroit: Silas Farmer & Co, 1884), 855. For the Hulls' route to Detroit, see *Documents Relating to Detroit and Vicinity,* 56–58.

117. [John Gentle], "On the Evils," nos. 19, 6. For the bank building's dimensions, see John Farmer, "Plat of streets in the southeast part of Detroit" (1825), fig. 10.3 of Brian Leigh Dunnigan, *Frontier Metropolis: Picturing Early Detroit, 1701–1838* (Detroit: Wayne State University Press, 2001), 180. Where the 1825 plat depicts a single-story building with double-high windows, the 1811 view of Detroit reproduced here, along with most contemporaneous documents, gives the bank two stories. The Detroit Bank purchased the lots on 18 October for $395; see "Transactions of the Governor and Judges of the Territory of Michigan: Land Titles, Book Number 1" (typescript), BHC-DPL, 21. Hull set the bank building's cost at $4,000 in a letter to Isaac McLellan, 11 December 1806, Grenville H. Norcross Autograph Collection, MHS. Given that Hull had reason to downplay the costs and Gentle had reason to exaggerate them, something in the middle—say $6,000—seems likely. For reports that "a Bank has been

established at *Detroit,* in the Michigan Territory," see *NEP,* 25 July 1806. That item traveled to newspapers in Vermont, Connecticut, and New Hampshire.

118. [John Gentle?] to William Duane, 16 October 1806, in Ford, "Letters of William Duane," 289, (emphasis added); [John Gentle], "On the Evils," nos. 19, 6; "A List of the Original Certificates of Stock in the Detroit Bank," *MPHS Collections* 8 (1886): 575. See also letters from Nathaniel Parker reprinted in Minns, "Detroit Bank," 523.

119. *Accompanying a Bill Disapproving of an Act, Passed by the Governor and Judges of the Territory of Michigan, Intituled "An Act Concerning the Bank of Detroit"* (Washington City: A&G Way, 1807); Hull to Isaac McLellan, 11 December 1806, Norcross Autograph Collection, MHS.

120. "Judge Woodward's Memorandum on the Fur Trade," *MPHS Collections,* 31 (1902): 589–91; compare to James Henry, William Brown, and William Flanigan [*sic*] to the Michigan legislature, 12 December 1808, *MPHS Collections,* 8 (1886): 577.

121. "A List of the Original Certificates of Stock in the Detroit Bank," *MPHS Collections* 8 (1886): 575; [John Gentle], "On the Evils," no. 19; and Jenks, "The First Bank in Michigan," 47–50.

122. The Detroit bills were Perkins stereotype bills, a new anticounterfeiting design. Gentle mocks this touch in [John Gentle], "On the Evils," no. 19.

123. [John Gentle], "On the Evils," no. 19; Hull to James Madison, 26 December 1807, *MPHS Collections* 36 (1908): 196–97. Letters from Nathaniel Parker on his journey east, dated 7, 18 November 1806, are reprinted in Minns, "Detroit Bank," 523–24. The first mention of Detroit bills in Boston appears in *BG,* 15 December 1806. They appeared in Portland nearly simultaneously; see "Detroit Bills," *CC,* 24 December 1806. For Appleton, Samuel Dexter, and Bradstreet staffing the Exchange Office's discount counter, see *BG,* 29 November, 20, 27 December 1806.

## CHAPTER TWO: ICARUS

1. William Bentley, *The Diary of William Bentley, D.D., Pastor of the East Church, Salem, Massachusetts* (Gloucester Mass.: Peter Smith, 1962), 3: 262, 264, 266, 269–70; "Remarks on Mr. Dexter's *Defense of Selfridge,*" *IC,* 19 January 1807, also 26 January; 5, 16, 22, 26 February 1807, 16 July 1807. On the Selfridge-Austin affray, see also Charles Warren, *Jacobin and Junto or, Early American Politics as Viewed in the Diary of Dr. Nathaniel Ames, 1758–1822* (Cambridge, Mass.: Harvard University Press, 1931), 182–89; Samuel Eliot Morison, *Harrison Gray Otis, 1765–1848: The Urbane Federalist* (Boston: Houghton Mifflin, 1969), 277–79; and Joanne B. Freeman, "Honor and Politics in Early National New England" (unpublished paper, 2001). Competing, contemporary accounts of the murder and the trial are found in *Trial of Thomas O. Selfridge, Attorney at Law . . . for Killing Charles Austin, on the Public Exchange, in Boston* (Boston: Russell & Cutler, 1807); Thomas O. Selfridge, *A Correct Statement of the Whole Preliminary Controversy Between Tho. O. Selfridge and Benj. Austin* (Charlestown, Mass.: Samuel Etheridge, 1807).

2. "Michigan Bank Notes," *BG,* 15 December 1806; advertisements in *Repertory,* 23 December 1806; *CC,* 17 December 1806; "Detroit Bank," by A Friend to the Public [pseud.], *NEP,* 23 December 1806. For evidence that Detroit bills have surfaced in other seaports, see *CC,* 24 December 1806.

3. "Detroit Bank," by A Friend to the Public [pseud.], *NEP*, 23 December 1806; "Some Reflections Respecting DETROIT BANK BILLS," by A Friend to the Public [pseud.], *CC*, 20 December 1806; "Bank Bills, a Few Facts Respecting Them," by One of the Public [pseud.], *BG*, 29 December 1806; "Michigan Bank Notes," *BG*, 15 December 1806.

4. *BG*, 18 December 1806; *IC*, 18 December 1806.

5. Boston Assessor's Records, BPL, 1806, tax books 4:10; see also taking books 4: 24; and transfer books 4:13. For the comparison to 1803, see Boston Assessor's Records, 1803: tax books 8: 6; transfer books 8:7; taking books 8:6. For Dexter's membership in the Massachusetts Charitable Fire Society, see *Act of Incorporation, Laws, and Regulations, Catalogue of the Members, and State of the Funds, of the Massachusetts Charitable Fire Society* (Boston: Russell & Cutler, 1805), 15; William Emerson, *A Discourse Delivered in the First Church, Boston, on the Anniversary of the Massachusetts Humane Society* (Boston: Munroe & Francis, 1807), 34.

6. For early real estate purchases, see William Pinchbeck to Andrew Dexter Jr., 5 June 1804; Norfolk County Deeds, Norfolk County Court House, Dedham, Mass., book 22:37–38; James Stimpson to Andrew Dexter Jr., 10 May 1806, Middlesex County Deeds, Middlesex County Court House, Cambridge, Mass., 164: 510–12; Thomas Pollock to Andrew Dexter Jr., 13 March 1806; Andrew Dexter Jr. to William Fenno, 13 March 1806; Andrew Dexter Jr., to Thomas Pollock, 14 March 1806; Dexter to Robert Fletcher, 13 August 1806; all SD, 214: 288–90, 216: 118r–119v.

7. Lobb to Dexter (3 parcels), 24 May 1806, SD 215: 124–25; Wright to Dexter, 27 May 1806, SD 219: 273–74.

8. John Lambert, *Travels Through Canada, and the United States of North America, in the Years 1806, 1807, and 1808: To Which Are Added Biographical Notices and Anecdotes of Some of the Leading Characters in the United States* (London: C. Cradock and A. Joy, 1816), 334, 331. For the neighborhood, see John Groves Hales, *Maps of the Street-Lines of Boston Made for the Selectmen in 1819 and 1820* (Boston: Rockwell & Churchill, 1894), 40–41; *Boston Directory for 1807;* and Boston Assessors' Records, 1807, taking and transfer books 8 (organized geographically).

9. John Lowell to Andrew Dexter Jr., missing deed; Andrew Dexter Jr. to John Lowell, 1 June 1806; Andrew Dexter Jr. to Alanson Tucker, 2 June 1806, SD 216: 205–6; Samuel Hall to Andrew Dexter Jr., 20 June 1806, SD 216: 55v–55r; Andrew Dexter Jr. to Samuel Hall, 20 June 1806, SD 216: 55r–56v; Andrew Dexter Jr. to Samuel Hall, 20 June 1806, SD 216, 57v–57r; Thomas Kendall to Andrew Dexter Jr., 26 June 1806, SD 216: 268–69; Andrew Dexter Jr. to Thomas Kendall, 26 June 1806, SD 216: 267–68; John McLane and wife to Andrew Dexter Jr., 28 June 1806, SD 216: 150v–150r; Andrew Dexter Jr. to John McLane, 10 July 1806, SD 216: 150r–151v; Josiah Quincy to Andrew Dexter Jr., 1 September 1806, SD 216: 251r–252r; Andrew Dexter Jr. to Josiah Quincy, 1 September 1806; SD 216: 252r–253r; John Coates to Andrew Dexter Jr., 7 October 1806, SD 217: 159v–160v; Andrew Dexter Jr. to John Coates, 8 October 1806, SD 217: 160v–6or; Andrew Dexter Jr. to John Coates, 8 October 1806; SD 217: 160r–61r. These calculations assume that the purchase price of the land described in Lowell's mortgage to Dexter (SD 216: 157–58) must be at least equal to the amount mortgaged, which is $15,000. See also Andrew Dexter Jr. to Robert Fletcher, 13 August 1806, SD 216: 118r–19v; Josiah Quincy to Andrew Dexter Jr., 1 September

1806, SD 216: 251r–52r; see also Andrew Dexter Jr. to Josiah Quincy, 1 September 1806, SD 216: 252r—53r, where Quincy extends Dexter a mortgage on the property for $8,000, or half the purchase price. John Coates to Andrew Dexter Jr., 7 October 1806, SD 217: 159v–160v; and the mortgages in Andrew Dexter Jr. to John Coates, 8 October 1806, SD 217: 160v–60r; and Andrew Dexter Jr. to John Coates, 8 October 1806, SD 217: 160r–61r.

10. Appleton quoted in Pamela Fox, "Nathan Appleton's Beacon Street Houses," *Old-Time New England* 70 (1980): 114; Thomas Pemberton, "A Topographical and Historical Description of Boston, 1794," *Massachusetts Historical Society Collections* 3 (1794): 248. On the social geography of State Street, see also Gayle Elizabeth Sawtelle, "The Commercial Landscape of Boston in 1800: Documentary and Archaeological Perspectives on the Geography of Retail Shopkeeping" (Ph.D. dissertation, Boston University, 1999), 136–49; and Robert Blair St. George, *Conversing by Signs: The Poetics of Implication in Colonial New England Culture* (Chapel Hill: University of North Carolina Press, 1998), 260–68. The link between ritual spaces and marketplaces is, of course, much older than Boston; see Jean-Christophe Agnew, *Worlds Apart: The Market and the Theater in Anglo-American Thought, 1550–1750* (New York: Cambridge University Press, 1986); and Helen Tangires, *Public Markets and Civic Culture in Nineteenth-Century America* (Baltimore: Johns Hopkins University Press, 2003).

11. Shubael Bell, "An Account of the Town of Boston, Written in 1817," *Bostonian Society Publications,* 2nd ser., 3 (1919): 41, 22. For the notion of "creative destruction," see Joseph A. Schumpeter, *Capitalism, Socialism, and Democracy* (New York: Harper, 1942), 82–85; and Max Page, *The Creative Destruction of Manhattan, 1900–1940* (Chicago: University of Chicago Press, 1999).

12. Lisa Beth Lubow, "Artisans in Transition: Early Capitalist Development and the Carpenters of Boston, 1787–1837" (Ph.D. dissertation, UCLA, 1987), 208, 198. On traditional colonial building practices, see Lubow, "Artisans in Transition," 130–48, and Catherine W. Bishir, "A Proper Good Nice and Workmanlike Manner: A Century of Traditional Building Practice, 1730–1830," in Catherine W. Bishir et al., *Architects and Builders in North Carolina: A History of the Practice of Building,* (Chapel Hill: University of North Carolina Press, 1990), 48–129. Lubow sees these changes as declension, the transformation of craftsmen into wage laborers. In her study of Philadelphia during the same period, Donna Rilling finds that the luckiest small builders themselves *became* capitalists, successfully manipulating credit to speculate on their own work products; Donna J. Rilling, *Making Houses, Crafting Capitalism: Builders in Philadelphia, 1790–1850* (Philadelphia: University of Pennsylvania Press, 2001).

On the professionalization of architecture in the early decades of the nineteenth century, see Martha J. McNamara, *From Tavern to Courthouse: Architecture and Ritual in American Law, 1658–1860* (Baltimore: Johns Hopkins University Press, 2004), 81–110; Harold Kirker and James Kirker, *Bulfinch's Boston, 1787–1817* (New York: Oxford University Press, 1964); Edward Francis Zimmer, "The Architectural Career of Alexander Parris (1780–1852)" (Ph.D. dissertation, Boston University, 1984), 163–66, 246–69; Jack Quinan, "Some Aspects of the Development of the Architectural Profession in Boston Between 1800 and 1830," *Old-Time New England* 68, no. 1–2 (Summer-Fall 1977): 32–37; Dell Upton, "Pattern Books and Professionalism: Aspects of the Transformation of Domestic Architecture in America, 1800–1860," *Winterthur*

*Portfolio* 19, no. 2/3 (Autumn 1984): 107–50; and Kenneth Hafertepe and James F. O'Gorman, eds., *American Architects and Their Books to 1848* (Boston: University of Massachusetts Press, 2001).

13. Bell, "An Account of the Town of Boston," 22, 36 and n; Edward Augustus Kendall, *Travels Through the Northern Parts of the United States, in the Years 1807 and 1808* (New York: I. Riley, 1809), 246. For the most recent detailed account of Boston's nineteenth-century transformation, see Nancy S. Seasholes, *Gaining Ground: A History of Landmaking in Boston* (Cambridge, Mass.: MIT Press, 2003). Still useful if somewhat dated is Walter Muir Whitehill and Lawrence W. Kennedy, *Boston: A Topographical History,* 3d ed., reprint, 2000 (Cambridge, Mass.: Harvard University Press, 1959).

14. Ali Bey [Samuel L. Knapp], *Extracts from a Journal of Travels in North America, Consisting of an Account of Boston and Its Vicinity* (Boston: Thomas Badger, 1818), 10; Bell, "An Account of the Town of Boston," 25, 21; *Boston Directory for 1807,* 3. For comprehensive surveys of Boston architecture ca. 1800–1810, see Harold Kirker, *The Architecture of Charles Bulfinch,* reprint, 1998 (Cambridge, Mass.: Harvard University Press, 1969); and Whitehill and Kennedy, *Boston: A Topographical History,* 46–72. On the evolution of elite domestic housing in Federalist Boston, see Damie Stillman, "City Living, Federal Style," in *Everyday Life in the Early Republic,* ed. Catherine E. Hutchins (Winterthur, Del.: Winterthur Museum, 1994), 137–74; and the many examples that appear in Kirker, *The Architecture of Charles Bulfinch*. On controversies over theater in Boston, see T. A. Milford, "Boston's Theater Controversy and Liberal Notions of Advantage," *New England Quarterly* 72, no. 1 (March 1999): 61–88; and Joanna Frang, "'The Theater Is an Important Engine in the Hands of *Any Party*': Boston's Federal Street Theater, Haymarket Theater, and Columbian Museum in the Early Republic" (unpublished paper, Brandeis University, 2004).

15. Pemberton, "Topographical and Historical Description of Boston," 250, 273 (quoting from an anonymous source); Lubow, "Artisans in Transition," 35, 460–70; *Boston Town Records, 1796 to 1813,* Records Relating to the Early History of Boston (1905), 137–39.

16. See Kirker, *The Architecture of Charles Bulfinch,* 104, 144, 159, 175, 207, 211, 226; and "West Boston Society Records, 1805–1908," MHS.

17. Bell, "An Account of the Town of Boston," 23; "Remarks on the Progress and Present State of the Fine Arts in the United States," *Analectic Magazine* 6 (1815), 372–73, quoted in W. Barksdale Maynard, *Architecture in the United States, 1800–1850* (New Haven, Conn., and London: Yale University Press, 2002), 25. The availability of English and Renaissance architectural texts in Boston is documented by the catalog of the Architectural Library of Boston, ca. 1809, appended to *The Constitution of the Proprietors of the Architectural Library of Boston* (Boston: T. Kennard, 1809). See also Martha J. McNamara, "Defining the Profession: Books, Libraries, and Architects," in *American Architects and Their Books to 1848,* eds. Kenneth Hafertepe and James F. O'Gorman (Amherst, Mass.: University of Massachusetts Press, 2001), 73–90; and Upton, "Pattern Books and Professionalism."

18. Bell, "An Account of the Town of Boston," 23, 24; Robert Adam and James Adam, *The Works in Architecture of Robert & James Adam*, int. Henry Hope Reed, reprint, 1980 (New York: Dover, 1778), 1–2. This brief summary of British classicism

draws on Barbara Arciszewska, "Classicism: Constructing the Paradigm in Continental Europe and Britain," in *Articulating British Classicism,* eds. Barbara Arciszewska and Elizabeth McKellar (London: Ashgate, 2004), 1–34; Robin Middleton and David Watkin, *Neoclassical and 19th Century Architecture* (New York: Rizzoli, 1980), 1:65–176; Kirker and Kirker, *Bulfinch's Boston, 1787–1817,* chaps. 1 and 2.

19. Bentley, *Diary of William Bentley,* 3:270; *IC,* 26 February 1807.

20. See Andrew Dexter Jr. to Thomas Pollock, 14 March 1806, SD 214: 290v–91v; and Andrew Dexter Jr. to John McLane, 10 July 1806, SD 216: 150r–51v; along with the mortgages in SD 216: 157–158; 216: 55r–56; 216: 267–68; 216: 252–53; 216: 289–90.

21. Albert Gallatin to Thomas Jefferson, 25 November 1806, in Henry Adams, ed., *Writings of Albert Gallatin* (Philadelphia: Lippincott, 1879), 1: 322; William Duane to Thomas Jefferson, 8 December 1806, Papers of Thomas Jefferson, Library of Congress, 2nd ser., vol. 27, no. 34; James Madison to William Hull, 8 December 1806, *MPHS Collections,* 8 (1886): 574; Augustus B. Woodward to James Madison, 31 January 1807, *MPHS Collections* 31 (1902): 585–92; "Legislative," *CC,* 28 January 1807.

22. Public Works [pseud.], *BG* 1 January 1807; Manto [Sarah Morton?], "Lines on Visiting the Exchange Coffeehouse in Boston," *Port Folio* 1 (new series), no. 5 (May 1809): 452–53.

23. Public Works [pseud.], *BG,* 1 January 1807; Letters "from an English traveller [sic] in this country, to his friend in Jamaica," *The Ordeal,* 1 April 1809, 205; 15 April 1809, 234–235; Kendall, *Travels Through the Northern Parts of the United States,* 237; William Tudor, *Letters on the Eastern States,* 2nd ed. (Boston: Wells & Lilly, 1821), 356, 358. For comparisons of Boston and European cities, especially London, see also John M. Duncan, *Travels Through Part of the United States and Canada in 1818 and 1819* (Glasgow: Wardlaw & Cunninghame, 1823), 46; and Bey [Samuel L. Knapp], *Extracts from a Journal of Travels in North America,* 13.

My thinking on the logic of the grid is informed by the suggestions of Robert Blair St. George. See especially Sibyl Moholy-Nagy, *Matrix of Man: An Illustrated History of Urban Environment* (New York: Praeger, 1968), 232–35; John W. Reps, *The Making of Urban America: A History of City Planning in the United States* (Princeton, N.J.: Princeton University Press, 1965); John Archer, "Puritan Town Planning in New Haven," *Journal of the Society of Architectural Historians* 34, no. 2 (May 1975): 140–49; and John W. Reps, "C² + L² = S²? Another Look at the Origins of Savannah's Town Plans," in *Forty Years of Diversity: Essays on Colonial Georgia,* eds. Harvey H. Jackson and Phinizy Spalding (Athens: University of Georgia Press, 1984), 101–51. See also Dell Upton, "The Grid and the Republican Spatial Imagination" (unpublished paper, Charles Warren Center, Harvard University, 2004); Dell Upton, "Another City: The Urban Cultural Landscape in the Early Republic," in *Everyday Life in the Early Republic,* ed. Catherine E. Hutchins (Winterthur, Del.: Winterthur Museum, 1994), 63, 67–72; Dell Upton, "The City as Material Culture," in *The Art and Mystery of Historical Archaeology: Essays in Honor of James Deetz,* eds. Anne Elizabeth Yentsch and Mary C. Beaudry (Boca Raton, Fla.: CRC Press, 1994), 53–56; and David M. Henkin, *City Reading: Written Words and Public Spaces in Antebellum New York* (New York: Columbia University Press, 1998), 35–38. The grid, of course, was also the scaffolding for the "settlement" of the West, from the Northwest Ordinance forward. See Malcolm J.

Rohrbough, *The Land Office Business: The Settlement and Administration of American Public Lands, 1789–1837* (New York: Oxford University Press, 1968), chap. 1; and Andrew R. L. Cayton, *The Frontier Republic: Ideology and Politics in the Ohio Country, 1780–1825* (Kent, Ohio: Kent State University Press, 1986), 28–29. On the emergence of occupational and residential segregation in the "sorted" post-Revolutionary city, see Diane Shaw, *City Building on the Eastern Frontier: Sorting the New Nineteenth-Century City* (Baltimore: Johns Hopkins University Press, 2004); and Betsy Blackmar, "Rewalking the 'Walking City': Housing and Property Relations in New York City, 1780–1840," in *Material Life in America, 1600–1860,* ed. Robert Blair St. George (Boston: Northeastern University Press, 1988), 371–84.

24. Henry B. Fearon, *Sketches of America: A Narrative of a Journey of Five Thousand Miles Through the Eastern and Western States of America* (London: Longman, Hurst, 1819), 105, 109; David T. Gilchrist, ed., *The Growth of the Seaport Cities, 1790–1825,* Proceedings of a conference sponsored by the Eleutherian Mills-Hagley Foundation, March 17–19, 1966 (Charlottesville: University Press of Virginia, 1967).

25. Public Works [pseud.], *BG,* 5, 1 January 1807.

26. Public Works [pseud.], *BG,* 1, 5 January 1807.

27. *Spectator* number 69, 19 May 1711, in Joseph Addison, *The Spectator,* ed. Donald F. Bond (Oxford: Clarendon Press, 1965), 1: 293–94; see also Guy Miege, *The Present State of Great-Britain and Ireland: In Three Parts,* 3d ed. (London, 1715), 119–20. On commercial architecture in London and Europe more broadly, see also Nikolaus Pevsner, *A History of Building Types* (Princeton, N.J.: Princeton University Press, 1976), 194–203; Roy Porter, *London: A Social History* (London: Hamish Hamilton, 1994), 131–59; John Summerson, *Georgian London* (New York: Scribner's, 1946), 36–48, 243–53; and Daniel M. Abramson, *Building the Bank of England: Money, Architecture, Society, 1694–1942* (New Haven, Conn., and London: Yale University Press, 2005). On the domestication of market relations in the early modern period, see Agnew, *Worlds Apart,* chap. 1.

28. Public Works, [pseud.] *BG,* 1, 5 January 1807. See also Walter R. Danforth, "Pictures of Providence in the Past, 1790–1820: The Reminiscences of Walter R. Danforth," ed. Clarkson A. Collins, *Rhode Island History* no. 10:1–11:2 (January 1951–April 1952): 93–96.

29. A. K. Sandoval-Strausz, "Why the Hotel? Liberal Visions, Merchant Capital, Public Space, and the Creation of an American Institution," *Business and Economic History* 28, no. 2 (Winter 1999): 5–6; and Agnes Addison Gilchrist, "John McComb, Sr. and Jr., in New York, 1784–1799," *Journal of the Society of Architectural Historians* 31, no. 1 (March 1972): 17–18.

30. Agnes Addison Gilchrist, "John McComb, Sr. and Jr.," 16–17; see also Henkin, *City Reading,* 123; James Grant Wilson, ed., *The Memorial History of the City of New-York from Its First Settlement to the Year 1892* (New York: New-York History Company, 1892), 2: 284, 448.

31. *Philadelphia in 1824 . . . A Complete Guide for Strangers* (Philadelphia: H. C. Carey & I. Lea, 1824), 93; see also Joseph J. Kelley Jr., *Life and Times in Colonial Philadelphia* (Harrisburg, Penn.: Stackpole Books, 1973), 167–68; and A. K. Sandoval-Strausz, "A Public House for a New Republic: The Architecture of Accommodation and the American State, 1789–1809," in *Constructing Image, Identity, and*

*Place,* eds. Alison K. Hoagland and Kenneth A. Breisch, *Perspectives in Vernacular Architecture* IX (Knoxville, Tenn.: University of Tennessee Press, 2003), 56. On the Bank of Pennsylvania, see William H. Pierson Jr., *The Colonial and Neoclassical Styles,* vol. 1 of *American Buildings and Their Architects* (New York: Oxford University Press, 1970), 348–57.

32. Sandoval-Strausz, "Why the Hotel?" 3–4; Sandoval-Strausz, "A Public House for a New Republic," 57–58. On real estate speculation in 1790s Washington, see also Bob Arnebeck, *Through a Fiery Trial: Building Washington, 1790–1800* (Lanham, Md.: Madison Books, 1990).

33. See Sandoval-Strausz, "Why the Hotel?" 7–8.

34. Public Works [pseud.], *BG,* 1, 5 January 1807

35. Public Works [pseud.], *BG,* 1, 5 January 1807; *BG,* 17 November 1806. For evidence that Selfridge and Dexter associated closely, see *NEP,* 6 December 1803.

36. Daniel Defoe, "The Anatomy of Exchange Alley, or, a System of Stock-Jobbing [1719]," in John Francis, *Chronicles and Characters of the Stock Exchange,* (Boston: Crosby and Nichols, 1850), 148, 136. See also Abramson, *Building the Bank of England.*

37. On the relationship between architecture and the legibility of credit, see Abramson, *Building the Bank of England.*

38. Public Works [pseud.], *BG,* 1, 5 January 1807; "Annuity Fund," *NEP,* 12 December 1806; see also "Annuity Fund," *Repertory,* 12, 23, 26 December 1806; 2, 9 January 1807; "Annuity Fund," *IC,* 18, 22, 29 December 1806; and "Massachusetts Legislative," *BG,* 15 January, 19 February 1807. On legal interest rates for banks, see Fritz Redlich, *The Molding of American Banking: Men and Ideas* (New York: Hafner Publishing, 1951), 1: 10–11.

39. Public Works [pseud.], *BG,* 5 January 1807.

40. For New York's example, see *Constitution and Nominations of the Subscribers to the Tontine Coffee-House* (New York, 1796).

41. Doris Elizabeth King, "Early Hotel Entrepreneurs and Promoters, 1793–1860," *Explorations in Entrepreneurial History* 8 (1955–1956): 149–50; Arnebeck, *Through a Fiery Trial,* 148–49, 202–3, 332–33.

42. Harrison Gray Otis to Robert Goodloe Harper [Baltimore], 19 April 1807, in Harrison Gray Otis Papers, MHS, microfilm edition, reel 4. On risk in the early national economy more broadly, see Bruce H. Mann, *Republic of Debtors: Bankruptcy in the Age of American Independence* (Cambridge, Mass.: Harvard University Press, 2002).

43. Boston Assessors' Records, 1807: tax books 4: 2; taking books 4:26–27; transfer books 4:15. For Cody, see *Boston Directory for 1807,* 52. I have not found deeds to corroborate Dexter's purchase of these properties from Jonathan Lucas. For the weather and the Selfridge affair, see Bentley, *Diary of William Bentley,* 3:286–87.

44. For Dexter's eighth ward holdings, see Boston Assessors' Records, 1807, taking books 8: 17–18; transfer books 8: 8, 17, 25, 27. I am including in this total the properties assessed to the Exchange Coffee House "Proprietors" as well as those credited to Andrew Dexter; he remains, at this point, the sole known owner of the venture. On Exchange Wharf, see Samuel Dexter Jr. to Andrew Dexter Jr., 16 October 1806, SD 217: 292. For a description of the wharf, which Samuel Dexter bought from Thomas

Lewis, see Thomas Lewis to Samuel Dexter, 11 August 1806, SD 216: 253; and several subsequent transactions: Thomas Lewis to Andrew Dexter, 16 June 1807, SD 222:31r–32v; Thomas Lewis to Andrew Dexter, 29 September 1807, SD 223: 100; and Thomas Lewis to Andrew Dexter, 5 October 1807, SD 223:95r–96r; and Andrew Dexter Jr. to Ebenezer Francis, 7 October 1807. See also "House and Wharf," *BG,* 7 April 1814.

45. *Repertory,* 31 March 1807. On the annuity fund, see "Massachusetts Legislature," *BG,* 19 February 1807; "Massachusetts Annuity Fund," *CC,* 18 March 1807. The bill nullifying the Detroit Bank cleared the Senate on 3 March 1807, and news reached Boston roughly two weeks later; see *CC,* 7, 18 March 1807, *BG,* 19 March 1807; *Berkshire Reporter* (Pittsfield), 25 April 1807. For Dexter's purchase of Parker and Bradstreet's shares, see [John Gentle], "On the Evils Which Have Proved Fatal to Republics . . . History of the Government of Michigan Territory, from Its Commencement, in June 1805, Till Nov. 1806," no. 19 (*Commonwealth,* 17 February 1808). Advertisements from Boston shopkeepers willing to accept Detroit bills throughout the spring of 1807 are numerous; see, for example, *CC,* 27, 30 May 1807.

46. *NEP,* 3, 6, 13, March 1807; 2 April 1807; *IC,* 5, 9, 30 March 1807; *BG,* 9, 16, 23 March 1807; 16 April 1807. Per the SD, Dexter did not actually sell any of these lands before July. Caleb Hayward, the auctioneer, had been a trustee of the Exchange Office in 1805; see *Massachusetts Register for 1806,* 54.

47. [Samuel Gilbert and Thomas Dean?], "Description of the Boston Exchange Coffee-House," *Omnium Gatherum* 1, no. 1 (November 1809): 3. This anonymous description is written by somebody both very close to the project—the author knows yet-unexecuted "ideas of the founder" (4)—and is very sympathetic with Dexter: perhaps Dexter himself? On Whitney's and Jarvis's residence, see *Boston Directory for 1807,* 95, 156. On the old West End as a "carpenters' ghetto," see Anne Elizabeth Macdonald, "Asher Benjamin: Architect, Author, Teacher and Entrepreneur" (unpublished MA thesis, Northeastern University, 1993), 80.

48. "Autobiographical fragment by Charles Bulfinch," box 3, Bulfinch Family Papers, 1720–1923, MHS. On Bulfinch's Federalist sympathies and aesthetics, see Evelyn Marie Walsh, "The Effects of the Revolution Upon the Town of Boston: Social, Economic, and Cultural" (Ph.D. dissertation, Brown University, 1964), part 1; and Thomas Conroy, "Before *Bulfinch's Boston*: Working Through the Challenges of a Successful Revolution" (unpublished paper, Annual Meeting of the Organization of American Historians, Boston, 2004).

49. On Benjamin's early life and works, see Abbott Lowell Cummings, "An Investigation of the Sources, Stylistic Evolution, and Influence of Asher Benjamin's Builders' Guides" (Ph.D. dissertation, Ohio State University, 1950), chaps. 1 and 2; John Francis Quinan Jr., "The Architectural Style of Asher Benjamin, a Study in Provincialism" (Ph.D. dissertation, Brown University, 1973), chap. 1; Macdonald, "Asher Benjamin"; and Kenneth Hafertepe, "*The Country Builder's Assistant:* Text and Context," in *American Architects and Their Books to 1848,* eds. Kenneth Hafertepe and James F. O'Gorman (Boston: University of Massachusetts Press, 2001), 129–48.

50. *IC,* 22 January 1807; Asher Benjamin, *The American Builder's Companion; or, a System of Architecture Particularly Adapted to the Present Style of Building,* 2nd ed. (Boston: Etheridge & Bliss, 1811), v–vii; see also Cummings, "Asher Benjamin's Builders' Guides," 74–136.

51. *Boston Directory for 1807,* 36; Boston Assessors' Records 1807, transfer books 7: 4. For a list of Benjamin commissions, see Jack Quinan, "Asher Benjamin and American Architecture," *Journal of the Society of Architectural Historians* 38, no. 3 (1979): 253–54. On the relationship of the West Church to Bulfinch's church commissions, see Nancy S. Voye, "Asher Benjamin's West Church: A Model for Change," *Old-Time New England* 67, no. 245 (Fall 1976): 8. For the Housewright's Society and its role in the town's artisanal community, see Lubow, "Artisans in Transition," 450–57. Benjamin was a trustee in 1804 and 1805, and later became vice president of the society; "Minutes Book, 1804–1837," in Associated Housewrights Society of Boston Records, series 6 , Massachusetts Charitable Mechanics Association Records, 1791–1995, MHS.

52. Boston Assessors' Records: 1803 on Poplar Street (transfer books 7:4); 1804 on Poplar Street (transfer books 7: 4); 1805 on Chamber Street (transfer books 7: 5); 1806 on Chestnut Street (transfer books 7: 3); 1807 on "New Street," which the following year is renamed Charles Street (transfer books 7: 4).

53. "Copy of the Accounts of Mungo Mackay, Thomas Dennie and James Prints Agents for Rebuilding the West Boston Meeting House in the Year 1806," West Boston Society Records, 1805–1908, MHS, line 123. For drawing the plans and supervising the construction of the Suffolk County Court House between 1810 and 1813, Charles Bulfinch earned $700; see "Bill for Plans and Supervision," 19 July 1813, in "Documents Relating to the Construction and Occupancy of the Suffolk County Court House in School Street," Adlow (Elijah) Collection, Boston Public Library, item Ms.Adl.S.C52.

54. Sarah Wentworth (Apthorp) Morton to Joseph Dennie, 27 March 1797, series 2, item 113, Joseph Dennie Papers, Houghton Library, Harvard University. Bulfinch is often credited as the architect of the Mortons' Dorchester estate; see, for example, Kirker, *The Architecture of Charles Bulfinch,* 135–40. But Morton's claim in this letter seems definite, and Walter Muir Whitehill deems her claim credible on stylistic grounds as well; see Walter Muir Whitehill, "Perez Morton's Daughter Revisits Boston in 1825," *Proceedings of the Massachusetts Historical Society* 82 (1970): 31.

55. James Smith Colburn, *The Personal Memoirs of James Smith Colburn 1780–1859, Who in the Year 1808 Built 54 and 55 Beacon Street, Boston, Massachusetts,* ca. 1859 (typescript) ([Boston]: Massachusetts Society of the Colonial Dames of America, 1949), 66–67; Benjamin, *American Builder's Companion,* vi. See also Fox, "Nathan Appleton's Beacon Street Houses." In addition to new editions of *The American Builder's Companion,* Benjamin published *The Rudiments of Architecture* (1814), *The Practical House Carpenter* (1830), *The Practice of Architecture* (1833), *The Builder's Guide* (1839), and *The Elements of Architecture* (1843).

56. Asher Benjamin's plans for the Coffee House do not survive. This description is based on the plans Thomas W. Sumner drew in September 1817, following extensive renovation, and on textual sources describing the Exchange as built. See Thomas W. Sumner and W. Bradley, "Exchange Coffee House Architectural Plans," Bostonian Society (1817); and [Samuel Gilbert and Thomas Dean?], "Description of the Boston Exchange Coffee-House." For the suggestion that the Exchange was planned for four stories (plus basement and cellars), and grew to seven with Dexter's bubble, see Nathaniel Dearborn, *Boston Notions; Being an Authentic and Concise*

*Account of 'That Village,' from 1630 to 1847* (Boston: W. D. Ticknor, 1848), 211; "First Sky-Scraper," *Boston Herald,* 3 November 1901. The exterior of the building—which seems to end twice—supports the contention.

57. Rilling, *Making Houses.*

58. The records of the construction of the Coffee House do not exist. Here I use the very detailed minutes of the construction of the West Boston Meeting House in 1806, along with those for the construction of the Suffolk County Court House, ca. 1810–1813, to approximate the wages and stages of building the Boston Exchange Coffee House the following year. See "Minutes of Agents Overseeing the Construction of a New Meeting House, 1805–1809," West Boston Society Records, 1805–1908, MHS.

59. Rough calculation based on the West-Boston Meeting House (75 feet by 75 feet, at two stories plus a center tower) requiring 400,000 bricks and 300 hogsheads of lime. A four-man crew produced approximately 2,500 bricks daily; see Rilling, *Making Houses,* 103–11; and Richard P. O'Connor, "A History of Brickmaking in the Hudson Valley" (Ph.D. dissertation, University of Pennsylvania, 1987), 67–70, 85. For brick manufacture in Massachusetts, see Tench Coxe, *A Statement of the Arts and Manufactures of the United States of America, for the Year 1810* (Philadelphia: A Cornman, 1814), 37.

60. "West Boston Church Construction Minutes." For Wait's brickyard, see *IC,* 16 February 1807, among many others. For the price of bricks ca. 1807 and the preconstruction stages of such projects, see "West Boston Church Construction Minutes"; and "Estimate of Brick Building," item Ms.Adl.S.A.8 of "Documents Relating to the Suffolk County Court House." Edward Kendall noted that red brick was also regularly imported to Boston from Philadelphia; see Kendall, *Travels Through the Northern Parts of the United States,* 237.

61. Bentley, *Diary of William Bentley,* 3: 288 (entry for 18 April 1807); "West Boston Church Construction Minutes"; *IC,* 13, 20, 27 April 1807.

62. Carroll D. Wright, *History of Wages and Prices in Massachusetts: 1752–1883* (Boston: Wright & Potter, 1885), 168, 164, 170; "Wages of Early American Building-Trades Workers," *Monthly Labor Review* 30, no.1 (January 1930): 5–15, esp. 12–13.

63. "West Boston Church Construction Minutes." On demolition and the sale of used materials, see also *BG,* 19 March 1807; Rilling, *Making Houses,* 168–69; and Lubow, "Artisans in Transition," 238. Per Rilling, 112, a wagonload holds thirty-five bushels. I am estimating that the Exchange Coffee House cellar was a minimum of 15 feet deep—enough for the unfinished cellar story (which includes a washroom and other areas that would require standing) and part of the basement story. Measuring 94 by 103 feet, the main building covers 9,682 square feet of surface area, or 145,230 cubic feet at a depth of 15 feet, divided by 1.244 to get 116,744 bushels, or 3,336 wagonloads.

64. [Samuel Gilbert and Thomas Dean?], "Description of the Boston Exchange Coffee-House," 3 ("spacious cellars"); Charles Bulfinch to William Donnison, 10 August 1813, in "Documents Relating to the Suffolk County Court House." Cellar cave-ins were common; see Rilling, *Making Houses,* 169.

65. Rilling, *Making Houses,* 168–69; Harley J. McKee, *Introduction to Early American Masonry: Stone, Brick, Mortar and Plaster* (Washington, D.C.: National Trust for

Historic Preservation, 1973), 18–39. On the Massachusetts Charitable Mechanics Association [hereafter MCMA] and its role in Boston labor activism see Lubow, "Artisans in Transition," 375–431; and Gary John Kornblith, "From Artisans to Businessmen: Master Mechanics in New England, 1789–1850" (Ph.D. dissertation, Princeton University, 1983), 49–130. Whitney joined the MCMA in 1800; see "Membership ledger, 1795–1866," series 2, box 1, MCMA records.

Masons priced the laying of rough stone by the perch, a cubic measure equal to 1.5 feet thick, 1 foot high, and 16.5 feet long. The Exchange Coffee House perimeter measured 394 feet, so each layer of cellar wall would require roughly 24 perch of stone. By the conventions of the day, a solid masonry building of the Exchange's height would require walls over 44 inches thick at their base, which means the cellar walls would be 3 perches (54 inches) deep, assuming a cellar depth of about 15 feet yields 1,080 perches of stone. On the West Boston Meeting House, workers were paid "ninety cents per perch" for the cellar stone; "West Boston Church Construction Minutes." Boston masons' standard work rules price the job at $1.33 per perch including mortar; see *The Rules of Work of the Masons, in the Town of Boston* (Boston: Josiah Hall, 1809), 3. The cost of rough stone was approximately $3.00 per perch; see "Estimate of Stone Building," in "Documents Relating to the Suffolk County Court House," item Ms.Adl. S.A.8. Many thanks to John Horton and David Fischetti for their help calculating the needed thickness of the cellar walls.

66. McKee, *Introduction to Early American Masonry,* 15–22; John Morrill Bryan, "Boston's Granite Architecture, c. 1810–1860," Ph.D. dissertation in *Boston's Granite Architecture, c. 1810–1860.* (Boston University, 1972), 13–18; Bell, "An Account of the Town of Boston," 36–37; Tudor, *Letters on the Eastern States,* 358. That the Exchange rests on a "base of granite" is confirmed by [Samuel Gilbert and Thomas Dean?], "Description of the Boston Exchange Coffee-House," 4.

67. Susan Apthorp Bulfinch to Thomas Bulfinch, November 1804, in Ellen Susan Bulfinch, ed., *The Life and Letters of Charles Bulfinch Architect, with Other Family Papers* (New York: Burt Franklin, 1973), 154; Duncan, *Travels Through Part of the United States and Canada,* 63–66.

68. Bentley, *Diary of William Bentley,* 3:292.

69. Neil Harris, *Building Lives: Constructing Rites and Passages* (New Haven, Conn.: Yale University Press, 1999), 18–31; "West Boston Church Construction Minutes."

70. "West Boston Church Construction Minutes"; *General Rules of Work, for Housewrights, in Newburyport* (Newburyport, Mass.: W. & J. Gilman, 1805), 10, 11. For wages for such work, see *The Rules of Work, of the Carpenters, in the Town of Boston* ([Charlestown, Mass.], 1800).

71. Rilling, *Making Houses,* 96–103; James Elliott Defebaugh, *History of the Lumber Industry of America* (Chicago: The American Lumberman, 1907), 2:22–23, 38–42, 222–26. For the location of Boston lumberyards, see Sawtelle, "The Commercial Landscape of Boston in 1800," 426–32.

72. Chester Kimball (New London, Conn.) to Simon Newton Dexter (Athens, N.Y.), 7 November 1811, Simon Newton Dexter Papers, Division of Rare and Manuscript Collections, Cornell University Library, folder 1. Other quarries that supplied marble to the Exchange were located in western Massachusetts and central Connecticut; *Northern Whig* (Hudson, N.Y.) 10 August 1812. See also O'Connor,

"Brickmaking in the Hudson Valley," 85; and William E. Verplanck and Moses W. Collyer, *The Sloops of the Hudson: An Historical Sketch of the Packet and Market Sloops of the Last Century* (New York: G. P. Putnam, 1908), part 1. For the cost of marble, see "Estimate of Brick Building," "Documents Relating to the Suffolk County Court House," item Ms.Adl.S.A.8.

73. "West Boston Church Construction Minutes"; *NEP,* 31 July 07; *BG,* 30 July 1807.

74. *NEP,* 31 July 1807; *BG,* 30 July 1807.

75. Bentley, *Diary of William Bentley,* 3: 315.

76. See Whitehill and Kennedy, *Boston: A Topographical History,* 61, for a scale rendering of the Exchange and its neighbors.

77. *CC,* 25 July 1807. For sheds and workshops, see Charles Bulfinch to Hannah Bulfinch, 7 January 1818, in Bulfinch, *Life and Letters of Charles Bulfinch,* 213. He finds "about 120 men" working on the Capitol site, even in (the capital's warmer) winter. Much of the exterior detail for the State House was likewise "moulded on the spot," *CC,* 10 January 1798, as quoted in Kirker, *The Architecture of Charles Bulfinch,* 106. Pemberton notes that "From July 15th, 1792, to December 26th, twenty to thirty-six men only were employed [on West Boston Bridge]. From April 8th, 1793, to November 23rd, following, from forty to two hundred and fifty men worked on it"; Pemberton, "Topographical and Historical Description of Boston," 246.

78. Bulfinch letter of 1795 quoted in Kirker, *The Architecture of Charles Bulfinch,* 103; *NEP,* 9 June 1807; *An Act to Incorporate Sundry Persons Into a Company, by the Name of the Proprietors of the Exchange Coffee-House* (Boston, 1807), esp. sects. 3, 5, and 7.

For Samuel Brown's ties to Morton and Dexter, see several promissory notes in Folder 1800–1829, Morton-Cunningham-Clinch Family Papers, 1754–1903, MHS; and folders 2 and 3, New England Mississippi Land Company Papers, Hargett Library, University of Georgia. On insider lending networks, see Naomi R. Lamoreaux, *Insider Lending: Banks, Personal Connections, and Economic Development in Industrial New England* (New York: Cambridge University Press, 1994). On the role of the Exchange Coffee House charter in the evolution of the limited liability corporation, see Oscar Handlin and Mary Flug Handlin, *Commonwealth: A Study of the Role of Government in the American Economy: Massachusetts, 1774–1861* (Cambridge, Mass.: Harvard University Press, 1969), 144–45.

79. Andrew Dexter to Augustus B. Woodward, 17 June 1807, *MPHS Collections* 8: 572. For the office and meetings of the Exchange proprietors, see *IC,* 30 July 1807; *CC,* 5 August 1807. No records suggest that anybody but Dexter, Hatch, and Brown became officers of the original Exchange Coffee House corporation or that any others bought shares.

80. "Bank Thermometer," *CC,* 23 September 1807; see also *CC,* 27 May, 31 August 1807; *IC,* 26 March 1807. For the action of the Massachusetts Bank, see N. S. B. Gras, *The Massachusetts First National Bank of Boston, 1784–1934* (Cambridge, Mass.: Harvard University Press, 1937), 392. For the annual trustee election of the Exchange Office, see *NEP,* 24 July 1807; and *Massachusetts Register for . . . 1808,* 56.

81. Andrew Dexter Jr. to James Prince, 31 July 1807, SD 222: 226v–226r; Andrew Dexter Jr. to James Prince, 13 August 1807, SD 222: 247r–48v; Andrew Dexter Jr. to

John Bradford, 11 September 1807, SD 223: 56r–7v; Andrew Dexter Jr. to Ebenezer Francis, 7 October 1807, SD 223: 109v–109r; Andrew Dexter Jr. to John Phillips, 6 November 1807; SD 223: 264r–65v. During this period, Dexter also bought a small additional parcel of land south of the coffeehouse, putting no money down: see Andrew Dexter Jr. to Martha Pritchard, 11 July 1807, SD 222: 259r–60v.

82. *NEP,* 31 July 1807; *BG,* 30 July 1807; Andrew Dexter Jr. to Thomas Wightman, 11 August 1807, SD 232: 58r–59v.

83. Quoted in Louis Martin Sears, *Jefferson and the Embargo* (Durham, N.C.: Duke University Press, 1927), 28, 59–61; see also John D. Forbes, "European Wars and Boston Trade, 1783–1815," *New England Quarterly* 11, no. 4 (December 1938): 722–24; and Thorp Lanier Wolford, "Democratic-Republican Reaction in Massachusetts to the Embargo of 1807," *New England Quarterly* 15, no. 1 (March 1952): 38–40.

84. *Boston Town Records, 1796 to 1813,* 222; *IC,* 10 September 1807; Bell, "An Account of the Town of Boston," 35–36; *IC,* 28 January 1808. See also Samuel Bond to Simon Newton Dexter, 11 December 1807, Simon Newton Dexter Papers, folder 1, Cornell University Library. On the impact of the embargo on New England politics, see Sears, *Jefferson and the Embargo,* 143–96; and Wolford, "Democratic-Republican Reaction."

85. Bentley, *Diary of William Bentley,* 3:334–37, quotation at 334; "Autobiographical fragment by Charles Bulfinch," Bulfinch Family Papers, box 3.

86. *Boston Town Records, 1796 to 1813,* 138; "Tremendous Conflagration," *New-England Galaxy,* 6 November 1818; *Calamity at Richmond, Being a Narrative of the Affecting Circumstances Attending the Awful Conflagration of the Theatre, in the City of Richmond, on the Night of Thursday, the 26th of December, 1811 . . . Collected from Various Letters, Publications, and Official Reports* (Philadelphia: John F. Watson, 1812), 36. Recipes for fireproof coatings appear in Joseph Coppinger, *On the Construction of Flat Roofed Buildings, Whether of Stone, Brick, or Wood, and the Mode of Rendering Them Fire Proof* (New York: C. S. van Winkle, 1819), 10–14; see also Sara E. Wermiel, *The Fireproof Building: Technology and Public Safety in the Nineteenth-Century City* (Baltimore: Johns Hopkins University Press, 2000), 62–65; and Joseph Kendall Freitag, *Fire Prevention and Fire Protection as Applied to Building Construction: A Handbook of Theory and Practice* (New York: John Wiley, 1921), 664–87.

87. [Samuel Gilbert and Thomas Dean?], "Description of the Boston Exchange Coffee-House," 5. For the dome as "shining," see Bell, "An Account of the Town of Boston," 35. The State House dome was gilded in 1861; Kirker, *The Architecture of Charles Bulfinch,* 103; and Bulfinch, *Life and Letters of Charles Bulfinch,* 111.

88. [Samuel Gilbert and Thomas Dean?], "Description of the Boston Exchange Coffee-House," 5.

89. "West Boston Church Construction Minutes."

90. Matthew 7:24–25. The epigraph appears on the frontispiece to one of the eighteenth century's most popular building manuals: J. Leadbeater, *The Gentleman and Tradesman's Compleat Assistant: or the Whole Art of Measuring and Estimating, Made Easy* (London: Webley and Todd, 1770).

## CHAPTER THREE: RECKONING

1. For the Morton estate, see Harold Kirker, *The Architecture of Charles Bulfinch,* reprint, 1998 (Cambridge, Mass.: Harvard University Press, 1969), 135–40; and David Clapp, "The Old Morton and Taylor Estates in Dorchester," *New England Historic and Genealogical Register* 46 (1892): 78–84. On the South Boston Bridge, see Walter Muir Whitehill and Lawrence W. Kennedy, *Boston: A Topographical History,* 3d ed., reprint, 2000 (Cambridge, Mass.: Harvard University Press, 1959), 76–78.

2. For Stuart as "celebrated," see CC, 31 July 1805; *Boston Town Records, 1796 to 1813,* Records Relating to the Early History of Boston (1905), 194. Information about the Dexters' sittings with Stuart, and the thunderstorm of 25 April 1808, comes from the sole surviving page of his account book, reproduced in Mabel M. Swan, "Paging Gilbert Stuart in Boston," *Antiques* 34 (December 1938): 308–9. On his reputation for drink and slowness, see Catherine Byles to Mather Brown, 18 November 1817, reprinted in Mabel M. Swan, "Gilbert Stuart in Boston," *Antiques* 29, no. 2 (February 1936): 65–67 (quotation at 67); Dorinda Evans, *The Genius of Gilbert Stuart* (Princeton, N.J.: Princeton University Press, 1999), 97. There is no evidence that both paintings were bound for the Dexters' new household. Stuart scholar Ellen Miles suggests that the sitters' parallel orientation may indicate that Charlotte's image was commissioned by and for the Mortons, and Andrew's by and for himself.

3. This reconstruction of Washington Street follows the *Boston Directory for 1807* and the Boston Assessors' Records for 1808, taking book 12:6. Stuart's landlord was Lucy Cobb, the widow of distiller Benjamin Cobb. Their house, as it stood in 1798, stood two stories high, encompassed 2,937 square feet, and had 40 windows. For the Cobb house and Washington Street land values more generally, see *The Statistics of the United States' Direct Tax of 1798, as Assessed on Boston,* Records Relating to the Early History of Boston (1890), 405, 100–119.

4. Quoted in Evans, *Genius of Gilbert Stuart,* 59. In September 1809, Stuart had asked the Reverend Stephen Peabody for one hundred dollars to paint him, a price Peabody deemed too high; Stephen Peabody diary quoted in Georgia Barnhill and et al., "Portraits in the Collection of the American Antiquarian Society," *Proceedings of the American Antiquarian Society* 111, part 1 (2001): 262; and William Thomas Whitley, *Gilbert Stuart* (Cambridge, Mass.: Harvard University Press, 1932), 143–44.

5. Interview with Henry Pickering, ca. 1810, 1817, quoted in Evans, *Genius of Gilbert Stuart,* 99, see also 85–89.

6. Swan, "Paging Gilbert Stuart," 308; David Humphries quoted in Whitley, *Gilbert Stuart,* 139. The contents of Stuart's painting rooms are listed in "Gilbert Stuart Inventory," Suffolk County Probates, 18 July 1828, no. 28699. For Stuart's use of drawing instruments and life masks, see Evans, *Genius of Gilbert Stuart,* 42, 85. For the effect of the embargo on canvas supplies, see Charles Merrill Mount, *Gilbert Stuart, a Biography* (New York: W. W. Norton, 1964), 283–84.

7. Sarah A. Clinch to Griselda Clinch, 11 August [1825], Morton-Cunningham-Clinch Family Papers, 1754–1903, MHS, folder 1800–1829. For descriptions of Stuart's "picturesque" dress and enormous snuff box, see diary of John Quincy Adams, 19 September 1818, Adams Papers, MHS, microfilm edition, reel 33, 399. Adams estimated that Stuart used perhaps a half pound of snuff per day. See also William Dunlap, *A*

*History of the Rise and Progress of the Arts of Design in the United States,* ed. Alexander Wyckoff, int. William P. Campbell, reprint, 1834 (New York: Benjamin Blom, 1918), 1: 224–25, 251–53. One recent and generally cautious biography concludes that Stuart suffered from bipolar disorder; see Evans, *Genius of Gilbert Stuart,* 118–19; and Dorinda Evans, "Gilbert Stuart and Manic Depression: Redefining His Artistic Range," *American Art* 18, no. 1 (Spring 2004): 10–31.

8. Sarah Morton's "To Mr. Stuart, on His Portrait of Mrs. M.," *Port Folio* 3: 25 (18 June 1803). Stuart's response, "To Mrs. M——," appears in the same issue. Sarah Morton later republished her ode under her own name, locating the portrait sessions "at Philadelphia, in the beginning of the present century"; "To Mr. Stuart," in Sarah Wentworth Morton, *My Mind and Its Thoughts, in Sketches, Fragments, and Essays,* reprint, 1823 (Delmar, N.Y.: Scholars' Facsimiles & Reprints, 1975), 74–75; see also "Stanzas to Gilbert Stuart, on His Intended Portrait of Mrs. H. . . . " in ibid., 213–14. On the Stuart portraits of Sarah Morton, see "Gilbert Stuart, *Sarah Wentworth Apthorp Morton (Mrs. Perez Morton),* 1802–1820," http://www.worcesterart.org/Collection/ Early_American/Artists/stuart/sarah/discussion.html. The theory that Stuart and Morton were lovers is advanced by Mount, *Gilbert Stuart,* 244–48, 277–78, 281; and dismissed by Evans, *Genius of Gilbert Stuart,* 110, 154 n. 27.

9. Swan, "Paging Gilbert Stuart"; Whitley, *Gilbert Stuart,* 137. For the length of a sitting with Stuart, see John Quincy Adams diary, 18 and 19 September 1818, Adams Papers, MHS, reel 33, 399.

10. Nathan Appleton, *An Examination of the Banking System of Massachusetts, in Reference to the Renewal of the Bank Charters* (Boston: Stimpson and Clapp, 1831), 10–11; Nathan Appleton to Ebenezer Appleton, 20 July 1809, Appleton Family Papers, 1539–1910, MHS, box 2, folder 18; Frances W. Gregory, *Nathan Appleton, Merchant and Entrepreneur, 1779–1861* (Charlottesville: University Press of Virginia, 1975), 43–44.

11. "Banks," *IC,* 26 March 1807. The article is signed "A." My attribution to Appleton is based on the pseudonym and the closeness of the argument to his published works. Compare, for example, Appleton, *Examination of the Banking System,* 10–12; Robert C. Winthrop, ed., "Memoir of Hon. Nathan Appleton," *Proceedings of the Massachusetts Historical Society* 5 (October 1861): 284.

12. Nathan Appleton, *Memoir of the Hon. Abbott Lawrence, Prepared for the Massachusetts Historical Society* (Boston: J. H. Eastburn, 1856), 5; *Port Folio,* 18 June 1803; see also "Stanzas to Gilbert Stuart," in Morton, *My Mind and Its Thoughts,* 213–14. For William Doyle, see *IC,* 16 February 1807. Doyle appears in the *Boston Directory for 1807* as a "miniature painter," 62.

13. Samuel L. Knapp, *Extracts from the Journal of Marshal Soult: Addressed to a Friend* (Newburyport, Mass.: William B. Allen, 1817), 19 ("Promethean impiety"); John Neagle's obituary for Stuart quoted in Evans, *Genius of Gilbert Stuart,* 110 ("counterfeit the soul"); compare to Whitley, *Gilbert Stuart,* 139. On dilemmas of representation in money and art in the nineteenth century, see Jose R. Torre, "The Political Economy of Sentiment: Money and Emotions in the Early Republic" (Ph.D. dissertation, SUNY Binghamton, 2002), chap. 6.

14. Swan, "Paging Gilbert Stuart," 308; Carol Damon Andrews, "John Ritto Penniman (1782–1841), an Ingenious New England Artist," *Antiques* 120, no. 1 (July

1981): 147–70. In the *Boston Directory for 1807,* Penniman appears as a "painter," not yet a "portrait painter" like Stuart, John Johnson, or Henry Sargent; see 96, 121, 132, 141. For pigments for sale in Boston, see the advertisement for Samuel Tuck's paint and color store, *IC,* 26 January 1807.

15. Gregory, *Nathan Appleton,* 31–40, 269–96, 319; Winthrop, "Memoir of Hon. Nathan Appleton," 260; Pamela Fox, "Nathan Appleton's Beacon Street Houses," *Old-Time New England* 70 (1980): 111–23. On conventions of mercantile portraiture, see Margaretta M. Lovell, *Art in a Season of Revolution: Painters, Artisans, and Patrons in Early America* (Philadelphia: University of Pennsylvania Press, 2005), chap. 4.

16. Morton's notes to "Apostrophe, to the Memory of My Beloved Daughter Charlotte. Fragment," in Morton, *My Mind and Its Thoughts,* 282–83, 67–68, see also 264–65.

17. Charlotte Morton to Mrs. General Knox, 15 August 1806, in Henry Knox Papers, MHS, 46: 145–47.

18. "Apostrophe, to the Memory of My Beloved Daughter Charlotte. Fragment," in Morton, *My Mind and Its Thoughts,* 265; See Andrew Oliver and James Bishop Peabody, eds., *The Records of Trinity Church, Boston, 1728–1830,* Publications of the Colonial Society of Massachusetts (1982), 623, 740. For Charlotte's birth, see "Fragment of a Genealogy of the Children of Perez Morton and Sarah Apthorp," Morton-Cunningham-Clinch Family Papers, 1754–1903, folder 1754–99. Sarah Morton's biographers place the birth of Fanny's "female child" at "about the end of 1787"; Emily Pendleton and Milton Ellis, *Philenia; the Life and Works of Sarah Wentworth Morton, 1759–1846,* University of Maine Studies, 2nd ser. (Orono: University of Maine Press, 1931), 32, see also 32–40. Literary representations of the scandal include *Occurrences of the Times. Or, the Transactions of Four Days . . . a Farce in Two Acts* ([Boston], 1789), 11, 18, 23; and William Hill Brown, *The Power of Sympathy: Or, the Triumph of Nature, Founded in Truth* (Boston: Isaiah Thomas, 1789), letters xxi–iii. If *this* were a novel, Charlotte Morton would not only live in the shadow of her concealed half sister; she would *be* Fanny Apthorp's illegitimate child.

19. Sarah Morton, "Marriage," essay 15 in Morton, *My Mind and Its Thoughts,* 180–81; see also "The Sexes," essay 25, ibid., 219–21. For the ages and marital statuses of the Morton children, see "Fragment of a Genealogy of the Children of Perez Morton and Sarah Apthorp." Sarah Morton Cunningham, who married in Nova Scotia in the summer of 1809, was the only one of Charlotte's siblings to find a mate.

20. Dunlap, *Rise and Progress of the Arts of Design,* 237. On his custom to demand partial payment, see ibid., 223; Evans, *Genius of Gilbert Stuart,* 53.

21. William Bentley, *Diary of William Bentley, D.D., Pastor of the East Church, Salem, Massachusetts,* reprint, 1911 (Gloucester, Mass.: Peter Smith, 1962), 3: 336–56 (weather); John Lambert, *Travels Through Canada, and the United States of North America, in the Years 1806, 1807, and 1808: To Which Are Added Biographical Notices and Anecdotes of Some of the Leading Characters in the United States* (London: C. Cradock and A. Joy, 1816), 334–35. Lambert arrived in Boston on Saturday, April 23, 1808.

22. "The Embargo, an Elegy . . . Being a Parody on Gray's 'Elegy in a Country Church Yard,' " *BG,* 14 July 1808; Gregory, *Nathan Appleton,* 34. See also John Tucker

Prince, "Boston in 1813, Reminiscences of an Old School-Boy," *Bostonian Society Publications* 3 (1906): 84.

23. Anonymous letter to Thomas Jefferson, Boston, 19 September 1808, Papers of Thomas Jefferson, Library of Congress, 1st series: General Correspondence. The author claimed to have raised $400 to pay an assassin to shoot Jefferson if he didn't lift the embargo by October 10.

24. *Democrat,* 9 January 1808; *CC,* 9 January 1808; *NEP,* 8 January 1808; William Bentley, *The Diary of William Bentley, D.D., Pastor of the East Church, Salem, Massachusetts* (Gloucester, Mass.: Peter Smith, 1962), 3:337; *Minutes of the Selectmen's Meetings, 1799 to and Including 1810,* Records Relating to the Early History of Boston (1904), 362. The Non-Intercourse Act of 1 March 1809 essentially repealed the embargo but left trade restrictions in place between the United States and Great Britain.

25. See *OED,* 2nd ed.; Colbert Jr., [Mathew Carey], *The Age of Paper, or, an Essay on Banks and Banking* (London, 1795).

26. Winthrop, "Memoir of Hon. Nathan Appleton," 284; Public Works [pseud.], *BG* 1, 5 January 1807.

27. For the second Detroit Bank, see Robert Sanders to John Sanders, 25 July 1807, Sanders Papers, BHC-DPL; Andrew Dexter Jr. to James Henry, 29 September 1807, Solomon Sibley Papers, BHC-DPL, box: July–December 1807; Augustus B. Woodward, "Considerations of the Affairs of the Michigan Territory," no. 6, *Commonwealth,* 24 February 1808.

28. "Promissory Notes of a New Form," *Enquirer* (Richmond, Va.), 22 September 1809; Elizabeth A. Perry, *A Brief History of the Town of Glocester, Rhode Island: Preceded by a Sketch of the Territory While a Part of Providence* (Providence, R. I.: Providence Press Co., 1886), 29–34, 44, 66, 94; Daniel P. Jones, *The Economic and Social Transformation of Rural Rhode Island, 1780–1850* (Boston: Northeastern University Press, 1992), 8–10, 33–35. On the difficult roads leading into the western parts of the tiny state see also Timothy Dwight, *Travels in New England and New York,* ed. Barbara Miller Solomon (Cambridge, Mass.: Harvard University Press, 1969), 2:20–22, 3: 42. (orig. pub. 1821); Milton Halsey Thomas, ed., *Elias Boudinot's Journey to Boston in 1809* (Princeton, N.J.: Princeton University Press, 1955), 27–29; and Glocester Bicentennial Commission, *Glocester: The Way Up Country* (Gloucester, R.I.: By the town, 1976), 11–14, 22. For licenses to sell "strong Liquor," see Gloucester Town Council Records, vol. 2 (1784–1816), 411, microfilm copy, NEHGS.

29. *Repertory,* 31 March 1807; Perry, *Brief History of the Town of Glocester,* 29, 46; Jones, *Transformation of Rural Rhode Island,* 81.

30. *Report of the Committee Appointed by the General Assembly of the State of Rhode-Island . . . to Inquire Into the Situation of the Farmers' Exchange Bank in Glocester* [hereafter *RICR*] ([Providence, R.I.]: n.p., March 1809), 4–6.

31. *RICR,* 3–6.

32. "To the Public," *PG,* 25 April 1807. For counterfeit Farmers' Exchange Bank notes, see: *PG,* 19, 26 July 1806; *Massachusetts Register and United States Calendar for . . . 1807* (Boston: Manning and Loring, [1806]), 182; *Massachusetts Register and United States Calendar for . . . 1808* (Boston: Manning and Loring, [1807]), 182.

33. Andrew Dexter to the president and directors of the Farmers' Bank [sic], December 1807, *RICR,* 29; Deposition of Daniel Smith, *RICR,* 23–24.

34. Judgments for debt on behalf of Dexter appear in the Records of the Suffolk County Court of Common Pleas, MArch: *Dexter v. Galloope* (July 1807, 279); *Dexter v. Welch* (October 1807, 255); *Dexter v. Bennett* (October 1807, 256); *Dexter v. Hern* (January 1808, 75).

35. *Private and Special Statutes of the* Commonwealth of Massachusetts *from February 1806 to February 1814* (Boston: Wells and Lilly, 1823), 1807: 78, passed 3 March 1808. No mortgage deeds follow the passage of the amendment. For delays paying out Berkshire Bank notes, see "Bank Thermometer," *CC,* 9, 23 January 1808, and numerous advertisements in January, February, and March. On Detroit notes in Pittsfield, see Caution [pseud.], *Berkshire Reporter,* 5 March 1808, and the rebuttal by Fair Play [Andrew Dexter?], *Berkshire Reporter,* 12 March 1808.

36. Caroline Hazard, ed., *Nailer Tom's Diary: Otherwise the Journal of Thomas B. Hazard of Kingstown Rhode Island, 1778 to 1840* (Boston: Merrymount Press, 1930), 303; Perry, *Brief History of the Town of Glocester,* 76; Glocester Bicentennial Commission, *Glocester: The Way Up Country,* 23, 24.

37. Deposition of William Colwell, 20 March 1809, *RICR,* 11.

38. *RICR,* 6, 12, 19–20, 21, 23. For Smith and Harris, see Jones, *Transformation of Rural Rhode Island,* 64–65. Dexter obviously trusted Fairbanks, telling Harris and Colwell on subsequent occasions to tell "no person whatever except Mr. Fairbanks" of their plans; see Dexter to Harris and Colwell, 10 December 1808, *RICR,* 37. I have been unable to document Fairbanks's links to the Dexter family. He appears to have been born in 1771, graduated from Brown in 1791 (seven years before Andrew Dexter), practiced law briefly in Providence before moving to New Hampshire, where he committed suicide in 1824. See *Historical Catalogue of Brown University, 1764–1894* (Providence, R.I.: The University, 1905), 35; Lorenzo Sayles Fairbanks, *Genealogy of the Fairbanks Family in America, 1633–1897* (Boston: n.p., 1897), 135.

39. *RICR,* 17, 7, 12.

40. Thomas Watts, "An Essay on the Proper Method for Forming the Man of Business" (London, 1716), quoted in Tamara Plakins Thornton, *Handwriting in America: A Cultural History* (New Haven, Conn.: Yale University Press, 1996), 39; see also 37–40. On clerks and carpenters more broadly, see Thomas Augst, *The Clerk's Tale: Young Men and Moral Life in Nineteenth-Century America* (Chicago: University of Chicago Press, 2003); Lisa Beth Lubow, "Artisans in Transition: Early Capitalist Development and the Carpenters of Boston, 1787–1837" (Ph.D. dissertation, UCLA, 1987); and Donna J. Rilling, *Making Houses, Crafting Capitalism: Builders in Philadelphia, 1790–1850* (Philadelphia: University of Pennsylvania Press, 2001).

41. Winthrop, "Memoir of Hon. Nathan Appleton," 257. Appleton learned from what he called "Mair's Treatise"; see John Mair, *Book-Keeping Modernized, or, Merchant-Accounts by Double Entry According to the Italian Form,* 8th ed. (Edinburgh: W. Creech, 1800).

42. Advertisement for a hardware store clerk, *PG,* 28 March 1807; James Smith Colburn, *The Personal Memoirs of James Smith Colburn, 1780–1859, Who in the Year 1808 Built 54 and 55 Beacon Street, Boston, Massachusetts,* ca. 1859 (typescript) ([Boston]: Massachusetts Society of the Colonial Dames of America, 1949), 2, 67.

43. For Colwell's ancestry, see Ruth Devereux Eddy, *Robert Colwell of Providence and His Descendants,* reprint, 1936 (Salem, Mass.: Higginson Book Company, 1977), 20, 29–30 (entries 43, 103). The family's residence in 1790 and 1800 is documented in the Rhode Island returns for the Federal Census: 1790 schedule for the town of Foster (p. 282), and 1800 schedule for the town of Smithfield (p. 524). On his role as a primary teacher in Gloucester, see Richard M. Bayles, *History of Providence County, Rhode Island* (New York: W. W. Preston, 1891), 2:142. Colwell's kin settled in Gloucester before 1774; see Perry, *Brief History of the Town of Glocester,* 100. He died in Foster in March 1817 at the age of thirty-six; *PG.*

44. "Deposition of Mowry Smith," *RICR,* 17; "Deposition of William Colwell," *RICR,* 11; bond for William Flanagan (Detroit Bank), 26 May 1806, in *MPHS Collections* 8:573 ("fidelity and faithfulness"). On the duties of the cashier, see *An Act to Incorporate Sundry Persons by the Name of the President, Directors, and Company of the Coos Bank* (Hanover, N.H.: Moses Davis, 1805), 11; and J. S. Gibbons, *The Banks of New-York, Their Dealers, the Clearing House, and the Panic of 1857* (New York: D. Appleton, 1858), 70–104.

45. Gibbons, *The Banks of New-York,* 71; *RICR,* 11; Eddy, *Robert Colwell of Providence,* 31. Bonds of $10,000 were typical in Massachusetts at the time. See "An Act to Incorporate Simon Larned and Others, by the Name and Stile of the President, Directors and Company of the *Berkshire Bank,*" sec. 3; and "An Act to Incorporate Sundry Persons, by the Name of *The President, Directors, and Company of the Penobscot Bank,*" sec. 4; both in *Laws of The Commonwealth of Massachusetts Passed at Several Sessions of The General Court Holden in Boston . . . February 1806* (Boston: Young & Minn, 1806), 50, 140.

46. "Regulations Agreed to by the President and Directors of the Bank," 24 March 1784, in N. S. B. Gras, *The Massachusetts First National Bank of Boston, 1784–1934* (Cambridge, Mass.: Harvard University Press, 1937), 233; Carroll D. Wright, *History of Wages and Prices in Massachusetts: 1752–1883* (Boston: Wright & Potter, 1885), 72.

47. Samuel Dexter to William Colwell, 16 November 1808; see also Charles Edwards to Colwell, 14 September 1808; Charles Edwards to Colwell, 22 October 1808; in *RICR,* 31–33.

48. *Massachusetts Register for 1806,* 54; bond for William Flanagan (Detroit Bank), 26 May 1806, in *MPHC Collections* 8: 573.

49. *RICR,* 14, 7, 12. As the bills that paid his extra salary depreciated, Colwell was left with less than he started with; see *RICR,* 14.

50. Jacob Perkins, *The Permanent Stereotype Steel Plate, with Observations on Its Importance, and an Explanation of Its Construction and Uses* (Boston: C. Stebbins, 1806), 8, 5; Jacob Perkins Petition to the General Assembly of Massachusetts, 28 February 1806, in Greville Bathe and Dorothy Bathe, *Jacob Perkins: His Inventions, His Times, & His Contemporaries* (Philadelphia: Historical Society of Pennsylvania, 1943), 29, see also 25, 32.

51. Perkins obtained the patent for his process in 1799 and began promoting the system in 1804. Sixteen Massachusetts banks had adapted the stereotype method by 1805, and another ten did so in 1806. See *BG,* 10 May 1804; Bathe and Bathe, *Jacob Perkins,* 23–24; Perkins, *The Permanent Stereotype Steel Plate,* 7. For country bank charters that compelled the use of Perkins plates, see "An Act to Incorporate Sundry

Persons by the Name of *The President, Directors and Company of the Penobscot Bank*,"
Massachusetts Laws 1805: 112, sec. 9; and "An Act to Incorporate Simon Larned and
Others, by the Name and Style of *The President, Directors and Company of the Berkshire
Bank*," Massachusetts Laws 1805: 44, sec. 15. The Massachusetts legislature directed
banks to use the Perkins plate in March 1809; see "An Act Requiring the Several
Incorporated Banks . . . to Adopt the Stereotype Steel Plate," Massachusetts Laws
1808: 99.

52. Jacob Perkins, "Notice to Banks," *BG*, 25 February 1808; Abel Brewster, "A
General Explanation of Bank Bills," *IC*, 7 March 1808. Brewster's critique, though
trenchant, was self-interested; he promotes his own process, which he deems the "*Universal Virtriolic Test*" against fraud. On the ironies of various anticounterfeiting
technologies, see Stephen A. Mihm, "Making Money, Creating Confidence: Counterfeiting and Capitalism in the United States, 1789–1877" (Ph. D. dissertation, New
York University, 2003), chap. 6.

53. Andrew Dexter to William Colwell, 21 May 1808, in *RICR*, 30; "A Bank
Cause . . . Report of a Case, argued and decided, at the late July term of the Court of
Common Pleas, . . . Gilbert & Dean, Plaintives [*sic*], versus The Nantucket Bank," *BG*,
15 September 1808. For weighing specie, see *Suffolk Bank v. Lincoln Bank*, May 1821,
23 F. Cas. 346; 1821 U.S. App.

54. Andrew Dexter to the president and directors of the Farmers' Exchange Bank,
25 May 1808; Charles Edwards to William Colwell, 14 September 1808; Charles
Edwards to Samuel Dexter, 11 May 1808; Charles Edwards to William Colwell,
30 August 1808; in *RICR*, 29, 30, 31–32. For Edwards's occupation, see *Boston Directory for 1809*, 52; and Boston Assessors' Records, 1809, taking books 8:43, BPL; for his
residence, see *Boston Directory for 1809*, 52.

55. *RICR*, 12, 31–32. Colwell reckoned the amount at $42,000, but Edwards dis-
puted the total, finding the parcels Dexter carried "925 dollars short of the amount
[Colwell] mentioned." Since 998 sheets of bills totaled, by Edwards' calculation,
$24,950, each sheet contained a total of $25 worth of bills. For names and occupations
of some of the finish workers on the Exchange, see Dexter's assignment of the revenues generated by the Exchange Coffee House lease to pay debts: Andrew Dexter Jr.
to George Odiorne, 6 May 1809, SD 231: 14–16.

56. *RICR*, 31–33, 8, 14–15. By the committee's reckoning, the blanket receipt promised $507,071.

57. *RICR*, 31–34, 37–39.

58. Samuel Dexter to William Colwell, 19 July 1808, *RICR*, 30–31; Andrew Dexter to John Harris and William Colwell, 8 October 1808, ibid., 32.

59. Jacob Sanders to John Sanders, 15 May 1809, Sanders Papers, BHC-DPL;
"Farmers' Exchange Bank," [Cincinnati, Ohio] *The Whig*, 19 July 1809; Andrew Dexter to William Colwell, 20 December 1808, *RICR*, 37.

60. Andrew Dexter to president and cashier of the Farmers' Exchange Bank, 10
December 1808; Colwell to Andrew Dexter, 12 December 1808, *RICR*, 36. For the
merchandise for sale at Appleton's store, see *BG*, 28 April 1808. For Appleton at the
Exchange Office, see *Appleton & al vs. Prs. & Trus. of Exchange Office*, Suffolk County
Court of Common Pleas, January 1809, 2:508.

61. Bentley, *Diary of William Bentley*, 3:396, 392, 393, 394; "Jeffersonian Gloom" in

Nathan Appleton to Ebenezer Appleton, ca. 1808, quoted in Louise Hall Tharp, *The Appletons of Beacon Hill* (Boston: Little, Brown, 1973), 7.

62. Entry for 31 December 1808, Georgia Brady Barnhill, "'Extracts from the Journals of Ethan A. Greenwood': Portrait Painter and Museum Proprietor," *Proceedings of the American Antiquarian Society* 103, no. 1 (April 1993): 110.

63. William H. Wheildon, *Memoir of Solomon Willard, Architect and Superintendent of the Bunker Hill Monument* (Boston: Bunker Hill Monument Association, 1865), 28, 27. Willard billed Dexter for the completed staircase on 8 December 1808, and for the six carved pillars that held up the portico on the building's north side in February 1809. See also *BG,* 18 August 1808 (bricks); *NEP,* 28 October 1808 (carpenters needed).

64. *NEP,* 12 August 1808 (Rufus Davenport's brokerage); *BG,* 3 October 1808 (Perkins's studio), and 10 November 1808 (post office). For the post office lease, see Andrew Dexter Jr. to Aaron Hill, 1 November 1808, SD 231: 175. The locations of these businesses are mapped in [Samuel Gilbert and Thomas Dean?], "Description of the Boston Exchange Coffee-House," *Omnium Gatherum* 1, no. 1 (November 1809): 7, 8.

65. The post office's four-year lease appears as Andrew Dexter Jr. (for Exchange Coffee House proprietors) to Aaron Hill, 1 November 1808; SD 231: 175v–175r. The post office was to pay $150 per year for two years, and $200 per year thereafter.

66. Thomas Coffin to Andrew Dexter, 4 November 1808, SD 228: 241; Charlotte Dexter to John Bradford, 21 August 1816, SD 252: 153–154. For residents of the neighborhood and their occupations, see *Boston Directory for 1809,* 43, 48, 57, 92, 97, 105, 124, 131, 144, 151.

67. Appleton's letters quoted in Fox, "Nathan Appleton's Beacon Street Houses," 114.

68. "Banking," by Smith [Nathan Appleton]," *NEP,* 20 December 1808.

69. Appleton, *Memoir of Abbott Lawrence,* 4–5; Winthrop, "Memoir of Hon. Nathan Appleton," 284–85; "Banking," by Smith [Nathan Appleton], *NEP,* 20 December 1808; "The Banking System," by A Merchant [pseud.], *CC,* 23 November 1808. On the "entrepreneurial ethos" that animated Appleton and other Federalist merchants turned Whig industrialists, see Daniel Walker Howe, *The Political Culture of the American Whigs* (Chicago: University of Chicago Press, 1979), 96–108; Paul Goodman, "Ethics and Enterprise: The Values of a Boston Elite, 1800–1860," *American Quarterly* 18, no. 3 (Autumn 1966): 437–51; and William F. Hartford, *Money, Morals, and Politics: Massachusetts in the Age of the Boston Associates* (Boston: Northeastern University Press, 2001).

70. Winthrop, "Memoir of Hon. Nathan Appleton," 285; "Manuscript Draft of a Bank Circular," Miscellaneous Bound Manuscripts, 1809 [misdated], MHS; Appleton, *Examination of the Banking System,* 13.

71. *Appleton & al vs. Prs. & Trus. of Exchange Office,* Suffolk County Court of Common Pleas, January 1809, 2: 508; Records of the Massachusetts Bank and the Union Bank reproduced in Gras, *Massachusetts Bank,* 393–94.

72. Appleton, *Memoir of Abbott Lawrence,* 5. "The Banking System," by A Merchant [pseud.], *CC,* 23 November 1808, is the first such article I have found. It doesn't appear to be Appleton's own writing, but clearly comes from a signatory of the circular. Dexter later adopted the pseudonym as his own.

73. "Banks Again," by Smith [Nathan Appleton], *NEP,* 25 November 1808.

74. "The Banking System," by One of the Deluded [pseud.], *BG*, 24 November 1808. Appleton himself attributed the unsigned article to Dexter; see letter signed "P," *BG*, 1 December 1808. Among other things, the two engaged in a war of Shakespearian quotations. "By flood and field" comes from *Othello*, act 1, scene 3, line 149. The lines that conclude Dexter's essay paraphrase the fool's soliloquy in *King Lear*, act 1, scene 4:

> Have more than thou showest,
> Speak less than thou knowest,
> Lend less than thou owest,
> Ride more than thou goest,
> Learn more than thou trowest,
> Set less than thou throwest;
> Leave thy drink and thy whore,
> And keep in-a-door,
> And thou shalt have more
> Than two tens to a score.

75. "The Banks Loan Too Much Money," *NEP*, 29 November 1808; "The Banking System: Imposition Exposed," *BG*, 1 December 1808. The second essay is an ingenious satire, which interlines Dexter's own words with the text of A Merchant's "Banking System" essay of a week before, completely reversing its meaning. Compare also the argumentation in "Bank Bills" by "Plain Argument," *IC*, 15 December 1808. For *sinister* and *dexter* see *OED*, 2nd ed.

76. *BG*, 1 December, 1808. The reference is to *The Tempest*, act 4, scene 1.

77. "Banking," by Smith [Nathan Appleton], *NEP*, 20 December 1808. Appleton's descendants made the attribution of authorship; see "Nathan Appleton Scrapbook," in Appleton Family Papers, MHS, vol. 22.

78. "New Hobbies," *NEP*, 20 December 1808.

79. Jacob Sanders to John Sanders, 10 December 1808, Sanders Family Papers, BHC-DPL. Sanders refers to sections 27 and 28 of "An Act for the Punishment of Crimes and Misdemeanors," 9 December 1808; see *MPHC Collections* 8: 576. It is possible, if just barely, that word from Appleton's syndicate had reached Detroit by the second week of December. Advertisements, ca. December 1808, by Boston merchants promising to accept the bills, discounting them, or refusing them are too numerous to cite, but see especially *NEP*, 23, 27, 30 December 1808.

80. Draft of a letter from John Harris to Andrew Dexter, 5 December 1808, *RICR*, 34 (emphasis mine). See also Samuel Dexter to William Colwell, 18 November 1808; Samuel Dexter to William Colwell, 27 November 1808; and draft of a letter from William Colwell to Andrew Dexter, 12 December 1808; *RICR*, 33, 36.

81. See Andrew Dexter to John Harris and William Colwell, 8 October 1808; Andrew Dexter to William Colwell, 7 December 1808; Andrew Dexter to president and directors of the Farmers' Exchange Bank, 10 December 1808; Andrew Dexter to William Colwell, 19 December 1808; Andrew Dexter to William Colwell, 20 December 1808; *RICR*, 32, 34–37.

Dexter's investment in the Washington Bank of Westerly, Rhode Island, leaves only faint traces in the record. See Andrew Dexter to Colwell, 6 September 1808; Samuel Dexter to Colwell, 18 November 1808; *RICR*, 31, 33; and letter signed "P," *BG*,

1 December 1808. Histories of the bank don't mention Dexter's involvement, but make clear that the Washington Bank was otherwise a fairly typical operation, with a remote location and paper issues that greatly exceeded its specie reserves. See Howard Kemble Stokes, *Private and Public Finance. A History of the Finances of Rhode Island, 1636–1900, and of Chartered Banking in Rhode Island, 1791–1900* (Providence, R. I.: Mason Publishing, 1901), 271–73, 281; and *One Hundred Years of Banking in Westerly* (Westerly, R.I.: Washington Trust Company, 1908), n.p.

82. Andrew Dexter to William Colwell, 2 December 1808; Deposition of Jesse Armstrong, 17 March 1809; *RICR*, 33–34, 26. Unlike many bank charters of the day, the act of incorporation creating the Farmers' Exchange Bank did not impose a limit on note issues, only on total capital, which was to be paid in specie. See "An act to incorporate the Stockholders of the Farmers' Exchange Bank," *At the General Assembly of the State of Rhode Island . . . holden . . . at Providence . . . February . . . One Thousand Eight Hundred and Four* (Newport, [n.p.], 1804), 11–14.

83. Dexter to Harris and Colwell, 10 December 1808; *RICR*, 35–36.

84. Draft of a letter from Colwell to Andrew Dexter, 12 December 1808; Colwell deposition; *RICR*, 36, 9, 13.

85. Draft of a letter from William Colwell to Andrew Dexter, [16 December 1808]; draft of a letter from William Colwell to Andrew Dexter, [ca. 21–24 December 1808]; *RICR*, 38–39.

86. Draft of a letter from William Colwell to Andrew Dexter, [16 December 1808]; draft of a letter from William Colwell to Andrew Dexter, [ca. 21–24 December 1808]; Andrew Dexter to William Colwell, 20 December 1808; in *RICR*, 38–39, 37, 39.

87. *BG*, 22 December 1808; Bentley, *Diary of William Bentley*, 3: 405, 268; *CC* 21 December 1808. On the changing meanings of Christmas in nineteenth-century cities, see Stephen Nissenbaum, *The Battle for Christmas* (New York: Knopf, 1996).

88. Andrew Dexter to William Colwell, 25 December 1808; *RICR*, 37–38. For the identity of John Fullerton, see *Massachusetts Register . . . for 1808*, 56; *Boston Directory for 1808*, 73.

89. "Vermont State Bank," *Rhode Island American*, 27 December 1808; Winthrop, "Memoir of Hon. Nathan Appleton," 284–85; Appleton, *Examination of the Banking System*, 12–13; Letter signed A Merchant and no Broker, [Portsmouth] *New Hampshire Gazette*, 22 August 1809.

90. Hastings and his partners Samuel Etheridge and Elam Bliss had to sue Dexter to recover the debt; see *Hastings et al. v. Dexter*, Suffolk County Court of Common Pleas, July 1809, 61. In addition to being the town postmaster, Hastings was a printer; Hastings, Etheridge, and Bliss had published Asher Benjamin's *American Builder's Companion* the year before; *IC*, 22 January 1807.

91. For the mortgage, see Andrew Dexter Jr. to Berkshire Bank, 18 January 1809, SD 227: 259r–60r. On the extent of Dexter's indebtedness to the Berkshire Bank, see Nathan Appleton to Ebenezer Appleton, 20 July 1809, Appleton Family Papers, box 2, folder 18.

92. Andrew Dexter to Colwell, 8 February 1809; see also Edwards to Colwell, [9 January 1809]; Andrew Dexter to Colwell, 8 January 1809; *RICR*, 40–42, 7–8, 10, quotation at 41.

93. *BG*, 1 December 1808; "Bank Thermometer," *BG*, 2, 16, 23 January 1809;

"Money for Sale," *Rhode Island American*, 14 February 1809; "No Stockholder in Any Bank," *Rhode Island American* 17 February 1809; "A Key to the Bank," *Rhode Island American*, 24 February 1809; "Balloon," *NEP*, 24 February 1809. Rumors that Farmers' Exchange Bank notes were trading at a 50 percent discount and even then could not "be put off in any quantity" surfaced and were disputed in Boston; see "Bank Bills" by A Customer [pseud.]; "Bank Bills," by Fair Play [pseud.], *NEP*, 13, 17 January 1809. Farmers' Exchange Bank notes do not appear in the "Bank Thermometer" after January 23, indicating that the bills had become officially uncurrent in Boston by February; see, for example, "Bank Thermometer," *BG*, 13 February 1809. On the winter weather, see Bentley, *Diary of William Bentley*, 3: 406–20.

94. *Rhode Island American*, 17 February, 10 March, 28 April 1809; *PG*, 4 March 1809.

95. *RICR*, 14–15, 10.

96. *Rhode Island American*, 3 March 1809; *RICR*, 10. The first legislative session unfolded between February 28 and March 4, 1809; see Hazard, *Nailer Tom's Diary*, 319; *PG*, 4 March 1809.

97. Andrew Dexter to William Colwell, [28] February 1809, and two attached unsealed "memoranda"; *RICR*, 42; *PG*, 11 March 1809.

98. *PG*, 4, 11 March 1809.

99. Jacob Sanders (Detroit) to John Sanders, 15 May 1809, Sanders Papers, BHC-DPL; *Rhode Island American*, 24 March 1809. For farmers in the Town House, see Hazard, *Nailer Tom's Diary*, 320. For spreading reports of the circumstances of the bank's failure, see "Banking," by Smith [Nathan Appleton], *NEP*, 14 March 1809; *PS*, 15 April 1809.

100. Deposition of Samuel Dexter, 18 March 1809, *RICR*, 28; *Rhode Island American*, 24 March 1809; *PG*, 25 March 1809; "A Friend to Honesty," *Rhode Island American*, 28 April 1809. The pamphlet was available for purchase in Boston by May first; see *BG*, 1 May 1809; *Repertory, NEP*, 2 May 1809.

101. "Banking," by Smith [Nathan Appleton], *NEP*, 20 December 1808.

102. "Farmers' Exchange Bills," *CD*, 28 April 1809; "A Friend to Honesty," *Rhode Island American*, 28 April 1809. Many newspapers featured gleanings from the pamphlet; the Republican *Columbian Detector* (Boston) devoted the bulk of six issues to reprinting the *Report* in its entirety; see 2, 5, 9, 12, 16, 19 May 1809.

103. *PS*, 1 April 1809; *Rhode Island American*, 24 March 1809.

104. For the proposed Tontine, see *NEP*, 7, 14, 17 March 1809; *PG*, 4 March 1809.

105. *BP*, 28 March 1809, reprinted *PS*, 8 April 1809; *CD* 31 March, 11 April 1809; "Tontine Plan," *Rhode Island American*, 28 March 1809.

106. For the sale of the wharf and other properties, see Andrew Dexter Jr. to J. Goodwin et al., 21 March 1809, SD 228:92–93. Dexter is referred to as being "of Charlestown" by the date of this transaction. For the Exchange Office shares, see *BP*, 28, 31 March 1809. The sale of the south Boston house appears in Andrew Dexter Jr. to John Bradford, 8 April 1809, SD 228: 242–43. Charles Ward Apthorp Morton died 28 February 1808; see Sarah W. A. Morton, "Lamentation of an Unfortunate Mother over the Tomb of Her Only Son," in Morton, *My Mind and Its Thoughts*, 260, 281.

107. The judgments of the court in favor of the Berkshire Bank are recorded in *Daniel Pepoon v. Andrew Dexter Jr.,* 20 April 1809, SD 221: 141–44; and *Joseph Goodwin v. Andrew Dexter Jr.,* 20 April 1809; SD 221: 145v–146r. The two awards total $167,457.50. For the description of debtors' quarter in the Boston jail, see Charles Shaw, *A Topographical and Historical Description of Boston, from the First Settlement of the Town to the Present Period; with Some Account of Its Environs* (Boston: Oliver Spear, 1817), 227. The crowding of the Boston jail with Exchange building workers is reported in *CD,* 9 May 1809.

108. In the absence of bankruptcy protection, absconding was a recognized remedy for indebtedness; see Bruce H. Mann, *Republic of Debtors: Bankruptcy in the Age of American Independence* (Cambridge, Mass.: Harvard University Press, 2002). Dexter transferred a lease and granted power of attorney to his Exchange Office partner, George Odiorne, on 5 May 1809, which appears to be on or near the day he fled; see SD 229: 184; 231: 40–41.

## CHAPTER FOUR: BABEL

1. William Flanagan to Solomon Sibley, 15 May 1809, Solomon Sibley Papers, BHC-DPL, box Z7, "1809–1819 / Flanagan Papers."

2. William Flanagan to Solomon Sibley, 20 July 1809, Solomon Sibley Papers, BHC-DPL, box Z7, "1809–1819 / Flanagan Papers." Flanagan first wrote to Sibley from Boston on 17 June; the Coroner's Sale took place on 14 June; *CC,* 27 May 1809.

3. William Flanagan to Solomon Sibley, 20 July 1809; "'British Influence'—Up to the Hob," *New-Bedford Mercury,* 16 March 1810 ("amiable and afflicted"). Deeds place the Dexters in Windsor by early August; Andrew Dexter to Joseph Goodwin, 7 August 1809, SD 229: 293r–93v. Charlotte's sister Sarah was there as well. At the end of the month, she married Richard Cunningham of Windsor, the second of the Morton children to wed; *Nova Scotia Royal Gazette,* 29 August 1809. Andrew Alfred Dexter was born in Windsor on 10 September 1809. On the connections among the families, see also Orrando Perry Dexter, Henry L. Mills, and John Haven Dexter, *Dexter Genealogy, 1642–1904; Being a History of the Descendants of Richard Dexter of Malden, Massachusetts, from the Notes of John Haven Dexter and Original Researches* (New York: J. J. Little, 1904), 125; Walter Muir Whitehill, "Perez Morton's Daughter Revisits Boston in 1825," *Proceedings of the Massachusetts Historical Society* 82 (1970): 23–24, 28–29; Brian C. Cuthbertson, *The Loyalist Governor: Biography of Sir John Wentworth* (Halifax, N.S.: Petheric Press, 1983); and L. S. Loomer, *Windsor, Nova Scotia: A Journey in History* (Windsor, N.S.: West Hants Historical Society, 1996).

4. William Flanagan to Solomon Sibley, 20 July 1809.

5. Benjamin Davies, *The Bank Torpedo; or, Bank Notes Proved to be a Robbery on the Public, and the Real Cause of the Distresses of the Poor* (New York: McCarthy and White, 1810), 53; "Farmers' Exchange Bank," *CD,* 16 May 1809; see also "Axioms," *BP,* 25 October 1809.

6. William Flanagan to Solomon Sibley, 27 August 1809, Sibley Papers, box 1790–1816, folder 1809–1814; Flanagan to Sibley, 20 July 1809.

7. "Bank Bills," by a Broker [pseud.], *BP*, 12 August 1809; "Bank Bills," by *Smith* [Nathan Appleton], *NEP*, 29 August 1809; William Bentley, *The Diary of William Bentley, D.D., Pastor of the East Church, Salem, Massachusetts* (Gloucester Mass.: Peter Smith, 1962), 3: 452, 454. For New England bank failures in 1809–1810 see *BG*, 16 November 1809; N. S. B. Gras, *The Massachusetts First National Bank of Boston, 1784–1934* (Cambridge, Mass.: Harvard University Press, 1937), 75, 394–97; "Report Respecting 'the Doings of the Berkshire Bank and the Present State Thereof,'" *PS*, 21 March 1810; *Report of the Committee Relative to the Penobscot Bank* ([Boston?], 1811); Walter W. Chadbourne, *A History of Banking in Maine, 1799–1930*, University of Maine Studies (Orono: University Press of Maine, 1936), 13–21; *Official Papers Containing the Speeches of the Respective Governors of Vermont in the Years 1808, and 1809* (Montpelier, Vt.: Derick Sibley, 1809), 12–18; *Report of the Committee Appointed by Act of the Last Session . . . to Examine Into and Report the Situation of the Vermont State Bank* (Montpelier, Vt.: Wright & Sibley, 1812); Kenneth A. Degree, "Malfeasance or Theft? What Really Happened at the Middlebury Branch of the Vermont State Bank," *Vermont History* 68 (Spring 2000): 5–34; and *Reports of the Committees, Appointed in June, 1810, to Investigate the Situation of the Coos, Cheshire and Hillsborough Banks* (Concord, N.H., 1811).

8. "Money Is Money," *BP*, 18 October 1809 ("paper mania"); "Bank Bills and Brokers," *BP*, 9 August 1809 ("paper-phobia").

9. "Bank Bills," *BP*, 12 August 1809; "Banks—Banks—&c. &c.," by Justice [pseud.], *CD*, 9 May 1809; "Money Is Money," *BP*, 18 October 1809. For the use of *confide* as a verb in this context see "Farmers Exchange Bills," *CD*, 5 May 1809. On the fragility of confidence, see also Davies, *The Bank Torpedo*, 18; Loammi Baldwin, *Thoughts on the Study of Political Economy, as Connected with the Population, Industry and Paper Currency of the United States* (Cambridge, Mass.: Hilliard and Metcalf, 1809), 43, 49.

10. "Farmers Exchange Bank," *CD*, 16 May 1809. For Republican calls for legislative redress and debt relief, see, for example, "Bank Bills," *IC*, 3 April 1809; "Bank Bills," *BP*, 12 August 1809; "The Remedy, and the Only Effectual Remedy," *IC*, 30 August 1809. For Federalist rejoinders see "Banks," by Public Good [Nathan Appleton?], *NEP*, 11 August 1809 (quoted); "Banking," by Smith [Nathan Appleton], *NEP*, 29 August 1809; "Banks," *BG*, 31 August 1809.

11. Davies, *The Bank Torpedo*, 10, 48. For Davies's use of Dexter's case as an object lesson, see 57–59. More modulated arguments can be found in Baldwin, *Thoughts on the Study of Political Economy*; and Mathew Carey, *Nine Letters to Dr. Adam Seybert, Representative in Congress for the City of Philadelphia* (Philadelphia, 1810), which treat the Massachusetts currency collapse as instructive but anomalous in their calls for banking reform. On the first Bank of the United States, see James O. Wettereau, "New Light on the First Bank of the United States," *Pennsylvania Magazine of History and Biography* 61, no. 3 (July 1937): 263–85.

12. "Money Is Money," *BP*, 18 October 1809; "The Sovereign of Counterfeiters," *NEP*, 17 March 1809; "Grand Chance for Speculation," *Omnium Gatherum* 1:1 (November 1809): 34–35.

13. "Promissory Notes of a New Form," *Enquirer* [Richmond, Va.], 22 September 1809 ("fatal credulity"); "A Subject Too Serious to Joke With," *CD*, 9 May 1809 ("miserable stuff").

14. "Money Changers," by Poor Richard [pseud.], *IC*, 24 August 1809; "A Few Serious Remarks," by Poor Richard, *IC*, 28 August 1809; Letter to Gilbert and Dean signed "Peace," *BG*, 3 August 1809; "Bank Bills and Brokers," *BP*, 9 August 1809; "Bank Bills," by A Broker [pseud.], *BP*, 19 August 1809.

15. "Bank Bills," by A Merchant and No Broker [pseud.], *IC*, 28 August 1809; *CD*, 16 May 1809; "Uncurrent Bills in Demand!!!," *IC*, 21 September 1809. See also "Bank Bill Embargo," by Americanus, *IC*, 4 September 1809.

16. J. E. A. Smith, *The History of Pittsfield, Massachusetts, from the Year 1800 to the Year 1876* (Springfield, Mass.: C. W. Bryan, 1876), 183; *CD*, 12, 16 May 1809; *CC*, 24 May 1809. See also open letter from A Citizen of Massachusetts [pseud.], *NEP*, 1 June 1809; open letter from "Fair Play [pseud.]," *CC*, 8 June 1809.

17. For a list of forty-seven creditors who made claims against the revenues to be generated by the building, see Andrew Dexter Jr. to George Odiorne, 6 May 1809, SD 231: 14–16. Using city directories, I have identified over half of these, twenty-five of forty-seven, as builders, suppliers, or finish workers on the Exchange Coffee House.

18. [Charleston, S.C.] *City Gazette and Daily Advertiser*, 5 September 1810; "British Influence," *IC*, 1 March 1810; "Democratic Runaways," [Worcester] *Massachusetts Spy*, 21 March 1810; see also "'British Influence'—Up to the Hob," *New-Bedford Mercury*, 16 March 1810.

19. "Gloucester Bills," *PS*, 1 April 1809; "Banks—Banks," by Justice [pseud.], *CD*, 9 May 1809; "Farmers Exchange Bills," *CD*, 5 May 1809.

20. William Flanagan to Solomon Sibley, 20 July 1809.

21. "Banks—Banks," *CD*, 9 May 1809; "Farmers Exchange Bills," *CD*, 31 Mar 1809; "To the Editors," signed "N" [Nathan Appleton?], *NEP*, 30 December 1808. For other references to the Exchange as a modern Babel see "Gloucester Bills," *PS*, 1 April 1809; "Farmers Exchange Bills," *CD*, 5 May 1809.

22. André Parrot, *The Tower of Babel*, trans. Edwin Hudson, Studies in Biblical Archaeology (New York: Philosophical Library, 1955), 16–17; Michael Oakeshott, "The Tower of Babel," in *On History and Other Essays* (Oxford: Basil Blackwell, 1983), 165–94.

23. Genesis 11:1–9; see also the early commentary discussed in Oakeshott, "The Tower of Babel," 170–71; Flavius Josephus, *The Antiquities of the Jews*, in *The Genuine Works of Flavius Josephus, the Learned and Authentic Jewish Historian*, trans. William Whiston (Boston: Thomas and Andrews, 1809), 1: 21–22.

24. John Milton, *Paradise Lost* (1667), book 3, lines 467–68. On early-modern Babel imagery, see Parrot, *The Tower of Babel*, 52–56; and the "Art" section of the amazing *Virtual Babel Encyclopedia*, http://www.towerofbabel.info/.

25. Donald Fraser, *The Young Gentleman and Lady's Assistant* (Danbury, Conn.: N. Douglass, 1794), 34–35; see also Edward G. Gray, *New World Babel: Languages and Nations in Early America* (Princeton, N.J.: Princeton University Press, 1999).

26. Thomas Paine, *Letter from Thomas Paine to George Washington, Dated Paris, July 1796* (Baltimore: G. Douglas, 1802), 6. For the search for the tower by early-nineteenth-century travelers, see Donald Campbell, *A Journey Over Land to India, Partly By a Route Never Gone Before by Any European* (Philadelphia: Thomas Dobson, 1797), 280; Abraham Parsons, *Travels in Asia and Africa* (London: Longman, 1808); "The Tower of Babel," [Worcester] *Massachusetts Spy*, 28 November 1810.

27. For the 1809 banking crisis in Vermont, see Degree, "Malfeasance or Theft?"; *Report of the Committee Appointed by Act of the Last Session . . . to Examine Into and Report the Situation of the Vermont State Bank.*

28. Washington Allston, "A draft of poem 'On the Domes of the State House and the Exchange Coffee House,'" (Boston, ca. 1808–1818), in James Russell Lowell Papers, 1st ser., item 43M-862, Houghton Library, Harvard University.

29. [Samuel Gilbert and Thomas Dean?], "Description of the Boston Exchange Coffee-House," *Omnium Gatherum* 1, no. 1 (November 1809): 5; Manto [Sarah Morton?], "Lines on Visiting the Exchange Coffeehouse in Boston," *Port Folio* 1 (new series), no. 5 (May 1809): 452.

30. Bentley, *Diary of William Bentley,* 3: 396; *CC,* 22 March 1809; *BG,* 9 July 1810; *NEP,* 19 October 1810.

31. Letter dated 1 September 1808, "from an English traveller [*sic*] in this country, to his friend in Jamaica," in *The Ordeal: A Critical Journal of Politics and Literature,* 1:12 (25 March 1809), 192.

32. "Promissory Notes of a New Form," *Enquirer,* 22 September 1809; Letter to the editor, signed "P," *BG,* 1 December 1808; "Gloucester Bills," *PS,* 1 April 1809.

33. "Banks—Banks," by Justice [pseud.], *CD,* 9 May 1809. For a range of adjectives used to describe the size of the Exchange, see, among many others, John Lambert, *Travels Through Canada, and the United States of North America, in the Years 1806, 1807, and 1808: To Which Are Added Biographical Notices and Anecdotes of Some of the Leading Characters in the United States* (London: C. Cradock and A. Joy, 1816), 334 (very lofty); Ali Bey [Samuel L. Knapp], *Extracts from a Journal of Travels in North America, Consisting of an Account of Boston and Its Vicinity* (Boston: Thomas Badger, 1818), 10 (vast, immense); Charles Tyng, *Before the Wind: The Memoir of an American Sea Captain, 1808–1833,* ed. Susan Fels (New York: Viking, 1999), 12 (immense, magnificent); Milton Halsey Thomas, ed., *Elias Boudinot's Journey to Boston in 1809* (Princeton, N.J.: Princeton University Press, 1955), 81 (monstrous).

34. Charles Shaw, *A Topographical and Historical Description of Boston, from the First Settlement of the Town to the Present Period; with Some Account of Its Environs* (Boston: Oliver Spear, 1817), 229–30.

35. Thomas, *Elias Boudinot's Journey to Boston,* 80; Tyng, *Before the Wind,* 12; Bey [Samuel L. Knapp], *Extracts from a Journal of Travels in North America,* 9.

36. [Samuel Gilbert and Thomas Dean?], "Description of the Boston Exchange Coffee-House," 4, 3; Bey [Samuel L. Knapp], *Extracts from a Journal of Travels in North America,* 9. For the sale of the land that Dexter conceived of as his arcade, see Andrew Dexter Jr. to John Phillips, 6 November 1807; SD 223: 264r–65v. On the architectural and cultural history of arcades, see Johann Friedrich Geist, *Arcades, the History of a Building Type* (Cambridge, Mass.: MIT Press, 1983); Walter Benjamin, *The Arcades Project,* ed. Rolf Tiedeman, trans. Howard Eiland and Kevin McLaughlin (Cambridge, Mass.: Harvard University Press, 1999). The arcade would have been the first in the United States; the earliest examples date from the 1820s; see Robert Alexander, "The Arcade in Providence," *Journal of the Society of Architectural Historians* 12, no. 3 (October 1953): 13–16.

37. [Samuel Gilbert and Thomas Dean?], "Description of the Boston Exchange Coffee-House," 4, 7–8. Unless otherwise noted, in this paragraph and throughout the

chapter, I draw on the floor plans to the Exchange to describe interior layouts and social pathways through the building. See Thomas W. Sumner and W. Bradley, "Exchange Coffee House Architectural Plans," Bostonian Society (1817).

38. [Samuel Gilbert and Thomas Dean?], "Description of the Boston Exchange Coffee-House," 4, 8.

39. Bentley, *Diary of William Bentley,* 3: 396. For the number of steps, see Thomas Wightman's engraving "North East View of the Boston Exchange Coffee House," which illustrates [Samuel Gilbert and Thomas Dean?], "Description of the Boston Exchange Coffee-House." Wightman's illustration (and every subsequent representation based on it) shows ten bays of windows on the north side of the building, where Sumner's plans show nine. The plans seem the more careful and reliable indicator.

40. [Samuel Gilbert and Thomas Dean?], "Description of the Boston Exchange Coffee-House," 6. The shelves and boxes are described in the lease for the post office; see Andrew Dexter Jr. (for Exchange Coffee House proprietors) to Aaron Hill, 1 November 1808, SD 231: 175v–75r. On the post in the early national period, see Richard R. John, *Spreading the News: The American Postal System from Franklin to Morse* (Cambridge, Mass.: Harvard University Press, 1995).

41. [Samuel Gilbert and Thomas Dean?], "Description of the Boston Exchange Coffee-House," 6–7. Subsequent newspaper articles make clear that the Reading Room didn't begin to operate until the spring of 1810; see "Exchange Coffee House," *BG,* 29 March 1810.

42. Asher Benjamin, *The American Builder's Companion; or, a System of Architecture Particularly Adapted to the Present Style of Building,* 2nd ed. (Boston: Etheridge & Bliss, 1811), 34; [Samuel Gilbert and Thomas Dean?], "Description of the Boston Exchange Coffee-House," 5. Jack Quinan points out that on dark days, the effect may have been more like that of an air shaft; the perimeter of the 'Change Floor measures over 200 feet, while the circumference of the skylight, nearly 100 feet above, is only 45 feet. Jack Quinan, "The Boston Exchange Coffee House," *Journal of the Society of Architecture Historians* 38, no. 3 (1978): 258–59.

43. [Samuel Gilbert and Thomas Dean?], "Description of the Boston Exchange Coffee-House," 5; "The Exchange Coffee House," *BG,* 4 January 1810; "The Exchange Coffee House," by A Merchant [pseud.], *BG,* 11 January 1810.

44. [Samuel Gilbert and Thomas Dean?], "Description of the Boston Exchange Coffee-House," 6. For the types of servants used at the Coffee House, see "Four Waiters Wanted," *NEP,* 9 June 1809; "Wanted" advertisement of Palmer's Information Office, an employment service located on the second floor of the Exchange, *NEP,* 12 October 1810.

45. [Samuel Gilbert and Thomas Dean?], "Description of the Boston Exchange Coffee-House," 6. Dexter's debt to William Lemon is documented in Andrew Dexter Jr. to George Odiorne, 6 May 1809, SD 231: 14–16. For the clock and the values of the furnishings in the Coffee Room, see inventories of the Coffee Room, the Reading Room, and the china closet in "Schedule of Furniture &c. Belonging to the Proprietors of the Exchange Coffee House," MS0174, Bostonian Society (1812).

46. On the quantity of coffee flowing into the United States, ca. 1809, see Timothy Pitkin, *A Statistical View of the Commerce of the United States* (Hartford, Conn.: Charles Hosmer, 1816), 137–43. In this and the following paragraphs I'm summarizing a great

deal of research on coffee culture. For my own work on the topic, see "Coffeehouses Everywhere and Not a Drop to Drink: Coffee and Identity in Provincial America" (unpublished paper delivered to the 1999 Berkshire Conference on the History of Women). The most careful and comprehensive study of the culture of coffee during the English Enlightenment—ground zero for coffee historians—is Brian W. Cowan, *The Social Life of Coffee: The Emergence of the British Coffeehouse* (New Haven, Conn.: Yale University Press, 2005). On English coffee culture, see also Lawrence E. Klein, "Coffeehouse Civility, 1660–1714: An Aspect of Post-Courtly Culture in England," *Huntington Library Quarterly* 59, no. 1 (Summer 1997): 1–22; and Steve Pincus, " 'Coffee Politicians Does Create': Coffeehouses and Restoration Political Culture," *Journal of Modern History* 67, no. 4 (December 1995): 807–34. The history of coffee in the United States and its colonial predecessors is less developed, but see William H. Ukers, *All About Coffee* (New York: Tea and Coffee Trade Journal, 1922); Francis B. Thurber, *Coffee: From Plantation to Cup. A Brief History of Coffee Production and Consumption.* (New York: American Grocer Publishing Association, 1881); Mary R. M. Goodwin, *The Coffee-House of the 17th & 18th Centuries,* typescript, Colonial Williamsburg Foundation Research Report Series (Williamsburg, Va., 1956). A recent journalistic overview of American coffee culture centering in the modern era is Mark Pendergrast, *Uncommon Grounds: The History of Coffee and How It Transformed Our World* (New York: Basic Books, 1999). Books in progress on coffee in British North America and the United States by Michelle Craig and Stephen Topik will enrich this literature considerably.

47. *A Cup of Coffee: Or, Coffee in Its Colours* (London, 1663); see also *News from the Coffee-House; in Which Is Shewn Their Several Sorts of Passions, Containing Newes from All Our Neighbour Nations* (London, 1667). On *Publick Occurrences,* see Charles E. Clark, "The Newspapers of Provincial America," *Proceedings of the American Antiquarian Society* 100, no. 2 (October 1990). Quantities of liquor and groceries in the Exchange's cellars on 21 July 1812 are listed in "Agreement between John Jones and the Proprietors of the Boston Exchange Coffee House, July 1812," Records of Hotels and Taverns in New England and New York, 1753–1912, Baker Library, Harvard Business School. (This document is tipped into the front of an account book from John Jones's wine business in the 1820s and 1830s, mistakenly labeled as the accounts of the second Exchange Coffee Hosue.)

48. Great Britain; Public Record Office, *Calendar of State Papers, Domestic Series . . . Preserved in the Public Record Office,* vol.17: *March 1st, 1675, to February 29th, 1676,* ed. F. H. Blackburne Daniell (London: H.M. Stationery Office, 1907), 465; see also 496–97, 503.

49. Hunter Dickinson Farish, ed., *Journal & Letters of Philip Vickers Fithian 1773–1774: A Plantation Tutor of the Old Dominion* (Charlottesville: University Press of Virginia, 1957), 110. In other words, the coffeehouse was alleged, by Enlightenment thinkers and their modern historians, to be the *locus classicus* of the public sphere; see Jürgen Habermas, *The Structural Transformation of the Public Sphere: An Inquiry Into a Category of Bourgeois Society,* trans. Thomas Burger, reprint, 1962 (Cambridge, Mass.: MIT Press, 1989), 32–43, 59 ff; and David S. Shields, *Civil Tongues and Polite Letters in British America* (Chapel Hill: University of North Carolina Press, 1997), Introduction. On the links between tea and femininity in the eighteenth century, see

Beth Kowaleski-Wallace, "Tea, Gender, and Domesticity in Eighteenth-Century England," eds. Carla H. Hay and Syndy M. Conger, *Studies in Eighteenth-Century Culture* 23 (1994): 131–45; and Rodris Roth, "Tea-Drinking in Eighteenth-Century America: Its Etiquette and Equipage," in *Material Life in America, 1600–1860*, ed. Robert Blair St. George (Boston: Northeastern University Press, 1988), 439–62.

50. *News from the Coffee-House*; *New-England Weekly Journal,* 30 October 1727. David Shields attributes this anonymous contribution, signed "C," to Mather Byles; Shields, *Civil Tongues and Polite Letters,* 237. On the Crown Coffee House, see also David W. Conroy, *In Public Houses: Drink and the Revolution of Authority in Colonial Massachusetts* (Chapel Hill: University of North Carolina Press, 1995), 73, 77, 93, 119–23. For the reputation of coffeehouses as penny universities, see Aytoun Ellis, *The Penny Universities: A History of the Coffee Houses* (London: Secker & Warburg, 1956).

51. Review of *Georgick Papers for 1809*, *Monthly Anthology and Boston Review* 7, no. 7 (July 1809): 56. For the coffeehouse and discourses of refinement in early national America see Richard L. Bushman, *The Refinement of America: Persons, Houses, Cities* (New York: Vintage, 1993); and Shields, *Civil Tongues and Polite Letters*. On the many limitations to the "public sphere" paradigm, see Christopher Looby, et al., "Forum: Alternative Histories of the Public Sphere," *William and Mary Quarterly,* 62, no. 1 (January 2005): 3–112.

52. [Samuel Gilbert and Thomas Dean?], "Description of the Boston Exchange Coffee-House," 6. For New York mineral waters being sold in the Coffee Room, see *NEP,* 25 Jul 1809. On the staircase, see William H. Wheildon, *Memoir of Solomon Willard, Architect and Superintendent of the Bunker Hill Monument* (Boston: Bunker Hill Monument Association, 1865), 28–29.

53. The dimensions and colors of the Dining Room appear in [Samuel Gilbert and Thomas Dean?], "Description of the Boston Exchange Coffee-House," 6; and Manto [Sarah Morton?], "Lines on Visiting the Exchange Coffeehouse," 452–53. For its seating capacity, see Charles Shaw, *A Topographical and Historical Description of Boston, from the First Settlement of the Town to the Present Period; with Some Account of Its Environs,* 232; and for values of the Dining Room's furnishings, see "Schedule of Furniture &c. Belonging to the Proprietors of the Exchange Coffee House."

54. The three banquets are announced in *CC,* 21 December 1808; 25 January, 25 March 1809. "Green Turtle Soup," *NEP,* 5 September 1809. For the critique of a lack of system and schedule in the Dining Room, see "The Exchange," by A Merchant [pseud.], *BG,* 11 January 1810.

55. For uses of the other rooms on the first gallery level, see [Samuel Gilbert and Thomas Dean?], "Description of the Boston Exchange Coffee-House," 9. Notices of the commissioners' sittings appear regularly in the Boston papers, especially the *NEP.*

56. [Samuel Gilbert and Thomas Dean?], "Description of the Boston Exchange Coffee-House," 8; Manto [Sarah Morton?], "Lines on Visiting the Exchange Coffeehouse," 452.

57. [Samuel Gilbert and Thomas Dean?], "Description of the Boston Exchange Coffee-House," 7.

58. This discussion is heavily indebted to the suggestions of Danny Abramson on the ways classical architecture embodies and rationalizes credit; see Daniel M.

Abramson, *Building the Bank of England: Money, Architecture, Society, 1694–1942* (New Haven, Conn., and London: Yale University Press, 2005), chap. 2.

59. [Samuel Gilbert and Thomas Dean?], "Description of the Boston Exchange Coffee-House," 7; "Ball Room" in "Schedule of Furniture &c. Belonging to the Proprietors of the Exchange Coffee House," n. p. On the cost and social meanings of mirrors in the late eighteenth and early nineteenth centuries, see Elisabeth Donaghy Garrett, "Looking Glasses in America 1700–1850," in *American Tables and Looking Glasses in the Mable Brady Garvan and Other Collections at Yale University,* ed. David L. Barquist (New Haven, Conn.: Yale University Press, 1992), 26–36.

60. [Samuel Gilbert and Thomas Dean?], "Description of the Boston Exchange Coffee-House," 7; Anna Cabot Lowell to Eliza Susan Quincy, 22 November 1809, in Anna Cabot Lowell Papers, 1795–1810, folder 3, MHS; Manto [Sarah Morton?], "Lines on Visiting the Exchange Coffeehouse," 452. On the alliance of mirrors and artificial light, see John E. Crowley, *The Invention of Comfort: Sensibilities and Design in Early Modern Britain and Early America* (Baltimore: Johns Hopkins University Press, 2001), 122–40.

61. [Samuel Gilbert and Thomas Dean?], "Description of the Boston Exchange Coffee-House," 5.

62. [Samuel Gilbert and Thomas Dean?], "Description of the Boston Exchange Coffee-House," 8; Bey [Samuel L. Knapp], *Extracts from a Journal of Travels in North America,* 9. For the furnishings of various hotel chambers and their values, see "Schedule of Furniture &c. Belonging to the Proprietors of the Exchange Coffee House."

63. "Proposals for Forming a Company to Purchase the 'Exchange Coffee House,'" *BG,* and *CC,* 12 July 1809; *Repertory,* 21 July 1809; *IC,* 20 July 1809. Joseph Goodwin of the Berkshire Bank purchased Dexter's rights to the property at the "coroner's sale" to dispose of the Exchange Coffee House on 14 June 1809 for $133,000. The bank then put up the building as security for their obligations to Samuel Gilbert and Thomas Dean, who held $138,000 worth of its bills; Homans [Suffolk County coroner] to Goodwin, et al., 3 July 1809, SD 229:293–295; and Goodwin, by attorney, to Gilbert and Dean, 4 September 1809, SD 229:295r–296v. On the financial relationship between the Berkshire Bank and Gilbert and Dean, see Curtis Guild, "Reminiscences of Old Boston or The Exchange Coffee House," bound clippings from the *Commercial Bulletin,* BPL, Rare Books Department (ca. 1872), 1: 2–3.

64. "Proposals for Making Sale of the Exchange Coffee House," *BG,* 18 September 1809; "Proposals for Making Sale of the Exchange Coffee House [and] Abstract of a Minute Estimate of the Yearly Income of Said Property," broadside, Bostonian Society; [Samuel Gilbert and Thomas Dean?], "Description of the Boston Exchange Coffee-House," 9. The similarity of this language to Gilbert and Dean's many grandiose advertisements for their lotteries and bank bill guides in the Boston press for their lotteries and their printing business, together with the "Description's" insider knowledge of the Exchange's finances, lead me to attribute authorship to Gilbert and Dean. See also "To the Concerned," *BG,* 14 September 1809; "Valuable Real Estates," *IC,* 2 October 1809.

65. *NEP,* 12 September, 21 November 1809; *CC,* 21 February 1810; *BG,* 2 April 1810. Hamilton had failed before as a hotelier; see Lambert, *Travels Through Canada*

*and the United States,* 334. He does not appear in the *Boston Directory for 1810,* having presumably left town before that June.

66. Manto [Sarah Morton?], "Lines on Visiting the Exchange Coffeehouse"; [Samuel Gilbert and Thomas Dean?], "Description of the Boston Exchange Coffee-House," 9, 3. The logic of my attribution of Manto's "Lines" to Sarah Morton is as follows. First, the author is both sympathetic to Dexter and familiar with his situation, as the mother of his exiled bride would be. Morton, of course, was also a much-published poet, with prior work appearing in the *Port Folio* and a documented friendship with its editor, Joseph Dennie. "Manto" was a Roman oracle, the daughter of Tiresias, imprisoned at the fall of Thebes—in sort, a seer and sufferer, as Sarah Morton often described herself. The attribution must remain tentative. Though Morton exposed her authorship of many anonymous poems in Sarah Wentworth Morton, *My Mind and Its Thoughts, in Sketches, Fragments, and Essays,* reprint, 1823 (Delmar, N.Y.: Scholars' Facsimiles & Reprints, 1975), the poem does not appear there, neither is it one of the items attributed in Randolph C. Randall, "Authors of the *Port Folio* Revealed by the Hall Files," *American Literature* 11, no. 4 (January 1940): 379–416. On the *Port Folio* and Dennie's editorship see also Harold Milton Ellis, *Joseph Dennie and His Circle: A Study in American Literature from 1792 to 1812,* Bulletin of the University of Texas Studies in English, no. 3 (Austin: University of Texas, 1915), 199–208.

67. For comparisons of Dexter's tower to other once-fatherless buildings, since adopted, see [Samuel Gilbert and Thomas Dean?], "Description of the Boston Exchange Coffee-House," 9; "Exchange Coffee House," *BG,* 28 September 1809; "Exchange Coffee House," *NEP,* 21 November 1809.

68. For the reincorporation of the proprietors of the Exchange Coffee House, see *BG,* 27 November, 28 December 1809 (lists directors); and "An ACT in further addition to an Act, entitled, 'An Act to incorporate sundry persons into a company by the name of the Proprietors of the Exchange Coffee House,'" *Mass. Laws* 1809: 66, passed 27 Feburary 1810.

Apthorp and Weld are designated Dexter's assignees in *Pepoon v. Dexter,* 15 May 1809, SD 221:141–44. Payne's tenancy in the Coffee House is mentioned in [Samuel Gilbert and Thomas Dean?], "Description of the Boston Exchange Coffee-House," 8; see also Suffolk Coroner to J. Goodwin et al., 14 July 1809, SD 229:290–93. For Coolidge's purchase of the Morton estate, see Emily Pendleton and Milton Ellis, *Philenia; the Life and Works of Sarah Wentworth Morton, 1759–1846,* University of Maine Studies, 2nd s. (Orono: University of Maine Press, 1931), 88. Coolidge, Ebenzer Larkin, and West Indies merchant John D. Williams appear as Gilbert and Dean's Trustees in "To the Concerned," *BG,* 18 September 1809. For the signatures of Coolidge and Ebenezer Francis on Appleton's bank circular, see "Manuscript Draft of a Bank Circular," Miscellaneous Bound Manuscripts, 1809 [*sic*], MHS.

The membership of Timothy Bigelow and Ebenezer Francis in the West Boston Church is documented in the West Boston Society Papers, MHS. On Thomas W. Sumner, see Associated Housewright Society Papers, 6th ser. of Massachusetts Charitable Mechanics Association Records, 1791–1995, MHS; and Christopher P. Monkhouse, "Thomas Waldron Sumner: A Biographical Sketch of the Architect of East India Marine Hall," in *East India Marine Hall: 1824–1974,* ed. Philip Chadwick Foster Smith (Salem, Mass.: Peabody Museum of Salem, 1974), n.p. Samuel Eliot

Morison describes Harrison Gray Otis's long and largely successful career in real estate speculation in *The Life and Letters of Harrison Gray Otis, Federalist, 1765–1848* (Boston: Houghton Mifflin, 1913). Gamaliel Bradford, Timothy Bigelow, Isaac P. Davis, Simon Elliot, Samuel G. Perkins, and William Sullivan completed the new directorate. Sullivan, a Federalist, was the son of the Republican governor James Sullivan, author of the anti-paper-money tract *The Path to Riches*, which was reprinted in the wake of Dexter's failure; see "Memoir of the Hon. William Sullivan," *Proceedings of the Massachusetts Historical Society* 2 (1835–1855): 150–60.

I have not found records of their ownership stakes in the corporation, or of the number of shares eventually issued. Gilbert and Dean continued to own some 760 shares; see "To Our Creditors and the Public," *BG,* 5 October 1814.

69. Letter on the Exchange Coffee House, *NEP,* 18 July 1809. For estimates of the building's profitability, see "Proposals for Making Sale of the Exchange Coffee House [and] Abstract of a Minute Estimate of the Yearly Income of Said Property," broadside, ca. 18 September 1809, Bostonian Society (25 percent); and "Exchange Coffee House," *BG,* 28 September 1809 (12 to 15 percent). Dexter's prospectus had projected an annual return of 10 to 11 percent; Public Works [pseud.], *BG,* 1 January 1807.

70. "Exchange Coffee House," *BG,* 4 January 1810 (emphasis mine); "Exchange Coffee House," *NEP,* 21 November 1809.

71. "The Exchange," by A Merchant [pseud.], *BG,* 11 January 1810; "Exchange Coffee House," *BG,* 29 March 1810; "Exchange Coffee House" (advertisement), *CC,* 28 March 1810; "Exchange Coffee House" (advertisement), *CC,* 20 June 1810.

72. Bey [Samuel L. Knapp], *Extracts from a Journal of Travels in North America,* 9.

73. Creating the "new street" was a longstanding plan. Gilbert and Dean had "purchased land on the north side of the building sufficient to leave an avenue from State-street to the building of 35 feet in width and 35 feet from Congress-street to *Dawes'* buildings" in the spring of 1809; *BG,* 12 July 09. The new directors also had to change their corporate charter to enable them to make such purchases as a corporate body; see "An ACT in further addition to an Act," *Mass. Laws* 1809: 66. For negotiations with the city, see *Minutes of the Selectmen's Meetings, 1799 to and Including 1810,* Records Relating to the Early History of Boston (1904), 441–42, 444, 445; and "Bond of Indenture from Proprietors of Exchange to Town of Boston," 1 September 1810, SD 237:252–53. The assessment against shareholders is announced in *CC,* 20 March 1811. The existence of "the new street in front of the Coffee-House" was mentioned in an advertisement in *NEP,* 15 January 1811, and the selectmen appointed a committee to oversee its paving on 23 July 1811; *Minutes of the Selectmen's Meetings, 1811 to 1817, and Part of 1818,* Records Relating to the Early History of Boston (1908), 28. But the street is not named or mapped in the 1810, 1813, 1816, or 1818 editions of the *Boston Directory.*

74. [Samuel Gilbert and Thomas Dean?], "Description of the Boston Exchange Coffee-House," 4. On the problem of the male gaze as women ventured into the new commercial spaces of the early Republic and antebellum public sphere, see Carolyn Brucken, "In the Public Eye: Women and the American Luxury Hotel," *Winterthur Portfolio* 31, no. 4 (Winter 1996): 203–20; Carolyn E. Brucken, "Consuming Luxury: Hotels and the Rise of Middle-Class Public Space, 1825–1860" (Ph.D. dissertation, George Washington University, 1997), 180–231; and Diane Shaw, *City Building on the*

*Eastern Frontier: Sorting the New Nineteenth-Century City* (Baltimore: Johns Hopkins University Press, 2004), 96–102.

75. The purchases of the lands south of the Exchange building were made possible by an amendment to the building's charter; see "An act in further addition to an Act, entitled, 'An Act to incorporate sundry persons into a company by the name of the Proprietors of the Exchange Coffee House,'" *Mass. Laws* 1813: 36. For the conveyances, see Patrick Whall to the Exchange Coffee House (ECH) Proprietors, 7 May 1813, SD 242:83; John Driscoll to ECH Proprietors, 6 July 1813, SD 242:175–75; Elizabeth Thayer to ECH Proprietors (2 deeds), 30 September 1816, SD 252:246–47; Joseph Thayer to ECH Proprietors, 30 September 1816, SD 252:245; Robert Thayer to ECH Proprietors, 30 September 1816, SD 252:245–46; S. Stevenson Thayer to ECH Proprietors, 30 September 1816, SD 252:246; Robert Thayer to ECH Proprietors, 24 July 1817, SD 256:44–45; Samuel Thayer to ECH Proprietors, 24 July 1817, SD 256:43–44.

76. These changes are reflected in the plans Thomas Sumner drew in September 1817, and described in Charles Shaw, *A Topographical and Historical Description of Boston,* 230–31; and "Destruction of the Exchange Coffee House by Fire," *NEP,* 6 November 1818.

77. "Exchange Coffee House," *BG,* 29 March 1810; "Exchange Coffee House Reading Room," *BG,* 2 April 1810; "Indenture Between Proprietors of the Exchange Coffee House & John Jones 1812 [Reading Room]," MS 47.21.2, Bostonian Society (1812); "To the Subscribers for the Exchange Coffee House Marine Books," *NEP,* 2 July 1811; "The Reading Room and Marine Diary in the Exchange Coffee House, 1810," *Bostonian Society Publications* 8 (1911): 123–31.

78. *NEP,* 27 April 1810. For the ECH boats, see Guild, "Reminiscences," 1: 2; and "Exchange Reading and News Room," *BG,* 19 November 1818.

79. *NEP,* 27 April, 4 May, 1 May, 27 July 1810; *BG,* 24 May 1810.

80. "A Hint to Merchants," *NEP,* 31 July 1810.

81. "A Card," *BG,* 26 November 1810; "To the Subscribers for the Exchange Coffee House Marine Books," *NEP,* 2 July 1811; "Exchange Coffee-House Hotel," *IC,* 5 August 1813; "Exchange Reading and News Room," *IC,* 25 July 1814; "Rules and Regulations of the Boston Exchange Coffee House News Room," *CC,* 3 August 1816.

82. "Exchange Reading and News Room," *IC,* 25 July 1814; "Rules and Regulations of the Boston Exchange Coffee House News Room," *CC,* 3 August 1816. See also "News Room," *CC,* 13 March 1816; "Exchange Coffee-House Reading and News Room," *IC,* 12 September 1816.

83. Gilbert and Dean's September 1809 "Abstract of a Minute Estimate of the Yearly Income of Said Property" enumerates 36 offices or rooms for long-term rental, in addition to the cellars and an unspecified number of rooms in the third, fourth, and fifth galleries. The tabulation of the "Number of Rooms which are for Hire to different Tenants" that accompanies Thomas Sumner's plan for the Exchange's fifth gallery lists a total of 30 rooms for hire outside those that leased with the Coffee House: Sumner and Bradley, "Exchange Coffee House Architectural Plans," plate 10. The tax assessors enumerated tenants in the building annually: 11 in 1809 (see Boston Assessors Records, taking books 8:43); 13 in 1810 (ibid. 8: 20); 22 in 1811 (ibid. 8: 41–42); 20

in 1812 (ibid. 8:41–42); 15 in 1813 (ibid. 8:41); 20 in 1814 (ibid. 8:34); 20 in 1815 (ibid. 8:36); 11 in 1816 (ibid. 8:40); 14 in 1817 (ibid. 8:48). See also "Offices to Let" (advertisement), which offers "20 or 30" offices and other rooms "which may be had at easy rents," *NEP,* 19 July 1811. The annual rent paid by the post office varied between $150 and $200; see Andrew Dexter Jr. (for Exchange Coffee House Proprietors) to Aaron Hill, 1 November 1808, SD 231:175v–75r. For the income of the hotel, ca. 1813–1814, see "Statement of Account of the Exchange Coffee House," MS 42.21.3, Bostonian Society (1813). (The "Statement of Account" is dated 1810–1811 in a later hand, but internal evidence strongly suggests that it correlates with the July 1813–June 1814 lease.) For Dexter's statement about the hotel department, see Public Works [pseud.], *BG,* 1 January 1807.

84. "Indenture Between Proprietors of the Exchange Coffee House & John Jones," MS 0174, Bostonian Society (1812); "Indenture Between Proprietors of the Exchange Coffee House & John Jones," MS 42.21.4, Bostonian Society (1813), with a rider for 1814–1815; "Statement of Account of the Exchange Coffee House."

85. "To Our Creditors and the Public," by Gilbert and Dean, *CC,* 5 October 1814; see also *CC,* 30 March 1811; Guild, "Reminiscences," 2:4; Nathan Appleton, *An Examination of the Banking System of Massachusetts, in Reference to the Renewal of the Bank Charters* (Boston: Stimpson and Clapp, 1831), 13; Robert C. Winthrop, ed., "Memoir of Hon. Nathan Appleton," *Proceedings of the Massachusetts Historical Society* 5 (October 1861): 284.

For sales of Exchange shares (no price mentioned unless noted), see *NEP,* 20 July 1810; *BG,* 27 December 1810; *NEP,* 15 January 1811; *CC,* 19 October 1811 ($410 per share); *CC,* 23 May 1813; *CC,* 13 October 1813; *CC,* 6 May 1815. The only records I have found of dividends paid to ECH shareholders appear in *CC,* 27 May 1815 ($6), and *CC,* 2 December 1815 (unspecified). At $12 per year on a share price of $410, the dividend represents a return of less than 3 percent.

86. For this day in the life of the Exchange, I have made a composite of actual events and types of events described in newspapers and personal documents from 1810, when the building achieved a kind of stability, through 1818. Citations that follow document the specific events mentioned.

87. "The President of the United States," *IC,* 2 July 1817 ("tour of personal examination"); "Arrival of the President," *IC,* 4 July 1817 ("political distinctions . . ."); "Era of Good Feelings," *CC,* 12 July 1817.

88. "Arrival of the President," *IC,* 4 July 1817.

89. *CC,* 4 August 1813; 15 June, 14, 21 August 1816; 26 September, 11 November 1818; *IC,* 29 July, 19 August 1816; 26, 30 September 1818.

90. "New-York and Boston New Line Enterprize," *CC,* 2 July 1814; "Schedule of Furniture &c. Belonging to the Proprietors of the Exchange Coffee House"; Letter to the editor, signed E.M., *CC,* 11 November 1818.

91. *BG,* 30 August 1810; see also *NEP,* 21 August, 28 September 1810; 8 January, 6 August 1811.

92. For panoramas on display, see *BG,* 11, 18 June, 9 August 1810; *IC,* 2 July 1810; *NEP,* 8 February 1814; *CC,* 25 May 1814. Elijah Pope Clark recorded a visit to see the "Panorama of the Battle of Lake Erie" in the ECH in "the forenoon"; see entry for 19 May 1814, Elijah Pope Clark Diary, 1813–1814, MHS. On the panorama genre and

other large-scale ephemeral art forms of the day, see Peter Benes, *American Rarities: Itinerant Callings and the Reshaping of Culture in Early New England* (Boston: Dublin Seminar and Boston University Scholarly Publications, forthcoming), chap. 21, "Public Painters, Public Artifacts."

93. *NEP,* 23 October, 7 December 1817. For other morning meetings, see *BG,* 2 April 1810, 21 September 1814.

94. For waiters among the city's "coloured persons," see *Boston Directory for 1818,* 252–53. Noontime auctions appear in *BG,* 5 February, 15 March, 2, 21 June, 2 July 1810; "Weekly Sale of Stocks," *CC,* 29 December 1813, 23 November 1814. For families stopping to dinner in the Exchange, see Thomas Wetmore to Joseph Story, ca. 1811, reel 1, Joseph Story Papers, 1797–1857, MHS; "Exchange Coffee House" (advertisement), *CC,* 28 March 1810.

95. For these and other offices, see Boston Assessors' Records for 1817, taking books 8:48; *City Directory for 1818;* "Fashionable Hair Cutter and Dresser," *NEP,* 23 November 1810; *BG,* 13 November 1817 (British consulate).

96. For Mr. Wifford's writing school, see *BG,* 23 April, 14 May, 5 November, 3, 27 December 1810 (quoted). Wifford moved the school from room number 84, where he didn't accept female pupils, to room 129, "directly over the *Ladies' Drawing-Room,*" which offered a more suitable location for young women. For Fennell's elocution school, see *BG,* 28 June, 12 July 1810. I've deduced the number of pupils from the furniture inventoried in room 129 in "Schedule of Furniture &c. Belonging to the Proprietors of the Exchange Coffee House."

97. Anna Cabot Lowell to Eliza Susan Quincy, 22 November 1809, in Anna Cabot Lowell Papers, 1795–1810, folder 3, MHS; Eliza Susan Quincy Journal, 1814–1821, item QP43, Quincy Family Papers, MHS, 29; see also 63; Elijah Pope Clark Diary, entries for 8, 17 March 1814. For the porcelains used in the ECH, see "Exchange Coffee House plate," object number A5406/1922.3, Bostonian Society.

98. *NEP,* 18 October 1811; *CC,* 24 February 1812, 21 September 1814, 16 May 1818.

99. On the "era of association," see Mary P. Ryan, *Cradle of the Middle Class: The Family in Oneida County, New York, 1790–1865* (New York: Cambridge University Press, 1981), chap. 3. For Harvard reunions in the building, see, for example, *CC,* 5 August 1818. On the MCMA membership and meetings, see *BG,* 24 December 1810; *CC,* 19 February 1814; 2nd ser., Membership Records, in MCMA Records, 1791–1995, MHS. For the building of the hall of the Grand Lodge on the Exchange's top two stories, see Charles Shaw, *A Topographical and Historical Description of Boston,* 233. The Masonic Lodge, dedicated on 23 July 1817, is described at length in "Masonic," *New-England Galaxy and Masonic Magazine,* 7 November 1817; see also Sumner and Bradley, "Exchange Coffee House Architectural Plans," Plan of the fourth gallery. On Masonic culture and ritual in early America more generally, see Steven C. Bullock, *Revolutionary Brotherhood: Freemasonry and the Transformation of the American Social Order, 1730–1840* (Chapel Hill: University of North Carolina Press, 1996).

100. Quotations from the Washington Benevolent Society [hereafter WBS] Constitution, vol. 1:1–3; Washington Benevolent Society Records, 1812–1824, MHS. For the contents of room 110, see "Schedule of Furniture &c. Belonging to the Proprietors of the Exchange Coffee House." On the WBS, see also *The First Book of the*

'Washington Benevolents'; Otherwise Called the Book of Knaves (Boston: Nathaniel Coverly, [1813]); and Matthew H. Crocker, *The Magic of the Many: Josiah Quincy and the Rise of Mass Politics in Boston, 1800–1830* (Amherst: University of Massachusetts Press, 1999), chap. 2. For the dinner service at such meetings, see "Receipt from Thomas Dean, payment for room rental, September 1810," Boston Theater (Federal Street) Papers, Ms. Th. 1, item D214, BPL; and "Dinner Bill for Assistant Fire Society," MS. A. 1808 (35), BPL.

101. WBS records, vol. 1, item 16-c, n.d.; see also 1:55-c (13 April 1813); 1:62-c (30 April 1813); 2: 65 (January 1817).

102. [Samuel Gilbert and Thomas Dean?], "Description of the Boston Exchange Coffee-House," 8; "Masonic," *New-England Galaxy and Masonic Magazine,* 7 November 1817.

103. "Washington and Naval Ball," *CC,* 10 March 1813.

104. Benes, *American Rarities,* chap. 21.

105. See, for example, *NEP,* 10, 17 October, 1 November, 5 December 1809; 22 May 1810; 11 January 1811; *CC,* 30 April 1814.

106. *NEP,* 15 May 1810, 9 April 1811.

107. "Novel Exhibitions," *NEP,* 16 April 1811; "Rannie's Exhibition," *IC,* 24 December 1810; "Ventriloquism," 3 January 1811; "The Choice of One from a Hundred," *BG,* 27 December 1810. For fraud as a theme in antebellum entertainments, see James W. Cook, *The Arts of Deception: Playing with Fraud in the Age of Barnum* (Cambridge, Mass.: Harvard University Press, 2001), 163–213.

108. "Ventriloquism," *NEP,* 6 December 1810; see also *IC,* 24 December 1810; "The Little Devil," *BG,* 26 November 1810.

109. Charles Shaw, *A Topographical and Historical Description of Boston,* 233.

110. *IC,* 3 August 1812; *CC,* 5 August 1812.

111. Charles Shaw, *A Topographical and Historical Description of Boston,* 232; "Exchange Coffee House," *BG,* 20 November 1817.

112. *IC,* 18 November 1818.

## CHAPTER FIVE: CONFLAGRATION

1. Thomas Jefferson to John Holmes, 22 April 1820, Papers of Thomas Jefferson, Library of Congress, Series 1: General Correspondence, 1651–1827.

2. Richard Cullen Rath, *How Early America Sounded* (Ithaca, N.Y.: Cornell University Press, 2003), 43–69, esp. 64; Alain Corbin, *Village Bells: Sound and Meaning in the 19th-Century French Countryside,* trans. Martin Thom (New York: Columbia University Press, 1998). For bells regulating civic time and space in Boston, see, for example, *Boston Town Records, 1796 to 1813,* Records Relating to the Early History of Boston (1905), 43, 127, 164, 166, 171, 180, 182, 205, 211, 213.

3. "Odd Freak of a Sailor," *Commercial Advertiser* (New York), 3 June 1807; Eva A. Speare, *Historic Bells in New Hampshire* (Plymouth, N.H.: n.p., 1944), 44–47. See also "Fire," *Federal Gazette and Baltimore Daily Advertiser,* 20 February 1801; "Further Particulars of the Late Fire at New-Orleans," *Commercial Advertiser,* 3 October 1816.

4. "Tremendous Conflagration," *New-England Galaxy and Masonic Magazine,* 6 November 1818 ("resistless"); "Conflagration," *Boston Idiot,* 7 November 1818 ("pow-

erful . . . possessed on earth"); Alexander Townsend, *An Address, to the Charitable Fire Society, on the Principles of Their Institution* (Boston: Russell & Cutler, 1809), 10, 12 ("thief . . . wealth," "reverses"); George Smith Tyack, *A Book About Bells* (London: William Andrews, 1898), 84–85. On the tocsin, see Corbin, *Village Bells,* 191–201. Satis Coleman, *Bells: Their History, Legends, Making, and Uses* (Chicago: Rand McNally, 1928), 79, 108–9, 391, features other similar inscriptions.

5. Jeremiah 50:32, quoted in Jonathan Mayhew, *God's Hand and Providence to Be Religiously Acknowledged in Public Calamities: A Sermon Occasioned by the Great Fire in Boston, New-England, Thursday March 20, 1760* (Boston: Richard Draper, 1760), 11–12. On fire and early urban life more generally, see Johan Goudsblom, *Fire and Civilization* (London: Allen Lane/The Penguin Press, 1992), 143–53; and William J. Novak, *The People's Welfare: Law and Regulation in Nineteenth-Century America* (Chapel Hill: University of North Carolina Press, 1996), 51–82.

6. *To the Citizens of the Town of BOSTON,* broadside (Boston, 1802); Sara E. Wermiel, *The Fireproof Building: Technology and Public Safety in the Nineteenth-Century City* (Baltimore: Johns Hopkins University Press, 2000), 2–3; Paul C. Ditzel, *Fire Engines, Firefighters: The Men, Equipment, and Machines, from Colonial Days to the Present* (New York: Crown, 1976), 13–16; John C. Weaver and Peter de Lottinville, "The Conflagration and the City: Disaster and Progress in British North America During the Nineteenth Century," *Histoire Sociale-Social History* 13, no. 26 (November 1980): 417–49.

7. Arnold Welles, *An Address, to the Members of the Massachusetts Charitable Fire Society* (Boston: Samuel Etheridge, 1797), 18; John Quincy Adams, *An Address to the Members of the Massachusetts Charitable Fire Society* (Boston: Russell & Cutler, 1802), 11; William Henry Whitmore, *An Historical Summary of Fires in Boston* (Boston: n.p., 1872), 8. For Boston fires, ca. 1816–1818, see Arthur Wellington Brayley, *A Complete History of the Boston Fire Department* (Boston: John P. Dale, 1889), 123, 124, 126.

8. John Gallison, "Journal, Volume K," Boston Athenaeum, 86.

9. Brayley, *Boston Fire Department,* 60–62; Whitmore, *An Historical Summary of Fires in Boston,* 6–7; *Rhode Island American* 28 March 1809; Elijah Pope Clark Diary, 1813–1814, MHS, entry for 26 December 1813.

10. "Appropriate Reflections," by Caution [pseud.], *IC,* 11 November 1818. The tally of cooking and heating fires in the ECH comes from Thomas W. Sumner and W. Bradley, "Exchange Coffee House Architectural Plans," Bostonian Society (1817); and "Schedule of Furniture &c. Belonging to the Proprietors of the Exchange Coffee House," MS0174, Bostonian Society (1812). For ice on the ponds by December 3, see William Bentley, *The Diary of William Bentley, D.D., Pastor of the East Church, Salem, Massachusetts* (Gloucester, Mass.: Peter Smith, 1962), 4:562. For sun and moon rise and set on any given date see http://aa.usno.navy.mil/data/docs/RS_OneDay.html.

11. For the "bonfires" that consumed the War and Treasury buildings during Samuel Dexter's tenure as secretary of each department, see [Philadelphia] *Aurora,* 2, 24, 26 January; 4 February 1801. For Gilbert and Dean's losses, which included stacks of bank bills and lottery tickets, see "Fires," *CC,* 25 January 1804; "Fire!," *BG,* 23 January 1804.

12. "Destructive Fire," *CC,* 7 November 1818; "Masonic," *New-England Galaxy and Masonic Magazine,* 7 November 1817. The Boston Marine Society meeting appears in

Nathaniel Spooner, comp., *Gleanings from the Records of the Boston Marine Society, Through Its First Century, 1742–1842* (Boston: Boston Marine Society, 1879), 91. For the Masons' convocation see also *IC,* 7 November 1818; *Centenary of Columbian Lodge A.F. and A.M.* (Boston: By Order of the Lodge, 1895), 104–5.

13. "The Late Fire," *BG,* 9 November 1818; Gallison, "Journal," 86; "Destructive Fire," *CC,* 7 November 1818. For Clay's presence, see *BG,* 2 November 1818; Bentley, *Diary of William Bentley,* 4:557.

14. "Destructive Fire," *CC,* 7 November 1818. On the Billiard Room, see *New-England Galaxy* 7, 14 November 1818. For the role of the town watch taking the alarm, see *Minutes of the Selectmen's Meetings from September 1, 1818, to April 24, 1822,* Records Relating to the Early History of Boston (1909), 48; and Benjamin L. Carp, "Fire of Liberty: Firefighters, Urban Voluntary Culture, and the Revolutionary Movement," *William and Mary Quarterly,* 3rd. ser., 58, no. 4 (October 2001): 783–84. William Brooks's address and occupation appear in Boston Assessors Records for 1818, Ward 8 Valuation Book, 21; *Boston Directory for 1818,* 239. I have reconstructed the order of the alarm bells from John Hales's 1814 map of Boston and the listing of churches in the *Boston Directory for 1818,* 246–47. For the Old South's refusal to ring the alarm, see *BP,* 7 November 1818.

15. Georgia Brady Barnhill, " 'Extracts from the Journals of Ethan A. Greenwood': Portrait Painter and Museum Proprietor," *Proceedings of the American Antiquarian Society* 103, no. 1 (April 1993): 140 ("general alarm"); *Minutes of the Selectmen's Meetings, 1799 to and Including 1810,* Records Relating to the Early History of Boston (1904), 131, 4, 321; Brayley, *Boston Fire Department,* 119. Engine companies were required by town ordinance to meet at least monthly to inspect and ready their equipment. Their duties were deemed significant enough to exempt them from military service and jury duty; see *The By-Laws and Orders of the Town of Boston: Passed at Several Legal Town Meetings* (Boston: Thomas G. Bangs, 1818), 150–52, 155.

16. William C. Hunneman (advertisement), *IC,* 7 November 1808; Greville Bathe and Dorothy Bathe, *Jacob Perkins: His Inventions, His Times, & His Contemporaries* (Philadelphia: Historical Society of Pennsylvania, 1943), 26, 36; Edward R. Tufts, *Hunneman's Amazing Fire Engines: Paul Revere's Apprentice Changed Firefighting in Colonial America* (New Albany, Ind.: Fire House Buff Publishers, 1995), 78.

17. Brayley, *Boston Fire Department,* 111, 118, 105, 393. On the responsibilities and social composition of Boston's municipal fire companies, see also Carp, "Fire of Liberty," 792–98.

18. *Act of Incorporation, Laws, and Regulations, Catalogue of the Members . . . of the Massachusetts Charitable Fire Society* (Boston: Russell & Cutler, 1805), 15; Charles Paine, *An Address Delivered Before the Members of the Massachusetts Charitable Fire Society . . . May 27, 1808* (Boston: Russell & Cutler, 1808), 22. See also Brayley, *Boston Fire Department,* 37–39. From Brayley, the early American imprints collection, and the manuscript records of Boston fire societies in the collections of the Bostonian Society and the MHS, it is possible to assemble at least a partial list of fire companies active ca. 1818, including the Alert Relief, Amicable, Argus, Assistant, Conservative, General Eaton, Philanthropic, Suffolk, Union, True, Volant, and Vigilant clubs. On the class, ethnic, gender, and partisan politics of volunteer fire companies from the Revolution to the Jacksonian period, see Carp, "Fire of Liberty"; Amy S. Greenberg, *Cause for Alarm:*

*The Volunteer Fire Department in the Nineteenth-Century City* (Princeton, N.J.: Princeton University Press, 1998); and Daniel A. Cohen, "Passing the Torch: Boston Firemen, 'Tea Party' Patriots, and the Burning of the Charlestown Convent," *Journal of the Early Republic* 24, no. 4 (Winter 2004): 527–86.

19. *Rules and Regulations of the Attentive Fire Society: Instituted in Boston, April 9, 1810* (Boston: Greenough and Stebbins, 1810), 3, 6–7, 4–5.

20. Gallison, "Journal," 86.

21. "The Exchange Coffee-House," *Intelligencer,* 7 November 1818.

22. Brayley, *Boston Fire Department,* 102; "Destructive Fire," *CC,* 7 November 1818 ("house aqueduct," buckets). For the office of the Aqueduct Corporation Office, see *Boston Directory for 1818,* 30. The selectmen mandated that each public school "have twenty fire buckets"; see *Minutes of the Selectmen's Meetings, September 1818 to April 1822,* 131.

23. "Act providing in case of fire for the more speedy extinguishment thereof" (1711), quoted in Brayley, *Boston Fire Department,* 32 (quotation), 17–18; "The Late Fire," *BG,* 9 November 1818 (Clay in the ranks, fire wards on the spot); "Destruction of the Exchange Coffee House by Fire," *NEP,* 6 November 1818 ("instantly"). On the relative social status of fire wards, fire club members, and engine company men, see also Carp, "Fire of Liberty," 794–96. For a list of those holding this office in 1818, see *Boston Directory for 1818,* 238. The pump appears in Sumner and Bradley, "Exchange Coffee House Architectural Plans," Plan of the Basement Story. On the (sometimes false) trope of the bucket brigade as a "triumph of brotherly solidarity," see Jill Lepore, *New York Burning: Liberty, Slavery, and Conspiracy in Eighteenth-Century Manhattan* (New York: Alfred A. Knopf, 2005), 41–42.

24. *Minutes of the Selectmen's Meetings, 1799–1810,* 86, 307, 320; Brayley, *Boston Fire Department,* 113, 125; "Destructive Fire," *CC,* 7 November 1818.

25. "Destructive Fire," *CC,* 7 November 1818 ("confident hopes"); Gallison, "Journal," 86; "Tremendous Conflagration," *New-England Galaxy,* 6 November 1818 ("not very alarming"); "Extract of a Letter. . . ," [Philadelphia] *Poulson's American Daily Advertiser,* 9 November 1818 ("cheering cry"); *Boston Weekly Messenger,* 5 November 1818 ("bells ceased").

26. "Destructive Fire," *CC,* 7 November 1818.

27. Gallison, "Journal," 87–88. "Destructive Fire," *CC,* 7 November 1818; and "Tremendous Conflagration," *New-England Galaxy,* 6 November 1818, both note the explosive composition of the building's roof; *Boston Weekly Messenger,* 5 November 1818 ("from almost every part"); "The Exchange Coffee-House," *Intelligencer,* 7 November 1818 ("one sheet").

28. "Destructive Fire," *CC,* 7 November 1818 ("so suffocatingly dense"); *Boston Weekly Messenger,* 5 November 1818 (". . . could not be saved"); "The Exchange Coffee-House," *Intelligencer,* 7 November 1818 ("elevated spot . . . out of the capacity"); Spooner, *Records of the Boston Marine Society,* 91. For the secretary's name and occupation, see William A. Baker, *A History of the Boston Marine Society, 1742–1967* (Boston: Boston Marine Society, 1968), 114; and *Boston Directory for 1818,* 36.

29. "Communication: Appropriate Reflections," by Caution [Benjamin Austin?], *IC,* 11 November 1818 ("peals of sonorous solemnity"); John A. Carr to Dabney S. Carr, 6 November 1818, in Carr-Cary Family Papers, 1785–1839, MSS 1231, Tracy

W. McGregor Library of American History, Special Collections, University of Virginia, box 1; Sophia Shuttleworth Simpson, "Two Hundred Years Ago," *Cambridge Historical Society Publications* 16: Proceedings for the Year 1922 (Cambridge, Mass.: Cambridge Historical Society, 1931), 66; *CC,* 14 November 1818 (light visible); "The Exchange Coffee-House," *Intelligencer,* 7 November 1818 ("the whole city . . ."); "Fire at Boston," *New York Evening Post,* 7 November 1818 ("frequently alarmed," "appearance of the light"); Gallison, "Journal," 89; "Tremendous Fire!! Representation of the Exchange Coffee-House in Flames," broadside, (Boston, [1818]), Wilton Historical Society, Wilton, N.H.

30. Gallison, "Journal," 89; "Fire!—Exchange Coffee-House," *Yankee,* 5 November 1818; *Boston Weekly Messenger,* 5 November 1818. For spectators in the windows and along rooftops and other visual details, see Penniman's *Conflagration of the Exchange Coffee-House* (1824). The fire wards comment on the presence of youth at fire scenes in *To the Citizens of the Town of BOSTON.*

31. *Repertory,* 7 November 1818; cards of thanks from the selectmen of Boston, *CC,* 7 November 1818 (engine companies); Wells & Lilly printers, *NEP,* 6 November 1818. For William Hunter, see also *Boston Directory for 1818,* 126.

32. For Bowen, see broadside entitled "Tremendous Fire!!" A week later, Bowen published an engraved version of the print; see *Boston Weekly Magazine,* 14 November 1818. Penniman's membership in the St. John's Lodge is established in Carol Damon Andrews, "John Ritto Penniman (1782–1841), an Ingenious New England Artist," *Antiques* 120, no. 1 (July 1981): 153, 162 n.30. On his "emblematic painting," see also *New England Galaxy,* 6 November 1818; *Centenary of Columbian Lodge,* 94–95, 104–5; John T. Heard, *A Historical Account of Columbian Lodge of Free and Accepted Masons of Boston, Mass.* (Boston: Alfred Mudge, 1856), 219–22. He exhibited his transparency, *The Conflagration of the Exchange Coffee House,* on the anniversary of the fire; *CC,* 3 November 1819.

33. "Destructive Fire," *CC,* 7 November 1818; Gallison, "Journal," 88–89. For items recovered from the fire, see *IC,* 7 November 1818; *BG,* 7 December 1818; *NEP,* 10 November 1818. For fire bags and bed keys, see *Rules and Regulations of the Attentive Fire Society,* 3–4; Donald J. Cannon, ed., *Heritage of Flames: The Illustrated History of Early American Firefighting* (Garden City, N.Y.: Doubleday, 1977), 80.

34. "Destructive Fire," *CC,* 7 November 1818; Gallison, "Journal," 88; Josiah Quincy, *Figures of the Past from the Leaves of Old Journals* (Boston: Roberts Brothers, 1883), 38; "Great Fire," [Hanover, N.H.] *Dartmouth Gazette,* 11 November 1818. Gallison would have known the younger Parsons (1797–1882) from the law offices of William Prescott, where both of them apprenticed, and from the *North American Review,* to which both contributed. See William Ellery Channing, *Memoir of John Gallison, Esq.* (Boston: Wells & Lilly, 1821), 6; Francis Helminski, "Parsons, Theophilus," *American National Biography Online* (February 2000), http://www.anb.org.ezp1.harvard.edu/articles/11/11-00664.html.

35. Gallison, "Journal," 89–91; "Fire!—Exchange Coffee House," *Yankee,* 5 November 1818 ("volcano"); "Tremendous Conflagration," *New-England Galaxy,* 6 November 1818 ("horizontal rockets"); see also "The Exchange Coffee-House," *Intelligencer,* 7 November 1818; *Boston Weekly Messenger,* 5 November 1818.

36. "The Exchange Coffee-House," *Intelligencer,* 7 November 1818.

37. "The Exchange Coffee-House," *Intelligencer,* 7 November 1818; Gallison, "Journal," 91–92; "Destruction of the Exchange Coffee House by Fire," *NEP,* 6 November 1818.

38. "The Exchange Coffee-House," *Intelligencer,* 7 November 1818; "Tremendous Conflagration," *New-England Galaxy,* 6 November 1818. Since the wall righted itself when it cooled, witnesses disputed whether it had in fact leaned into the street. "It is *fact,* that the upper parts of the front walls of the Exchange, from the pressure of the heat in it, was projected a foot or more into Congress-street, but when the pressure ceased, resumed its perpendicular direction," the *Centinel* reported on November 7. See also Gallison, "Journal," 92. On the overornamentation of the eastern elevation for its sight lines, see [Samuel Gilbert and Thomas Dean?], "Description of the Boston Exchange Coffee-House," *Omnium Gatherum* 1, no. 1 (November 1809): 4.

39. Letter from J. Hooper, [New York] *Commercial Advertiser,* 6 November 1818; "Conflagration of the Exchange Coffee-House," *IC,* 7 November 1818.

40. "The Exchange Coffee-House," *Intelligencer,* 7 November 1818 ("danger . . . too great"); "The Late Fire," *BG,* 9 November 1818; *NEP,* 10 November 1818. For the contents of a typical printing office of the day, see Jeffrey L. Pasley, *"The Tyranny of Printers": Newspaper Politics in the Early American Republic* (Charlottesville: University Press of Virginia, 2001), 25–26; and Rollo G. Silver, *The American Printer, 1787–1825* (Charlottesville: University Press of Virginia, 1967), 28–96.

41. Gallison, "Journal," 92–94; recollections of Charles H. Stearn, quoted in "The Exchange Coffee House: The Two Hotels Which Bore the Same Name," undated newspaper clipping from the *Boston Budget,* after 1876, Scrapbook Collection, Bostonian Society, box 10, item 43. Internal cues suggest that the account dates from the late 1870s.

42. Quincy, *Figures of the Past,* 37–39. The college soon closed the fire company for drunken behavior.

43. "Serious Fire," *BG,* 5 November 1818; *To the Citizens of the Town of BOSTON.*

44. "Fire at Boston," *New York Evening Post,* 7 November 1818; "Conflagration of the Exchange Coffee-House," *IC,* 7 November 1818; "Destructive Fire," *CC,* 7 November 1818; N. Sawyer advertisement, *Repertory,* 17 November 1818.

45. The literature on rites of festive inversion is immense, but see especially Natalie Zemon Davis, *Society and Culture in Early Modern France* (Stanford, Calif.: Stanford University Press, 1975) on early modern Europe; and David Waldstreicher, *In the Midst of Perpetual Fetes: The Making of American Nationalism, 1776–1820* (Chapel Hill: University of North Carolina Press, 1997) on the United States.

46. The scene allegorizes Hogarth's view of the Seven Years' War embroiling North America and Europe; William Pitt is the man on stilts, fanning the flames of war. For a detailed reading of Hogarth's allegory, see Ronald Paulson, ed., *Hogarth's Graphic Works,* 3d ed. (London: The Print Room, 1989), 179–80, 410.

47. Gallison, "Journal," 89, 93. For other accounts fixing the conclusion of the blaze around midnight, see *Boston Weekly Messenger,* 5 November 1818; *Intelligencer,* 7 November 1818. 48. *NEP,* 10 November 1818; *Intelligencer,* 7 November 1818.

48. *NEP,* 10 November 1818; *Intelligencer,* 7 November 1818.

49. *Boston Weekly Messenger,* 5 November 1818; "Destructive Fire," *CC,* 7 November

1818. See also Gallison, "Journal," 94. For the identification of Marsh and the Mc-Clennens, see "Tremendous Conflagration," *New-England Galaxy,* 6 November 1818; "The Exchange Coffee-House," *Intelligencer,* 7 November 1818; *Boston Directory for 1818,* 118, 150. The *Centinel's* allusion is to Joseph Addison, *Cato: A Tragedy* (1713), act 5 scene 1:

> The Stars shall fade away, the Sun himself
> Grow dim with Age, and Nature sink in Years;
> But thou shalt flourish in immortal Youth,
> Unhurt amidst the War of Elements,
> The Wrecks of Matter, and the Crush of Worlds.

The play was wildly popular in early national America, and Cato's virtues were strongly associated with the Exchange's patron saint, George Washington; see Meyer Reinhold, *Classica Americana: The Greek and Roman Heritage in the United States* (Detroit: Wayne State University Press, 1984), 98–99; Caroline Winterer, *The Culture of Classicism: Ancient Greece and Rome in American Intellectual Life, 1780–1910* (Baltimore: Johns Hopkins University Press, 2002), 25.

50. "Destructive Fire," *CC,* 7 November 1818.

51. Barnhill, "Extracts from the Journals of Ethan A. Greenwood," 140; see also Gallison, "Journal," 96. The *Centinel, Independent Chronicle,* and *Patriot* all missed their Wednesday issues; the *Repertory* remained unable to publish on Thursday. The *Recorder,* which normally published on Tuesdays and Saturdays, didn't put out a paper until a week after the fire. See especially *New-England Galaxy,* 6 November 1818.

52. Gallison, "Journal," 94; *Boston Weekly Messenger,* 5 November 1818.

53. "Fire at Boston," *New York Evening Post,* 7 November 1818; [New York] *Columbian,* 7 November 1818.

54. For the contents of the Billiard Room, see "Schedule of Furniture &c. Belonging to the Proprietors of the Exchange Coffee House," room 92. The chimney behind the Billiard Room without a hearth; see Sumner and Bradley, "Exchange Coffee House Architectural Plans," plan of the fifth gallery. For arson in Boston, see Brayley, *Boston Fire Department.*

55. "Destruction of the Exchange Coffee House by Fire," *NEP,* 6 November 1818; "Fire at Boston," *New York Evening Post,* 7 November 1818; "The Late Fire," *BG,* 9 November 1818; "Destructive Fire," *CC,* 7 November 1818; "Fires!," [Palmyra, N.Y.] *Palmyra Register,* 17 November 1818.

Though arson for profit was not unknown in early America, the business of fire insurance was in its infancy in the 1810s; see Dalit Baranoff, "Shaped by Risk: The American Fire Insurance Industry, 1790–1820" (Ph.D. dissertation, Johns Hopkins University, 2004), 32–52.

56. *NEP,* 10 November 1818.

57. *Boston Daily Advertiser,* 6, 7 November 1818.

58. Curtis Guild, "Reminiscences of Old Boston or The Exchange Coffee House," bound clippings from the *Commercial Bulletin,* BPL, Rare Books Department (ca. 1872), 3:3. On urban scavenging and the early-nineteenth-century family economy, see Christine Stansell, *City of Women: Sex and Class in New York, 1789–1860* (New York: Alfred A. Knopf, 1986), 50–51, 54.

59. "Tremendous Conflagration," *New-England Galaxy,* 6 November 1818;

"Destructive Fire," *CC*, 7 November 1818. Quilty is identified by name only in *CC*, 11 November 1818.

60. "Fire at Boston," *New York Evening Post*, 7 November 1818; "Fire!—Exchange Coffee House," *Yankee*, 5 November 1818; "Deaths," *CC*, 7 November 1818.

61. *NEP*, 10 November 1818; "Fire at Boston!," *New York Evening Post*, 7 November 1818; "Extract of a Letter. . . ," *Poulson's American Daily Advertiser*, 9 November 1818; *CC*, 7 November 1818.

62. *Rules and Regulations of the Alert Relief Fire Society: Formed in Boston, March, 1815* (Boston: Russell, Cutler, & Co., 1815), 8; advertisements for lost property in *CC*, 18 November 1818; *BG*, 9, 19 November 1818; *IC*, 7 November 1818. For the identification of the advertisers see *Boston Directory for 1818*, 44 (Blake), 112 (Haven).

63. Gallison, "Journal," 96; *Repertory*, 17 November 1818.

64. Lost property advertisements in *BP*, 7, 9 November 1818; *NEP*, 6 November 1818; *Repertory*, 7, 17 November 1818; and *Intelligencer*, 7 November 1818. For occupations, see *Boston Directory for 1818*.

65. *BP*, 7 November 1818; *BG*, 7 December 1818; "Tenement Wanted," *IC*, 11 November 1818, "Communication," *BG*, 5 November 1818. The fire wards' notice appeared in every Boston paper in the issue closest to 7 November 1818.

66. *Boston Weekly Messenger*, 5 November 1818 ("great loser," "effected an insurance"); "Destruction of the Exchange Coffee House by Fire," *NEP*, 6 November 1818 ("expectations blasted"). See also "Destructive Fire," *CC*, 7 November 1818; "The Exchange Coffee-House," *Intelligencer*, 7 November 1818; "Fire at Boston," *New York Evening Post*, 7 November 1818; "The Departed Exchange," *CC*, 11 November 1818.

67. "Destructive Fire," *CC*, 7 November 1818; "Tremendous Conflagration," *New-England Galaxy*, 6 November 1818.

68. "Fire at Boston," *New York Evening Post*, 7 November 1818; "The Late Fire," *BG*, 9 November 1818; "The Departed Exchange," *CC*, 11 November 1818; see also *Boston Weekly Messenger*, 5 November 1818.

69. Letter to the editor, signed E.M., *CC*, 11 November 1818.

70. Letter, signed "P," *BG*, 1 December 1808; "Fire!—Exchange Coffee-House," *Yankee*, 5 November 1818. This anonymous article closely echoes the letter datelined "Boston, Nov. 4th, 1818," which ran in New York's *Commercial Advertiser* on 7 November 1818. The New York version, written earlier and published later, is signed by J. Hooper, who superintended the Exchange's Reading Room.

71. "Fire!—Exchange Coffee-House," *Yankee*, 5 November 1818.

72. "The Departed Exchange," *CC*, 11 November 1818; "The Exchange Coffee-House," *Intelligencer*, 7 November 1818; Guild, "Reminiscences," 2:91. Even the proprietors of the Exchange had given up on it, voting to auction the land and anything else that might fetch a dollar, and then "to close the concern" for good; see "Notice to Proprietors of Exchange Coffee-House," *BP*, 7 November 1818.

73. "The Departed Exchange," *CC*, 11 November 1818. For the location of the Exchange's pigeon house, see Sumner and Bradley, "Exchange Coffee House Architectural Plans," plan of the third gallery. The swirling pigeons can also be seen in Penniman's *Conflagration*.

74. *BG*, 16 November 1818; see also "Conflagration," *The Idiot*, 7 November 1818.

75. *BG,* 16 November 1818.

76. *BG,* 9, 16 November 1818; *Minutes of the Selectmen's Meetings, September 1818 to April 1822,* 20; *Boston Town Records, 1814 to 1822,* Records Relating to the Early History of Boston (1906), 111–12; Brayley, *Boston Fire Department,* 126.

77. "Tremendous Fire!!" broadside (emphasis mine).

78. "The Late Fire," *BG,* 9 November 1818; "The Exchange Coffee-House," *Intelligencer,* 7 November 1818; Caution [Benjamin Austin?], "Communication: Appropriate Reflections," *IC,* 11 November 1818.

79. Caution [Benjamin Austin?], "Communication: Appropriate Reflections," *IC,* 11 November 1818.

80. Harold Kirker, *The Architecture of Charles Bulfinch,* reprint, 1998 (Cambridge, Mass.: Harvard University Press, 1969), 269–70, 293–94, 292, 282–87, 263–65, 311–17; Martha J. McNamara, *From Tavern to Courthouse: Architecture and Ritual in American Law, 1658–1860* (Baltimore: Johns Hopkins University Press, 2004), 83–91; John Morrill Bryan, "Boston's Granite Architecture, c. 1810–1850," (Ph.D. dissertation, Boston University, 1972).

81. David T. Gilchrist, ed., *The Growth of the Seaport Cities, 1790–1825,* Proceedings of a conference sponsored by the Eleutherian Mills-Hagley Foundation, March 17–19, 1966 (Charlottesville: University of Virginia Press, 1967); Henry C. Binford, *The First Suburbs: Residential Communities on the Boston Periphery, 1815–1860* (Chicago: University of Chicago Press, 1985).

82. Guild, "Reminiscences," 2:92; "Great Fire," *Dartmouth Gazette,* 11 November 1818.

83. Caution [Benjamin Austin?], "Communication: Appropriate Reflections," *IC,* 11 November 1818; Guild, "Reminiscences," 2:92.

84. "The Late Fire," *BG,* 9 November 1818; "To Our Creditors and the Public," *CC,* 5 October 1818; *CC,* 15 April 1818; *Boston Directory for 1818,* 100; Guild, "Reminiscences," 2:92.

85. Robert C. Winthrop, ed., "Memoir of Hon. Nathan Appleton," *Proceedings of the Massachusetts Historical Society* 5 (October 1861): 284, 304; "The Reading Room and Marine Diary in the Exchange Coffee House, 1810," *Bostonian Society Publications* 8 (1911): 129. See also Frances W. Gregory, *Nathan Appleton, Merchant and Entrepreneur, 1779–1861* (Charlottesville: University Press of Virginia, 1975), 269–97.

86. Winthrop, "Memoir of Hon. Nathan Appleton," 265, 304–5; A Conservative [Nathan Appleton], *Bank Bills or Paper Currency, and the Banking System of Massachusetts* (Boston: Little, Brown, 1856), 6. See also D. R. Whitney, *The Suffolk Bank* (Cambridge, Mass.: Riverside Press, 1878), 2–7; and Howard Bodenhorn, *State Banking in Early America: A New Economic History* (New York: Oxford University Press, 2003), 95–122.

87. Nathan Appleton, *An Examination of the Banking System of Massachusetts, in Reference to the Renewal of the Bank Charters* (Boston: Stimpson and Clapp, 1831), 12–14; Winthrop, "Memoir of Hon. Nathan Appleton," 284–85, 253; Nathan Appleton to Ebenezer Appleton, 24 October 1818, Appleton Family Papers, MHS, box 3, folder 7. For other transactions placing Appleton in Boston when the Exchange burned, see his account book for 1818, Appleton Family Papers vol. 20.

88. For a list of Benjamin's projects, see Jack Quinan, "Asher Benjamin and Amer-

ican Architecture," *Journal of the Society of Architectural Historians* 38, no. 3 (1979): 253–54. Quinan notes, but does suggest a convincing cause for the gap in his Boston commissions; see John Francis Quinan Jr., "The Architectural Style of Asher Benjamin, a Study in Provincialism" (Ph.D. dissertation, Brown University, 1973), 277–78, 305, 335. Figures for real and personal property come from the Boston Assessors Records: see 1803 tax book 7:4; 1809 tax book 7:4; 1818, tax book 7:n.p. On Benjamin's 1824 bankruptcy, after which he left Massachusetts for several years, see Quinan, "Architectural Style of Asher Benjamin," 359–64; and Anne Elizabeth Macdonald, "Asher Benjamin: Architect, Author, Teacher and Entrepreneur" (unpublished MA thesis, Northeastern University, 1993), 97–101.

Benjamin's role in the town's leading artisans' fraternity seems similarly bifurcated. Before the Exchange, he had cofounded and served for several years as a trustee of the Associated Housewrights Society. Post-Exchange, he took subordinate roles there, missing every meeting of the society in 1810 and 1811, and holding club offices only briefly thereafter. See "Minutes Book, 1804–1837," in Associated Housewrights Society of Boston Records, ser. 6, Massachusetts Charitable Mechanic Association Records, 1791–1995, MHS.

89. *BG,* 17 May 1810; *CC,* 24 November 1810. For the activities of the paint store, and for Benjamin's work for Ward Nicholas Boylston, see "Correspondence between Asher Benjamin and Ward Nicholas Boylston, 1815–1823," box 86, Boylston Family Papers, MHS.

90. *Minutes of the Selectmen's Meetings, September 1818 to April 1822,* 21, 23, 25.

91. "Benj. Austin—Lt. Governor," *IC,* 27 March 1819 ("high flying . . ."); Honestus, [Benjamin Austin], *Observations on the Pernicious Practice of the Law,* reprint, 1786 (Boston: True & Weston, 1819), 45 ("Exchange Alley traffic"); see also Benjamin Austin, *Remarks on a Late Proposition from the Boston and Roxbury Mill Corporation* (Boston: Rowe, 1818). For the lawsuit in which Samuel Dexter represented Austin, see "Benjamin Austin, jun. Esq. against Benjamin Russell, Printer," *CC,* 27 March 1793; *Massachusetts Mercury,* 14 March 1793. The catalog of some of the aspersions "Mr. Austin and other managers of the Chronicle . . . have for years" leveled against Dexter comes from "Reasons Why the Democrats Cannot Vote for Mr. Dexter," *Salem Gazette,* 18 March 1814.

92. "Fire at Boston," *New York Evening Post,* 7 November 1818; Nathaniel Dearborn, *Boston Notions; Being an Authentic and Concise Account of 'That Village,' from 1630 to 1847* (Boston: W. D. Ticknor, 1848), 211 ("brought forth . . . purified"); Austin, *Remarks on a Late Proposition from the Boston and Roxbury Mill Corporation,* 3.

The *Post* article reprints without signature a letter from Boston describing the author's sojourn with "Colonel Austin" in the Old State House. The article contains several internal clues to the anonymous author's identity. He is a tenant in the Old State House with a "key to the upper door." The tax valuation book of 1818 lists nineteen tenants in the building, of whom four had either cellars or street-level shops. The author of "Fire at Boston" was "setting alongside the bed of a sick-friend in Poplar-street" when the alarm bells rang. The only one of the Old State House's remaining fifteen tenants who lived near Poplar Street was the broker Jacob Bender, who lived in the sixth ward, two blocks away on Leverett Street, making Bender the likely author. See Boston Assessors' Records for 1818, valuation book 8:47; *Boston Directory for 1818,* 41. Long an essayist for the *Chronicle,* Austin may well have been the author of the "Caution" editorial, though Caution is not a known Austin pseudonym. But see, for example, the line of argument against self-interested speculation, and the Vesuvius reference, in Austin, *Remarks on a Late Proposition from the Boston and Roxbury Mill Corporation,* 6.

## CHAPTER SIX: PROMETHEUS

1. Charlotte Dexter to Perez and Sarah Morton, 19 April 1819, Morton-Dexter Letters, MHS; M. P. Blue, Jesse Beale, and John Dennis Phelan, *History of Montgomery, Alabama, with a Summary of Events in That History, Calendarically Arranged* (Montgomery, Ala.: T. C. Bingham, 1878), 3.

2. Charlotte Dexter to Perez and Sarah Morton, 19 April 1819, Morton-Dexter Letters, MHS; "Banking, No. 1," [Amherst, N.H.] *Farmer's Cabinet,* 20 March 1810; see also "Joseph Emerson vs. Andrew Dexter Jr.," *CC,* 26 January 1811. For Dexter's residence in River Philip see Andrew Dexter Jr. to John Ware, 2 May 1811, Middlesex Deeds 190: 359–60; and Orrando Perry Dexter, Henry L. Mills, and John Haven Dexter, *Dexter Genealogy, 1642–1904; Being a History of the Descendants of Richard Dexter of Malden, Massachusetts, from the Notes of John Haven Dexter and Original Researches* (New York: J. J. Little, 1904), 125. On the gypsum trade there, and Richard Cunningham's prominent role in it, see Gwendolyn Vaughan Shand, *Historic Hants County* (Halifax, N.S.: Petheric Press, 1979), 26, 79–97. See also Jean Layton, "River Philip: A Study of a Community's Changing Characteristics Through Time" (unpublished paper, Mount Allison University, 1974), esp. 6–9, on the early history of the community.

3. Jessie Rachel van Vechten Vedder, *History of Greene County, New York* (Catskill, N.Y.: Greene County Board of Supervisors, 1927), 19–28; *History of Greene County, New York, with Biographical Sketches of Its Prominent Men* (Cornwallville, N.Y.: Hope Farm Press, 1987), 151–66. (Orig. pub. 1884.) Simon Newton Dexter lived there by November 1811; see Chester Kimball (New London) to Simon Newton Dexter (Athens, N.Y.), 7 November 1811, Simon Newton Dexter Papers, Division of Rare and Manuscript Collections, Cornell University Library, folder 1. Andrew Dexter Sr. was there by December 1812; see Dexter, Mills, and Dexter, *Dexter Genealogy,* 82. Andrew and Charlotte Dexter's residence in Athens can be dated from the baptism of their daughter, Charlotte Sophia, at Trinity Episcopal Church in Athens on November 22, 1812, Episcopal Church Parish Register (copy), Greene County Historical Society, Catskill, N.Y. The sale of Dexter's property to satisfy his creditors, announced in August 1812, makes it likely that the family arrived during the summer; see "To Be Sold at Public Auction," [Hudson, N.Y.] *Northern Whig* 10, 24 August 1812.

4. For the Dexter family's Athens landholdings, see "Assessment Roll of 1813 for Greene County, New York," typescript, Greene County Historical Society, 11. Andrew Dexter's personal property, including "one Black child," is enumerated in "Inventory of Andrew Dexter [Sr.]," 13 June 1817, Greene County Surrogate's Court, box 97, packet 2437, Greene County Historical Society. For the elder Dexter's worries over his sheep, see Andrew Dexter Sr. to Jonathan Russell, 10 January 1814, box: "Desbassyns, Ph through Dortic, John," Jonathan Russell Papers, John Hay Library, Brown University.

5. "To Be Sold at Public Auction," *Northern Whig,* 10, 24, 31 August 1812; 8 March 1814. These sales were governed by "An Act for the Benefit of Insolvent Debtors and Their Creditors," *1811 N.Y. Laws 123.* For Dexter's property holding and loans from his father, see "Assessment Roll of 1813 for Greene County, New York"; "Inventory of Andrew Dexter [Sr.]," 13 June 1817, lists $1,280 due from Andrew Dexter Jr. at his father's death.

6. For Dexter's various enterprises ca. 1812–1817, see Dexter, Mills, and Dexter, *Dexter Genealogy,* 125–26; *History of Greene County,* 121; "Lands for Sale," *Northern Whig,* 29 March 1814. For the meaning of rural pursuits among urban gentlemen, see Tamara Plakins Thornton, *Cultivating Gentlemen: The Meaning of Country Life Among the Boston Elite, 1785–1860* (New Haven, Conn.: Yale University Press, 1989). Academy education spurred the ambition deemed crucial for commercial success; see J. M. Opal, "Exciting Emulation: Academies and the Transformation of the Rural North, 1780s–1820s," *Journal of American History* 91, no. 2 (September 2004): 445–70.

7. Charlotte Dexter to Frances Morton, June 1815; Charlotte Dexter to Sarah Morton, 31 August 1813; Charlotte Dexter to "my dear Pupils," 29 April 1815; Morton-Dexter Letters, MHS.

8. Charlotte Dexter to Sarah Morton, 31 August 1813.

9. *Northern Whig,* 23 April 1816; Dexter, Mills, and Dexter, *Dexter Genealogy,* 126.

10. Inventory of Samuel Dexter, 24 June 1816, Suffolk County Probate Record Books, MArch, 114: 429–38. For Samuel Dexter's death, see *Northern Whig,* 7 May 1816; Joseph Story, *Sketch of the Life of Samuel Dexter* (Boston: J. Eliot, 1816), 12–13. On the settlement of the Yazoo claims, see C. Peter Magrath, *Yazoo: Law and Politics in the New Republic* (Providence, R.I.: Brown University Press, 1966), 82–83, 97–99.

11. "Inventory of the Estate of Andrew Dexter [Sr.]"

12. Malcolm J. Rohrbough, *The Land Office Business: The Settlement and Administration of American Public Lands, 1789–1837* (New York: Oxford University Press, 1968), 115–18 (quotation at 115); Daniel Feller, *The Public Lands in Jacksonian Politics* (Madison, Wisc.: University of Wisconsin Press, 1984), 15; *Niles' Weekly Register,* 5 April 1817. See also Albert Burton Moore, *History of Alabama* (University, Ala.: University Supply Store, 1934), 75–77; J. Mills Thornton III, *Politics and Power in a Slave Society: Alabama, 1800–1860* (Baton Rouge: Louisiana State University Press, 1978), 10.

13. "The Times," by Economicus [pseud.], *Carolina Centinel* 12 June 1819; J. Van Fenstermaker, *The Development of American Commercial Banking, 1782–1837* (Kent, Ohio: Kent State University / Bureau of Economic and Business Research, 1965), Appendix A; Daniel Dupre, *Transforming the Cotton Frontier: Madison County, Alabama, 1800–1840* (Baton Rouge: Louisiana State University Press, 1997), 42–43; Feller, *The Public Lands in Jacksonian Politics,* 18–22; Howard Bodenhorn, *State Banking in Early America: A New Economic History* (New York: Oxford University Press, 2003), 219–48, 252.

14. Blue, Beale, and Phelan, *History of Montgomery, Alabama,* 6; Billie Riley Capell, *Early Land Patents of Montgomery County, Alabama* (Montgomery, Ala.: Montgomery Genealogical Society, 2001), 83–88; Clanton Ware Williams, "History of Montgomery, Alabama, 1817–1846" (Ph.D. dissertation, Vanderbilt University, 1938), 46–53. For

the pace of bidding, see John Taylor and Alexander Pope to Josiah Meigs, 2 August 1817, in Edwin Clarence Carter, ed., *The Territory of Alabama,* vol. 18 of *The Territorial Papers of the United States* [hereafter *TPUS*] (Washington, D.C.: U.S. Government Printing Office, 1952), 132–33.

15. William B. Hesseltine and Larry Gara, eds., "Across Georgia and Into Alabama, 1817–1818," *Georgia Historical Quarterly* 37, no. 4 (December 1953): 333–35. See also "Diary of Richard Breckenridge, 1816," *Transactions of the Alabama Historical Society* 3 (1898–1899): 142–53. On the Federal Road, see Henry DeLeon Southerland Jr. and Jerry Elijah Brown, *The Federal Road Through Georgia, the Creek Nation, and Alabama, 1806–1836* (Tuscaloosa: University of Alabama Press, 1989); Thomas Perkins Abernethy, *The Formative Period in Alabama, 1815–1828* (University, Ala.: University of Alabama Press, 1965), 17–27; and Peter A. Brannon, *Adventures on the High Road: Here and There in Alabama* (Montgomery, Ala.: Paragon Press, 1930), 49–50.

16. Hesseltine and Gara, "Across Georgia and Into Alabama, 1817–1818," 334–35; Karl Bernard, *Travels Through North America, During the Years 1825 and 1826, by His Highness, Bernhard, Duke of Saxe-Weimar Eisenach* (Philadelphia: Carry, Lea & Carey, 1828), 2: 30; John Read to Josiah Meigs, 4 September 1817, *TPUS: Alabama,* 144–45; "From the Montgomery Mail, Nov. 24, 1858—Letter from J. K. Klinck, of Tennessee," *Alabama Historical Quarterly* 18, no. 1 (Spring 1956): 35. Weekly stage service between Milledgeville and Montgomery began in January 1821; see Clanton Ware Williams, "History of Montgomery," 113.

17. "Letter from J. K. Klinck," 35; Clanton Ware Williams, "History of Montgomery," 16–18, 27–28.

18. [Huntsville] *Alabama Republican,* 14 August 1817, quoted in Clanton Ware Williams, "History of Montgomery," 51–52; see also Stuart Seely Sprague, "Alabama Town Production During the Era of Good Feelings," *Alabama Historical Quarterly* 36, no. 1 (Spring 1974): 15–20.

19. Col. A. J. Pickett, "Montgomery's History, 1852," *Montomery Advertiser,* 14 March 1937; Hesseltine and Gara, "Across Georgia and Into Alabama, 1817–1818," 336. On the other investments of the Alabama Town promoters, see Sprague, "Alabama Town Production," 18–19. See also W. Brewer, *Alabama: Her History, Resources, War Record, and Public Men from 1540 to 1872* (Montgomery, Ala.: Barrett & Brown, 1872), 447; *Northern Alabama: Historical and Geographical* (Birmingham, Ala.: Smith & DeLand, 1888), 575–76.

20. "New Towns in the West, &c.," *Richmond Enquirer,* 14 August 1818.

21. On the topography and value of the "big bend" lands, see Clanton Ware Williams, "History of Montgomery," 80.

22. John Gallison, "Journal, Volume K," Boston Athenaeum, 134 (entry for 5 January 1819); Curtis Guild, "Reminiscences of Old Boston or The Exchange Coffee House," bound clippings from the *Commercial Bulletin,* BPL, Rare Books Department (ca. 1872), 2: 90. For other accounts of hot coals lingering in the ruins, see *Connecticut Gazette,* 9 December 1818; [Natchez] *Mississippi Republican,* 9 February 1819. For references to the ruins in maps and directions, see John Groves Hales, *Maps of the Street-Lines of Boston Made for the Selectmen in 1819 and 1820* (Boston: Rockwell & Churchill, 1894), 3, 41, 45; "Both Hands Full!" *BG,* 28 January 1819; "Boston Soda & Rochelle Establishment," *BG,* 3 June 1819.

23. Charlotte Dexter to Sarah and Perez Morton, 19 April 1819, Morton-Dexter Letters, MHS. That Alfred stayed behind is established conclusively by Samuel Dexter to Andrew Dexter Jr., 13 August 1821, Dexter Family Papers, 1821–1941, ADAH. That Samuel and Sophia accompanied Charlotte south is suggested by the fact that Samuel Dexter sends his love to his brother Andrew "and the children," asking him to "give them each a [torn] for me and tell them not to forget this yankee unckle."

24. "Letter from J. K. Klinck," 37.

25. "John Owen's Journal of His Removal from Virginia to Alabama in 1818," *Publications of the Southern History Association* 1, no. 2 (April 1897): 93; David Brearley to Andrew Jackson, 21 February 1818; Israel Pickens to Josiah Meigs, 4 April 1818 (quotations); David Brearley to Andrew Jackson, 20 February 1818, in Carter, *TPUS: Alabama,* 262–63, 293–94. See also Southerland and Brown, *The Federal Road,* 57–60.

26. His instructions are discussed in Samuel Dexter to Andrew Dexter Jr., 13 August 1821, Dexter Family Papers, folder 1, ADAH. Samuel Dexter had been unable to "find the captain by whom you wished me to send him" and promised to ship the boy out the following fall "by some vessel that will go from here to Blakely or Mobile."

27. Abernethy, *The Formative Period in Alabama,* 91–94; Clanton Ware Williams, "History of Montgomery," 111–12; Blue, Beale, and Phelan, *History of Montgomery, Alabama,* 13–14.

28. Bernard, *Travels Through North America,* 2:30; Clanton Ware Williams, "History of Montgomery," 74–84; Pickett, "Montgomery's History, 1852." For the post office, see "Table of Post Offices," Carter, *TPUS: Alabama,* 507–9. This census of buildings refers to late 1820, so the number when Charlotte Dexter got there would have been smaller still. East Alabama, which combined with New Philadelphia in December 1819 to form Montgomery, had twenty buildings in total.

29. All these activities are based on the assumption that the early ordinances of the city indicate the presence of the behaviors they proscribe; see Clanton W. Williams, ed., "Extracts from the Records of the City of Montgomery, Alabama, 1820–1821," *Alabama Review* 1, no. 2 (April 1948): 131, 133–34, 136–39.

30. Bernard, *Travels Through North America* 2: 31–32; Clanton Ware Williams, "History of Montgomery," 80–86; Margaret Humphreys, *Yellow Fever and the South* (New Brunswick, N.J.: Rutgers University Press, 1992), 18–22.

31. Harriet E. Amos, *Cotton City: Urban Development in Antebellum Mobile* (Tuscaloosa: University of Alabama Press, 2001), 6, 90; Sarah Wentworth Morton, *My Mind and Its Thoughts, in Sketches, Fragments, and Essays,* reprint, 1823 (Delmar, N.Y.: Scholars' Facsimiles & Reprints, 1975), 282. On the epidemiology of yellow fever, see Humphreys, *Yellow Fever and the South,* 4–7. For the date of Charlotte Dexter's death, see Dexter, Mills, and Dexter, *Dexter Genealogy,* 124; and *CC,* 22 September 1819.

32. Morton, *My Mind and Its Thoughts,* 282–83; Clanton Ware Williams, "History of Montgomery," 94; Blue, Beale, and Phelan, *History of Montgomery, Alabama,* 6–7. Worshipers are known to have assembled in Vickers' Tavern on other occasions in 1819; see Pickett, "Montgomery's History, 1852." Charlotte Dexter's gravestone lies

in Montgomery's Old Oakwood Cemetery, called the "old graveyard" or "Scott free burying ground" in Dexter's day. The stone refers to New Philadelphia as Montgomery, a name the town didn't acquire until December 1819. Thomas Oliver IV, *Old Oakwood Cemetery: A Brief History* ([Montgomery, Ala.]: The Society of Pioneers of Montgomery, 1986), 4–7. A surviving abstract from the Alabama Territorial Census of 1818 shows that in Montgomery *County,* adult white men outnumbered adult white women by roughly 144:100; Carter, *TPUS: Alabama,* 462. No census of the city of New Philadelphia survives.

33. Bernard, *Travels Through North America,* 2: 32. The occupational structure of the town is detailed in *Montgomery Republican,* 17 February 1821.

34. "Letter from J. K. Klinck," 38. Klinck maintained that Dexter's Montgomery was named "after the county," which in turn was named for Major Lemuel Purnell Montgomery, a southern military man who fell at the Battle of Horseshoe Bend—the decisive engagement of the Creek war—on March 27, 1814. But virtually all contemporary sources point to Richard Montgomery as the town's, and Dexter's, Montgomery; see Clanton Ware Williams, "History of Montgomery," 72–73, 75; and *Montgomery Republican,* 6 January 1821. On the cult of Montgomery's martyrdom, see *Niles' Weekly Register,* 11 July 1818; see also the five-page narrative of the reburial in *Niles' Weekly Register,* 25 July 1818, 371–75; and Michael Meranze, "Major André's Exhumation," in *Mortal Remains: Death in Early America,* eds. Nancy Isenberg and Andrew Burstein (Philadelphia: University of Pennsylvania Press, 2003), 123–35.

35. Andrew Dexter Jr., *An Oration, on the Importance of Science and Religion, Particularly to American Youth* (Providence, R.I., 1798), 8.

36. "The Times," by Economicus [pseud.], *Carolina Centinel,* 12 June 1819; Dupre, *Transforming the Cotton Frontier,* 48–71. For cotton prices ca. 1815–1830, see Abernethy, *The Formative Period in Alabama,* 83–84. On the causes and consequences of the panic of 1819 nationwide, see Murray N. Rothbard, *The Panic of 1819: Reactions and Policies* (New York: Columbia University Press, 1962); Samuel Rezneck, "The Depression of 1819–1822: A Social History," *American Historical Review* 39, no. 1 (October 1933): 28–47; Sarah A. Kidd, "The Search for Moral Order: The Panic of 1819 and the Culture of the Early American Republic" (Ph. D. dissertation, University of Missouri-Columbia, 2002); and Scott A. Sandage, *Born Losers: A History of Failure in America* (Cambridge, Mass.: Harvard University Press, 2005), 22–43.

37. *Alabama Journal,* 12 September 1828; see also 1 September 1826; Thomas Hamilton, "Men and Manners in America" (1833), in Walter Brownlow Posey, ed., *Alabama in the 1830s as Recorded by British Travellers* (Birmingham, Ala.: Birmingham-Southern College, 1938), 12–13. For wealth and population statistics, see Clanton Ware Williams, "History of Montgomery," 83–85, 111–12; Clanton W. Williams, "Conservatism in Old Montgomery," *Alabama Review* 10, no. 2 (April 1957): 99–100; and Clanton Ware Williams, "Early Ante-Bellum Montgomery: A Black-Belt Constituency," *Journal of Southern History* 7, no. 4 (November 1941): 498–99, 512–13.

38. Tyrone Power, *Impressions of America; During the Years 1833, 1834, and 1835* (Philadelphia: Carey, Lea & Blanchard, 1836), 2: 100–101; Clanton Ware Williams, "History of Montgomery," 84.

39. *Alabama Journal,* 15 September 1826; Blue, Beale, and Phelan, *History of Montgomery, Alabama,* 9–22.

40. *Alabama Journal,* 4 November 1825; 30 June, 15 September 1826; 8 February, 13 June, 31 October 1828; 24 April 1829. See also Blue, Beale, and Phelan, *History of Montgomery, Alabama,* 9–22.

41. Clanton Ware Williams, "Extracts from the Records of the City of Montgomery," 138–39; *Alabama Journal,* ca. 1825–1833. On the evolution of slave society in Alabama, see J. Mills Thornton III, *Politics and Power in a Slave Society.*

42. Bernard, *Travels Through North America* 2:30–32; "Letter from J. K. Klinck," 39.

43. Bernard, *Travels Through North America* 2:31–32; "Letter from J. K. Klinck," 39; Thomas S. Woodward, *Woodward's Reminiscences of the Creek, or Muscogee Indians, Contained in Letters to Friends in Georgia and Alabama* (Montgomery, Ala.: Barrett & Wimbish, 1859), 134.

44. Samuel Dexter to Andrew Dexter Jr., 13 August 1821, Dexter Family Papers folder 1, ADAH.

45. Sarah Morton to Andrew Dexter, September 1825, Morton-Dexter Letters, MHS.

46. Wallace W. Screws [presumed author], William Warren Rogers, ed., "Andrew Dexter: Founder of Montgomery," *Alabama Historical Quarterly* 43, no. 3 (Fall 1981): 163, 165–66, 169. (Orig. pub. 19 March 1871.) For this sketch, which appeared in the *Montgomery Advertiser,* 12 March 1871, Screws appears to have relied heavily on the Blue Papers, ADAH.

Census data from early Alabama are frustratingly scarce, and frustratingly silent where Dexter is concerned. A territorial census taken in 1818 enumerates Montgomery County but does not include a schedule of its inhabitants; see Carter, *TPUS: Alabama,* 462. The manuscript schedules of the Federal Census of 1820 for twenty-one of Alabama's twenty-nine counties were destroyed, and Montgomery is not among the eight counties whose data survive; see "Alabama Census Returns 1820 and an Abstract of the Federal Census of Alabama 1830," *Alabama Historical Quarterly* 6, no. 3 (Fall 1944), esp. 332–33. Dexter is not enumerated in the schedules of the Federal Census of 1830 in either Montgomery County or Mobile County.

47. *Montgomery Republican,* 12 May 1821; Screws and Rogers, "Andrew Dexter," 168. See also Clanton Ware Williams, "History of Montgomery," 52–57. For Dexter's ceaseless land purchases, sales, and mortgages, see Montgomery County Probate Judge, Records of Conveyances, Containers LGM 82–83, ADAH.

48. *Alabama Journal,* 8 February 1828.

49. *Alabama Journal,* 15 August 1828. On the contested meanings of power in Jacksonian ideology, see Harry L. Watson, *Liberty and Power: The Politics of Jacksonian America* (New York: Noonday Press, 1990). For the role of Indian affairs and land policies in the regional politics of 1824–1829, see Abernethy, *The Formative Period in Alabama,* 135–51; and Feller, *The Public Lands in Jacksonian Politics,* 71–111.

50. *Alabama Journal,* 15 August 1828.

51. *Alabama Journal,* 15 August 1828; "No. I," by Andrew Dexter Jr., *Alabama Journal,* 22 August 1828.

52. "No. II," by Andrew Dexter Jr., *Alabama Journal,* 5 September 1828; "No. I," by Andrew Dexter Jr., *Alabama Journal,* 22 August 1828. Part 3 of this five-part series does not survive. The *Journal*'s 12 September 1828 issue announced that part 3 would

be inevitably "laid over until next week," but only a partial paper survives for 19 September 1828, neither does the essay appear in the 26 September or 3 October issues.

53. "No. IV," by Andrew Dexter Jr., *Alabama Journal*, 10 October 1828; "For the *Alabama Journal*," by Andrew Dexter Jr., *Alabama Journal*, 24 October 1828. For Dexter as secretary of the Montgomery auxiliary of the Alabama Bible Society, see *Alabama Journal*, 4 December 1829.

54. Andrew Dexter Jr., *On the Importance of Science and Religion*, 6; "For the *Alabama Journal*," by Andrew Dexter Jr., *Alabama Journal*, 24 October 1828.

55. *Alabama Journal*, 15 August 1828, 19 June 1829; Abernethy, *The Formative Period in Alabama*, 148.

56. Samuel Dexter to Andrew Dexter Jr., 13 August 1821, Dexter Family Papers, folder 1, ADAH.

57. Sarah Wentworth Morton to Andrew Dexter Jr., September 1825, Morton-Dexter Letters, MHS. My surmise that Alfred Dexter apprenticed to Simon Newton Dexter in the 1820s is based on the close relationship between the two evinced in various family letters in the Dexter Family Papers (ADAH) and the Simon Newton Dexter Papers, Cornell University Library. For Simon Newton Dexter's involvement in canal building, see Dexter, Mills, and Dexter, *Dexter Genealogy*, 130–31.

58. Andrew Alfred Dexter to Simon Newton Dexter, 20 July 1827, Simon Newton Dexter Papers, folder 2, Cornell University Library.

59. See Samuel Dexter to Charlotte Sophia Dexter, 31 January 1836, Dexter Family Papers, folder 1, ADAH. Andrew Dexter granted his son Samuel power of attorney over his lands in Montgomery in July 1834; Montgomery County Probate Judge Record of Conveyances, LGM 83, reel 2, vol. O, 373–74. See also Dexter, Mills, and Dexter, *Dexter Genealogy*, 122.

60. Sarah Morton to Andrew Dexter, September 1825, Morton-Dexter Letters, MHS. For the Morton family activities in the summer of 1825, see Walter Muir Whitehill, "Perez Morton's Daughter Revisits Boston in 1825," *Proceedings of the Massachusetts Historical Society* 82 (1970): 21–47. Sophia does not appear to have been with Sarah Morton and her daughter, Sarah Cunningham, when the two visited Gilbert Stuart's studio in August and saw the unfinished portrait of Charlotte Dexter; see Sarah A. Cunningham to Griselda Cunningham, 11 August 1825, Morton-Cunningham-Clinch Family Papers, MHS.

61. Louisa Morton to Charlotte Sophia Dexter, 1 June 1838; Louisa Morton to Charlotte Sophia Dexter, 20 May 1840; Andrew Alfred Dexter to Charlotte Sophia Dexter, 24 August 1844; all in Dexter Family Papers, folder 1, ADAH. Sophia was boarding with a Mrs. Bench in Fort Decatur, Alabama, in 1831 (Andrew Alfred Dexter to Charlotte Sophia Dexter, 9 April 1831); with the Mortons in Boston in 1836 (Samuel Dexter to Charlotte Sophia Dexter, 31 January 1836); with a "Mr. Williams" in Aiken, South Carolina, in 1838 (Louisa Morton to Charlotte Sophia Dexter, 1 June 1838); and with Samuel Dexter in Providence in 1844 (Andrew Alfred Dexter to Charlotte Sophia Dexter, 24 August 1844). According to Dexter, Mills, and Dexter, *Dexter Genealogy*, 122, she died unmarried. But Simon Newton Dexter refers to her recent marriage in Providence in his letter to Andrew Alfred Dexter, 25 November 1852. All letters in Dexter Family Papers, folder 1, ADAH.

62. Woodward, *Woodward's Reminiscences,* 94 (quotation), see also 42, 77, 89, 91; Samuel Monac [*sic*] to Andrew Dexter, 27 November 1827, Montgomery Probate Judge, Miscellaneous Records Conveyances, LGM 82, vol. B, 1. The price Dexter paid, $1.25 per acre, reflects the minimum price established by the Land Law of April 1820; see Rohrbough, *The Land Office Business,* 140–44. On the long history of colonial mistranslations between native beliefs in usufruct rights to land and English insistence on fee simple ownership, see William Cronon, *Changes in the Land: Indians, Colonists, and the Ecology of New England* (New York: Hill and Wang, 1983).

63. Dexter, Mills, and Dexter, *Dexter Genealogy,* 127; "Great Freshet," *Alabama Journal,* 3 September 1831. No issues of the *Alabama Journal* between April 1830 and April 1831 survive.

64. Samuel Dexter to Charlotte Sophia Dexter, 31 January 1836; Archie P. McDonald, comp., *Nacogdoches: Wilderness Outpost to Modern City, 1779–1979* (Burnet, Tex.: Eakin Press, 1980).

65. Samuel Dexter to Charlotte Sophia Dexter, 31 January 1836. Dexter's "Interesting Letter from Nacogdoches, Texas," dated August 1832, was printed in the [Montgomery] *Planters' Gazette,* 16 October 1832, according to "Montgomery in 1832," *Montgomery Daily Post,* 24 March 1860. Only scattered issues of the *Planters' Gazette* survive.

66. "Destructive Fire," *CC,* 17 November 1819 ("*wooden* part of town"); Nathan Negus "Memorandum Book," entries for 13–18 October 1819, Papers of Nathan Negus and Negus Family, Archives of American Art, reel 611. For Negus's apprenticeship to Penniman, see also Jessica Nicoll, " 'The Real Pioneer of Art in This City': Charles Codman and the Rise of Landscape Painting in Portland, Maine," in *Charles Codman: The Landscape of Art and Culture in 19th-Century Maine,* ed. Caroline F. Sloat (Portland, Me.: Portland Museum of Art, 2002), 12–17. For Penniman's drinking see Carol Damon Andrews, "John Ritto Penniman (1782–1841), an Ingenious New England Artist," *Antiques* 120, no. 1 (July 1981): 154–55. Penniman's residence is established in the *Boston Directory for 1818,* 168.

67. A search in the digital edition of the Early American Newspapers collection for news stories headlined HARD TIMES in the year 1819 yields 245 results. See esp. "Hard Times," [Worcester] *Massachusetts Spy,* 2 June 1819 (quotation); "Hard Times," *CC,* 26 June, 3 July, and 7 October 1819. On the impact of the panic of 1819 in Boston more generally, see Andrew R. L. Cayton, "The Fragmentation of 'A Great Family': The Panic of 1819 and the Rise of the Middling Interest in Boston, 1818–1822," *Journal of the Early Republic* 2, no. 2 (Summer 1982): 143–67.

68. Negus "Memorandum Book," 26 October 1819. On transparencies, see Peter Benes, *American Rarities: Itinerant Callings and the Reshaping of Culture in Early New England* (Boston: Dublin Seminar and Boston University Scholarly Publications, forthcoming), chap. 21; and Edward Orme, *An Essay on Transparent Prints, and on Transparencies in General* (London: J. G. Barnard, 1807).

69. Negus "Memorandum Book," entries for 26 October through 2 November 1819; Georgia Brady Barnhill, " 'Extracts from the Journals of Ethan A. Greenwood': Portrait Painter and Museum Proprietor," *Proceedings of the American Antiquarian Society* 103, no. 1 (April 1993): 141, 144 (quotation).

70. "Exchange Coffee-House," "Fire! Fire!! Fire!!!," *CC,* 3 November 1819.

71. Negus "Memorandum Book," 3 November 1819; "Splendid Transparent Painting," *BG*, 11 November 1819.

72. Negus "Memorandum Book," 25 December 1819; "Conflagration of the Exchange Coffee-House," *CC*, 10 November 1819; "New Exhibition and Transparent View of the Burning of the Late Exchange Coffee-House," *BG*, 13 January 1820. The second transparency was still showing in June 1820; see "Artillery Election, Grand Illumination," *IC*, 3 June 1820.

73. *BP*, 10 November 1818; *Boston Weekly Magazine*, 14 November 1818. Barnum's auction of the Exchange Coffee House furniture is advertised in *BG*, 22 July 1819. On the Staffordshire pattern, see Hayden Goldberg, "Two Newly Identified American Views on Historical Blue Staffordshire," *The Magazine Antiques* 125:1 (January 1984), 281–83.

74. For comparisons of the Exchange conflagration to the Richmond Theater Fire and the Capitol in ruins, see *NEP*, 6 November 1818; *IC*, 7, 11 November 1818; and *London Chronicle*, 12 December 1818. Gruesome images of the fire in Richmond, which killed scores of people, can be found in *The Burning of the Theatre in Richmond, Virginia, on the Night of the 26th. December 1811 . . .* (Philadelphia: B. Tanner); *Calamity at Richmond, Being a Narrative of the Affecting Circumstances Attending the Awful Conflagration of the Theatre, in the City of Richmond . . .* (Philadelphia: John F. Watson, 1812), frontispiece; *Distressing Calamity: A Brief Account of the Late Fire at Richmond* (Boston: Nathaniel Coverly, 1812), title page. For images of the Capitol in flames or in ruins, see "View of the Capitol of the United States, After the Conflagration, in 1814," frontispiece to Jesse Torre, *A Portraiture of Domestic Slavery in the United States* (Philadelphia, 1817); and *The Taking of the City of Washington* (London: G. Thompson, 1814). For Joseph Gandy's and Sir John Soane's watercolors of the Bank of England in ruins, see *Visions of Ruin: Architectural Fantasies and Designs for Garden Follies* (London: Sir John Soane's Museum, 1999), 28, 38–39, 46–47; and Daniel M. Abramson, *Building the Bank of England: Money, Architecture, Society, 1694–1942* (New Haven, Conn., and London: Yale University Press, 2005), 193–96.

75. For later images, see Caleb H. Snow, *A History of Boston, the Metropolis of Massachusetts, from Its Origin to the Present Period* (Boston: Abel Bowen, 1828), illustration facing p. 330; John Howard Hinton, *The History and Topography of the United States*, 2 vols. (London: J. T. Hinton and Simpkin and Marshall, 1830–32), frontispiece to vol. 2. For building views on porcelain, see Ellouise Baker Larsen, *American Historical Views on Staffordshire China* (1939; reprint New York: Dover, 1975).

76. "Old Exchange Coffee-House," *CC*, 18 December 1819; map in SD 266:51. The smallest of the lots measured 941 square feet, the largest 1,550.

77. *CC*, 29 December 1819; Proprietors of the Exchange Coffee House [ECH] to James Prince, 5 January 1820, SD 268:131–33; Proprietors of the ECH to John Parker, 5 January 1820, SD 266:57–58; Proprietors of the ECH to Edward H. Robbins Jr., 5 January 1820, SD 266:52–54. For Edward H. Robbins Sr.'s original landholdings on the block, see *The Statistics of the United States' Direct Tax of 1798, as Assessed on Boston*, Records Relating to the Early History of Boston (1890), 316–17; Thomas W. Sumner and W. Bradley, "Exchange Coffee House Architectural Plans," Bostonian Society (1817), plate 1.

78. Guild, "Reminiscences," 3:3; *BG*, 7 February, 11 May 1820. The sales are

recorded in Proprietors of the ECH to Edward H. Robbins Jr., 5 January 1820, SD 266:52–54; Edward H. Robbins Jr. to John D. Williams [for Proprietors of the ECH], 5 January 1820, SD 266:55–56. Compare John Coates to Andrew Dexter Jr., 7 October 1806, SD 217:158–59.

79. "Proposals for Forming a Company to Purchase the 'Exchange Coffee House,'" *CC*, 12 July 1809; *BP*, 7 November 1818; *CC*, 11, 14 November 1818; "Exchange Coffee House Land," *IC*, 18 November 1818.

80. See "New Exchange Coffee-House," by Public Good [pseud.], *BG*, 28 December 1818; "The Town of Boston," *IC*, 28 November 1818; "Letter," *IC*, 18 November 1818; "Exchange Coffee House," *BG*, 18 January 1819.

81. "Letter," *IC*, 18 November 1818; *BG*, 19 November 1818. See also "New Exchange Coffee-House," *BG*, 28 December 1818.

82. *BG*, 19 November 1818; "Town of Boston," *IC*, 28 November 1818; "New Exchange Coffee-House," by Public Good [pseud.], *BG*, 28 December 1818.

83. "Letter," *IC*, 18 November 1818; *BG*, 19 November 1818; "Exchange Coffee House," *Boston Weekly Messenger*, 19 November 1818.

84. "The Town of Boston," *IC*, 28 November 1818; "New Exchange Hotel," *BG*, 21 January 1819; "New Exchange Coffee-House," *BG*, 28 December 1818; "New Exchange Coffee House," *BG*, 31 December 1818; "Exchange Coffee House," *BG*, 18 January 1819; "Interesting Notice. New Exchange Coffee House," *IC*, 23 January 1819.

85. Lots 1 through 5, lying along Congress Street, sold for an average of $3.69 per square foot; lots 6 through 11, bordering Salter's Court and Devonshire Street, averaged $1.54; see *CC*, 29 December 1819. For Robbins's request to widen Congress Street, see *Minutes of the Selectmen's Meetings from September 1, 1818, to April 24, 1822*, Records Relating to the Early History of Boston (1909), 121, 127–28, 181–82. The gable end of this block of stores is visible on the left side of an Exchange Coffee House trade card, ca. 1836–1840, reprinted in Sally Pierce and Catharina Slautterback, *Boston Lithography 1825–1880: The Boston Athenaeum Collection* (Boston: Boston Athenaeum, 1991), plate 42. That these were "warehouses" is confirmed by "New Bank Building. Reminiscences of the Old Exchange Coffee House," unidentified newspaper clipping, Scrapbook Collection, Bostonian Society (Boston, 1878), vol. Z, 86–1.

86. The Branch Bank's new location was announced in *CC*, 2 September 1820. I have compiled a list of the other tenants in Congress Square from the *Boston Directory for 1822*.

87. "Exchange Coffee House," *CC*, 2 January 1822; Pierce and Slautterback, *Boston Lithography*, plate 42. The size of the footprint is established by the map of property lines in SD 266:51. I have estimated the height of the building, relative to its 72-foot length, from the Pendleton lithograph.

88. "The Exchange Coffee House, Congress Square," *CC*, 2 January 1822; see also "Exchange Coffee House," *Baltimore Patriot*, 18 July 1822.

89. *IC*, 28 August, 1 September, 24 November 1824; 30 July 1825; *Middlesex Gazette*, 3 August 1825; *New Hampshire Gazette*, 15 February, 11 October 1825; *Baltimore Patriot*, 20 July 1824; 13 September, 25 November 1828. Announcements of shareholders' and club meetings appear regularly in advertising pages of the *Boston Gazette*. For the popularity of the noon meal with merchants, see "The

Exchange Coffee House: The Two Hotels Which Bore the Same Name," undated newspaper clipping from the *Boston Budget,* after 1876, Scrapbook Collection, Bostonian Society.

90. "Exchange Coffee House," *Baltimore Patriot & Mercantile Advertiser,* 11 May 1829; *Bowen's Picture of Boston, of the Citizen's and Stranger's Guide to the Metropolis of Massachusetts, and Its Environs* (Boston: Otis, Broaders & Company, 1838), 204–206; *Bowen's New Guide to the City of Boston and Vicinity* (Boston: James Munroe, 1849), 9–11.

91. George Adams, *A Guide Book to Boston and Vicinity* (Boston: Boston Directory Office, 1853), 15; R. L. Midgley, *Sights in Boston and Suburbs, or Guide to the Stranger* (Boston: John P. Jewett, 1856), 16–19; "Merchants' Exchange Boston," *Farmer's Cabinet,* 29 April 1842. On the marine telegraph network operated in Boston ca. 1824–1845 by John Rowe Parker, see *Bowen's Picture of Boston,* 100–103; and William Upham Swan, "Early Visual Telegraphs in Massachusetts," *Proceedings of the Bostonian Society* 10 (1929–1933): 31–47, esp. 42–46. Thanks to Richard John for explaining these early telegraphy technologies.

92. *Bowen's Picture of Boston,* 205; *Bowen's New Guide to Boston,* 9–10; Midgley, *Sights in Boston,* 16–17.

93. *"Our First Men": A Calendar of Wealth, Fashion and Gentility; Containing a List of Those Persons Taxed in the City of Boston, Credibly Reported to be Worth One Hundred Thousand Dollars* (Boston, 1846), 39; "Exchange Coffee House, Boston," *PS,* 19 September 1850; "A Good Boarding House," *Boston Herald,* 23 March 1853. For the history of small fires in the house, see "Fire," *Farmer's Cabinet,* 19 September 1844, which references four blazes in the Exchange in the previous two years; and "Another Chapter of Fire," *Farmer's Cabinet,* 15 May 1845. The date of Robbins's death is furnished by Guild, "Reminiscences," 3: 3.

94. *Bowen's New Guide to Boston,* 13. The Exchange had reduced its rate to $1 per day in 1840, in the midst of yet another commercial depression; *New Bedford Mercury,* 13 November 1840. In 1849, the tariff was $1.25; "Exchange Coffee House," *PS,* 12 April 1850. For other contemporaneous hotel rates in Boston, see *A Guide Book to Boston and Vicinity* (Boston: Boston Directory Office, 1851), 7. A comprehensive listing of "public houses in Boston" in 1851 appears in Nathaniel Dearborn, *Dearborn's Reminiscences of Boston, and Guide Through the City and Its Environs* (Boston: W. D. Ticknor, 1851), 138–39.

95. *Boston Daily Atlas,* 18 January 1854; "The Exchange Coffee House: The Two Hotels Which Bore the Same Name", box 10, item 43. On the history of the idea of obsolescence in architecture, see Daniel M. Abramson, "Discourses of Obsolescence," paper presented to the Charles Warren Center for Studies in American History, Harvard University (2005).

96. Andrew Dexter to Michael Portier, 15 July 1833, Montgomery County Probate Judge Records of Conveyances, LGM 83, reel 1, vol. W, 567–69. The other deeds executed by Dexter in the second half of 1833 appear in this volume and in LGM 83, reel 1, vol. F.

97. *Alabama Journal,* 9 January 1829; see also E. Bryding Adams, "'True to Life . . . in the Highest Style': Painting in Alabama," in *Made in Alabama: A State Legacy,* eds. E. Bryding Adams and Leah Rawls Atkins (Birmingham, Ala.: Birmingham Museum

of Art, 1995), 151; and Richard S. Morgan, *Joseph Thoits Moore, 1796–1854, Portraitist of Maine, Ohio and Alabama* (State College, Penn.: n.p., 1977). For Moore's sitters in Alabama, see Robert Hosea Moore, comp., "List of Portraits Painted by Joseph Thoits Moore Between the Years 1825 and 1839," ADAH (1911).

98. The Stuart portrait of Charlotte Dexter remained in the artist's studio at his death in 1828, and eventually passed to Sophia and Alfred Dexter; see the provenance in Ellen G. Miles et al., *American Paintings of the Eighteenth Century* (New York: Oxford University Press / National Gallery of Art, 1995), 279–80. For Moore's gallery see E. Bryding Adams, "'True to Life . . . ,'" 162; and *Alabama Journal,* 9 January 1829.

99. *Alabama Journal,* 9 January 1829. For Moore's biography see Morgan, *Joseph Thoits Moore*; E. Bryding Adams, "'True to Life . . . ,'" 151–52; and George C. Groce and David H. Wallace, *The New-York Historical Society's Dictionary of Artists in America, 1564–1860* (New Haven, Conn.: Yale University Press, 1957), 452.

100. Robert Hosea Moore, "List of Portraits by Joseph Thoits Moore."

101. Amos, *Cotton City,* 1–17, 21, quotation at 16; Tyrone Power, *Impressions of America during the Years 1833, 1834, and 1835* (1836), reprinted in Posey, *Alabama in the 1830s,* 24 (shell streets).

102. Amos, *Cotton City,* 18–47, 120.

103. Dexter, Mills, and Dexter, *Dexter Genealogy,* 127–28. For Dexter's sales of Montgomery lands in 1834 and 1835, see Montgomery County Conveyances, LGM 83, reel 2, vols. G and H. On the sawmill, see Andrew Alfred Dexter to Simon Newton Dexter, 24 January 1841, Simon Newton Dexter Papers, folder 2, Cornell University Library.

104. "At New Orleans," *National Intelligencer,* 27 April 1837; see also "Running Upon a Bank," *National Intelligencer,* 29 April 1837; "Truth and Eloquence," *National Intelligencer,* 23 May 1837. Thanks to Jessica Lepler and contributors to the H-SHEAR listserv for supplying references likening the panic of 1837 to a fire. The path of the panic through the United States and beyond is the subject of Lepler's Brandeis University dissertation-in-progress, "1837: The Anatomy of a Panic."

105. Letter to the editor, *Mobile Register,* 18 October 1837. For Dexter's creditors, see Bens & Privost to Simon Newton Dexter, 13 July 1837, Simon Newton Dexter Papers, folder 3, Cornell University Library. On the impact of the panic on Mobile, see Amos, *Cotton City,* 122–29.

106. *Mobile Register,* 16, 18, 20, 23 (quotation), 30 October 1837. The frost, which people at the time thought eliminated disease-causing miasma, would in fact have killed the mosquitoes that carried the virus from host to host.

107. Screws and Rogers, "Andrew Dexter," 169; Col. Michael L. Woods, "Story of the Life of Andrew Dexter," *Montgomery Advertiser,* 8 November 1903, 1. For the location of Dexter's office, see *Mobile Directory, Embracing the Names of the Heads of Families and Persons in Business . . . for 1837* (Mobile, Ala.: McGuire & Fay), 21; and "Plan and View of the City of Mobile," 1824, Mobile Municipal Archives. Death notices have been excised from many surviving issues of the *Mobile Register,* including those for 3, 4 November 1837.

108. Notice from the *Mobile Advertiser,* reprinted in the *Connecticut Courant*, 2 December 1837; Samuel Dexter to Thomas M. Owen, [ca. 1896?], Dexter surname

clipping file, ADAH. Word of Dexter's death reached Boston by the end of the month; see *Boston Free Press,* 29 November 1837. The *Mobile Advertiser* of November 1837 does not survive. For Dexter's intestacy, see Mobile County Probate Court, Minute Books for 1837, 2: 251, 3: 538–84.

109. *Mobile Daily Commercial Register,* 28 February 1840, 20 October 1842.

110. Alfred Dexter to Simon Newton Dexter, 24 January 1841, Simon Newton Dexter Papers, folder 2, Cornell University Library.

111. Freeman Hunt, *Worth and Wealth: A Collection of Maxims, Morals and Miscellanies for Merchants and Men of Business* (New York: Stringer & Townsend, 1857), 41–42; Andrew Alfred Dexter to Simon Newton Dexter, 24 March 1849, Simon Newton Dexter Papers, folder 2, Cornell University Library. I have not located the "Memoir" Alfred describes.

112. Andrew Alfred Dexter to Charlotte Sophia Dexter, 24 August 1844, Dexter Family Papers, ADAH. Alfred calls this family failing "the want of Concentrativeness," using a phrenological term for "the propensity to inhabit a particular place"; see Amos Dean, *Lectures on Phrenology: Delivered Before the Young Men's Association for Mutual Improvement of the City of Albany* (Albany, N.Y.: Hoffman and White, 1834), 82–86. For Alfred Dexter's various attempts to get rich, see Andrew Alfred Dexter to the Proprietors of the Selma and Tennessee Railroad, 7 February 1837; Simon Newton Dexter to Andrew Alfred Dexter, 23 November 1852; Dexter Family Papers, ADAH; and Andrew Alfred Dexter to Simon Newton Dexter, 24 March 1849, Simon Newton Dexter Papers, folder 2, Cornell University Library.

## EPILOGUE: RELICS

1. *Celebration of the Introduction of the Water of Cochituate Lake Into the City of Boston, October 25, 1848* (Boston: J. H. Eastburn, 1848), 43; "Water for South Boston," *Excelsior,* 17 June 1848. On the project more broadly, see Nelson Manfred Blake, *Water for the Cities: A History of the Urban Water Supply Problem in the United States* (Syracuse, N.Y.: Syracuse University Press, 1956), 209–18; see also Fern L. Nesson, *Great Waters: A History of Boston's Water Supply* (Hanover, N.H.: University Press of New England, 1983), 4–7; Frank A. McInnes, "The Boston Water Supply," *Journal of the New England Water Works Association* 46, no. 1 (March 1932): 8–11.

2. Curtis Guild, "Reminiscences of Old Boston or The Exchange Coffee House," bound clippings from the *Commercial Bulletin,* BPL, Rare Books Department (ca. 1872), 2: 90–91, 88. For the growing fascination with archaeology among learned Bostonians, see Caroline Winterer, *The Culture of Classicism: Ancient Greece and Rome in American Intellectual Life, 1780–1910* (Baltimore: Johns Hopkins University Press, 2002), 157–63.

3. *Boston Courier,* 24 August 1848; *Boston Daily Times,* 25 August 1848; *Boston Daily Advertiser,* 25 August 1848; *Boston Herald,* 25 August 1848; *Boston Daily Republican,* 25 August 1848.

4. Will of Sarah Wentworth Apthorp Morton, 30 April 1838; Inventory of Personal Estate of Mrs. S. W. Morton, Morton-Cunningham-Clinch Family Papers, 1754–1903, folders 1830–39, 1840–49, MHS. See also Will of Perez Morton, 1 August 1836, Norfolk County Register of Probate, Dedham, Mass., #13228.

5. Freeman Hunt, *Worth and Wealth: A Collection of Maxims, Morals and Miscellanies for Merchants and Men of Business* (New York: Stringer & Townsend, 1857), 39.

6. *"Our First Men": A Calendar of Wealth, Fashion and Gentility; Containing a List of Those Persons Taxed in the City of Boston, Credibly Reported to Be Worth One Hundred Thousand Dollars* (Boston, 1846), 4, 3, 11; Will and Inventory of Nathan Appleton, Appleton Family Papers, box 13, folder 10, MHS. On Appleton's wealth ca. 1840s, see also Frances W. Gregory, *Nathan Appleton, Merchant and Entrepreneur, 1779–1861* (Charlottesville: University Press of Virginia, 1975), 293. On Appleton's second Beacon Street house, designed by Alexander Parris, see Pamela Fox, "Nathan Appleton's Beacon Street Houses," *Old-Time New England,* 70 (1980): 115–24.

7. Isaac Appleton Jewett, comp., *Memorial of Samuel Appleton of Ipswich, Massachusetts; with Genealogical Notices of Some of His Descendants* (Boston, 1850), 82; Louise Hall Tharp, *The Appletons of Beacon Hill* (Boston: Little, Brown, 1973), 103, 144. On Healy, see Lois Marie Fink, "Healy, George Peter Alexander," *American National Biography Online,* February 2000, http://www.anb.org.ezp1.harvard.edu/articles/17/17-00394.html.

8. Nathan Appleton, *Labor, Its Relations in Europe and the United States Compared* (Boston: Eastburn's Press, 1844), 4; Robert C. Winthrop, ed., "Memoir of Hon. Nathan Appleton," *Proceedings of the Massachusetts Historical Society* 5 (October 1861): 304–306.

9. *Our First Men,* 4; Appleton, *Labor,* 3.

10. Inventory of Nathan Appleton, Appleton Family Papers, box 13, MHS; Alexis de Tocqueville, *Democracy in America,* Arthur Goldhammer, (New York: Penguin / Putnam, 2004), 738 (Orig. pub. 1835); Hunt, *Worth and Wealth,* 253–54; see also Nathan Appleton, *Memoir of the Hon. Abbott Lawrence, Prepared for the Massachusetts Historical Society* (Boston: J. H. Eastburn, 1856), 4–6. At his death, in 1861, Appleton owned forty-three bound volumes of *Hunt's Merchants' Magazine.* Since volume 44 began that year, I am assuming that he had collected the whole run, with the current year's volumes still in paper. He also owned a first edition of de Tocqueville's *De la Démocratie en Amérique.*

11. Hunt, *Worth and Wealth,* vii, 72–73, 79–80. Hunt compiled but did not write all the wisdom in the volume.

12. Hunt, *Worth and Wealth,* 78; Orrando Perry Dexter, Henry L. Mills, and John Haven Dexter, *Dexter Genealogy, 1642–1904; Being a History of the Descendants of Richard Dexter of Malden, Massachusetts, from the Notes of John Haven Dexter and Original Researches* (New York: J. J. Little, 1904), 197; Susan M. Loring, ed., *Selections from the Diaries of William Appleton, 1786–1862* (Boston: [n.p.], 1922), 145–46, 148–49.

On the growing legal acceptance of failure as part and parcel of a capitalist economy, see Edward J. Balleisen, *Navigating Failure: Bankruptcy and Commercial Society in Antebellum America* (Chapel Hill: University of North Carolina Press, 2001); Bruce H. Mann, *Republic of Debtors: Bankruptcy in the Age of American Independence* (Cambridge, Mass.: Harvard University Press, 2002). On antebellum culture's increasing tendency to fault individuals for their own losses, see Scott A. Sandage, *Born Losers: A History of Failure in America* (Cambridge, Mass.: Harvard University Press, 2005). On related changes in conceptions of luck and chance, see T. J. Jackson Lears, *Something for Nothing: Luck in America* (New York: Viking, 2003).

13. Winthrop, "Memoir of Hon. Nathan Appleton," 284–86. Appleton drafted the autobiography in the mid-1850s. For the marriage of Franklin Dexter and Harriet Appleton, see Dexter, Mills, and Dexter, *Dexter Genealogy,* 197; Loring, *Selections from the Diaries of William Appleton,* 145–46, 148–49.

14. Guild, "Reminiscences"; "First Sky-Scraper," *Boston Herald,* 3 November 1901; Nixon Waterman, "Burning of the Exchange Coffee House," *Boston Globe,* 18 November 1924.

15. *Our First Men,* 5.

16. Letter from Lawrence Falater to the author, 19 March 2003; e-mail from Don C. Kelly to the author, 6 August 2003, among others. The collector's bible for obsolete banknotes is James A. Haxby, *Standard Catalogue of United States Obsolete Bank Notes,* 4 vols. (Iola, Wisc.: Krause Publications, 1988). I curse Stephen Mihm for introducing me to this source.

17. M. R. Friedberg, "Fractional Currency Fourth and Fifth Issues: Papers and Printing," *Paper Money* 4, no. 16 (1965): 110–13; see also Neil Carothers, *Fractional Money: A History of the Small Coins and Fractional Paper Currency of the United States* (New York: Wiley, 1930). On the move to a national currency in the United States and elsewhere see Eric Helleiner, *The Making of National Money: Territorial Currencies in Historical Perspective* (Ithaca, N.Y.: Cornell University Press, 2003).

18. E-mail communication from Cecelia Wertheimer, lead curator, Historical Resource Center, Bureau of Printing and Engraving, 10 August 2006.

# INDEX

Illustration and map page numbers are shown in *italics*.

## D

# ILLUSTRATION CREDITS

174   *The Tower of Babel*, from Athanasius Kircher, *Turris Babel*, 1679; courtesy of Trinity College.

177   *North-East View of the Exchange Coffee House*, by Thomas Wightman, 1809; courtesy of the Bostonian Society/Old State House.

177   Aerial view, east elevation of the Exchange Coffee House. Drawing by Elliott Hodges; rendering by Ana Pinto da Silva.

181   Aerial view, north and east elevations of the Exchange Coffee House. Drawing by Elliott Hodges; rendering by Ana Pinto da Silva.

182   Northeast view of the Exchange Coffee House, street level. Drawing by Elliott Hodges; rendering by Ana Pinto da Silva.

183   Exchange Coffee House and surrounding streets; map by David Lindroth, Inc.

184   South elevation of the Exchange Coffee House, street level. Drawing by Elliott Hodges; rendering by Ana Pinto da Silva.

186   Looking up from the 'Change Floor. Drawing by Elliott Hodges; rendering by Ana Pinto da Silva.

194   'Change Floor. Drawing by Elliott Hodges; rendering by Ana Pinto da Silva.

224   Hunneman Engine Number 39 ("Dexter"), ca. 1815. Author photograph; courtesy Newport Firefighters Association/Town of Newport, New Hampshire.

232   "Fire on State Street Near Old State House," detail from Massachusetts Fire and Marine Insurance Company Policy, ca. 1804. Courtesy of the Boston Public Library, Print Department.

238   Detail, certificate of membership, "Firemen of the City of New York," 1807; courtesy of the New York Fire Museum.

239   *The Times,* by William Hogarth, 1762. By permission of Houghton Library, Harvard College Library.

277   Dexter Avenue Memorial, Montgomery, Alabama; photograph by Robert Heinrich.

291   *Conflagration of the Exchange Coffee House,* by John Ritto Penniman, 1824. Private collection; photograph by Henry E. Peach.

292   Staffordshire teacup with a prospect of the Exchange Coffee House, ca. 1819; private collection.

294   "Boston Exchange Coffee House, Burnt 1818"; private collection.

295   Lots for sale on the Exchange Coffee House lands, December 1819; courtesy of Suffolk County Registry of Deeds.

300   The second Exchange Coffee House, ca. 1825–1835.

307   *Andrew Dexter,* by Joseph Thoits Moore, 1833; courtesy of Alabama Department of Archives and History.

318   *Nathan Appleton and the Calico Printing Machine*, by George Peter Alexander Healy, 1846; courtesy of Pollard Memorial Library, Lowell, Massachusetts.

325   Samuel Dexter fifty-cent note, ca. June 1873–January 1874; private collection.